INTRODUCTION TO DYNAMICS AX

BY MURRAY FIFE

ISBN: 1496043588

ISBN-13: 978-1496043580

Preface

What You Need For This Guide

All the examples shown in this blueprint were done with the Microsoft Dynamics AX 2012 virtual machine image that was downloaded from the Microsoft CustomerSource or PartnerSource site. If you don't have your own installation of Microsoft Dynamics AX 2012, you can also use the images found on the Microsoft Learning Download Center or deployed through Lifecycle Services. The following list of software from the virtual image was leveraged within this guide:

Microsoft Dynamics AX 2012 R3

Even though all the preceding software was used during the development and testing of the recipes in this book, they may also work on earlier versions of the software with minor tweaks and adjustments, and should also work on later versions without any changes.

Errata

Although we have taken every care to ensure the accuracy of our content, mistakes do happen. If you find a mistake in one of our books—maybe a mistake in the text or the code—we would be grateful if you would report this to us. By doing so, you can save other readers from frustration and help us improve subsequent versions of this book. If you find any errata, please report them by emailing editor@dynamicsaxcompanions.com.

Piracy

Piracy of copyright material on the Internet is an ongoing problem across all media. If you come across any illegal copies of our works, in any form, on the Internet, please provide us with the location address or website name immediately so that we can pursue a remedy.

Please contact us at legal@dynamicsaxcompanions.com with a link to the suspected pirated material.

We appreciate your help in protecting our authors, and our ability to bring you valuable content.

Questions

You can contact us at help@dynamicsaxcompanions.com if you are having a problem with any aspect of the book, and we will do our best to address it.

Table Of Contents

7   **INTRODUCTION**

9   **PART I: INTRODUCTION TO DYNAMICS AX**
11   The Dynamics AX Clients
29   Introduction To Portals
43   Introduction To Role Centers
51   The Role Center Parts
91   Navigating Menus
101   Navigating Forms
121   Personalizing Dynamics AX
141   Self Service Reporting and Analysis
169   Using Office With Dynamics AX
187   The Lifecycle Management Tools

199   **PART II: DYNAMICS AX OVERVIEW**
201   Product Management
209   Order To Cash
245   Sales & Marketing
257   Operations
281   Planning & Forecasting
291   Procure To Pay
313   Project Management
323   Service Management
331   Finance
349   Human Resources

355   **SUMMARY**

INTRODUCTION

When you are first introduced to Dynamics AX, it may seem a little overwhelming because there is so much that it is able to do. It may seem like you've been dropped in a completely foreign land, unable to speak the language, and not knowing which direction to start walking in.

It may be even worse if you are in the middle of a software selection where you are looking at a number of different options (including Dynamics AX) because you need to understand what the differences are, and also remember which feature applies to which application. In that case, you are in multiple foreign lands, and no-one is speaking the same language.

You may have picked up a book or two on Dynamics AX to start your self guided learning, but even then it may be too much because they usually assume that you have had some familiarity with the system, and you still don't have a basic foundation knowledge. Rather than wanting to read Lord of the Rings, you are at more of a See Spot Run level when it comes to Dynamics AX.

This is what this book is designed to achieve, and is aimed to give you a high level introduction to Dynamics AX. It is split into two parts as well, the first is an general overview of the system, showing you all of the usability features, and the second part is a functional overview that highlights all of the functional features within Dynamics AX.

In essence it teaches you the language of this new land, and also gives you a map of the land so that you can then start heading in the direction that is important to you.

Hopefully this will help you quickly get comfortable with Dynamics AX and get you on the right track.

PART I: AN INTRODUCTION TO DYNAMICS AX

Dynamics AX is a great product, and you can do so much with it to make your business successful. But before you dive into nuts and bolts of Product Management, Planning, Scheduling, or Sales & Marketing, it's probably a good idea to get an overview of what Dynamics AX is, how it works, and also what you can do with it just from a users point of view.

The Dynamics AX Clients

Everyone within the organization is special in their own way, and it makes sense that way to use Dynamics AX would never make everyone happy. So as a result, there are a number of different ways that users are able to use Dynamics AX based on their role, and also their needs within the company.

Dynamics AX has the traditional Rich Client interface that you would expect, but also includes web based clients for internal and external users to take advantage of while they are on the go, reporting clients for both analytical and financial reporting, and also Office integration for the users that need to bridge the gap between the business system, and the functional needs. Also there are modern Windows 8 applications that you can get directly from the Microsoft Store that give very focused task driven interfaces.

In this section we will show all of the different ways that you can use Dynamics AX. You can use any and all of them in order to make your workday just a little bit easier.

The Rich Client

The Rich Client is the interface that most users will take advantage of when accessing Dynamics AX. It runs locally on the clients workspace. Because it's a native Windows client, it also provides seamless integration between the Dynamics AX and all of the Microsoft Office tools, and also gives the user the ability to customize the layout and user experience themselves without any coding changes.

Although this is a Windows client, once installed, there is usually no need to update the client again since all of the processing and business logic is managed at the server level.

Role Centers

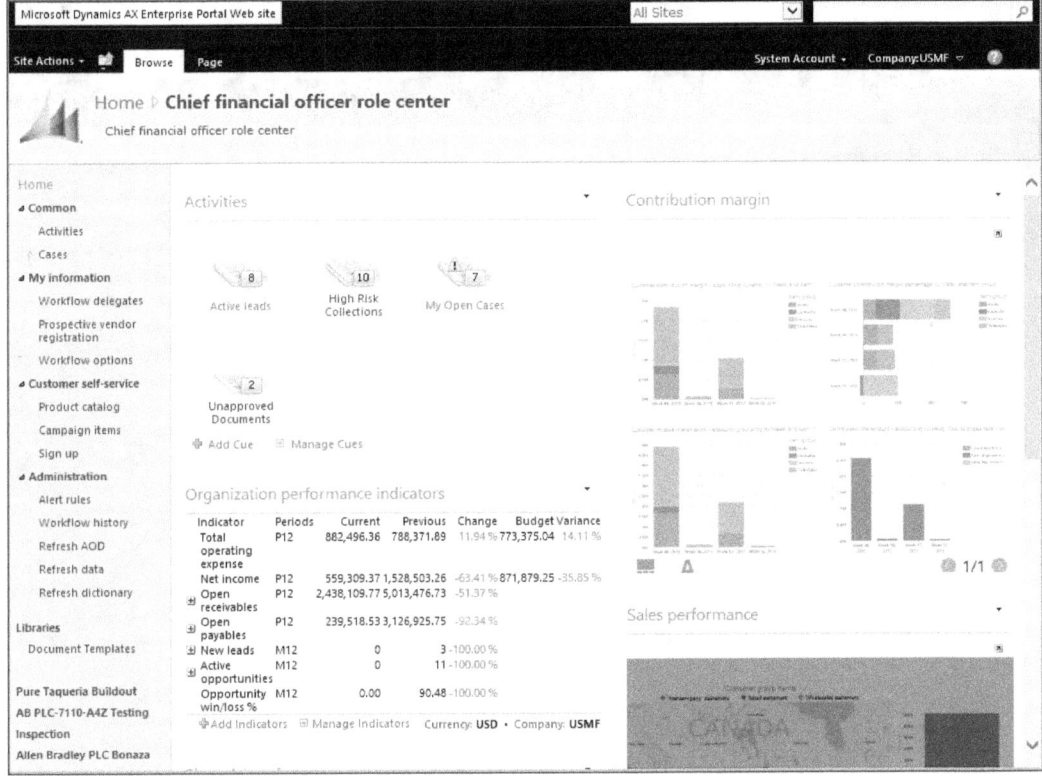

Dynamics AX Is also delivered with 38 web based Role Center Portals tailored to different user types within the organization providing an ideal way for users to access Dynamics AX through tablets integration, through a quick and secure interface to Dynamics AX functions without having to install any software.

Some of the Role Centers that are delivered by default with Dynamics AX include CEO/CFO, Controller, Human resources Manager, Marketing Manager, Production Manager, & Purchasing Manager.

Self Service Portals

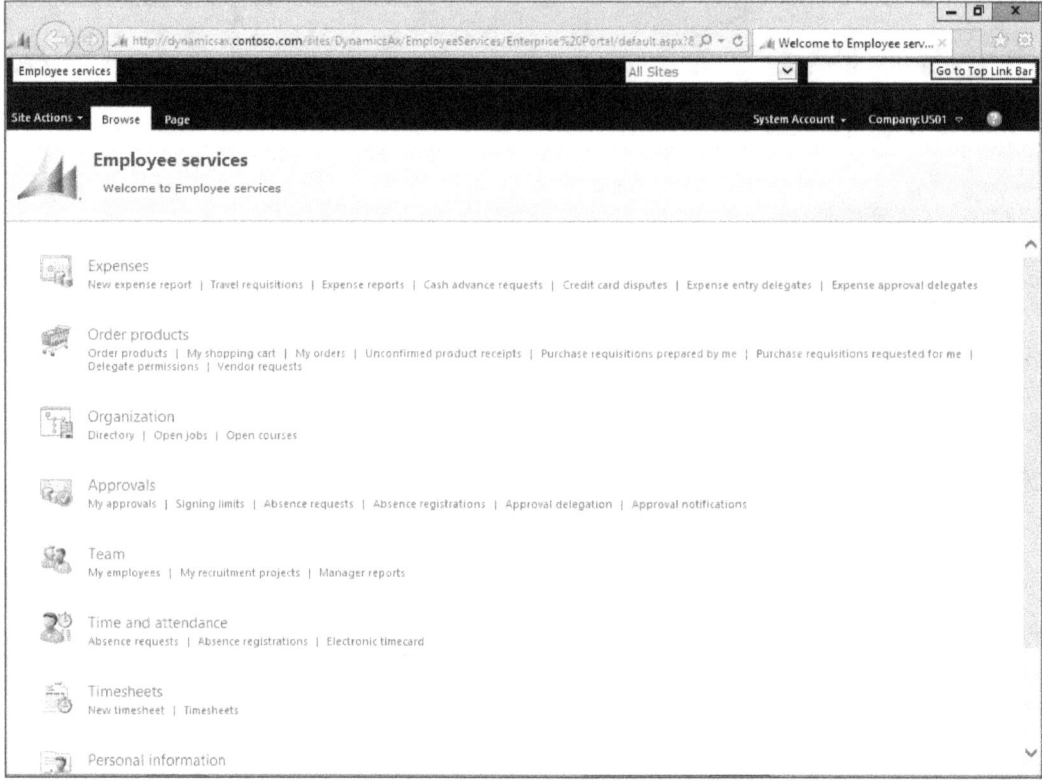

In addition to the Role Centers, Dynamics AX has 11 web based Self Service Portals for both internal and external user access.

Some of the default Portals that are delivered by default with Dynamics AX include Budgeting, Compliance, Customer Self-Service, Employee Services, Finance, Procurement, Projects, Retail, Sales, Service orders & Vendor.

Collaboration Portals

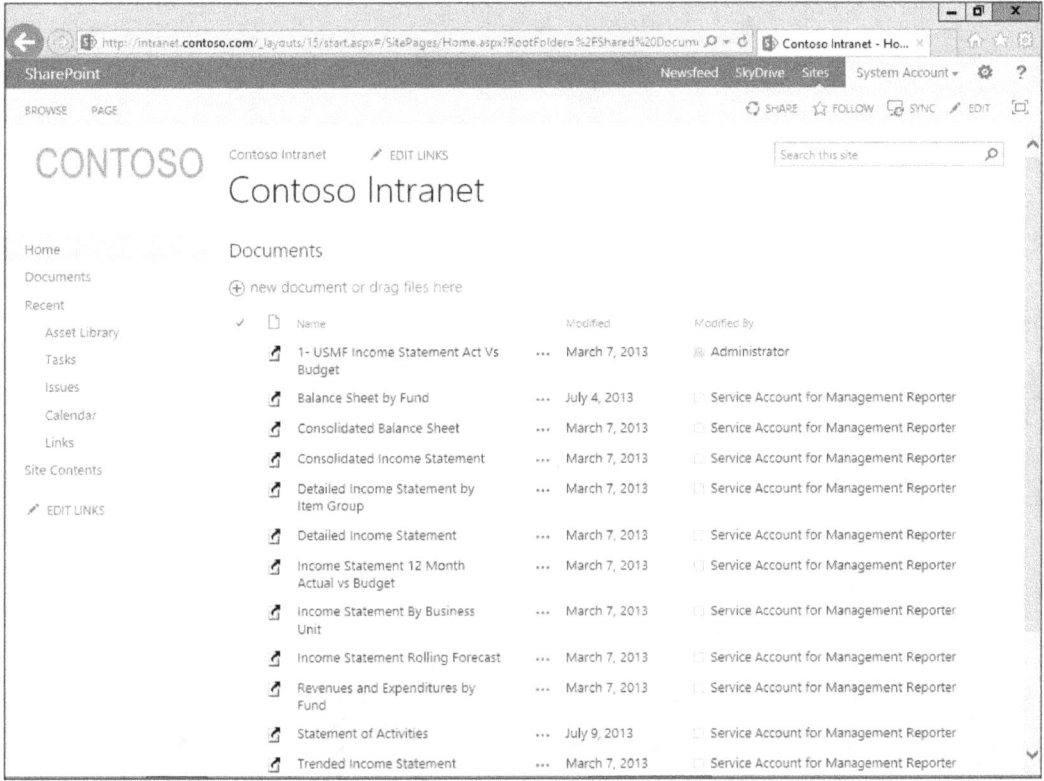

Along with the functional portals that are delivered with Dynamics AX, there are also more collaborative portals that are available for sharing information within particular groups within the organization. An example of this is the Financial portal where everyone (who has rights) is able to access all of the published reports and documents for the department.

Financial Reporting

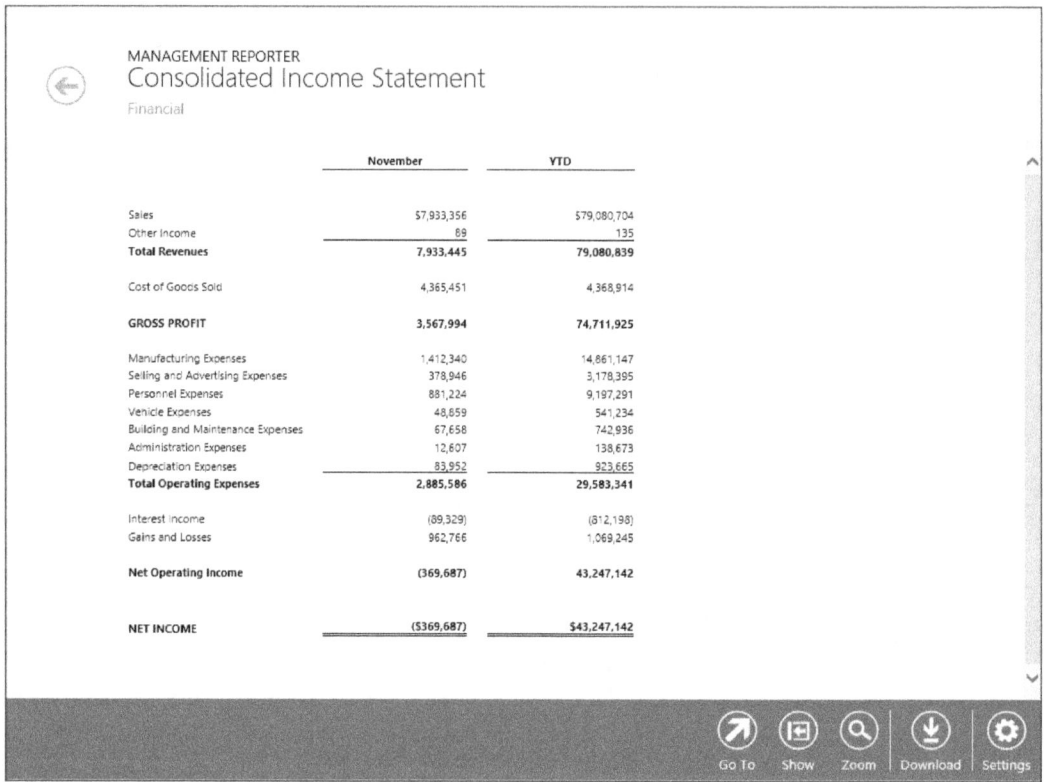

As a side note, all of the financial reports that are published to the Financial Portal can be accessed through the Management Reporter web client, so that you can browse through all the financial information at your leisure on your tablet or surface device.

PowerBI Canvas

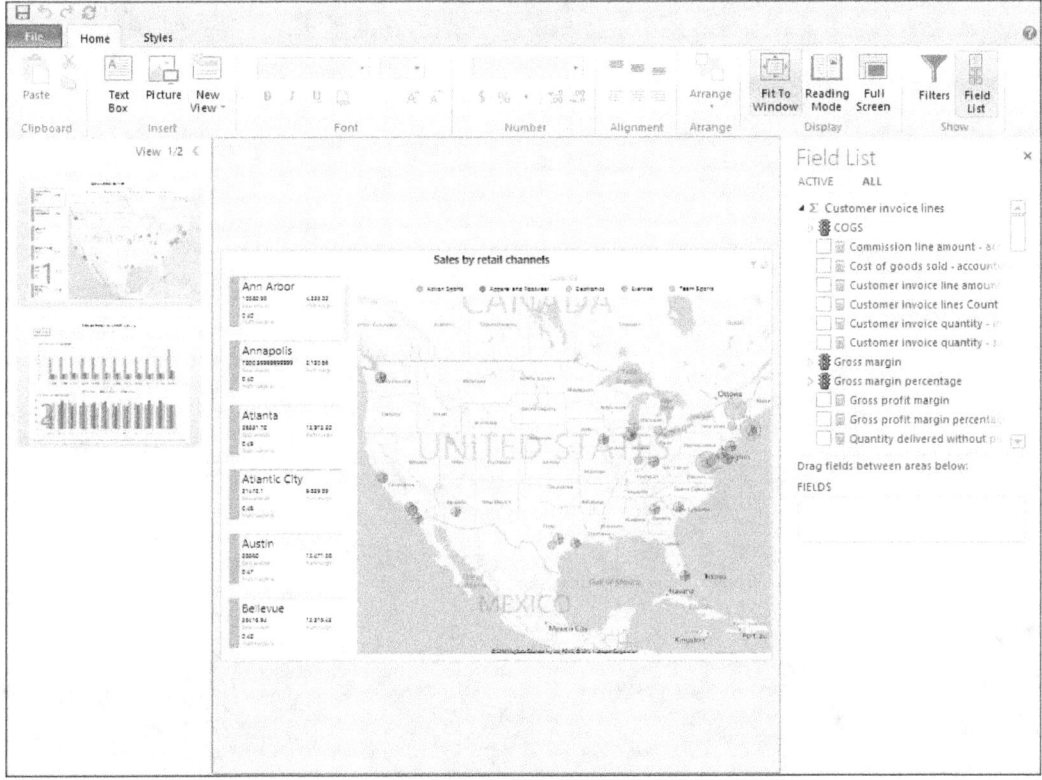

Since Microsoft Dynamics is built on the foundation products of Microsoft SQL Server, and SharePoint then it makes sense that all of the analytical reporting that you can do will also leverage Microsofts PowerBI stack of reporting tools. This allows you to report off all the data within Dynamics AX through the PowerView web client to create any of your dashboard reports without needing to get a developer involved.

Dynamics Business Analyzer

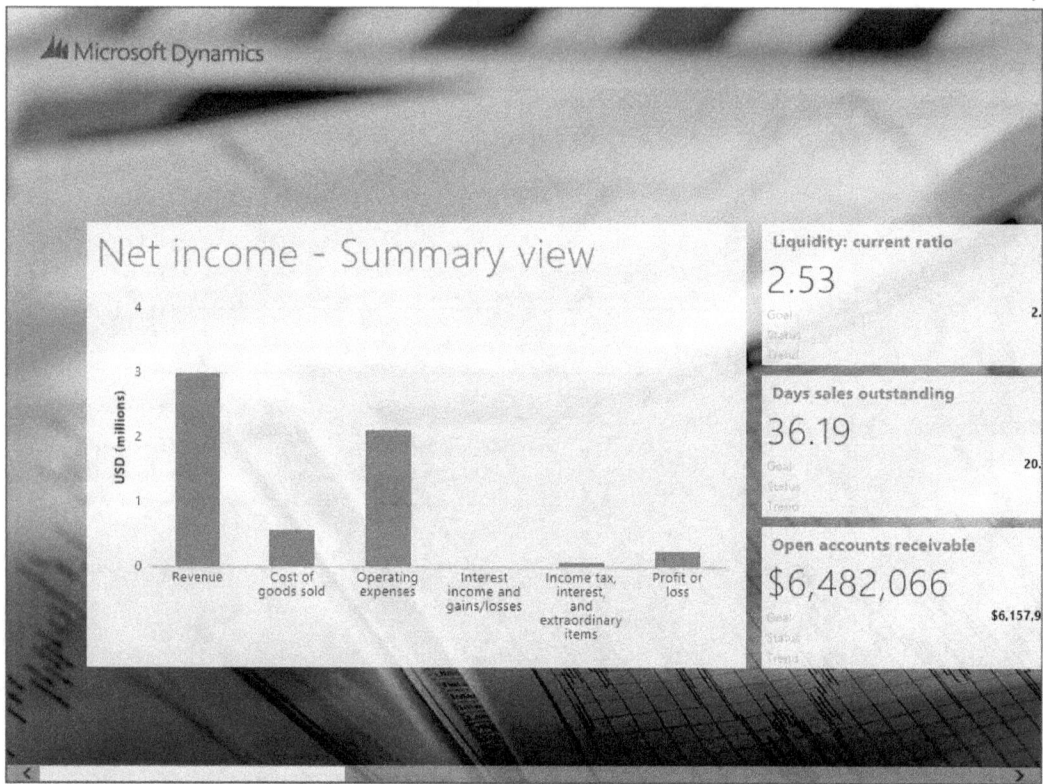

For the more mobile manager or executive, then you can access all of the reports that you like through the Business Analyzer client that you can run on any Windows 8 client or device, including the RT versions. This gives you a single place to view the state of the organization and also drill into the reporting detail through a simple and intuitive client.

Microsoft Office Integration: Excel

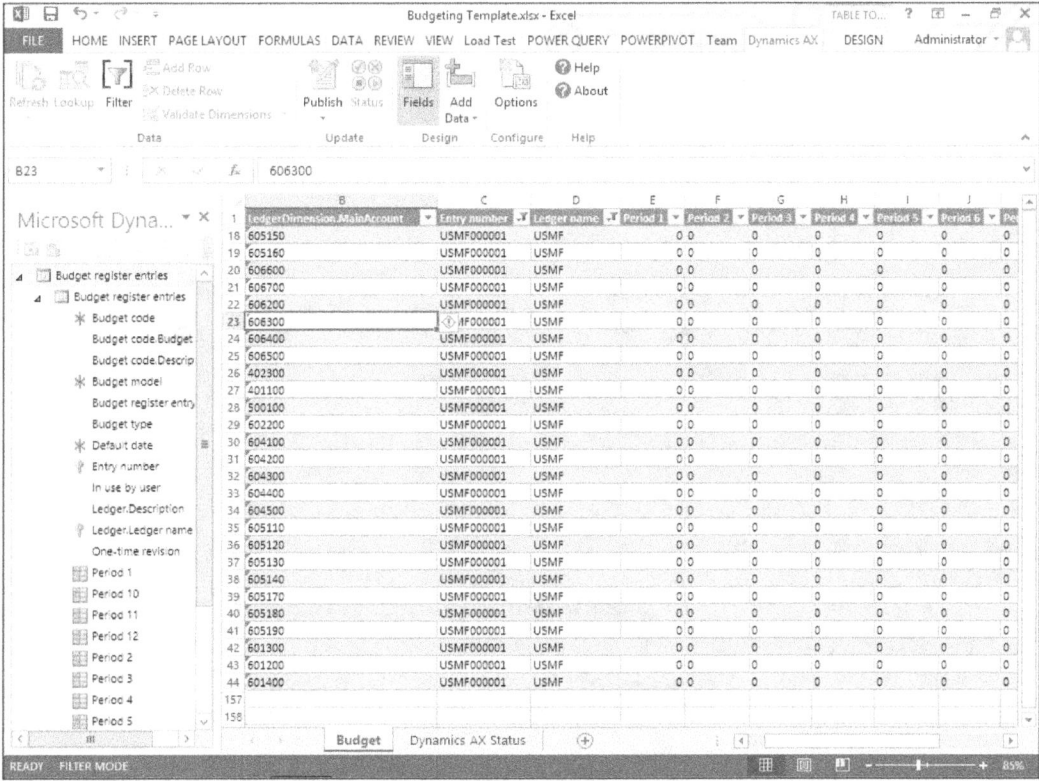

In addition to using the traditional clients for accessing Dynamics AX, you can also take advantage of the native integration with the Microsoft Office Suite of applications.

Almost every ERP client is able to export data to Excel, but Dynamics AX takes it to the next level by linking the data that is exported back to Dynamics AX, allowing the user to add additional fields to the exported data as needed, and also the ability to update data within Dynamics AX directly from Excel. This is a great (and secure) method of performing all of the mass updates that you may have to do when restructuring customers, or vendors, or products...

Microsoft Office Integration: Word

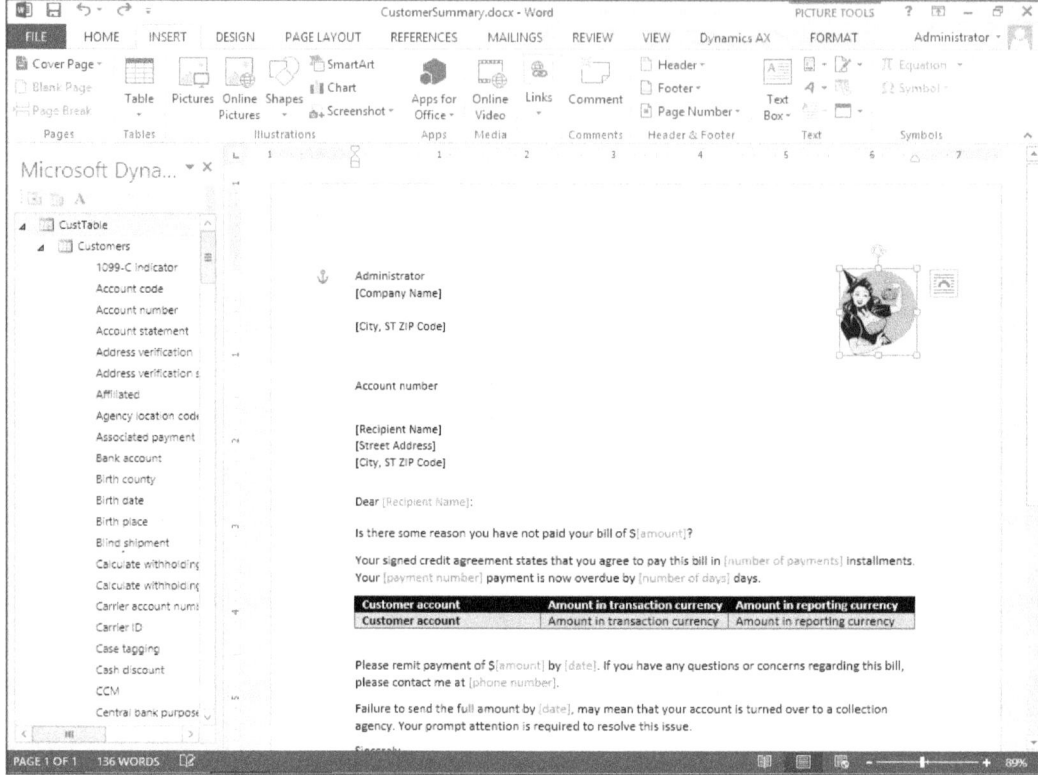

Additionally, you can query Dynamics AX data directly from within Word. This is a great way for users to create their own personalized form letters or mail-merge documents without having to get the IT department involved.

To make these even more useful, you can then save the templates back to the Dynamics AX form template library so that everyone is able to use the templates to generate standard correspondence.

Microsoft Office Integration: Project

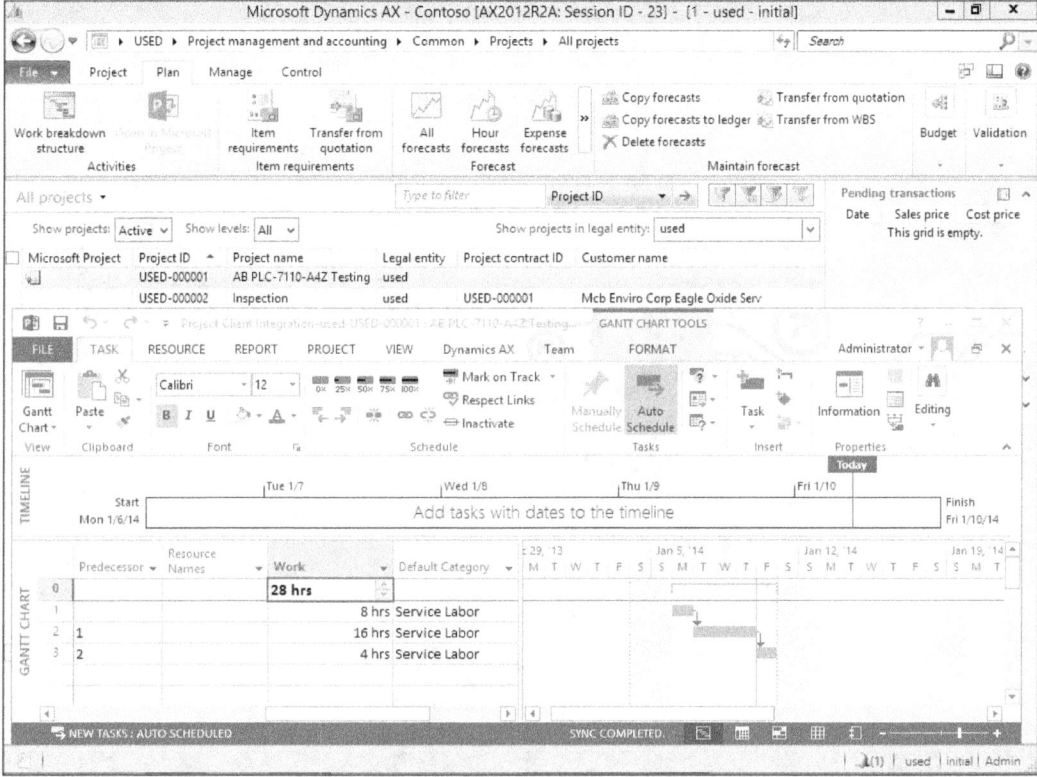

For those of you that manage projects, or standard processes, then you can take advantage of the standard integration with Microsoft Project that is built into Dynamics AX. This allows you to update plans and project data directly within Microsoft Project and then have all of the dates and project information automatically update within Dynamics AX.

Microsoft Office Integration: PowerPoint

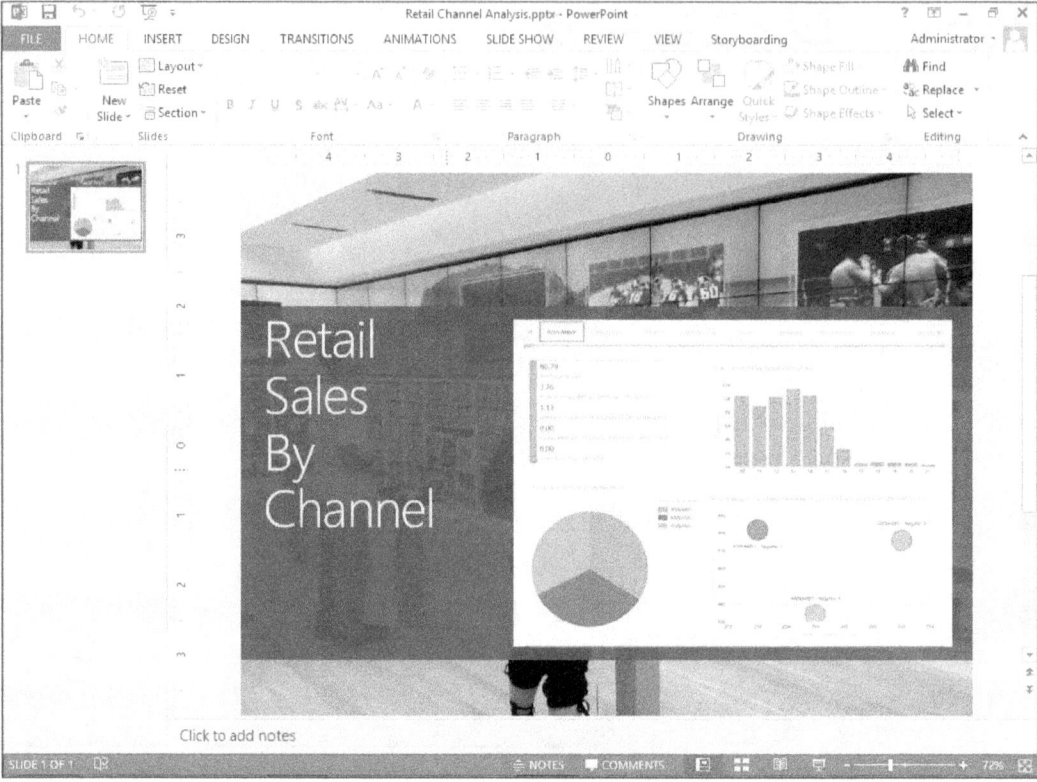

Forget cutting and pasting all of your standard dashboards into PowerPoint every time that you need to refresh the data. All of the dashboards that you create using PowerView can be embedded within PowerPoint, and then dynamically refreshed as you run the presentation. You can now have one presentation that rules them all.

Microsoft Office Integration: Outlook

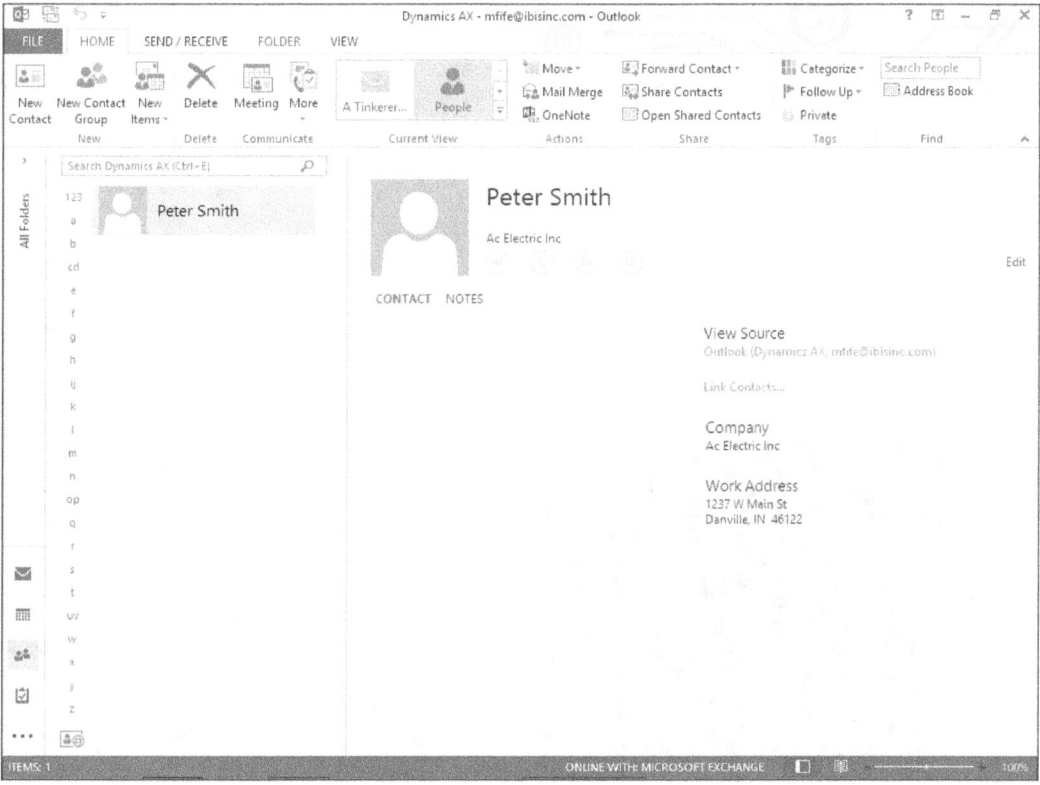

Dynamics AX also has native integration with Microsoft Outlook allowing you to synchronize your Contacts, Tasks, and Appointments with Dynamics AX. This synchronization can be either one way, or bi-directional, allowing you to always know what you have to do, when you have to do it, and also have quick access to all of your contacts so that you know who you need to contact.

Modern Clients

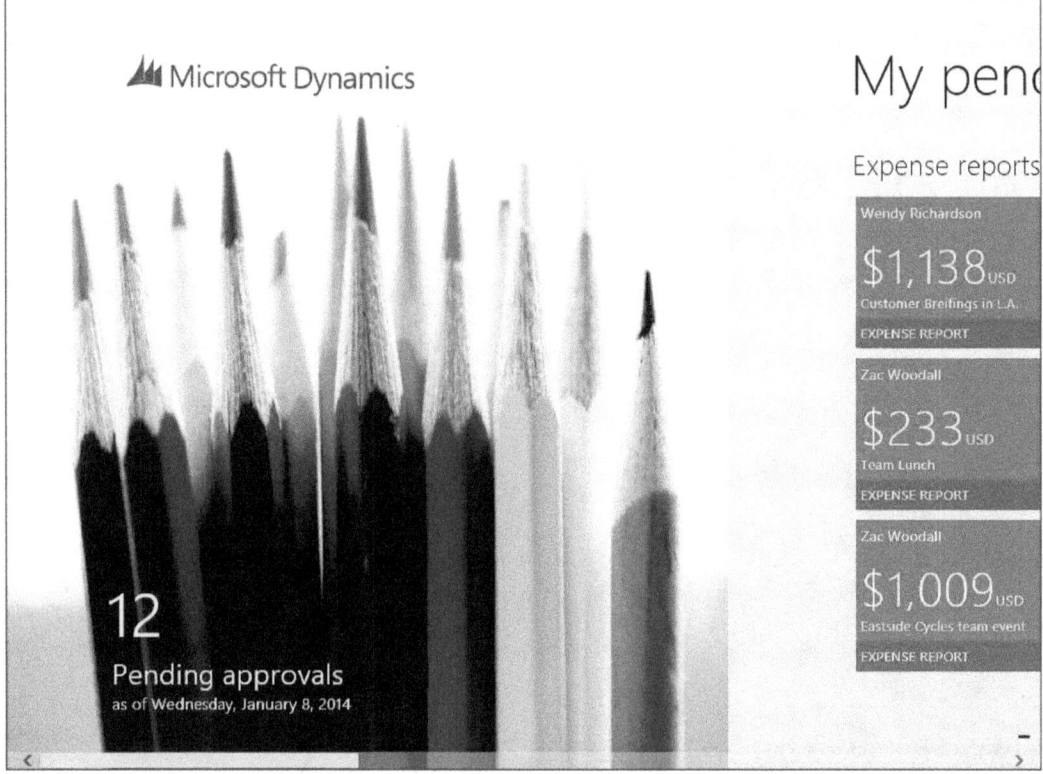

Finally, for the task oriented users that don't need the full functionality of Dynamics AX, but need to be involved in the processes, there are a number of modern style clients that they can use on and Windows 8 device or tablet. They are very focused on particular tasks and give the users a cooler way to do their job.

Examples of the different tasks that can be performed through the modern style clients are Timesheets, Expense Reports & Workflow Approvals.

Retail POS

Dynamics AX's retail module includes a Point Of Sale Register interface that you can deploy out to your stores without having to buy any additional software.

The POS register interface is a streamlined client that includes native integration with receipt printers, signature capture devices, and is also designed to be used with touch enabled screens making it a great way to capture your orders.

Online Store

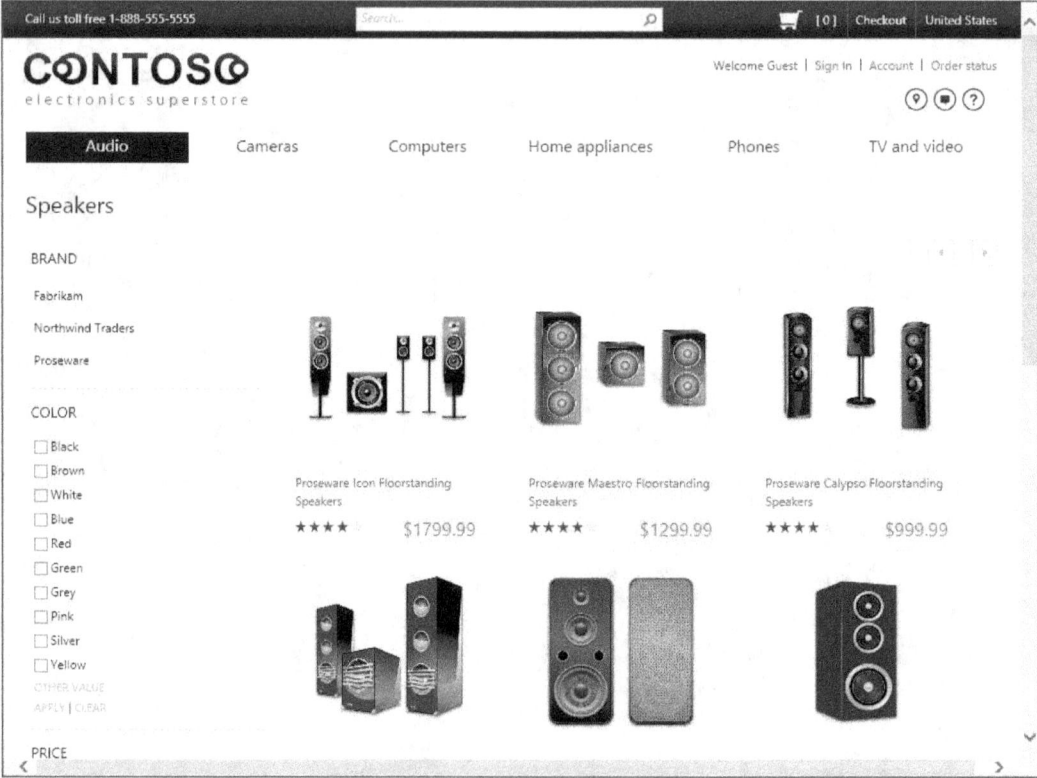

The Retail module within Dynamics AX also includes an ecommerce website out of the box that you can roll out to your customers and allow them to place orders, and also check on the status of their orders.

The Online Store provides the customers with all of the searching capabilities that you have come to expect from on-line stores, including ratings, price searches, and filtering based on product attributes and dimensions.

Introduction To Portals

The lightest way that users are able to access Dynamics AX is through the Portals that are delivered out of the box with the system. These portals are web clients that allow the user to perform many of the key functions without having to install any additional software, and are also tailored to fit a number of profiles both within the organization, and also external users as well.

Although they do not have the full experience that is offered through the Windows Rich Client, they are an quick and simple way for users to access data, and perform transactions through their tablets and remote clients. Also, because they are performing live transactions within Dynamics AX, then there is no synchronization or updates required, all of the data is always the most up to date.

Budgeting Portal

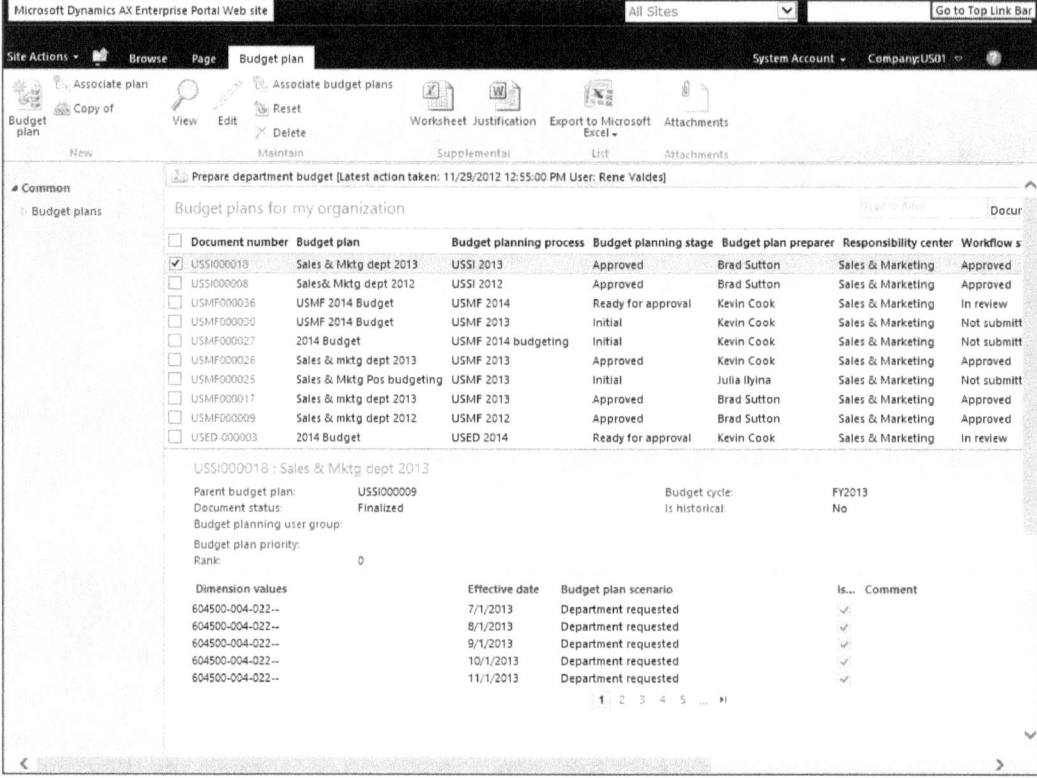

The Budgeting Portal provides a way for users that are not normally using Dynamics AX to still participate in the budgeting process, but still have access to all of the same budgeting functionality that is provided within the Rich Client.

Through the Budgeting Portal, the users are able to see all of the budgets that they have been assigned, update and approve budgets, and also take advantage of Office Integration through the Excel Worksheets and Word Justification documents.

Compliance Portal

The Compliance Portal is a one stop show for managing all of your Policies, Procedures, and Compliance/Risk Management documentation through a single website.

You can use this portal to track the progress of compliance documentation updates, and also leverages SharePoint to manage all of your compliance documentation, linked back to all of the Internal Controls that you have in place.

A lot of the other portals are alternatives to the standard functions within Dynamics AX, but this portal is a little different because it adds additional management functionality that augments all of the functions within Dynamics AX.

Customer Self Service Portal

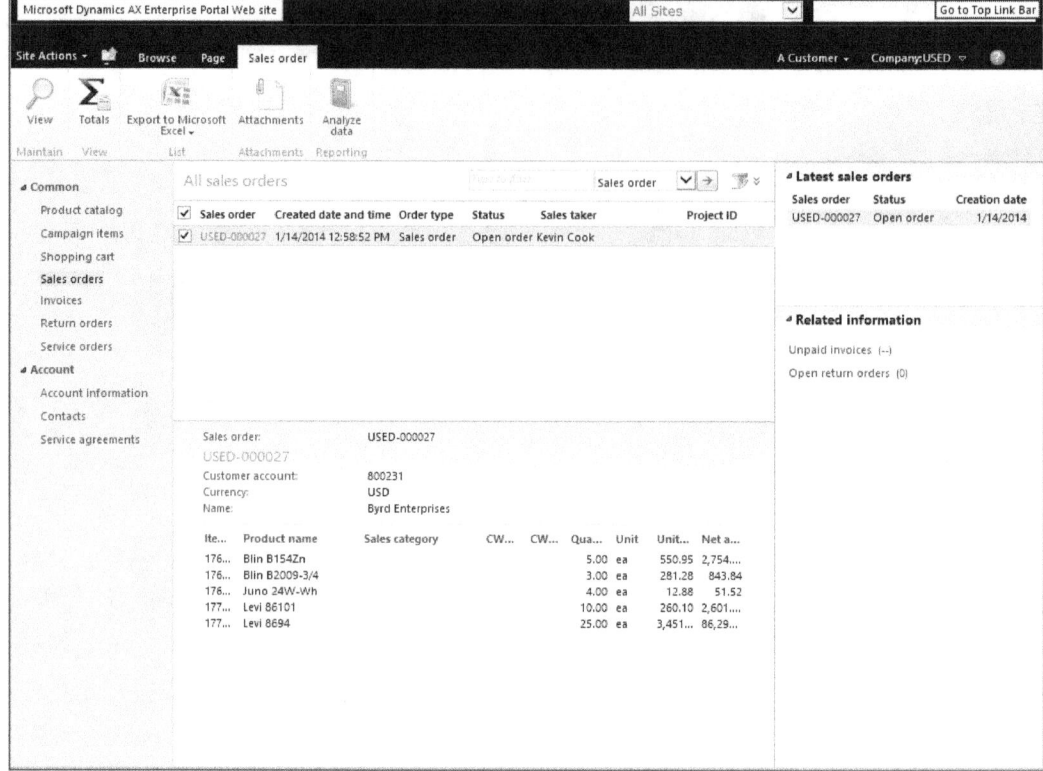

The Customer Portal is one of the two external portals that you can use to share information with the other parties that you work with, and in this case it provides a self service portal for your customers.

The customers are able to log into this portal, and view all of their transaction history, update their personal contact information, and even place orders through a simple product catalog function.

It's ideal for empowering your customers to access their own information, and also a great way to offload a lot of the small administrative questions that would normally have to be answered by customer service.

To make this an even better tool, there are no user licenses required for your external customer to access the portal.

Employee Self Service Portal

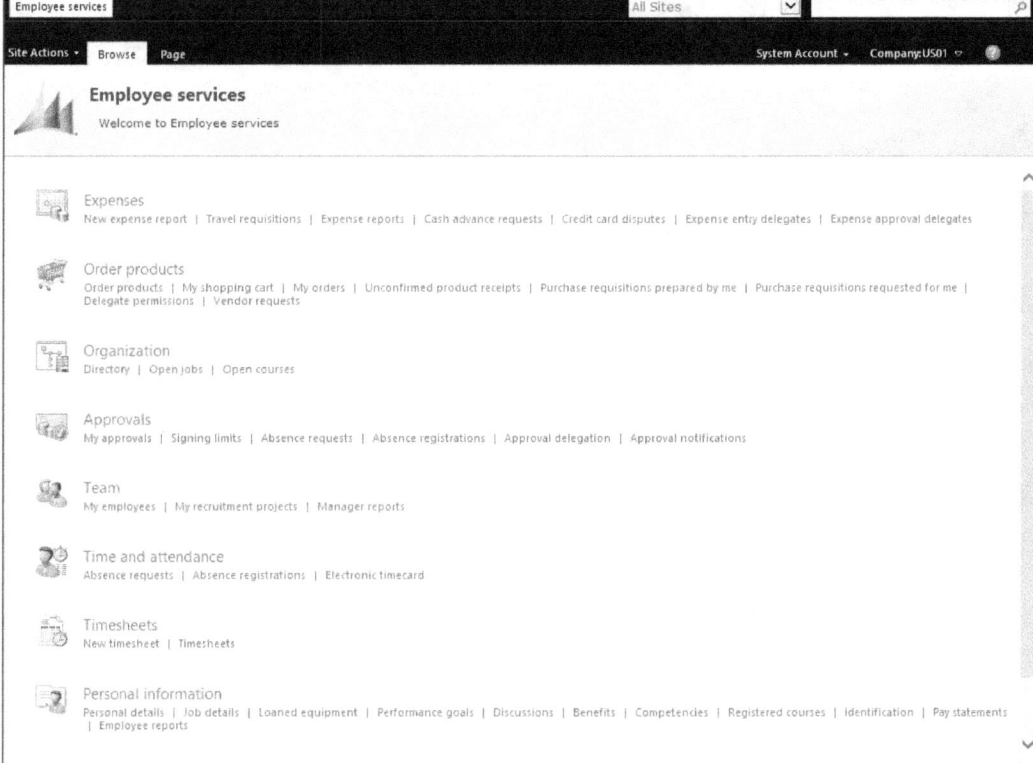

The Employee Self Service Portal provides a one-stop-shop for your employees to access all of their HR information, to perform administrative tasks such as entering and updating timesheets and expense reports, and also a place to requisition products and submit travel requests.

A majority of your users will probably not access Dynamics AX directly, but still need to perform administrative activities, so this portal is the ideal way to allow them to do that without having to install any applications on their desktops.

Finance Portal

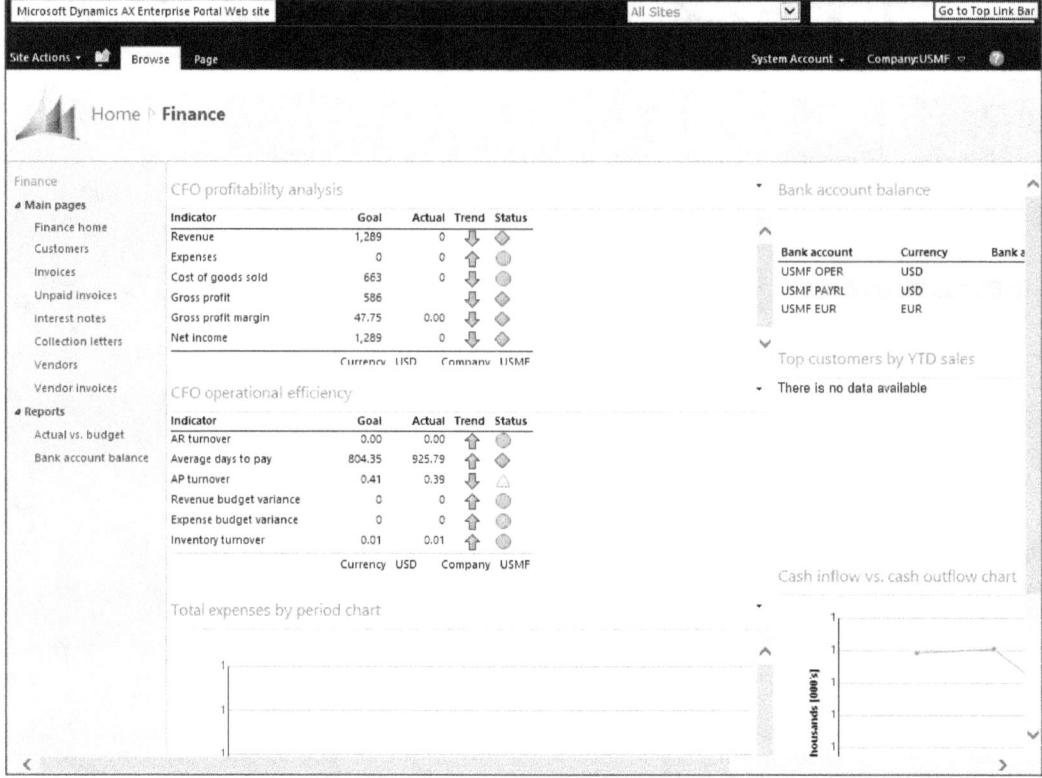

The Finance Portal provides a single portal to access all of the current invoicing, collection, and financial metrics.

This is an ideal tool for the CFO on the run to be able to keep tabs on all of the goings on within the organization, without having to log into the real Dynamics AX application.

Procurement Portal

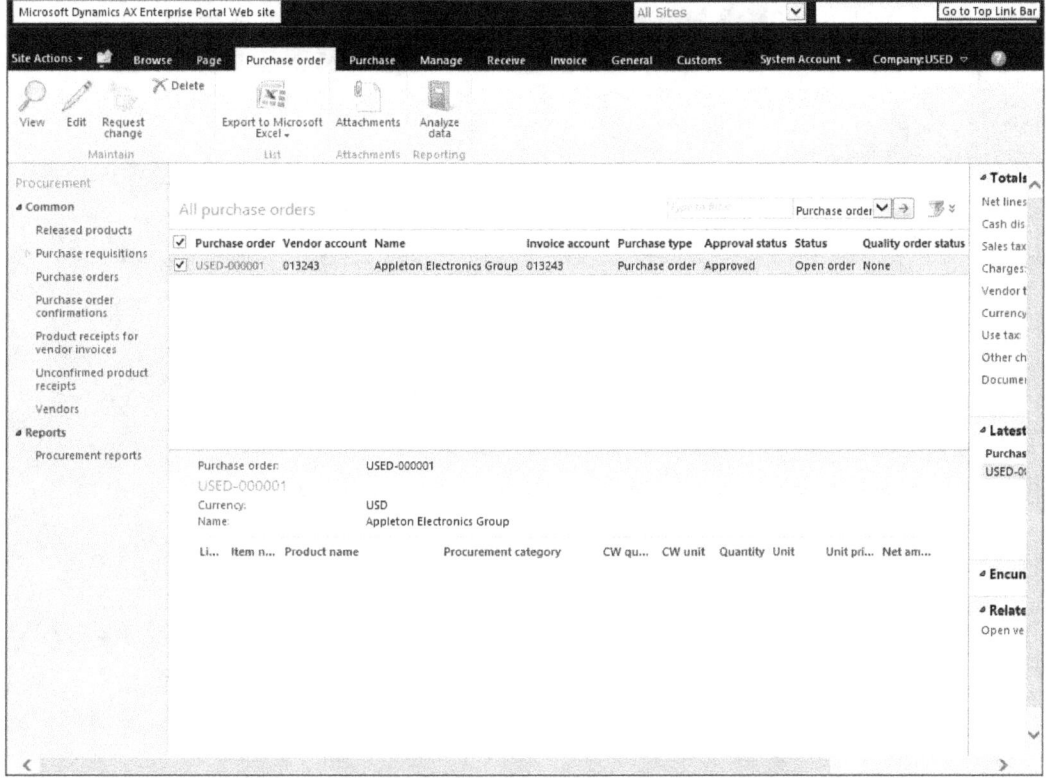

The Procurement Portal gives you access to all of the Purchasing information through a single website, and is a great tool for a Purchasing Agent to use when they are on-site with a vendor because they can quickly access all of the purchasing history through the web, and also create ad-hoc analysis through PowerView to support their negotiations.

Additionally the portal allows the user to create and manage purchase orders directly through the web, using the same functionality that they would normally have within the traditional Dynamics AX client. They can create a purchase order, confirm it, and have the confirmation sent to the vendor without leaving their tablet.

Projects Portal

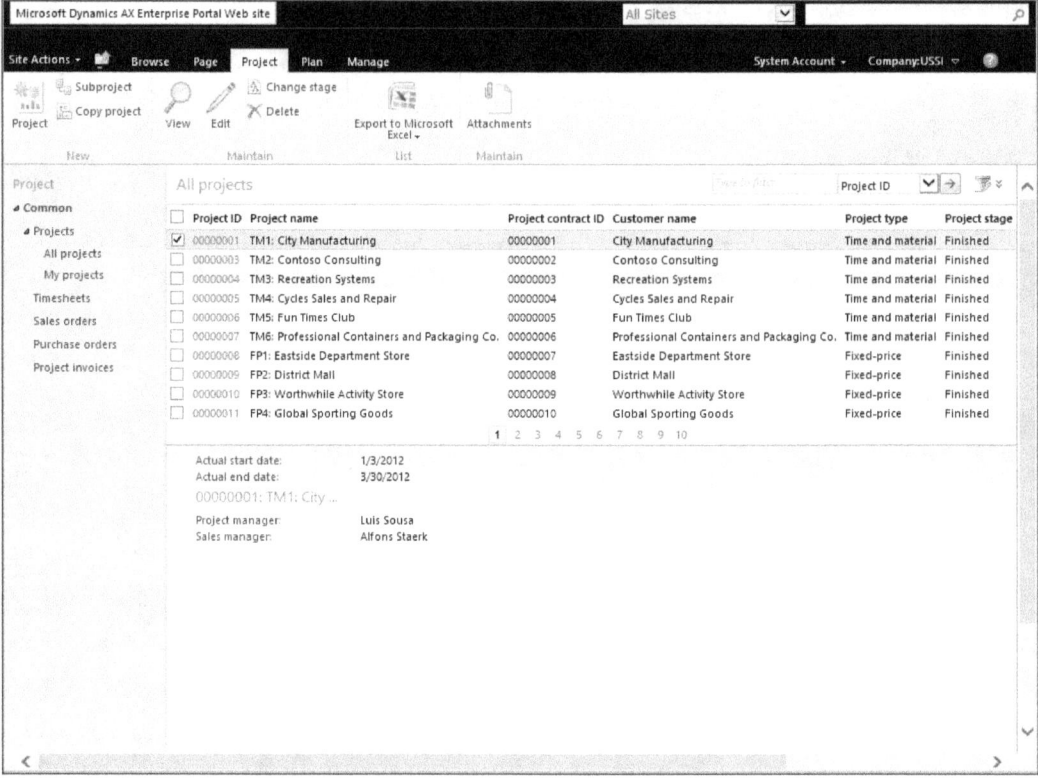

The Projects Portal allows Project Managers to see all of the current projects that they are involved with, and also for the project team members to update the project information directly through the web.

This is a great tool to allow the project members to have greater access to project details, and also to collaborate more closely than just posting time and expenses against projects through the Employee Self Service Portal.

Retail Portal

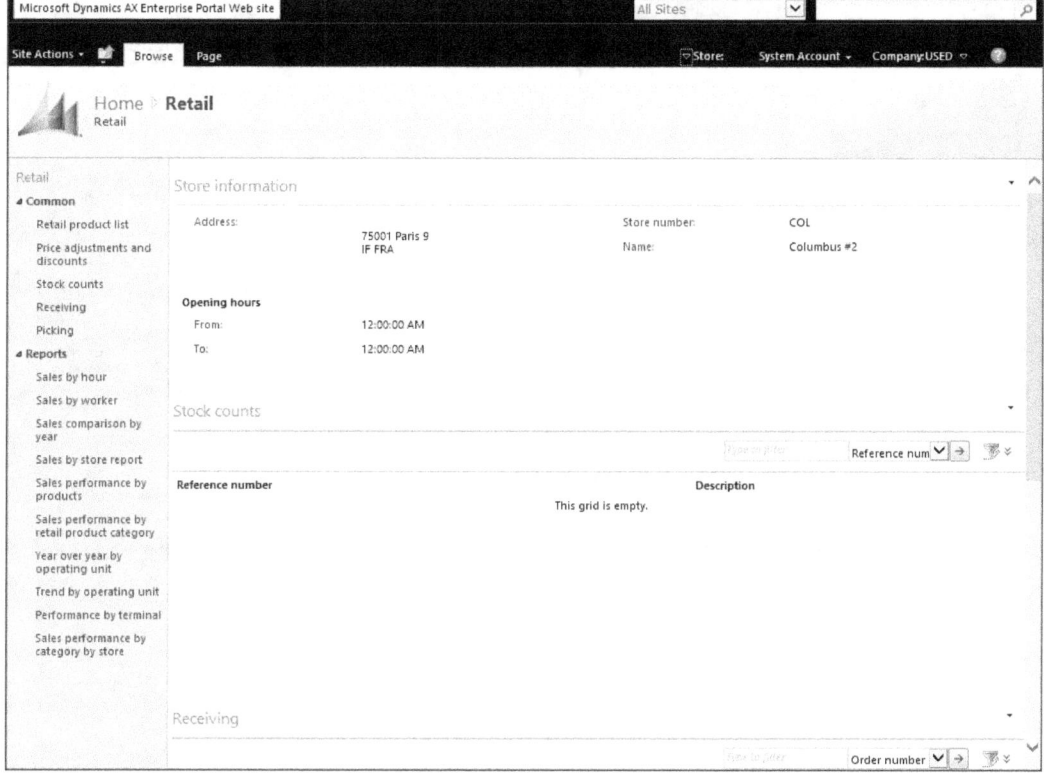

The Retail Portal allows the retail staff to get more insight into their store performance through the website as all of the POS information is synchronized back to Dynamics AX.

Since a lot of the transactions that are performed through the Retail locations are register based, this is a simple way to deliver the manager level information that is required on a day-to-day basis.

Sales Portal

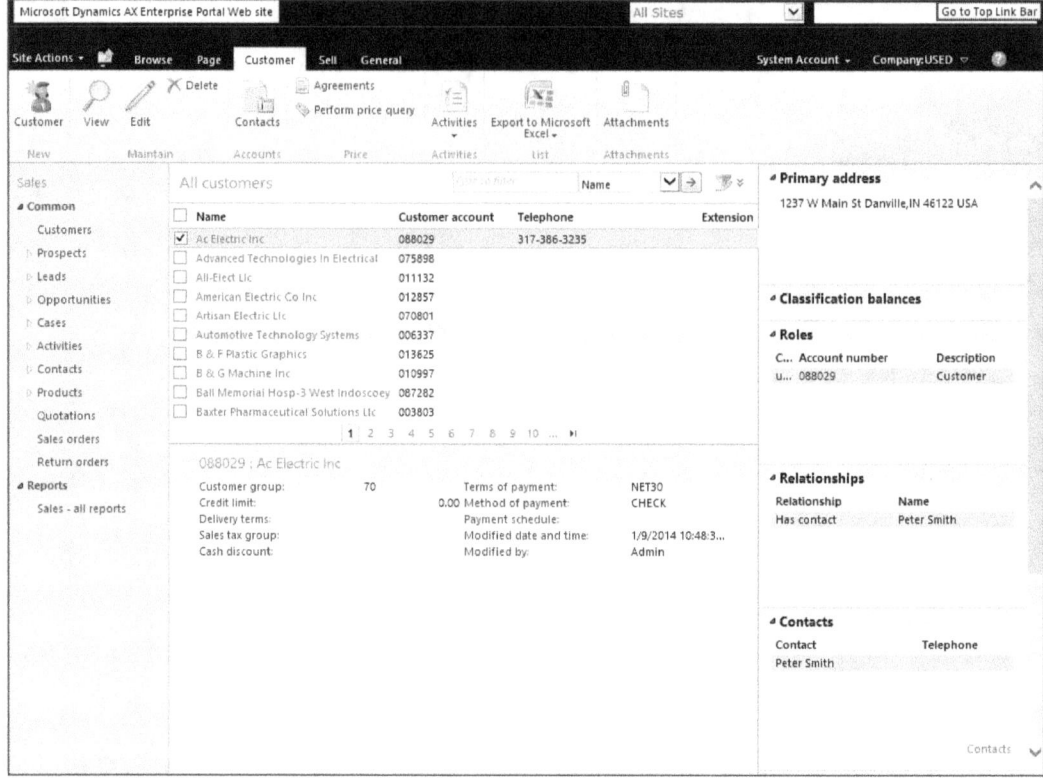

The Sales Portal is designed to give your mobile sales force a way to access and update all of the sales and marketing information with Dynamics AX through a thin web based interface.

This portal allows users to see all of the sales information as well as create new sales orders on the fly leveraging all of the standard pricing mechanisms that are built within Dynamics AX.

It also allows the user to access all of the CRM content such as Prospects, Leads, Opportunities, and Cases so that they can update their activities and progress through the sales cycle.

For the mobile sales force that are running on tablets, this is a must implement feature.

Service Management Portal

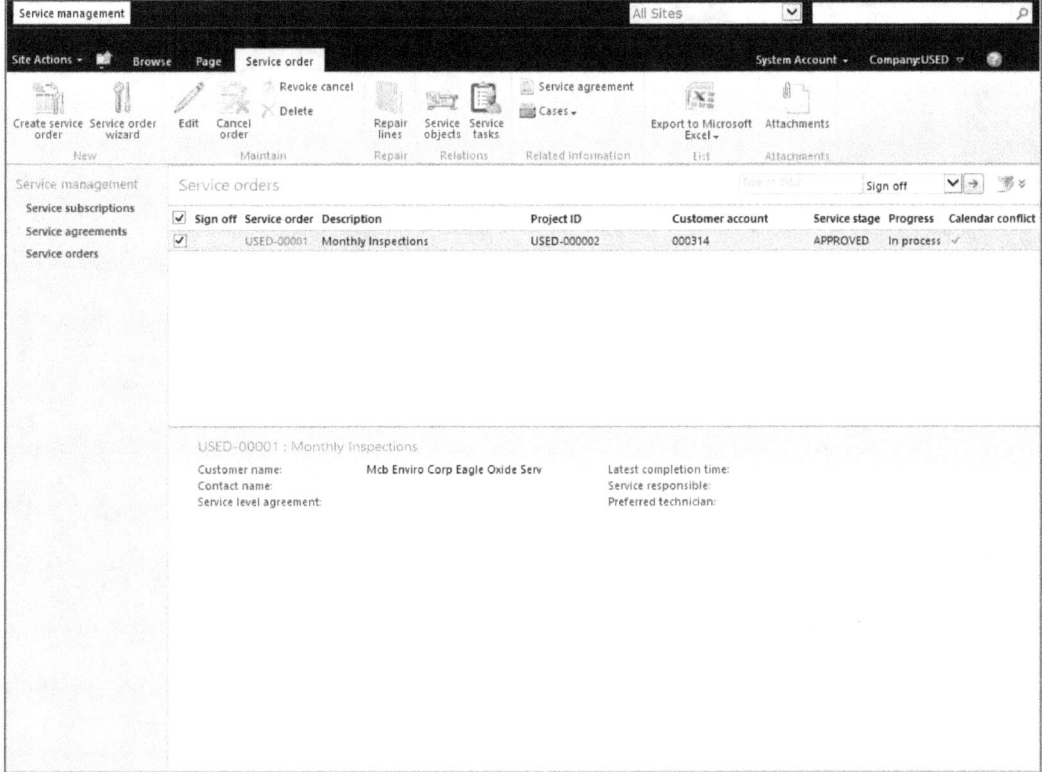

If you are taking advantage of the Service Management module within Dynamics AX, then the Service Management Portal allows your technicians and workers to access and update all of the service order information through a web client.

Since tablets rule when it comes to the mobile sales force, not having to install any client application in order to access your jobs and work orders, then this is a great way to keep up to date.

Vendor Self Service Portal

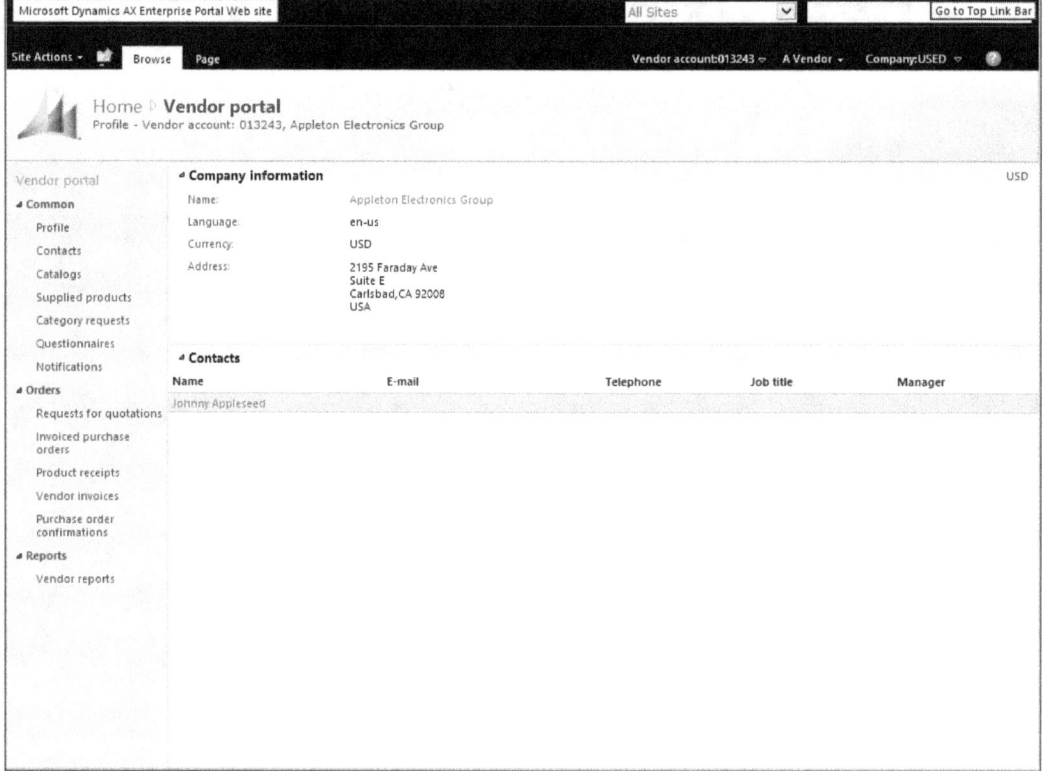

The Vendor Self Service Portal is the second external portal that is delivered with Dynamics AX. It allows your vendors to log into a secure site, and access and update all of their contact information, and even see all of the transactions that are associated with their account.

Additionally, the Vendor Portal allows you to collaborate with your vendors by allowing them to respond to Request For Quotations, answer certification questionnaires, receive notifications, and can also be used for on-boarding prospective vendors.

And one final point is that there are no user licenses required to allow your vendors to collaborate with you.

Introduction To Role Centers

Another way that users are different, is in the information that they need on a daily basis in order to get their jobs done. The CFO is interested in different information than the Production Manager, and they have different requirements than a Sales Manager as well.

To solve this problem, Dynamics AX comes pre-configured with about 45 or so Role Centers that are tailored to different roles and responsibilities within the organization that you can start using right away to deliver the right information to the right people.

The Role Centers are also the first view that the users will see when they log into Dynamics AX, making it a great place for the users to start their day and see what issues or events they may want to watch out for.

Additionally, with this feature, you get a template that you can use for the creation of your own Role Centers for the people within your organization that don't quite fit into the default profiles that are delivered with Dynamics AX. So if you have an Author role, or a Clinical Technician, don't worry, they can easily have their own custom Role Centers that show whatever information they may need for their job.

In this section we will show some of the default Role Centers, and the information that is available as a starting point for the users.

CFO Role Center

Cost Controller Role Center

HR Manager Role Center

Retail Merchandising Manager Role Center

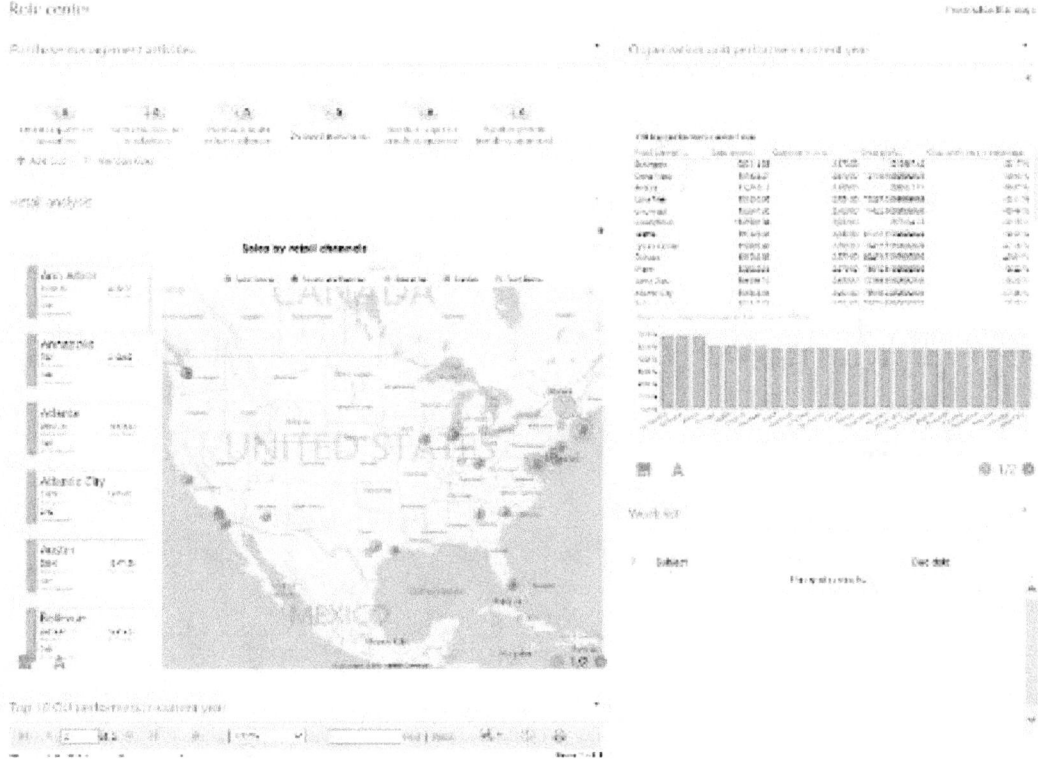

Shipping And Receiving Role Center

Role center

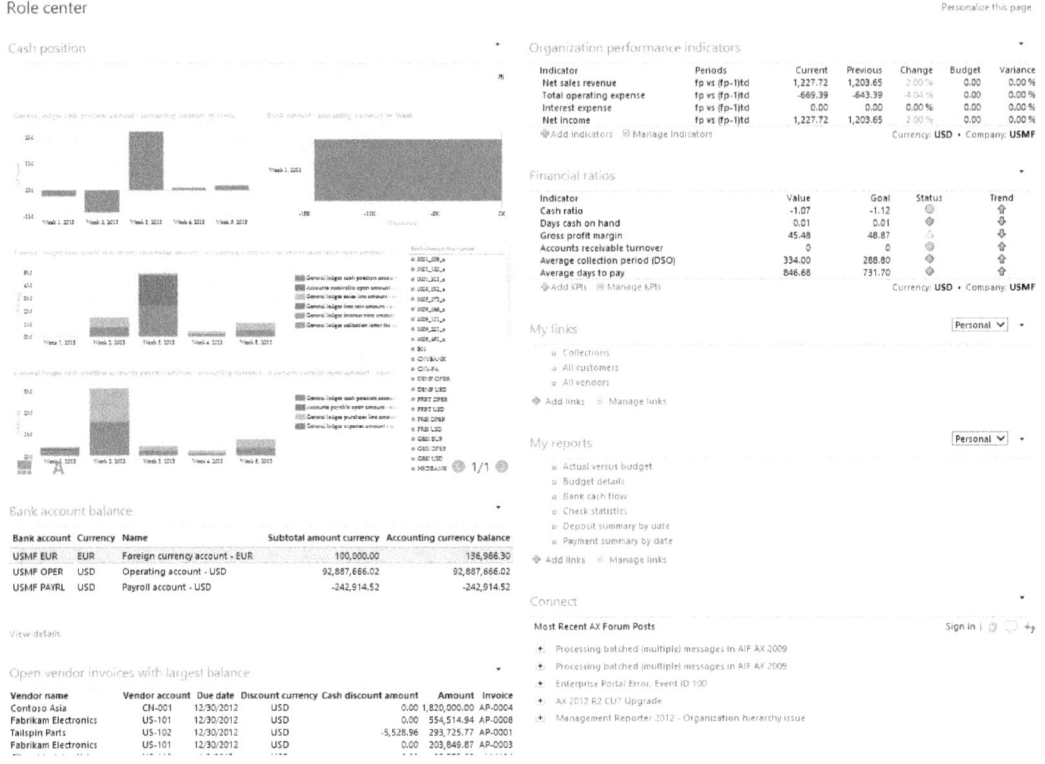

The Role Center Parts

One of the things that makes the Role Centers so useful is that it contains a lot of useful tools, all within one place so that you don't have to hunt through different screens in order to find everything that you are interested in.

In this section we will look at some of the typical things that you will find on your Role Centers, and also how you can use them to make your life just a little easier.

Activities and Cues

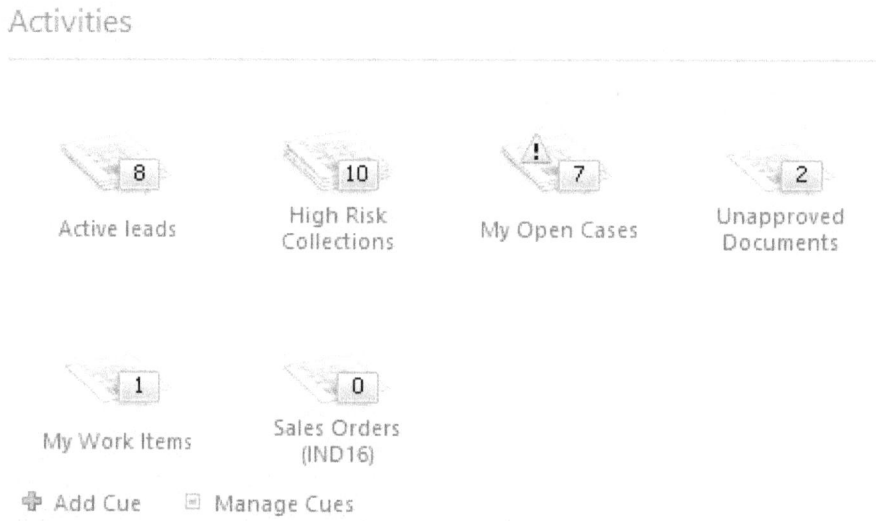

If you look at most peoples desks, then they probably have a number of stacks of paper that are there to remind them of what they need to work on, and also how much work they have to do.

Activities and Cues are a way to replace some of those stacks of paper on your desk, and replace them with virtual ones that are linked to tasks and processes within Dynamics AX. Apart from tidying up your desktop, they also give you direct links to the things that you are working on, and are also dynamics (unlike the piles of paper on your desk) so you can also use them to monitor what your direct reports are working on, and when things start to get out of hand, you can jump on it right away rather than getting blindsided.

You can create cues from almost any information that is available within Dynamics AX yourself, so these also work as your own personal tickler file, so if you want to track how many new customers there are, then just create a cue and add it to your Role Center.

Example: Using Cues To Jump Directly Into The Data You Are Interested In

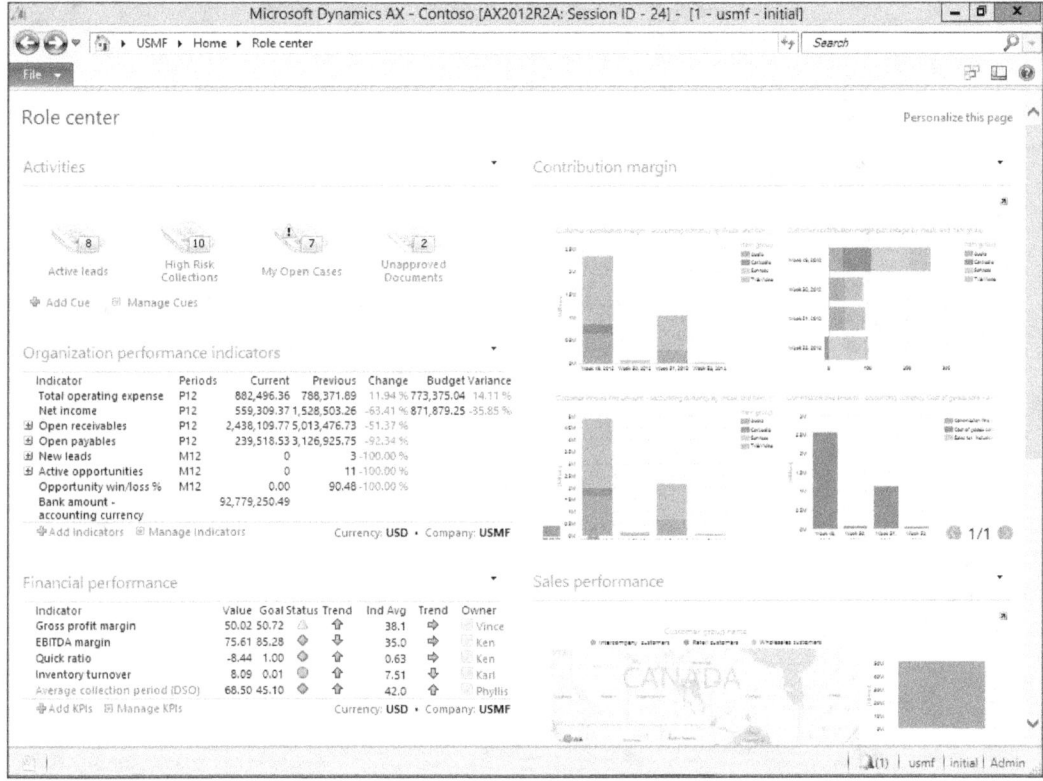

In this example when we look at the Activities area within the Role Center we notice that the Cue labeled "My Open Cases" is getting a little out of hand.

To view the open cases and see if we can resolve some of them we just click on the Cue.

Example: Using Cues To Jump Directly Into The Data You Are Interested In

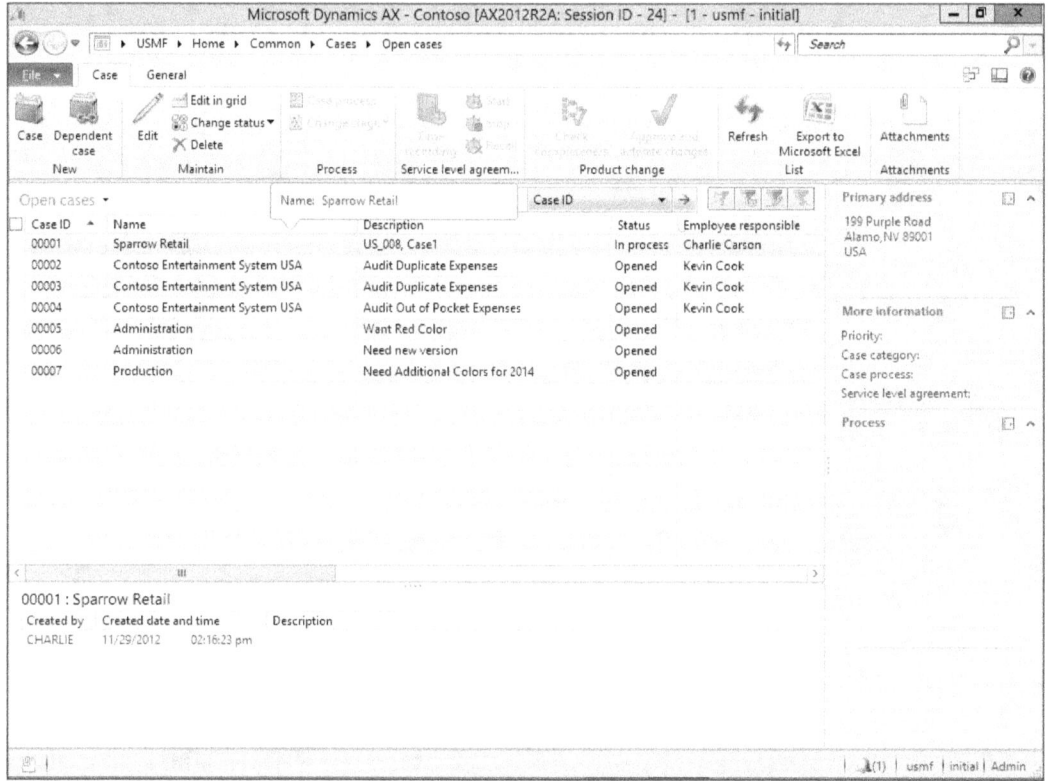

This will take us directly to the Open Cases list page within Dynamics AX and show us all of the Cases that are assigned to us, and we can start working on them right way.

David Allen would be so proud of us.

Performance Indicators
(a.k.a. Real Time Statistics)

Organization performance indicators

Indicator	Periods	Current	Previous	Change	Budget	Variance
Total operating expense	P12	10,901,693.92	7,555,285.58	44.29 %	1,306,647.29	734.33 %
Net income	P12	4,588,755.55	8,723,441.31	-47.40 %	120,405.00	3,711.10 %
⊞ Open receivables	P12	-40,075,956.40	16,645,096.74	-340.77 %		
⊞ Open payables	P12	11,943,964.78	10,316,920.40	15.77 %		
⊞ New leads	M12	0	3	-100.00 %		
⊞ Active opportunities	M12	2	13	-84.62 %		
Opportunity win/loss %	M12	100.00	98.15	1.89 %		
Bank amount - accounting currency		449,025,263.93				

⊹ Add Indicators   ▢ Manage Indicators   Currency: **USD** • Company: **All**

Financial performance

Indicator	Value	Goal	Status	Trend	Ind Avg	Trend	Owner
Gross profit margin	50.02	50.72	△	⇧	38.1	⇨	Vince
EBITDA margin	75.61	85.28	◇	⇩	35.0	⇨	Ken
Quick ratio	-8.44	1.00	◇	⇧	0.63	⇨	Ken
Inventory turnover	8.09	0.01	◯	⇧	7.51	⇩	Karl
Average collection period (DSO)	68.50	45.10	◇	⇧	42.0	⇧	Phyllis

⊹ Add KPIs   ▢ Manage KPIs   Currency: **USD** • Company: **USMF**

The next area of the Role Center that we will look at will be the Performance Indicators. These show all of the statistics that you are interested in all in one place, with trend information, and also links to the people within the organization that are responsible for them.

As an executive, or a manager, these give you a great way to track the state of the company, and if things are not quite going the direction that you like, then you can act upon them immediately and make small course corrections rather than waiting until there is a real problem and you need to make major corrections.

You can also personalize the statistics that are shown within the Performance Indicators so that you see just the information that you are interested in, getting rid of all the noise from company statistics that you are not interested in.

Example: Adding New Indicators To Your Watch List

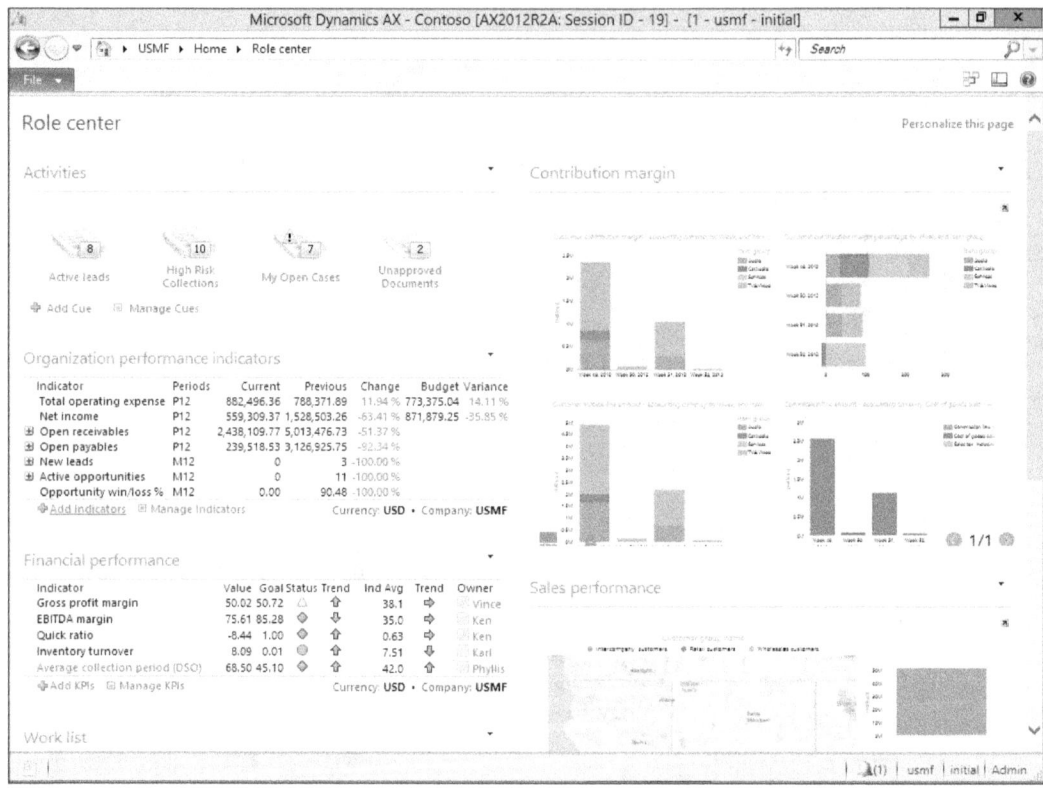

If you want to add another Performance Indicator to your watch list, then all you need to do is click on the Add indicators (or Add KPI's) link at the bottom of the Performance Indicators part of the Role Center.

Example: Adding New Indicators To Your Watch List

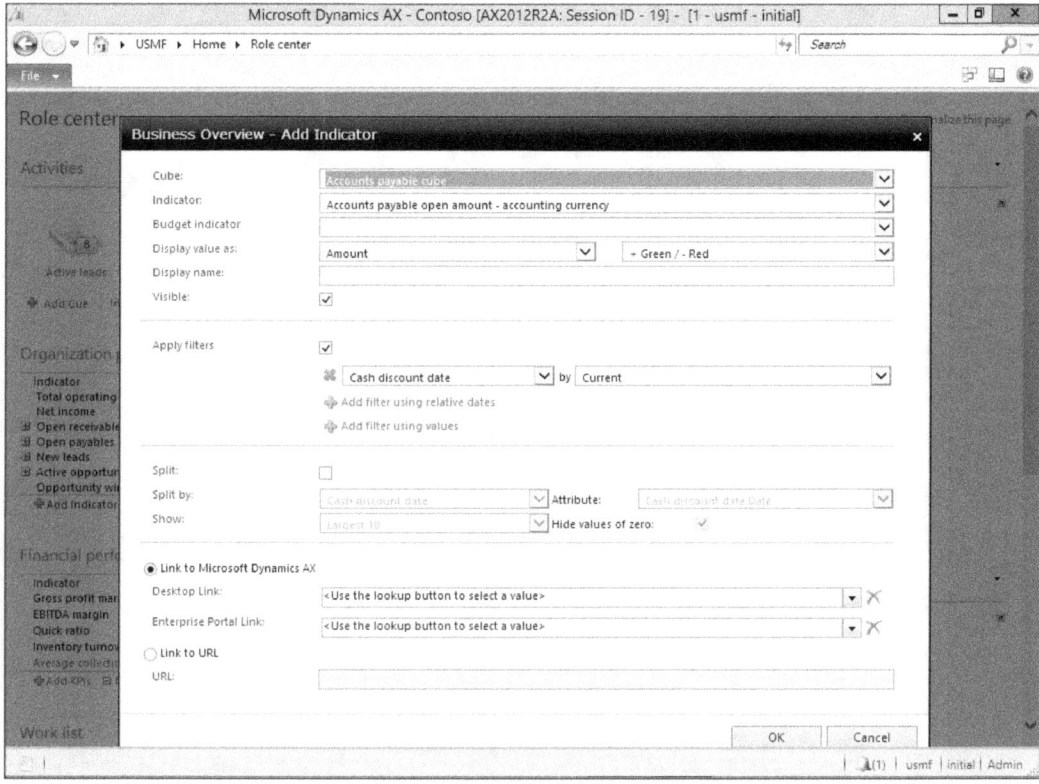

This will open up the Add Indicator form within the Role Center.

Example: Adding New Indicators To Your Watch List

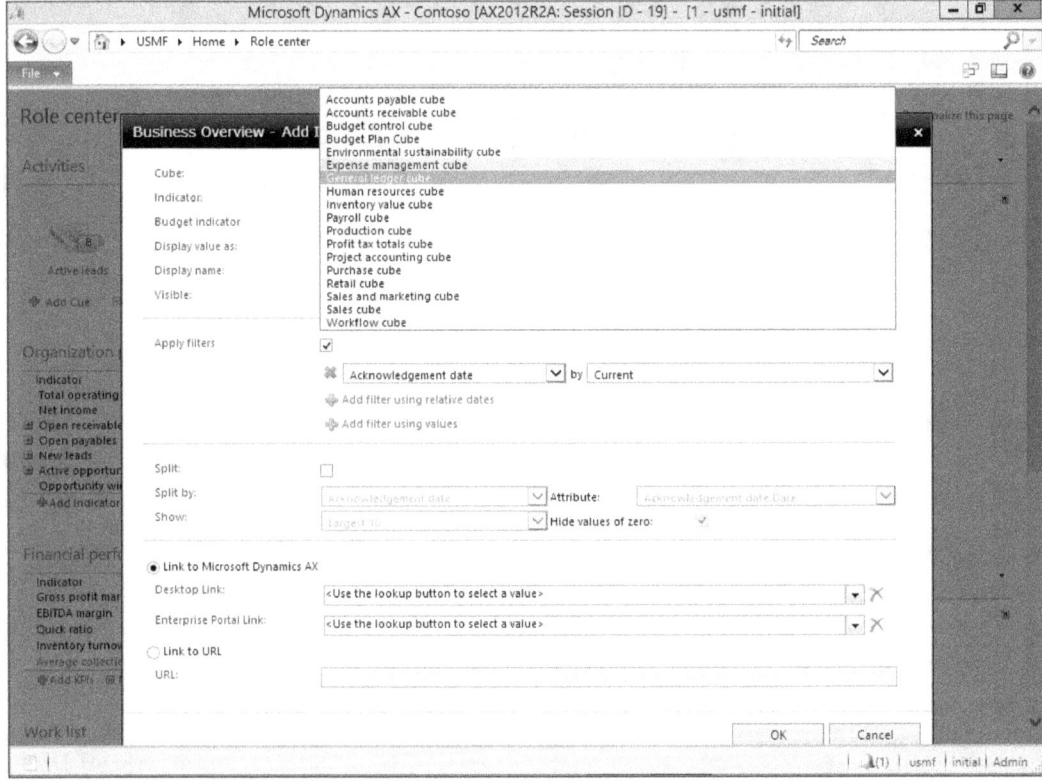

If you click on the Cube drop down box, you will see all of the different business areas that you can get information on.

Example: Adding New Indicators To Your Watch List

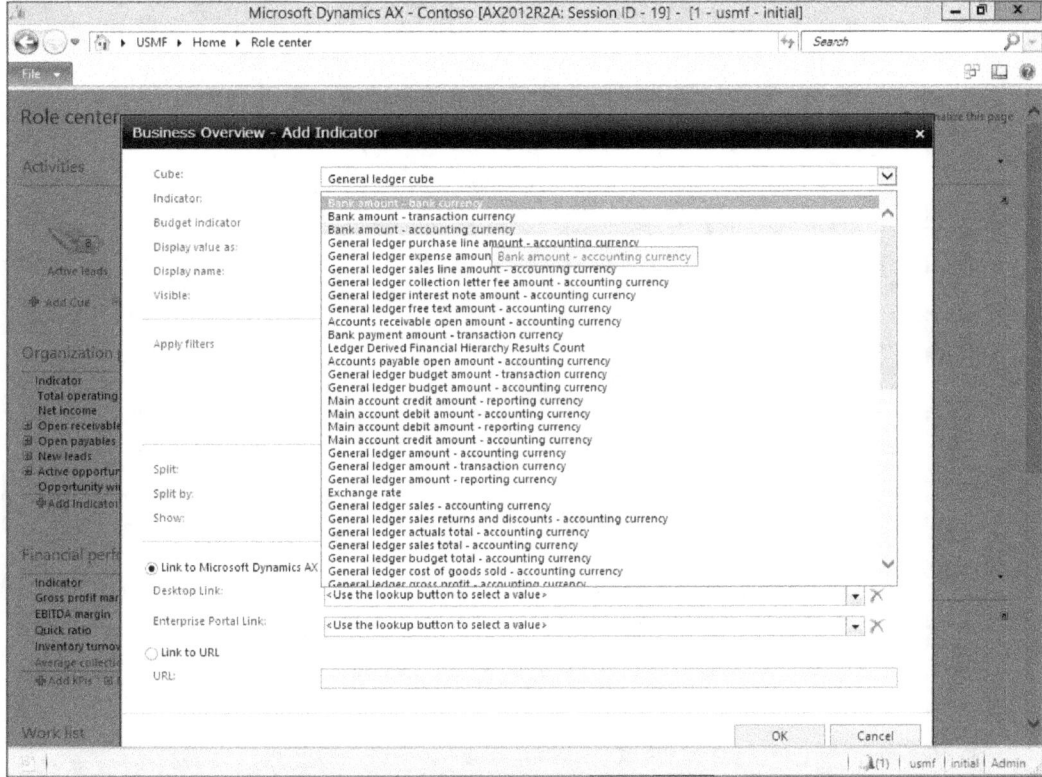

After selecting a business area, you can click on the Indicator dropdown, and you will see all of the standard indicators that you can add to your watch list.

Example: Adding New Indicators To Your Watch List

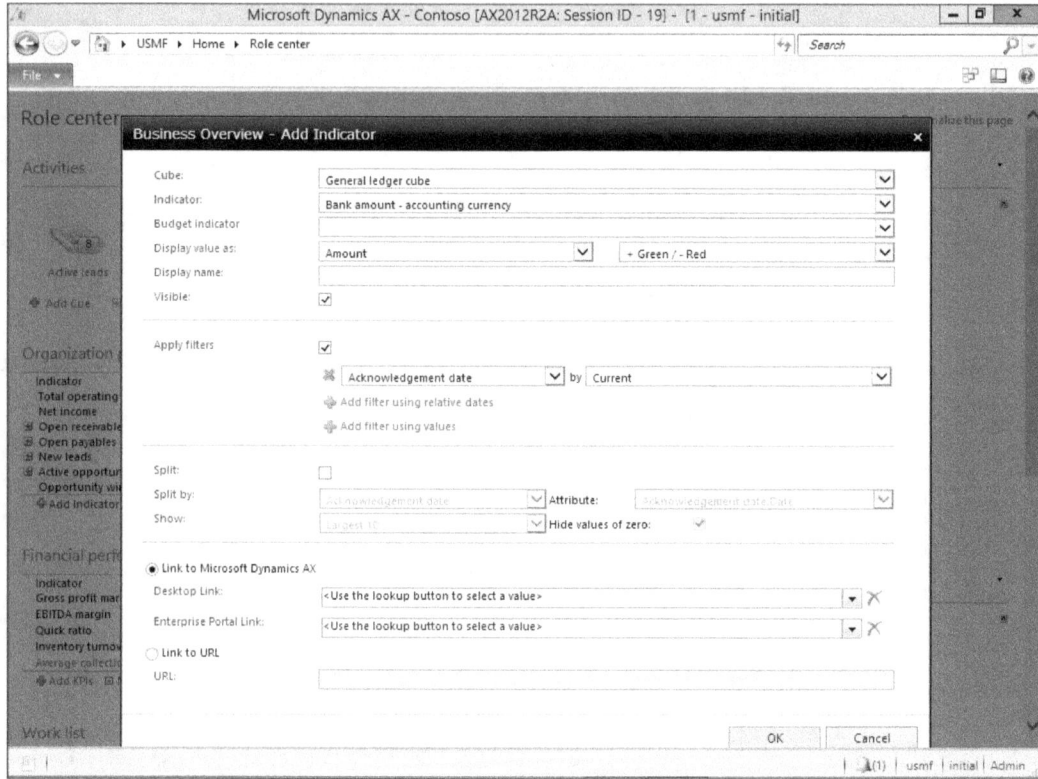

Once you have selected the Indicator, you can further refine the way that the information is displayed, relabel it, and even specify an area of Dynamics AX that you want to go to when you click on the link.

When you are done though, just click on the OK button.

Example: Adding New Indicators To Your Watch List

Now when you return to the Role Center, you will see your new Indicator has been added.

Example: Contacting The People Responsible Directly Through Lync

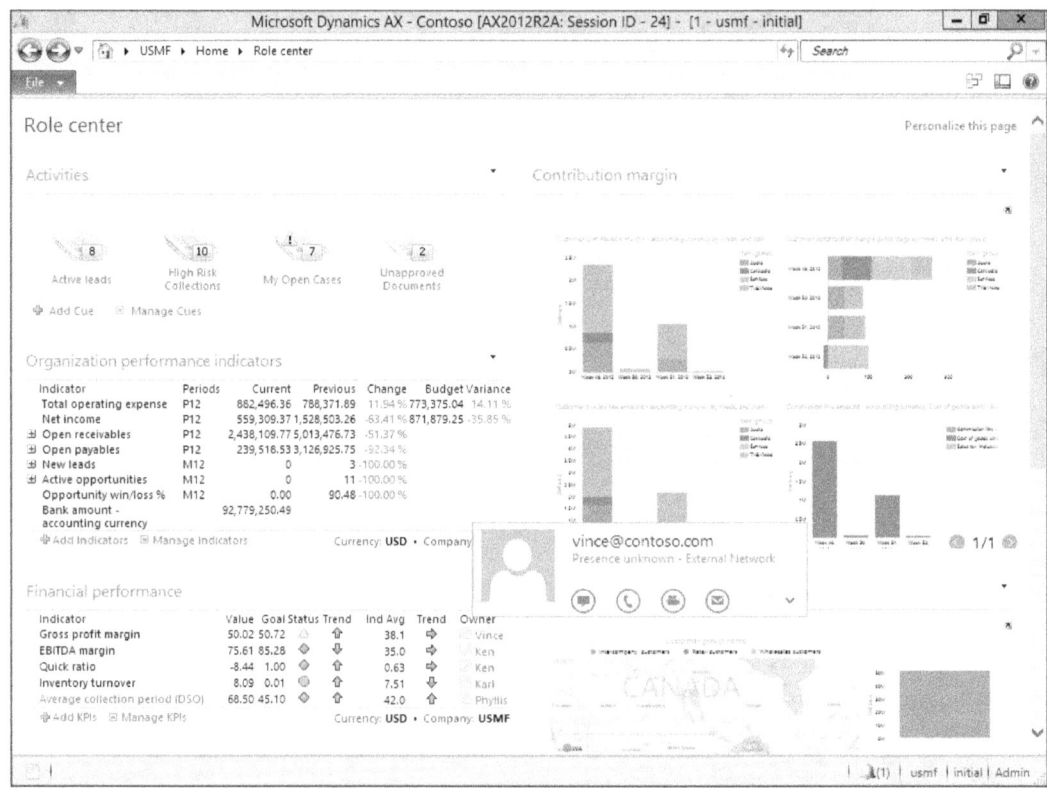

If you are just watching the performance indicators, and someone else (probably that works for you) is responsible for keeping the indicator in check, and you need to get things back in balance then you can hover over their name beside the indicator.

This will open up the Lync presence indicator with the person's information. If you want to contact them, then just click on the messaging, voice, video, or email icon.

Example: Contacting The People Responsible Directly Through Lync

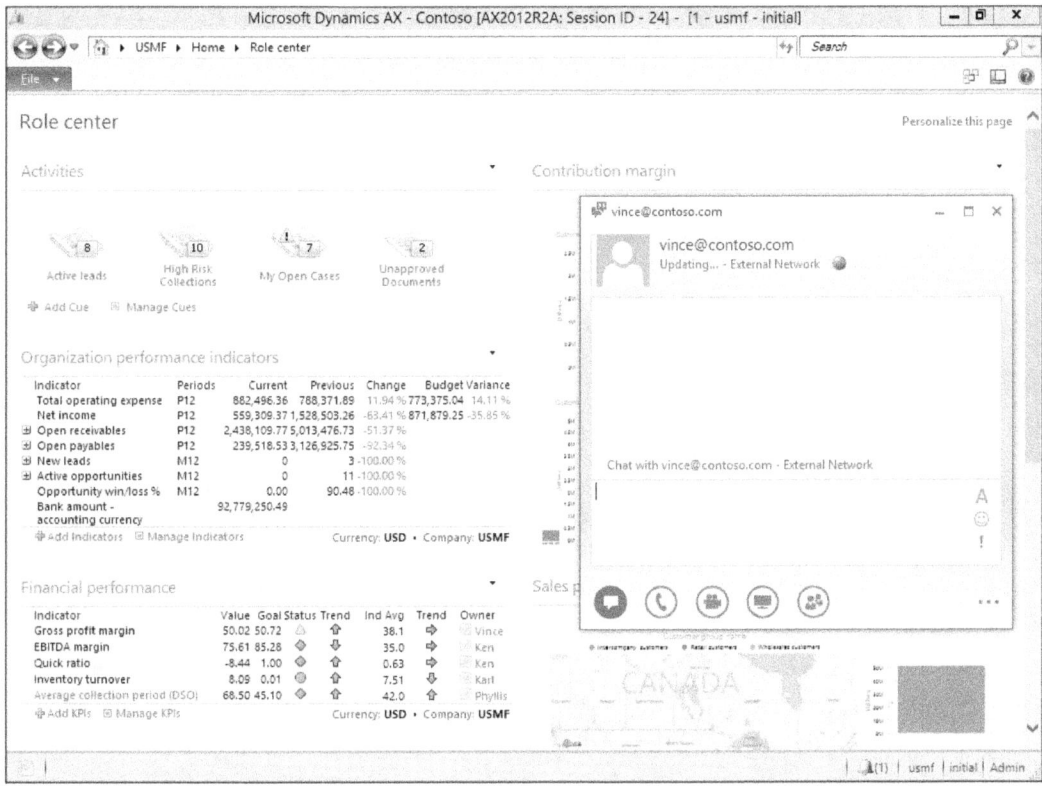

That will take you directly into Lync and you can start asking them what the heck is happening.

Example: Accessing The Owners Details Through MySites

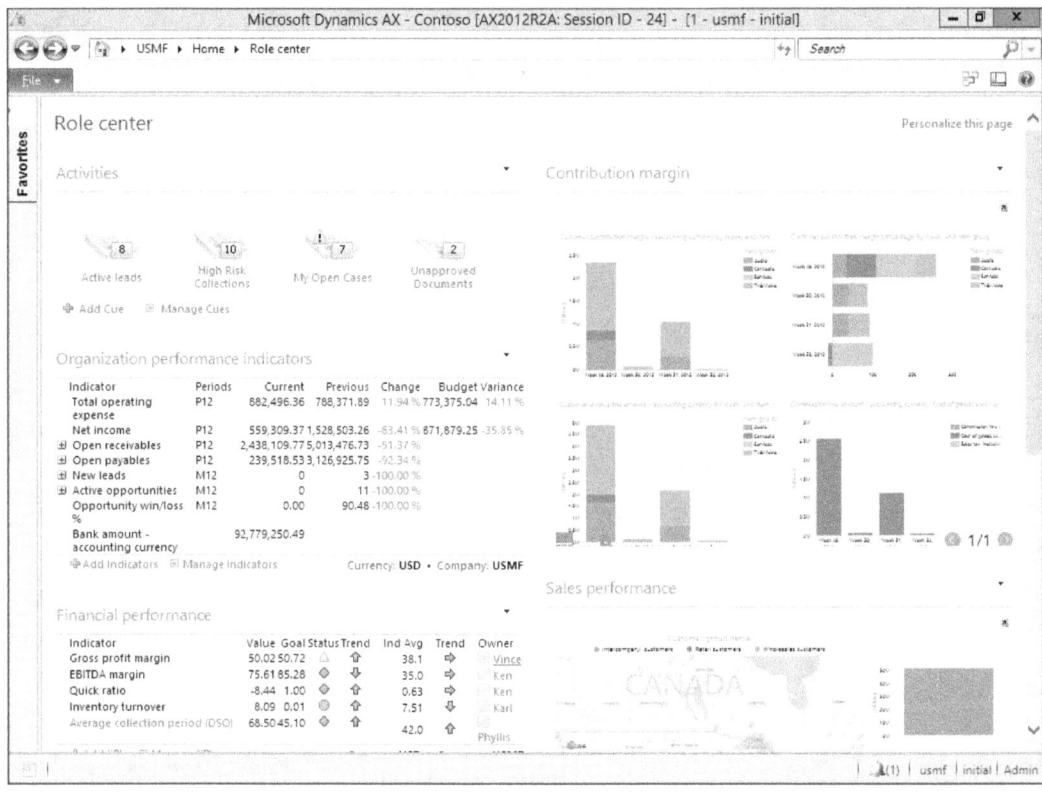

If you are using MySites within SharePoint, then you can also contact the people that are responsible for the indicators that way as well. All you have to do is click on their name.

Example: Accessing The Owners Details Through MySites

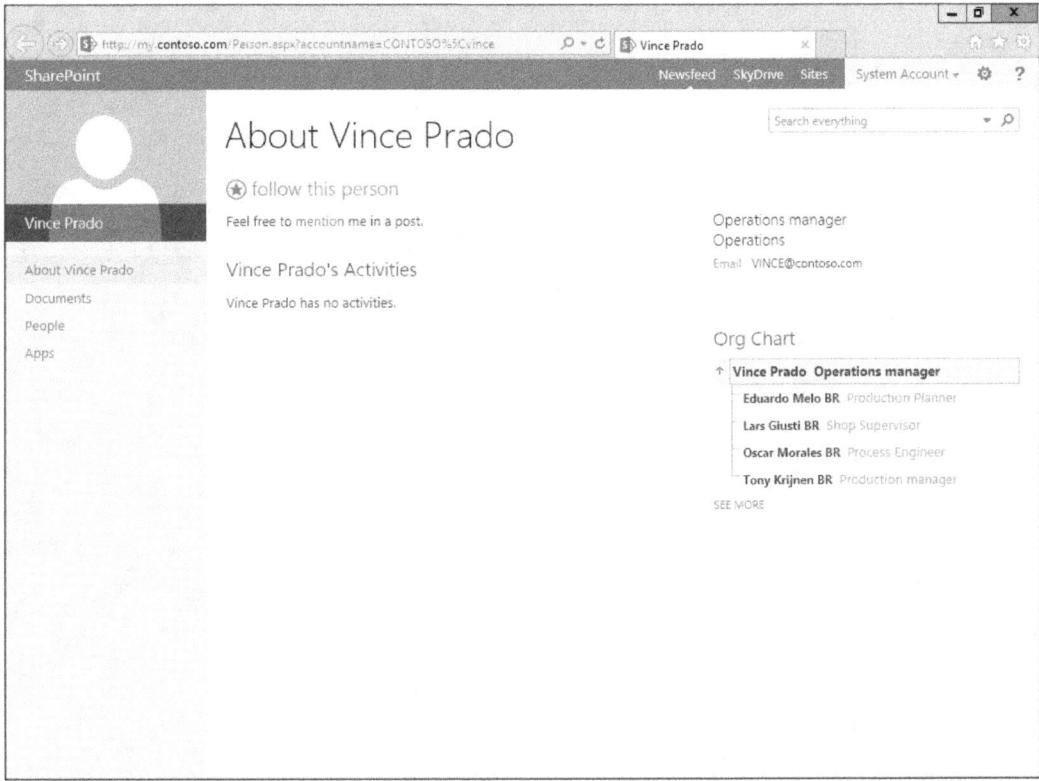

This will open up their MySite showing you what they are up to and also additional information like the Org Chart. If the person is on vacation for example, you can start trying to get in contact with their direct reports, or if they are micro-blogging, then maybe they have made a note on their MySite about certain situations that may be causing an issue.

This way you are still in the loop, but not bothering them while they are working.

PowerView Dashboards & Analytics

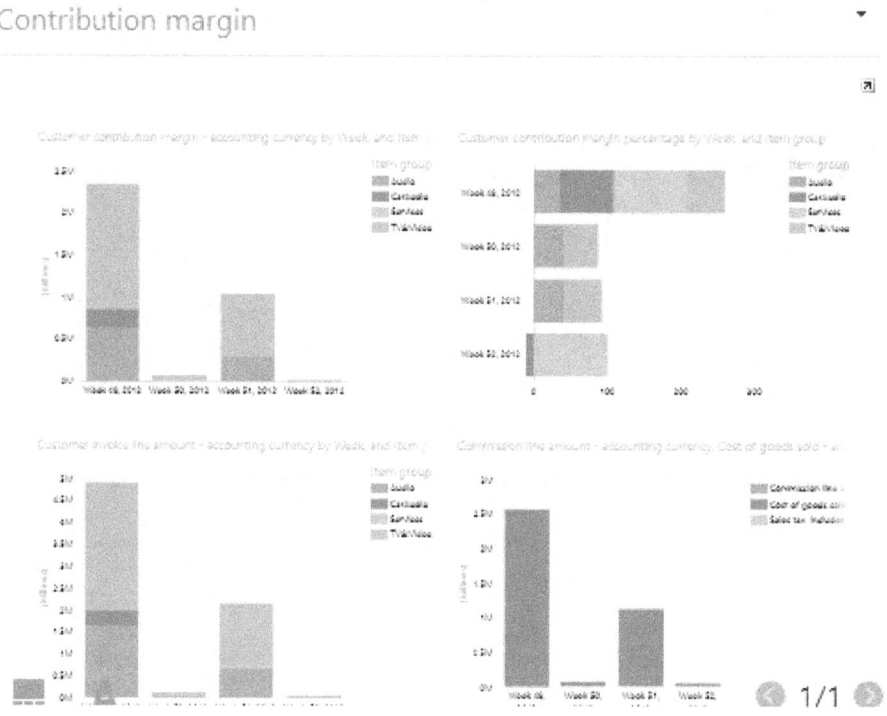

Everyone loves dashboards because they give you a more visual way to track your data, and also see the interrelationships between pieces of information. So that you don't have to go to another application or window in order to view your dashboards, you can embed them directly within the Role Center itself.

Example: Launching Dashboards In Full Screen Mode

The PowerView dashboards are useful within the Role Center because you can get a quick visual on how the business is running. But it's sometimes a little too small for clicking and filtering.

If you want to see all of the detail provided through the dashboard, all you need to do is click on the Launch the report in full screen icon to the top right of the dashboard.

Example: Launching Dashboards In Full Screen Mode

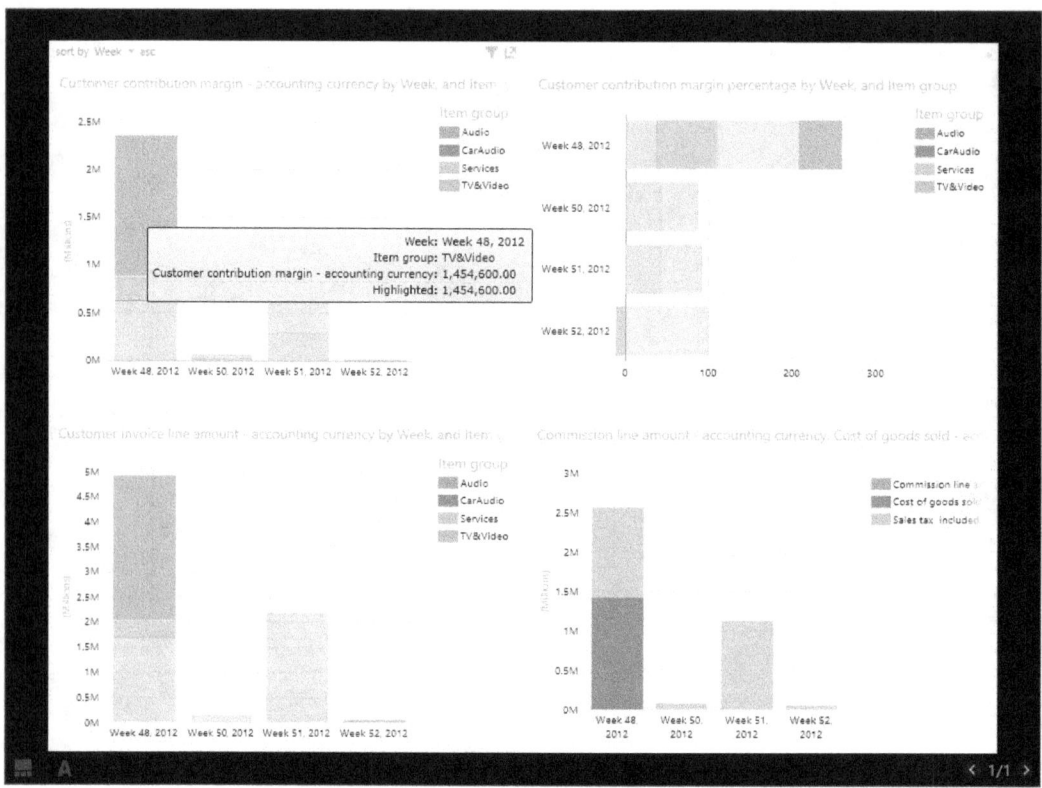

This will open up the dashboard in full screen mode and then you can click through the data to your hearts content.

The Workflow Task List

One of the strengths of Dynamics AX is the workflow functionality that allows you to route tasks within the organization automatically based on the procedures that you configure. So if you need someone to approve something, then you do it through workflows, and can stop using paper approvals that can get lost or circumvented.

The Role Centers keep everyone on point by showing all of the workflow tasks that they have been assigned through the Work List part that allows you to act upon any workflow task, and also drill into the task to see all the detail within Dynamics AX.

That way, everyone knows everything that they need to do, and just what they need to do.

Example: Approving A Workflow

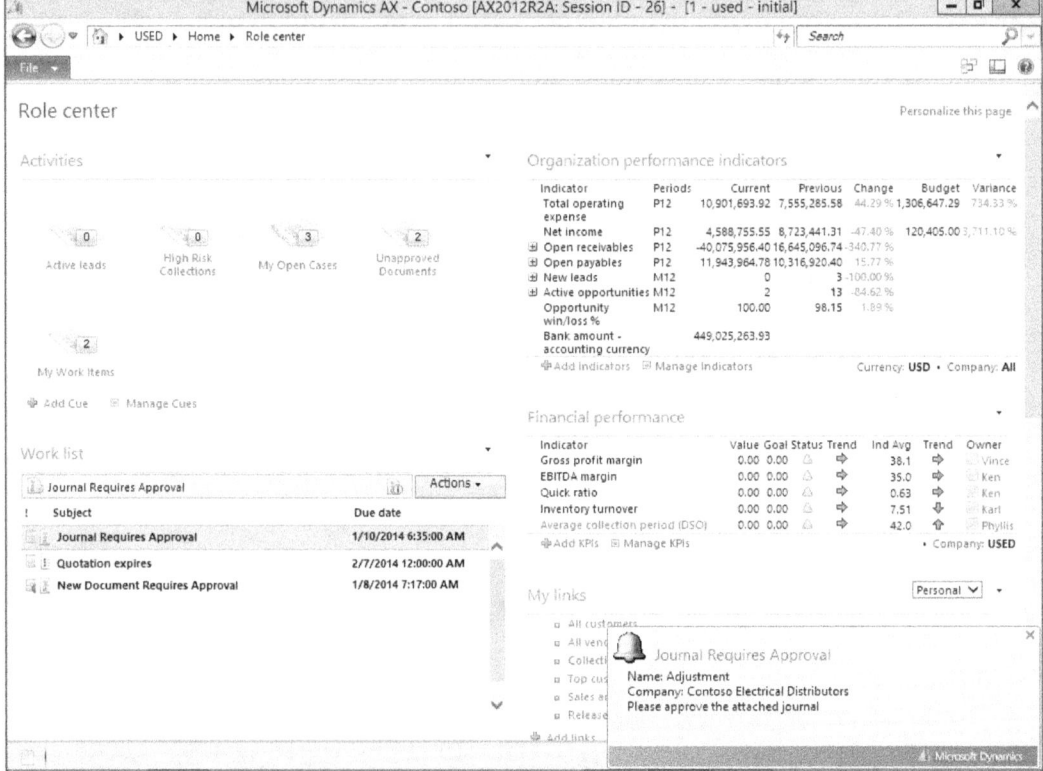

When a workflow task is assigned to you, then you will receive notifications a number of different ways, and you can act upon it immediately through your role center.

Immediately you will receive a pop-up notice that you have been assigned a task. If you happen to miss it though don't worry because Work List part within the Role Center will show that you have a task as well.

Example: Approving A Workflow

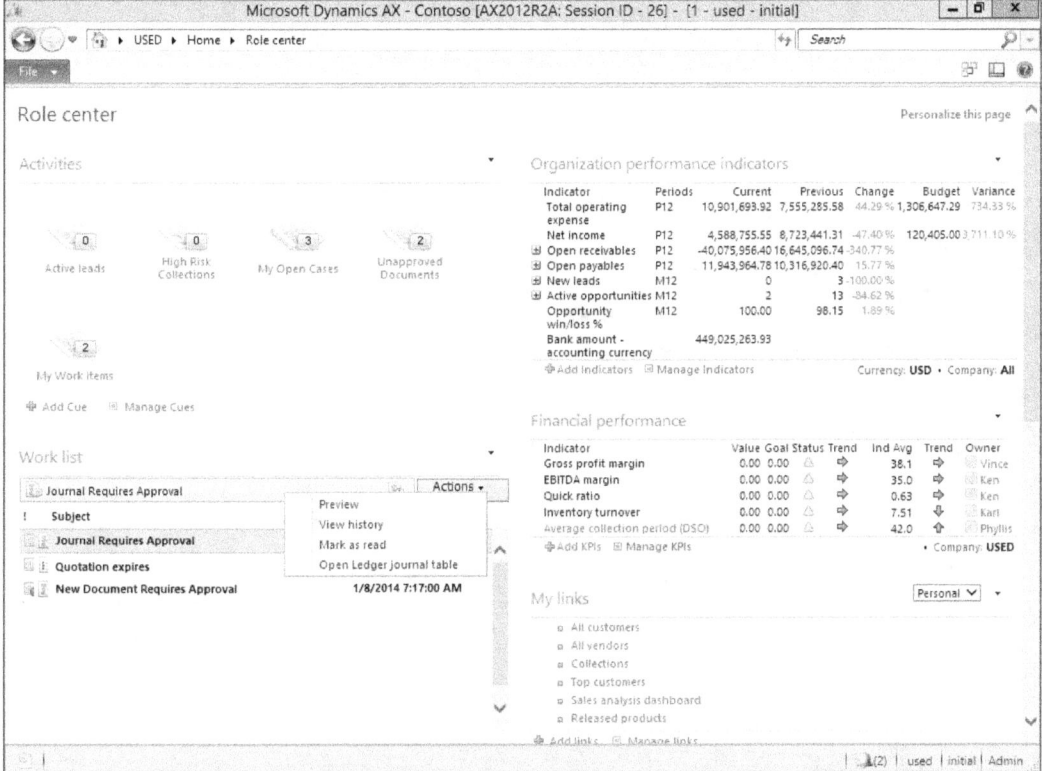

If you need more information about a workflow task that you have been assigned, just select it within the Work List and then click on the Actions menu button to see all the options that you have related to the task.

Depending on the type of workflow task that you have been assigned, you may be able to approve the task directly from here, or you can drill into the detail of the transaction that assigned you the task in the first place.

Example: Approving A Workflow

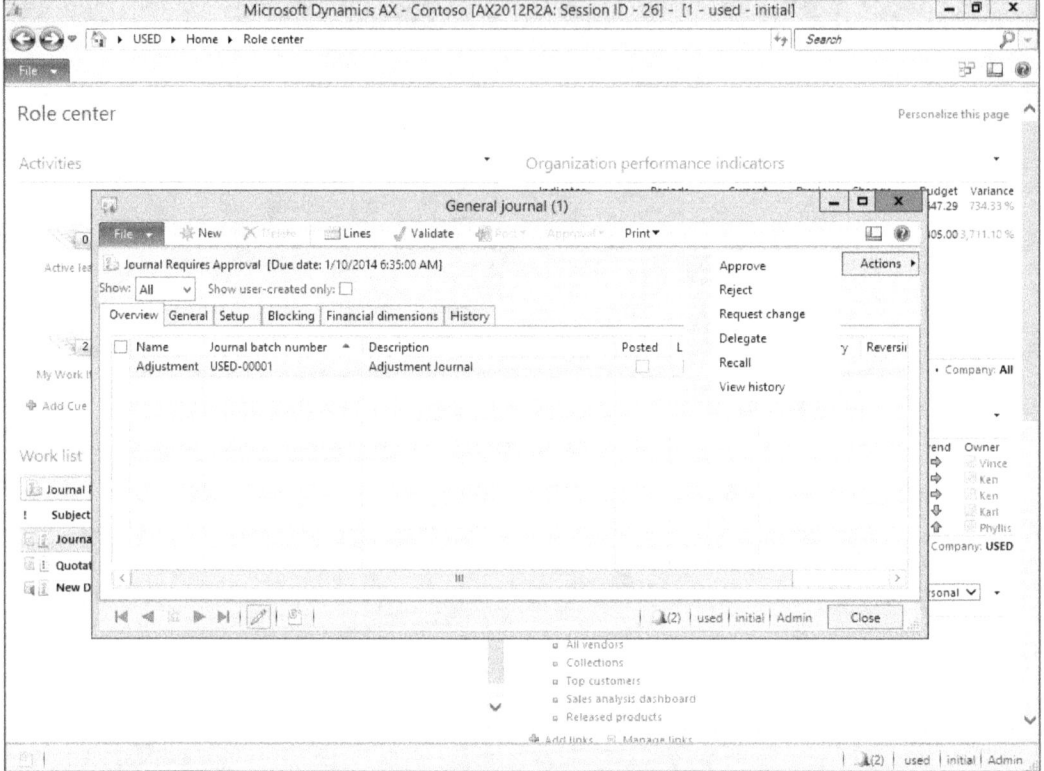

When you open up the transaction details, you can click on the Actions button and respond to the workflow task.

Example: Approving A Workflow

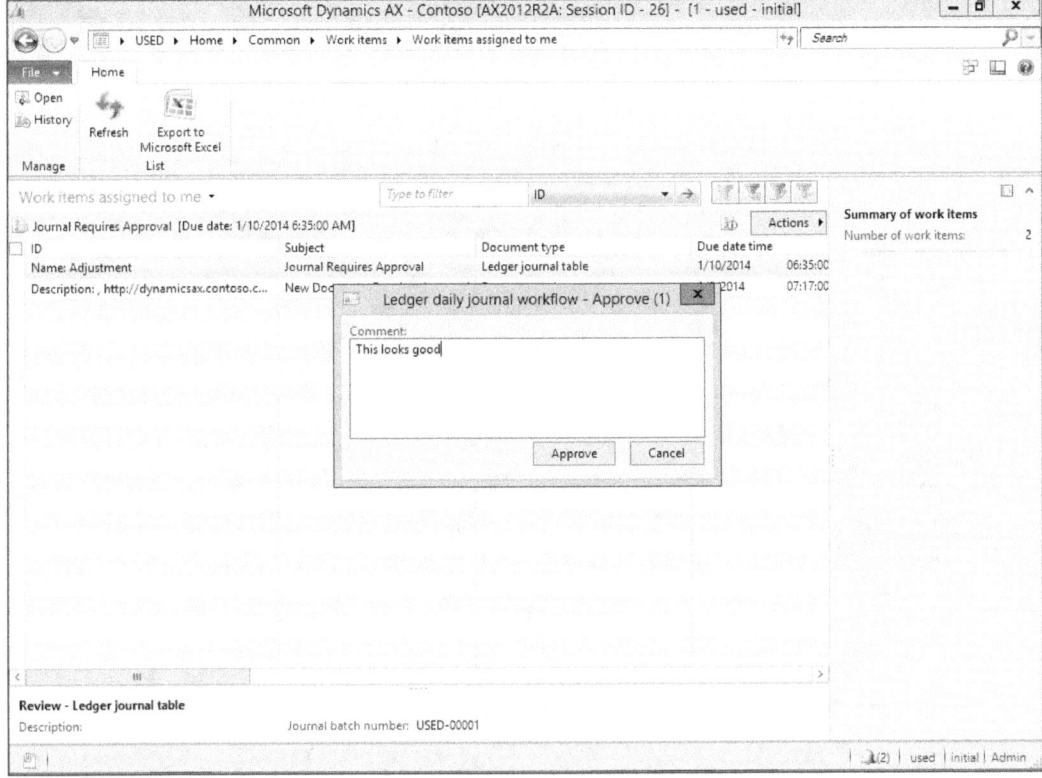

You can also attach any comments that you may have that are associated with the workflow, and then move it along to the next step in the workflow.

Example: Approving A Workflow

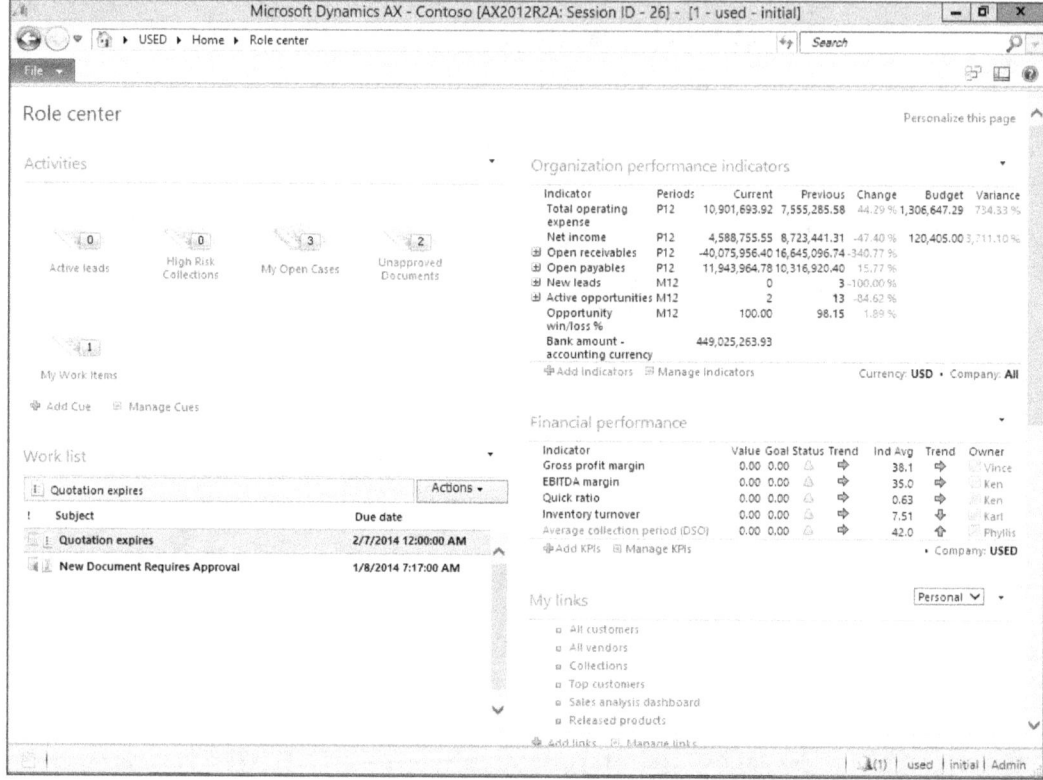

When you return to your Role Center, you will notice that the task that you just completed has been taken off your Work List and you can continue with your day.

Quick Links to Dynamics AX Forms and Reports

My reports   Personal ∨   ▾

    ▫ Actual versus budget report
    ▫ Budget detail report
    ▫ Bank cash flow report
    ▫ On-hand inventory
    ▫ Gross margin by customer
    ▫ Gross margin by item
    ▫ Financial reports

✚ Add links   ▣ Manage links

Most users will only need to access a handful of functions within Dynamics AX on a daily basis, so rather than having to find those functions each time through the normal menus within Dynamics AX, you can add them to you My Links and My Reports parts within the Role Center.

This gives you a quick and easy way to go to the functions within Dynamics AX that you use all the time.

Example: Using The My Links To Go To Dynamics AX Screens

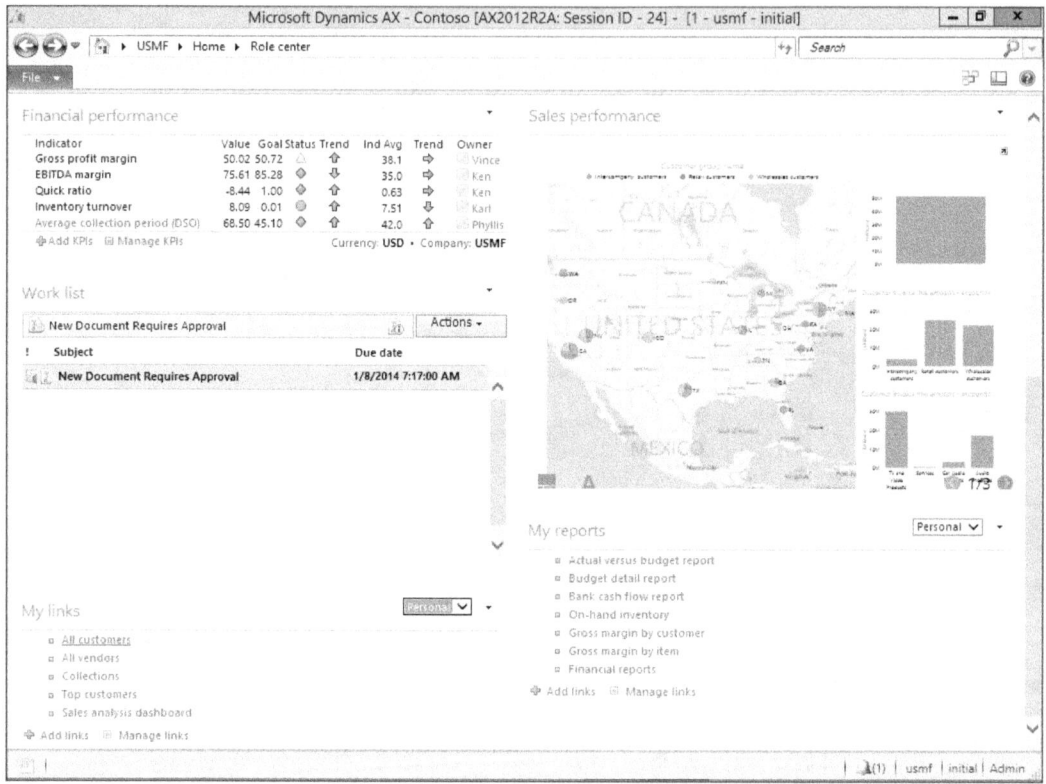

In this example we have added a number of the common forms within Dynamics AX to our My Links part of the Role Center. If we want to see all of our customers, then we can just click on the All Customers link.

Example: Using The My Links To Go To Dynamics AX Screens

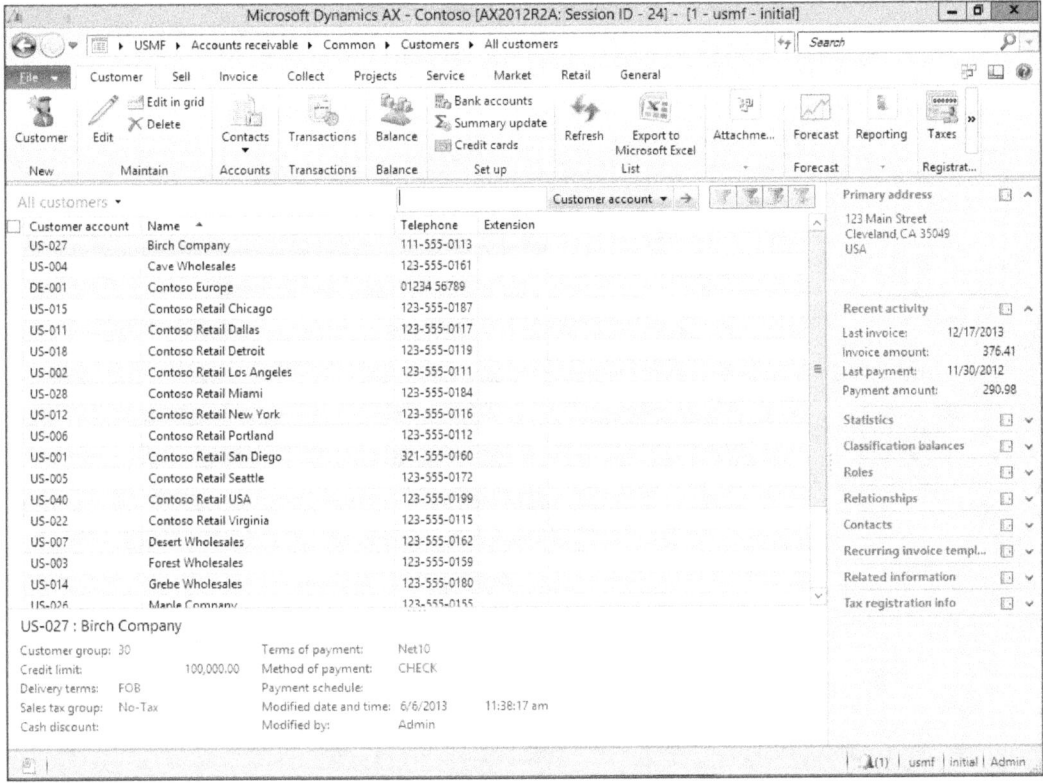

That will take us directly from the Role Center to the All Customers list page.

Example: Adding New Menu Item Links

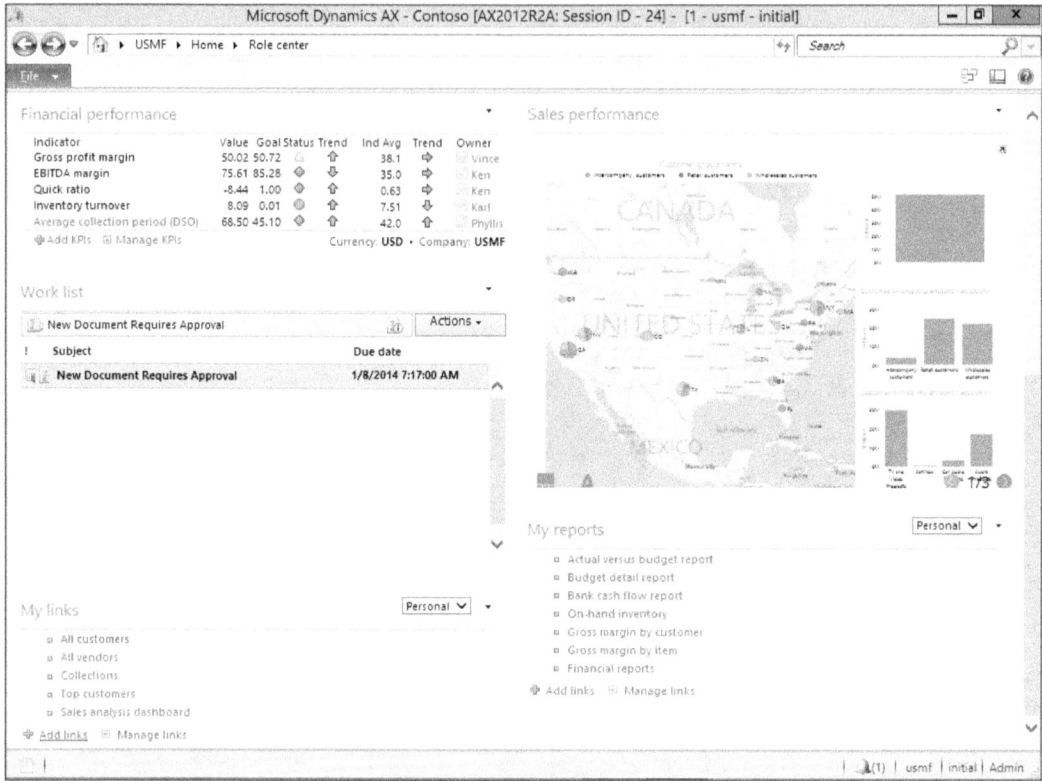

If you want to add a link to another form or report within Dynamics AX to the My Links part of the Role Center, just click on the Add Links at the bottom right of the My Links part.

Example: Adding New Menu Item Links

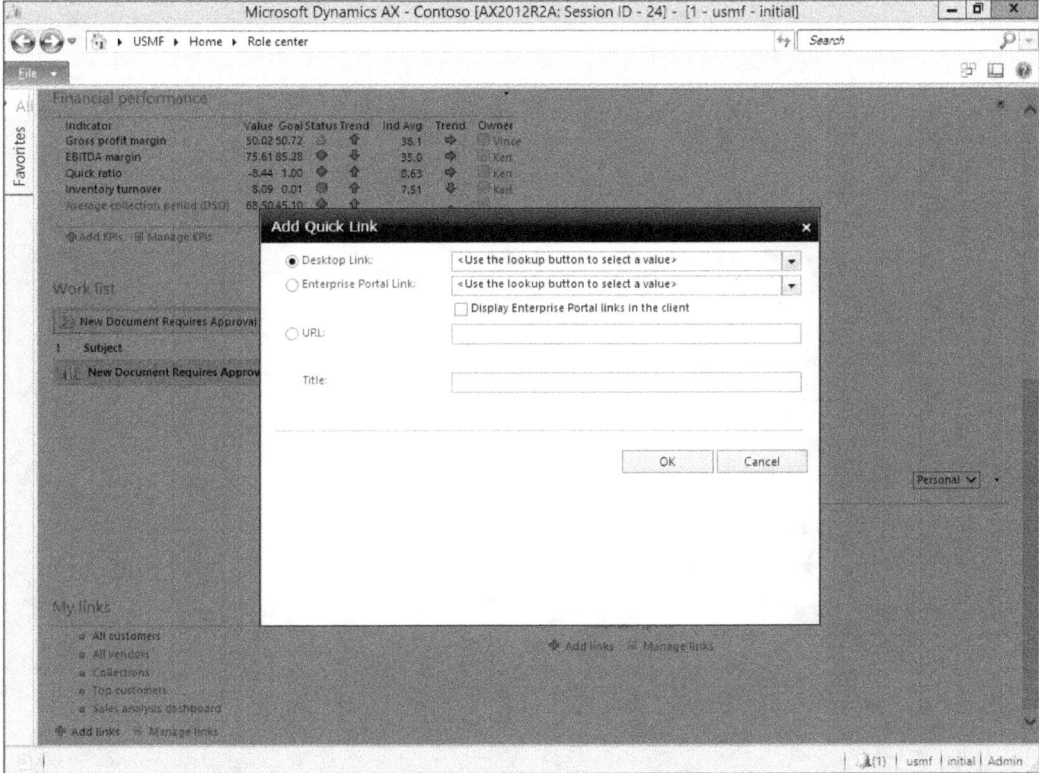

That will open up the Add Quick Link dialog box.

Example: Adding New Menu Item Links

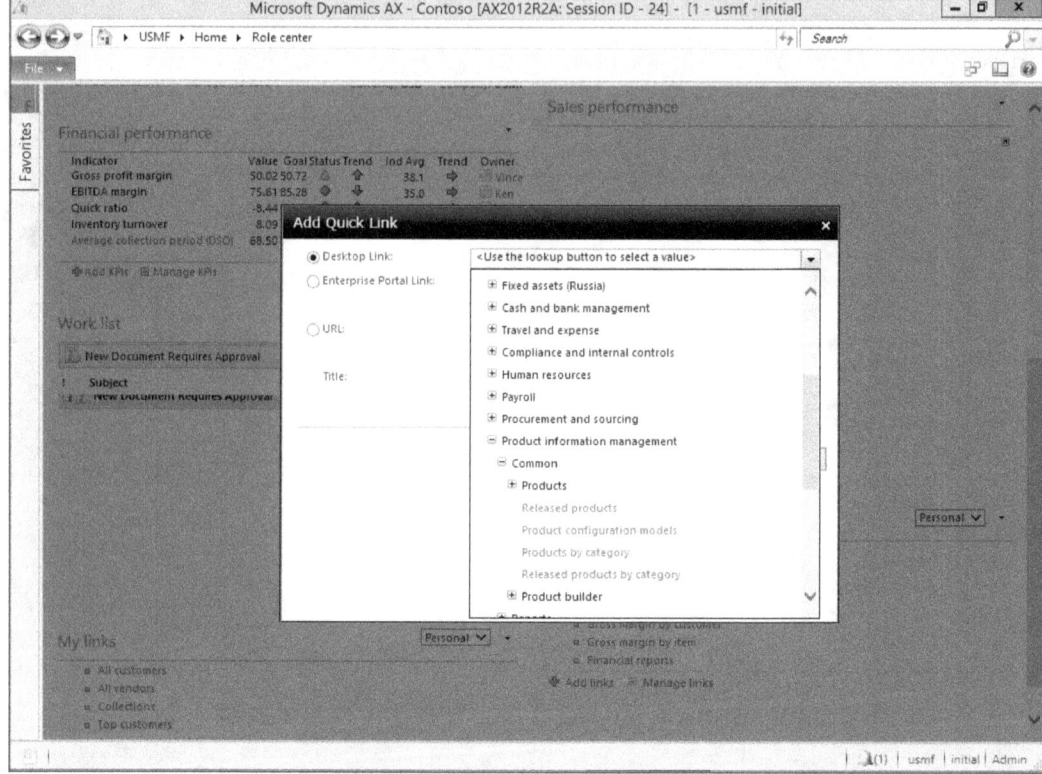

All you need to do is open up the Desktop Link dropdown box (or Enterprise Portal Link if you want to open up the web version of the form) and select the menu item that you want to add.

Example: Adding New Menu Item Links

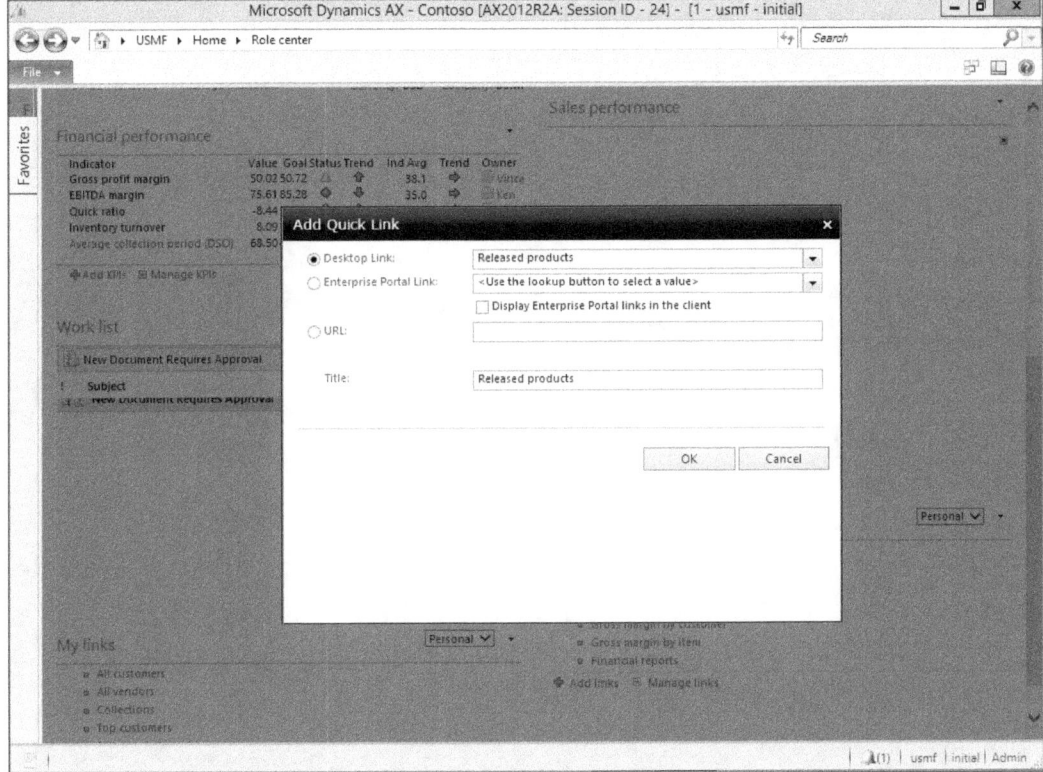

You can rename the form if you like from the default, and when you are done, just click on the OK button.

Example: Adding New Menu Item Links

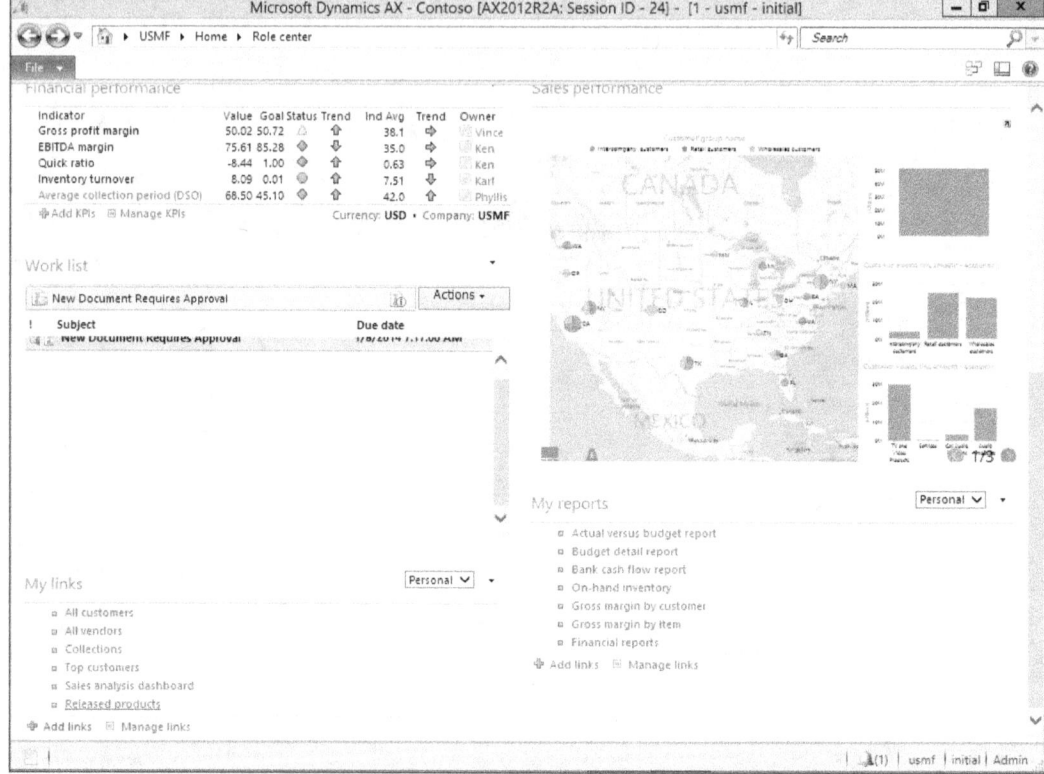

Now you will see the new quick link to the form in the My Links part.

Personalizing The Role Center Even More

Role center

Personalize this page

The Role Centers are built upon Microsoft SharePoint, so if you like (and have the privileges), you can personalize them even more by moving the parts of the Role Center around, and also by adding additional parts to the Role Center. These could be parts that link to Dynamics AX, or they could be any of the others that are available through SharePoint like document lists, tasks, RSS feeds and so much more.

Example: Personalizing The Role Center Page

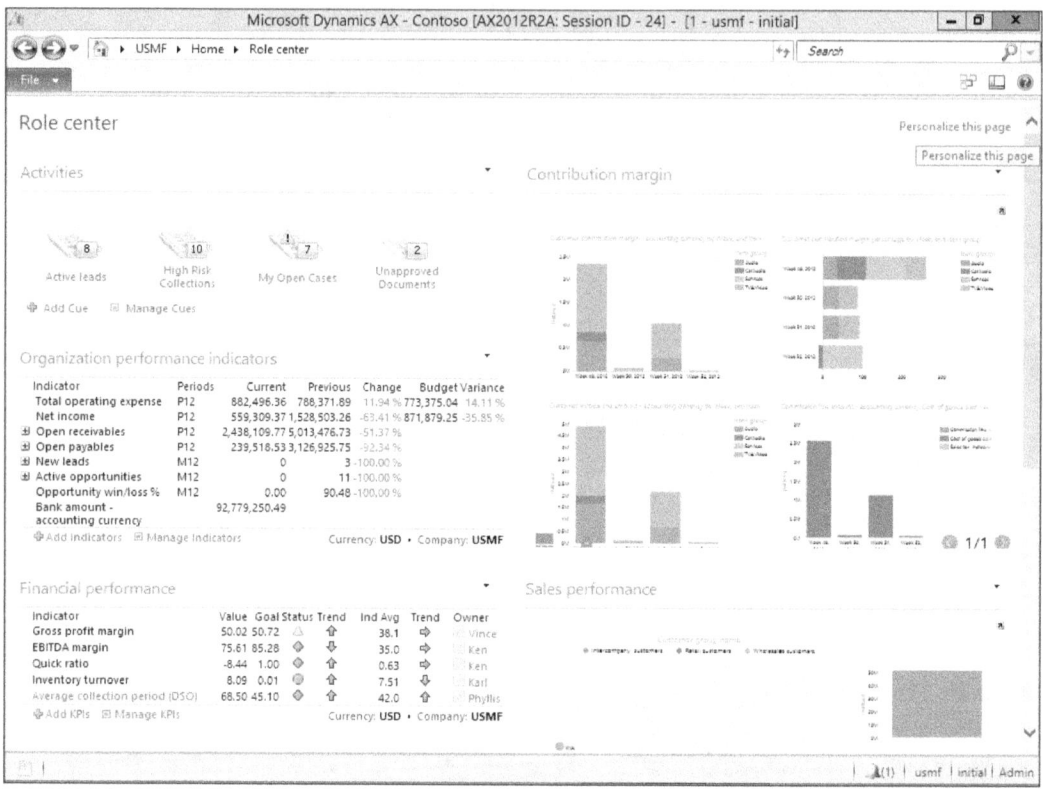

If you have the privilege to tweak the Role Center even more, then you will be able to see a Personalize this page link at the top right of the Role Center.

Just click it.

Example: Personalizing The Role Center Page

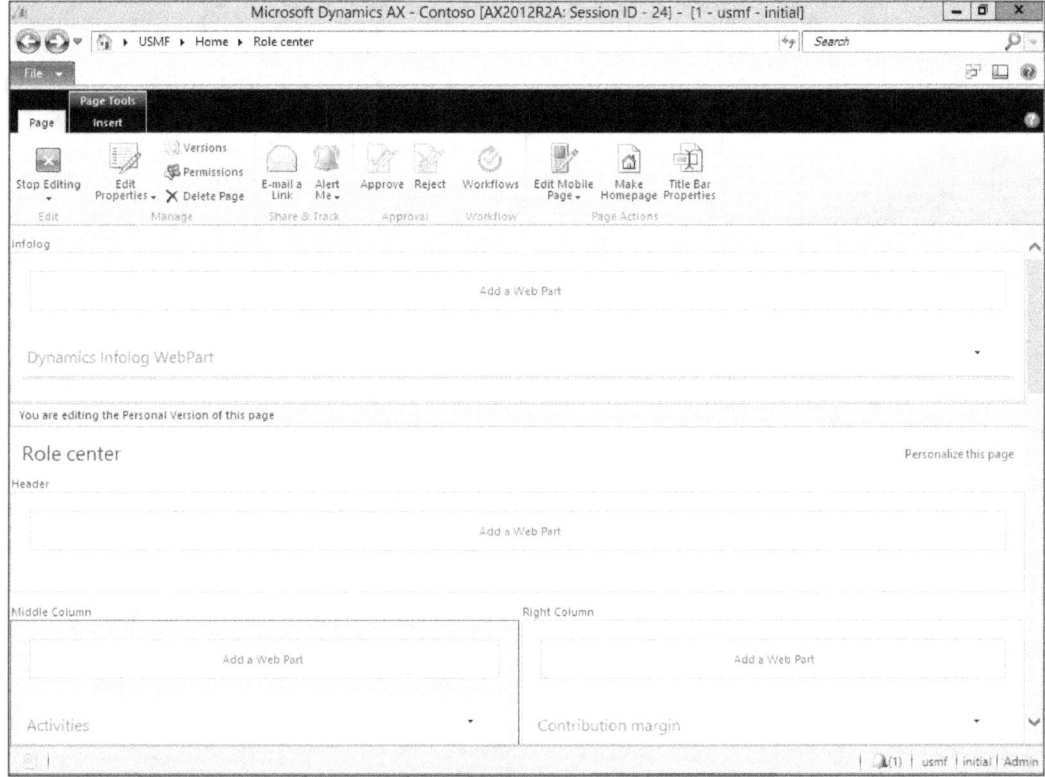

This will change the mode of the Role Center into design mode.

If you want to add a new part to the Role center just click on the Add a Web Part link in the area that you want to add it.

Example: Personalizing The Role Center Page

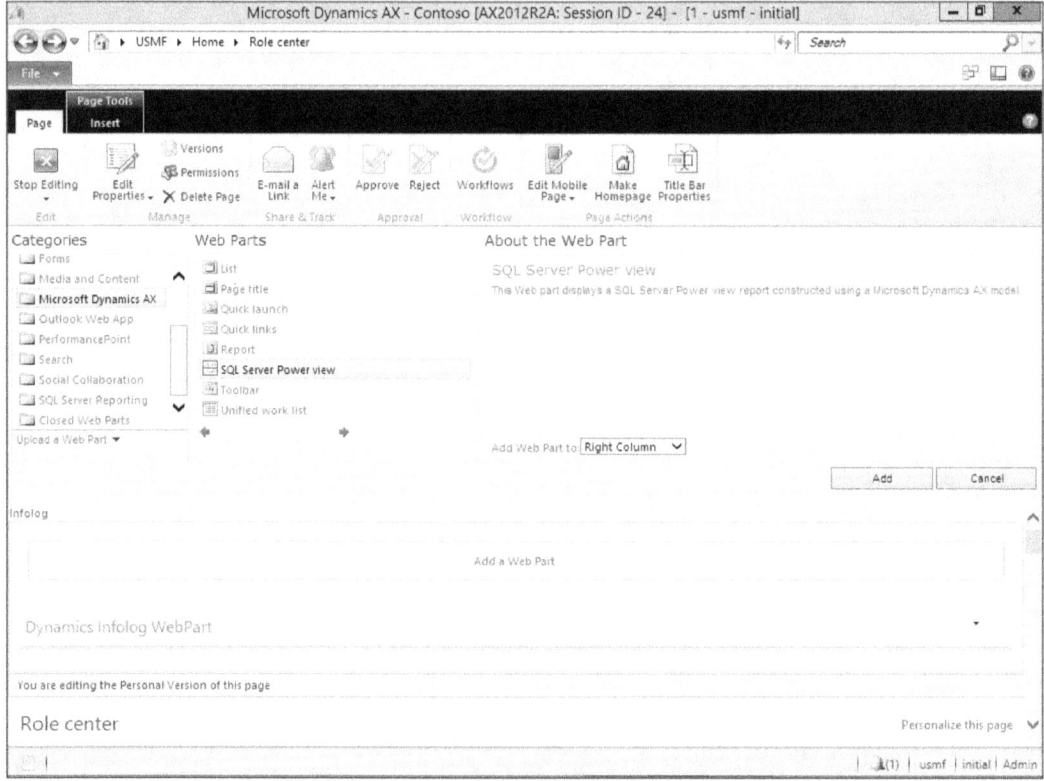

This will open up a browser in the header with all of the available web parts. Just select the one that you want to add and click the Add button.

Example: Personalizing The Role Center Page

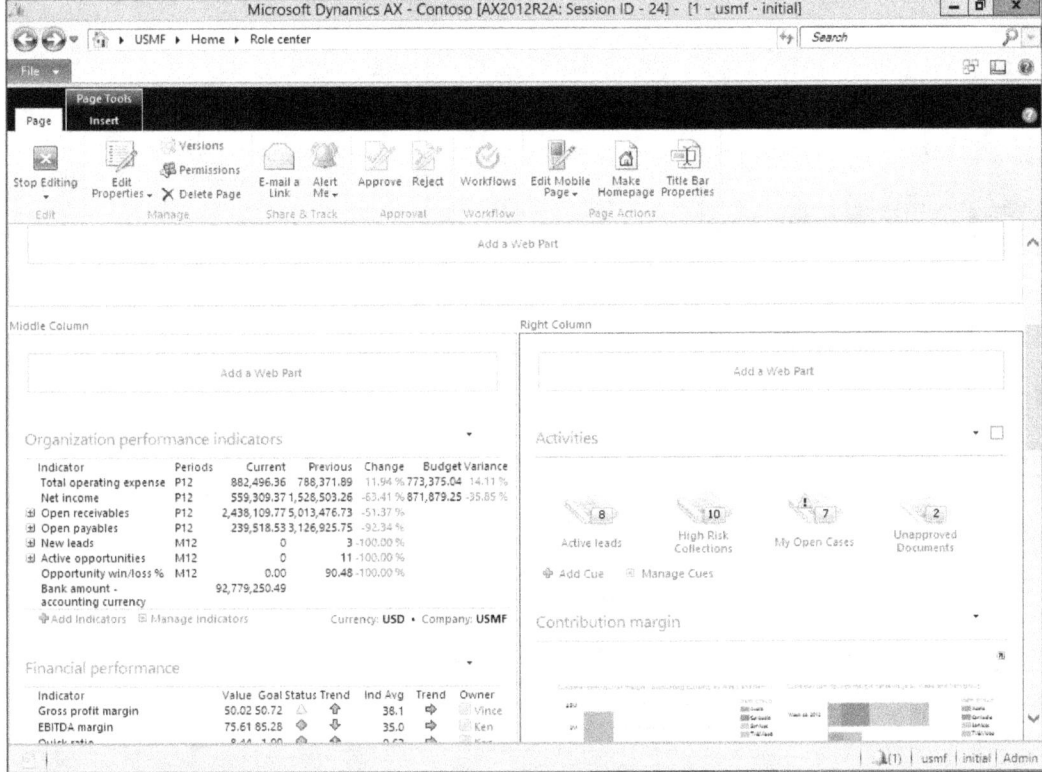

You can also grab any of the existing parts within the Role Center, and drag them to any other section. So if you don't like how the Role Center is laid out, then you can tweak your version to look just how you want.

When you are finished, just click on the Stop Editing button within the ribbon bar.

Example: Personalizing The Role Center Page

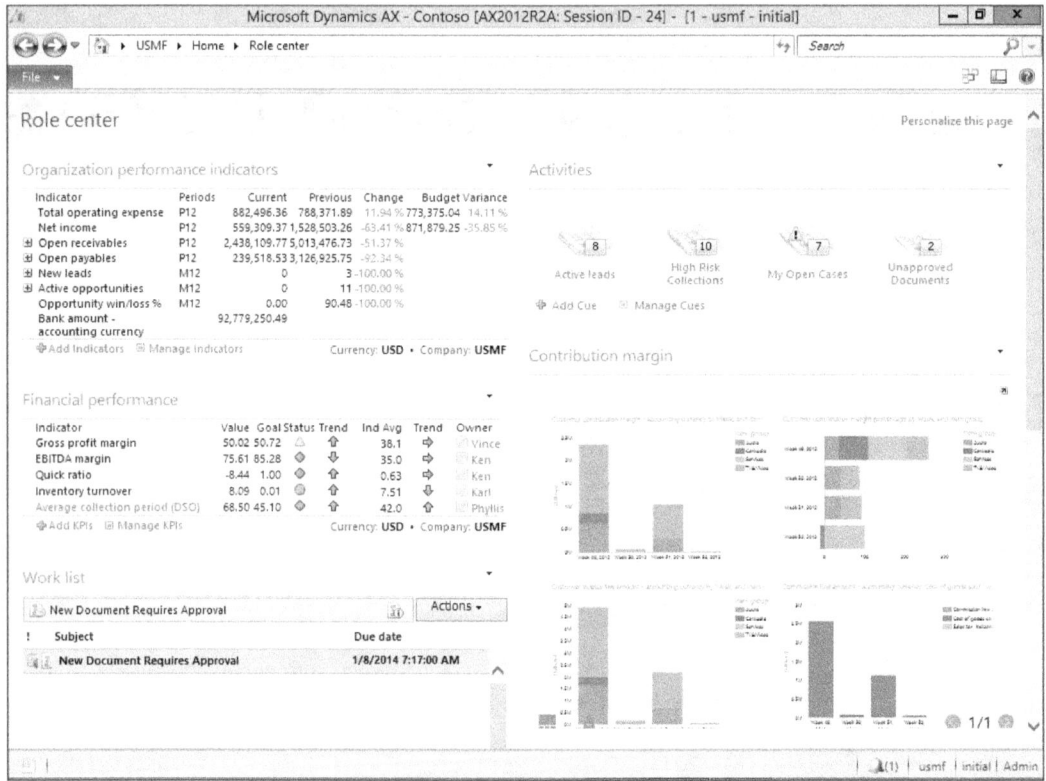

That will return you to the normal view for the Role Center with whatever changes you made.

Navigation Menus

We have already shown how you can navigate the system a number of different ways just through the Role Center, but if you are a power user that need to access a little more of the system, then you may want to step it up a notch and take advantage of the other Navigation menus that are built into Dynamics AX.

As with everything else within Dynamics AX, there are a number of different options to match the different ways that people want to plan their trips to the different forms.

Navigation Panels

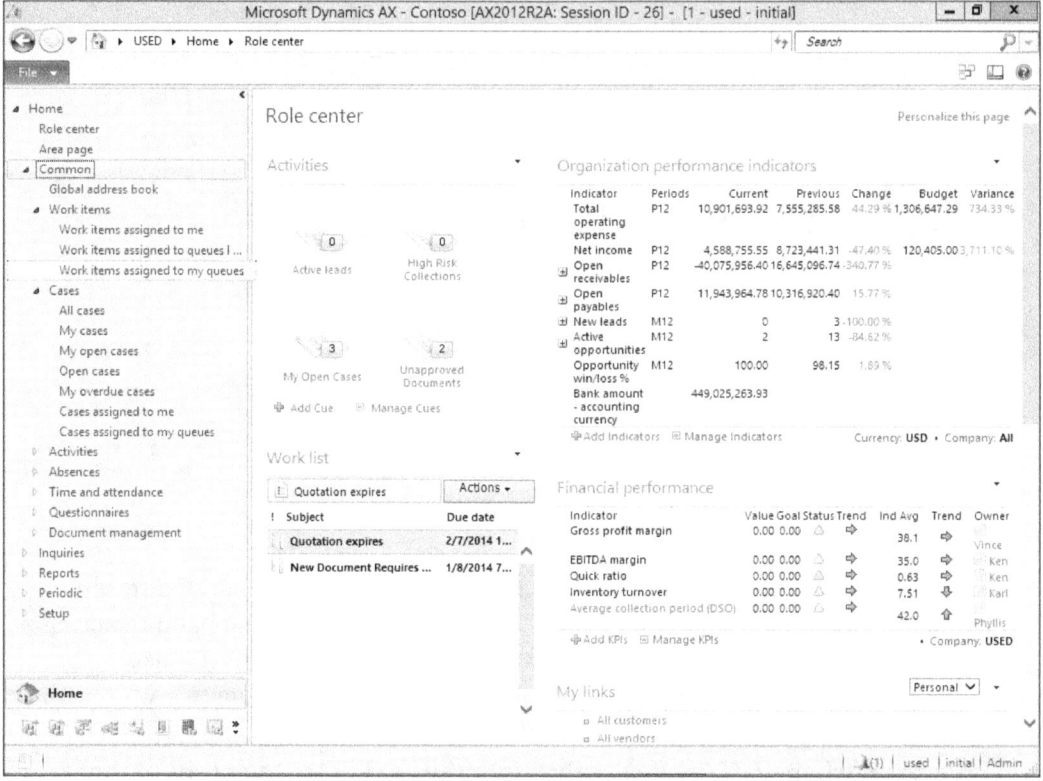

The most common way that users are able to access the functions within Dynamics AX is through the Navigation Panel on the left hand side of the form.

This will show you all of the different functions that are available to you within the current area (i.e. Sales & Marketing, Procurement etc.) that you are looking at.

To find a particular form and open it, you just expand the menu tree and click on the link.

Area Shortcuts

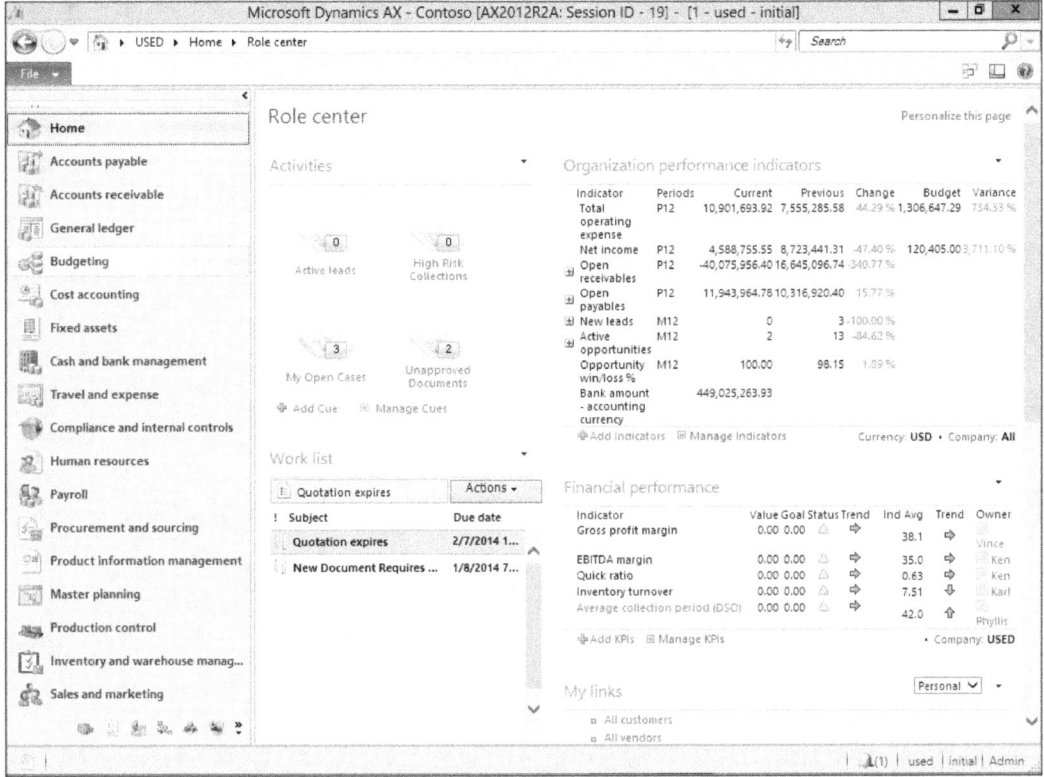

If you want to change your current area, then at the bottom of the Navigation Pane you will see all of the different functions within Dynamics AX listed out. You can expand the list just like you can within Outlook to see all of the available areas, and you just need to click on them to change.

Favorites Menu

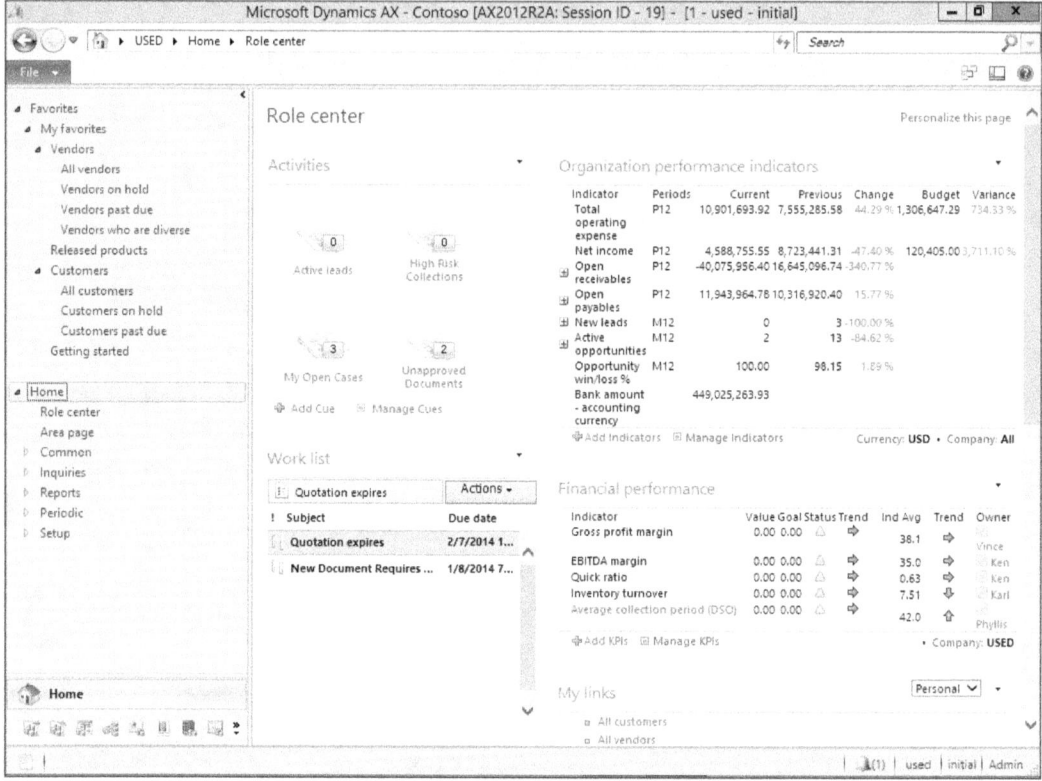

If you want to, you can also use a Favorites menu within the Navigation Pane. This allows you to add the common programs that you access to the Favorites (like you did within the Role Center) and use it as a quick link.

Breadcrumb Bar

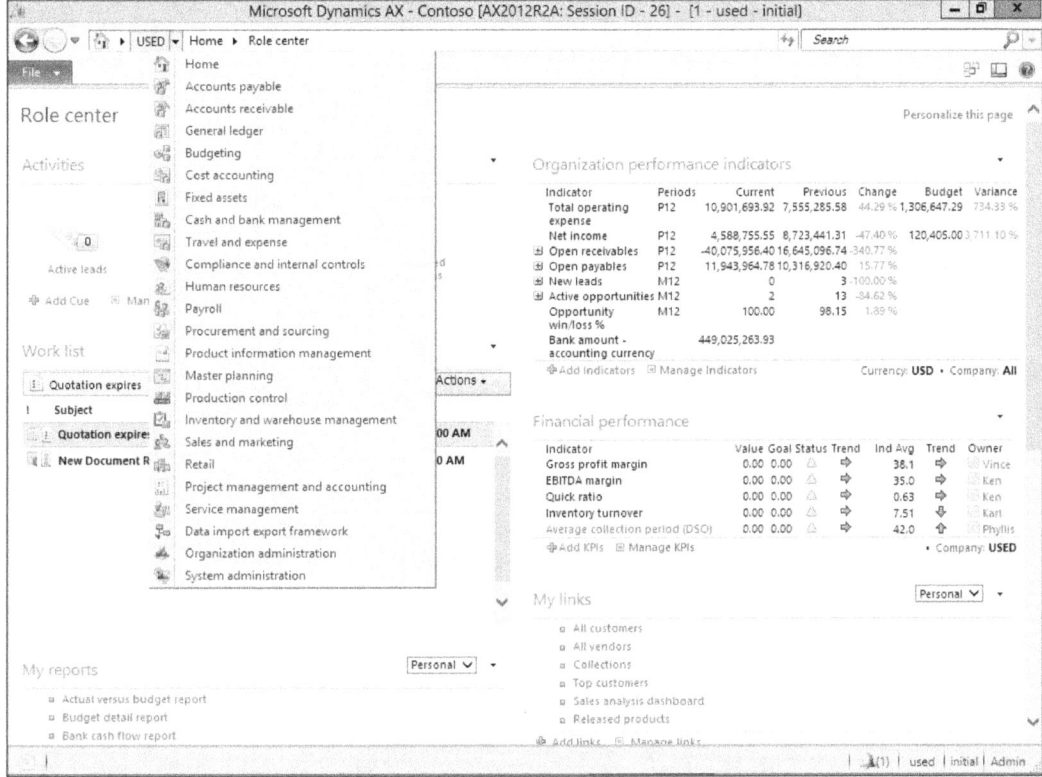

At the top you will also see a Breadcrumb Bar that shows you where you are within the application. It has an additional function that allows you to move around within the menus just by clicking on the section of the Breadcrumb bar that you want to change.

Note: This is useful if you hide the Navigation Panel, and is actually my favorite way to move from area to area within Dynamics AX.

Area Pages

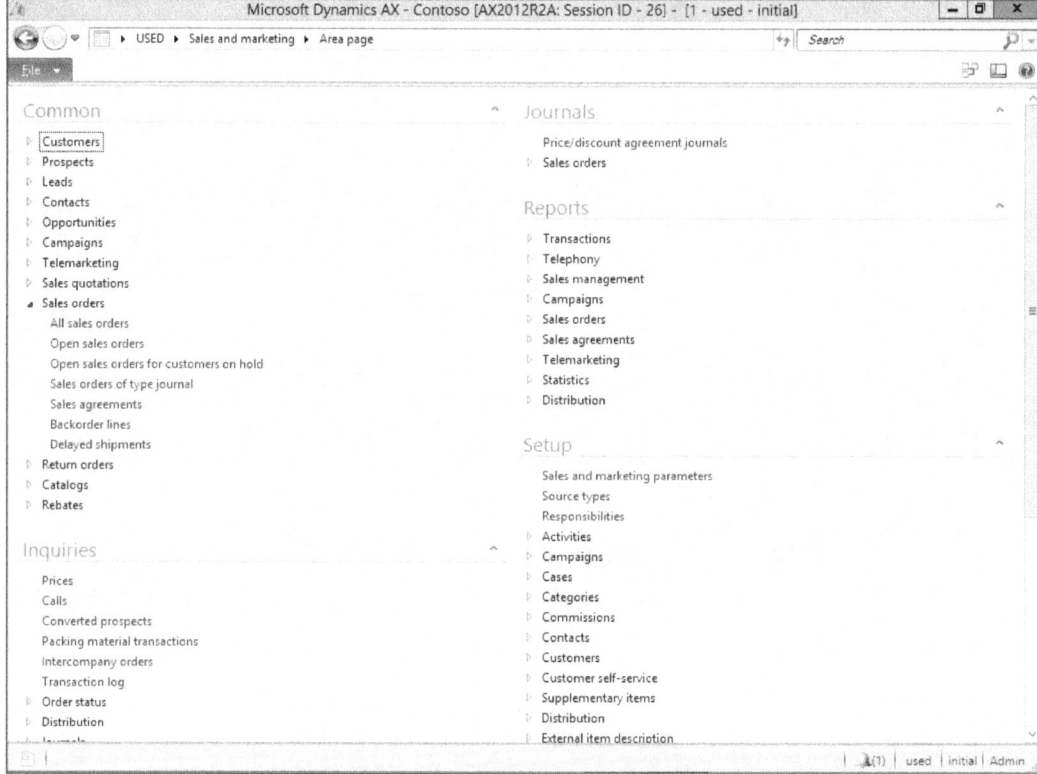

The final navigation option is to use the Area Page menu. If you select any of the general areas within Dynamics AX through the menus, then it will show you an index of all the menu items within the workspace so that you can get an overview of all the features and functions.

All you need to do is expand the group that you want to use and then click on the link.

Example: Adding Items To The Favorites Group

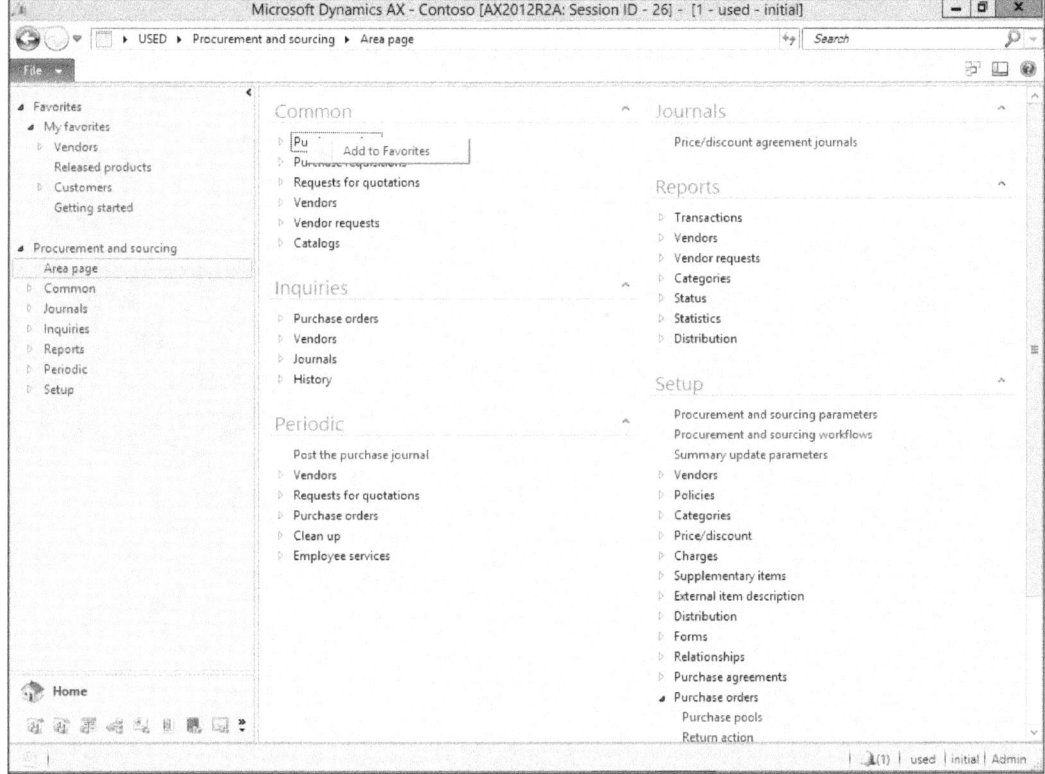

If you use the Favorites within the Navigation Panel, and you want to add a menu item, or a group of menu items to the favorites, just right-mouse-click on it and then select the Add to Favorites menu item.

Example: Adding Items To The Favorites Group

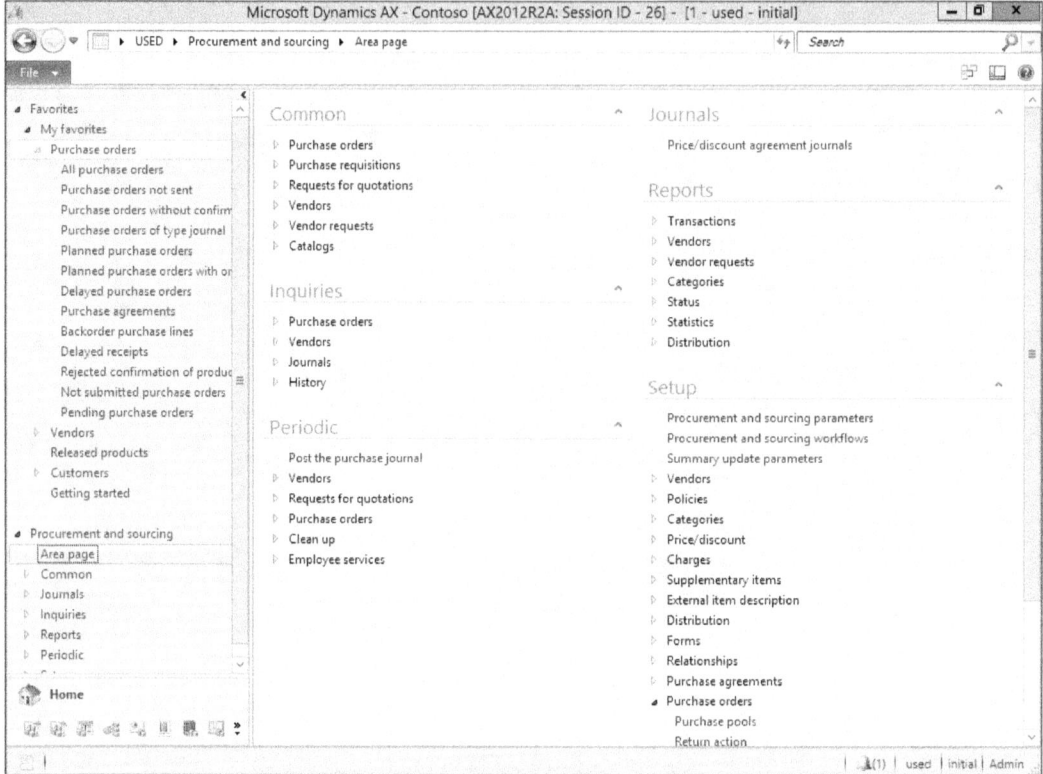

That will add the menu item(s) to the Favorites group.

Enterprise Search

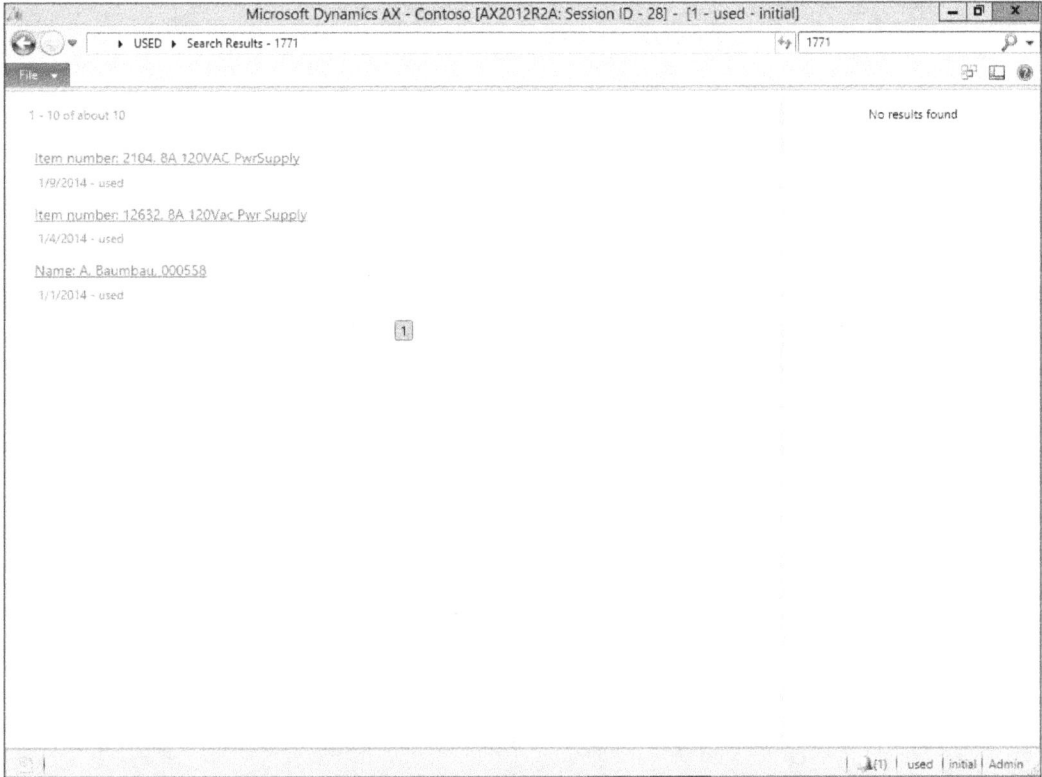

If you are having trouble finding exactly the location that a particular menu item is located, or if you are just plain lazy, then you can also use the Enterprise Search field that is in the top right for the Dynamics AX client.

This allows you to type in anything that you want to find and it will show you all the matches within the menu, and also the data.

If you find the item that you are interested in opening, all you need to do is click on the link.

Navigating Forms

Once you click on a menu item, you will be taken into the Form view. All of the forms will have pretty much the same structure, and there are a lot of different features that you can take advantage of within the forms so that you don't have to jump around a lot in order to find the information that you want.

List Pages

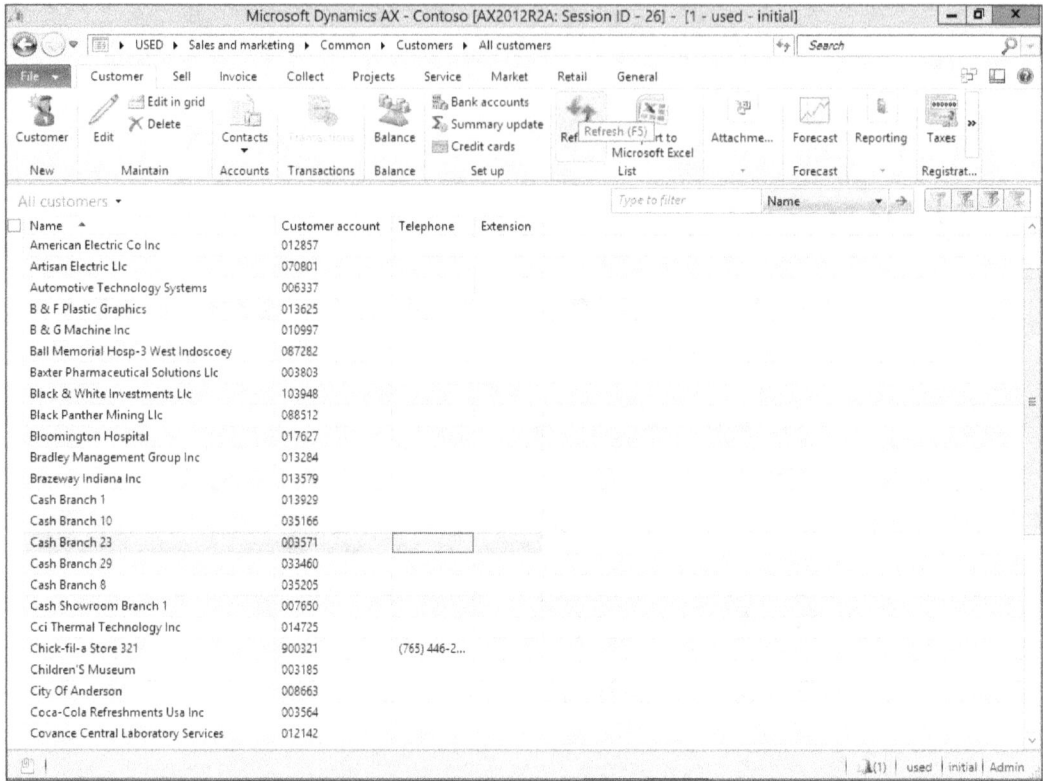

Usually when you open up a form, you will be taken into a list page that shows you all the records within the particular area.

As with any Microsoft application, you can move any of the fields around, and also select any of the headings to sort the data within the form.

Fact Boxes

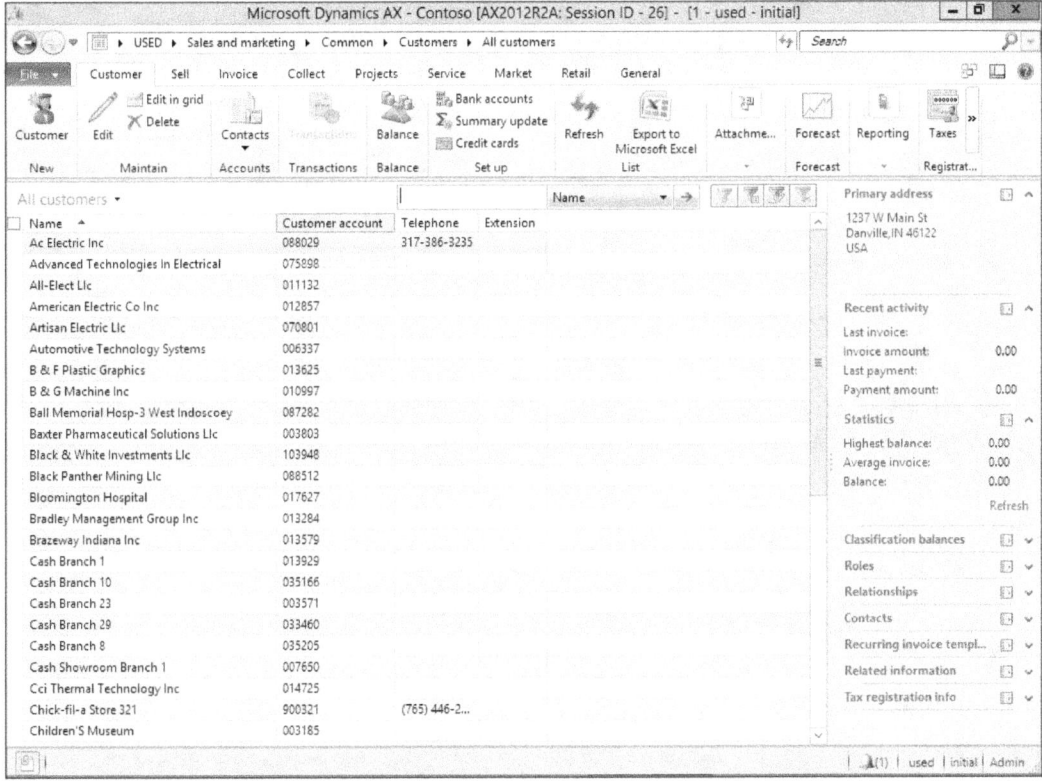

You can enable Fact Boxes on the right for most forms as well. The Fact Boxes give you little snapshots of information about the record that you have currently selected so that you don't have to drill into the document view.

Also the Fact Boxes can show you information that is related to the current record such as child table records, again to remove the requirement of drilling into the form to see the child data.

Preview Panel

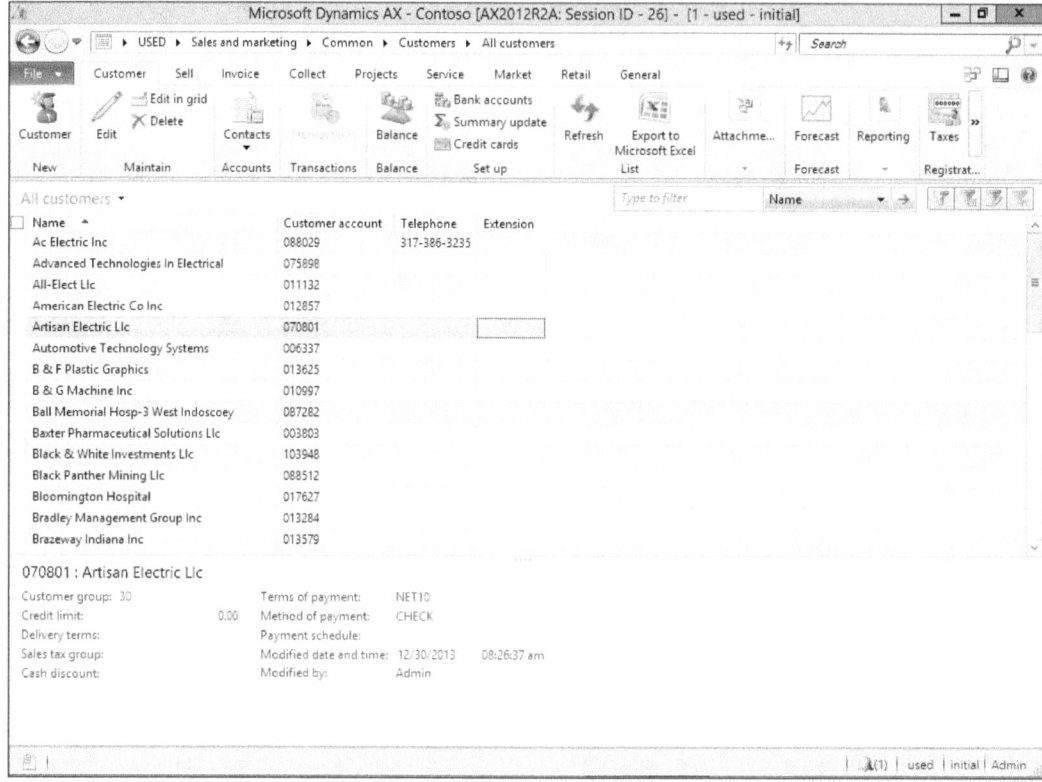

You can also turn on a Preview Panel within the List View. This shows you a thumbnail view of the key information about the record so that you can step through the records one by one if you are searching for particular information.

Ribbon Bars

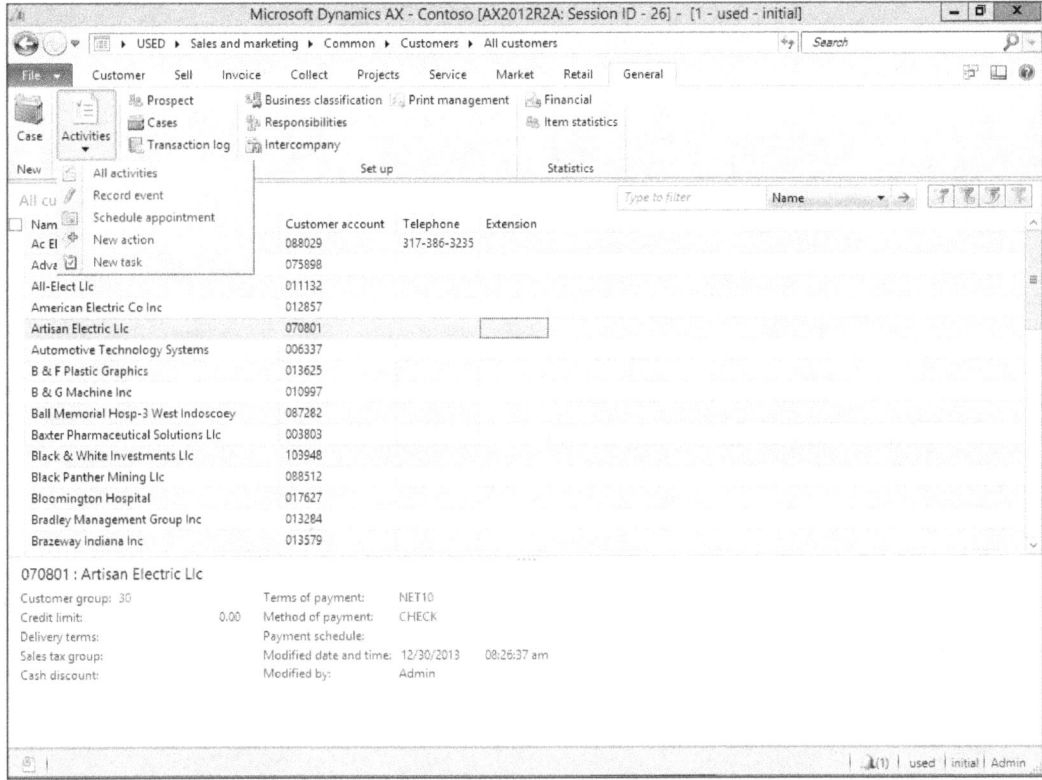

Finally, you will notice that all of the functions that are related to the current record are listed at the top within the Ribbon Bar. The Ribbon Bar is broken out by functional area to make it easier to navigate.

For example, on the Customers List Page, if you click on the Sell tab of the ribbon bar, you will find links to create new sales orders and quotations, if you click on the General tab, you will be able to create Cases and record CRM events.

Document View

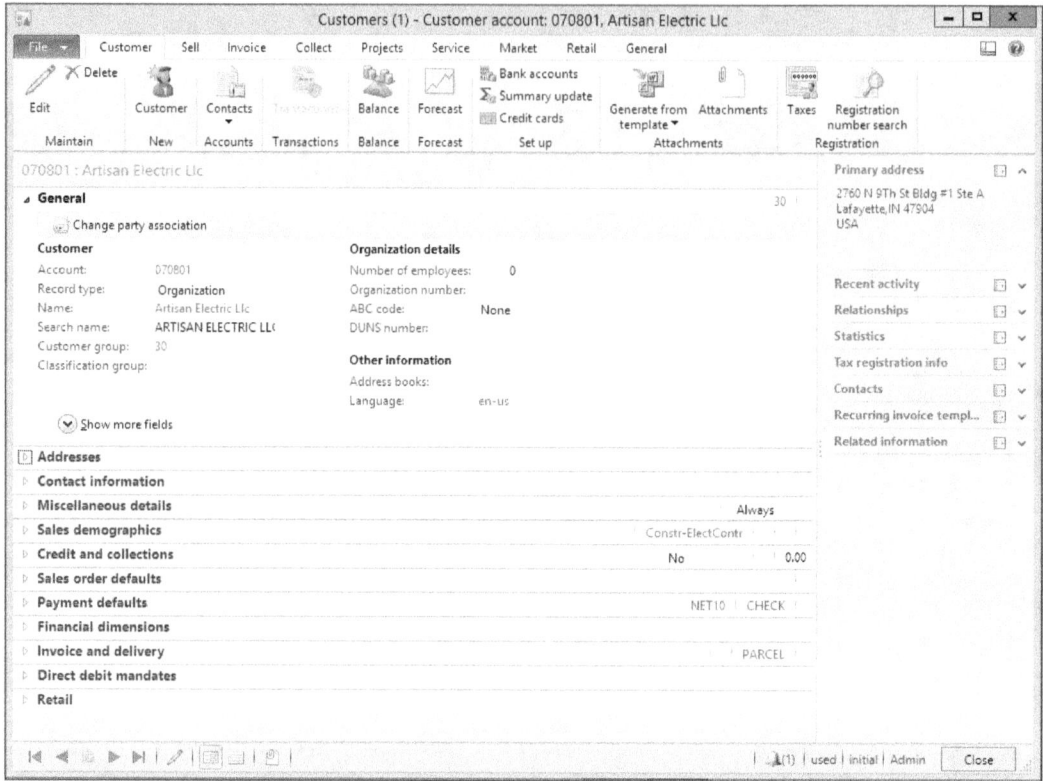

If you drill into a record from the list page, you will be taken into the document view where you will be able to update all of the key information relating to the record.

Notice that this does not have tabs list a old-fashioned application. All of the fields are separated by document groups that you can expand or contract depending on whet you are looking for. This makes it easier to find information if it's within different sections of the document.

Example: Expanding All The Document View Sections

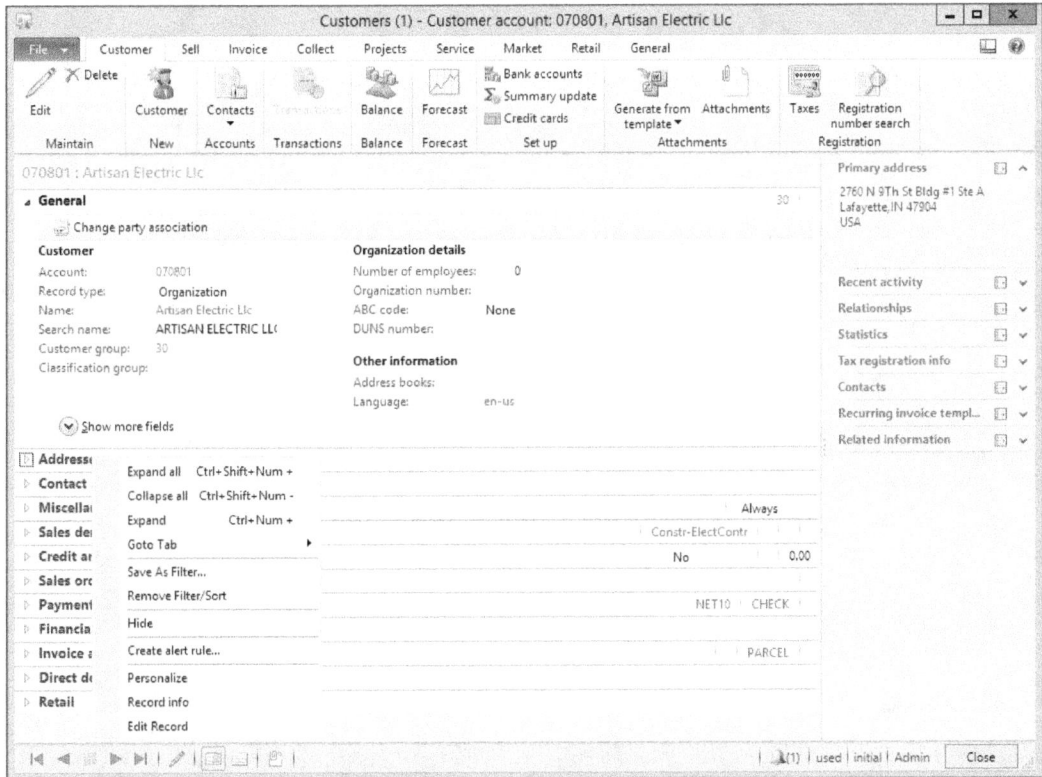

One trick that is useful to know is that you can collapse all of the document groups, and also expand all of the groups. If you are searching for a particular field to update, then sometimes quickly scrolling through all of the available fields is useful.

To do that, you just right-mouse-click on the document group header and select the Expand all option.

Example: Expanding All The Document View Sections

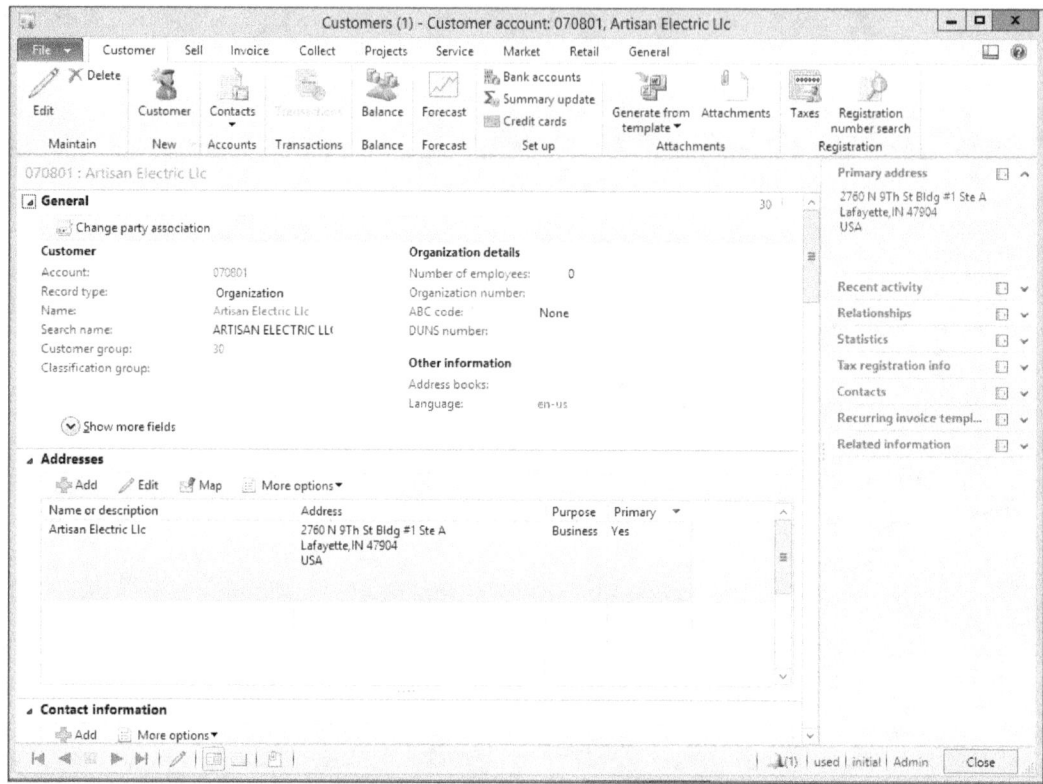

Now all of the groups will be expanded.

Example: Expanding All The Document View Sections

 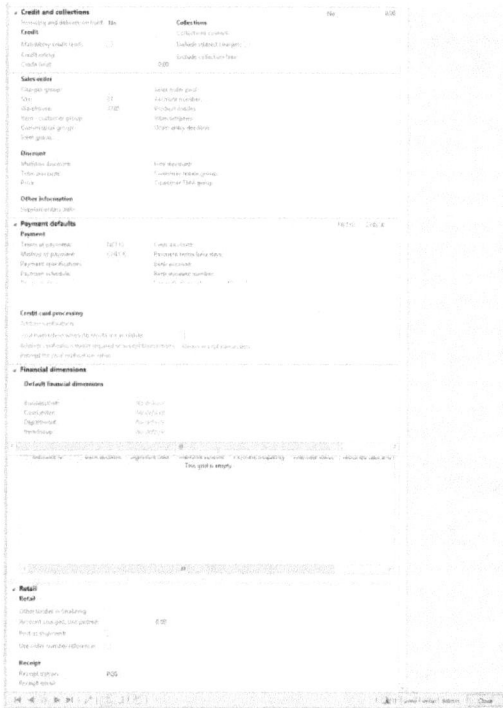

As you can see there is a lot of information that you can store against the customer record used in this example.

Example: Switching from View To Edit Mode

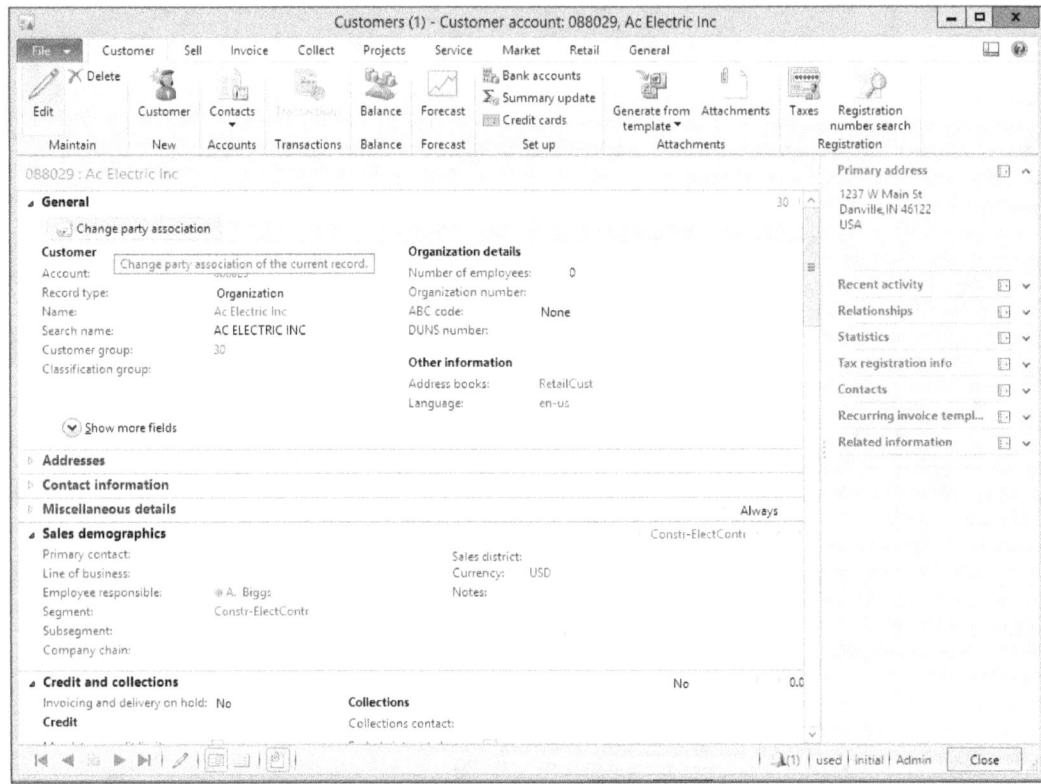

A form has two modes, View and Edit. Depending on your preferences, you can start in either one when you enter a form.

In this example we have opened the form in View mode. Switch to Edit mode, we just need to click on the Edit button within the ribbon bar.

Example: Switching from View To Edit Mode

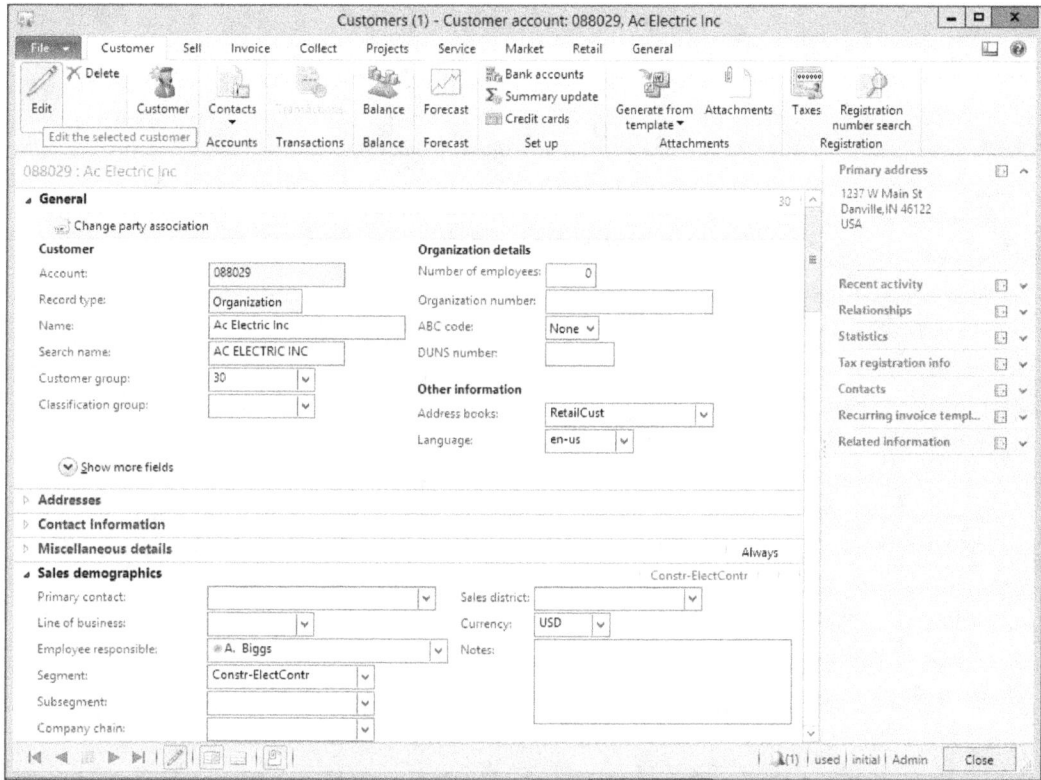

Now that I'm in edit mode, I can update the record.

Example: Accessing Related Details Mid-Stream

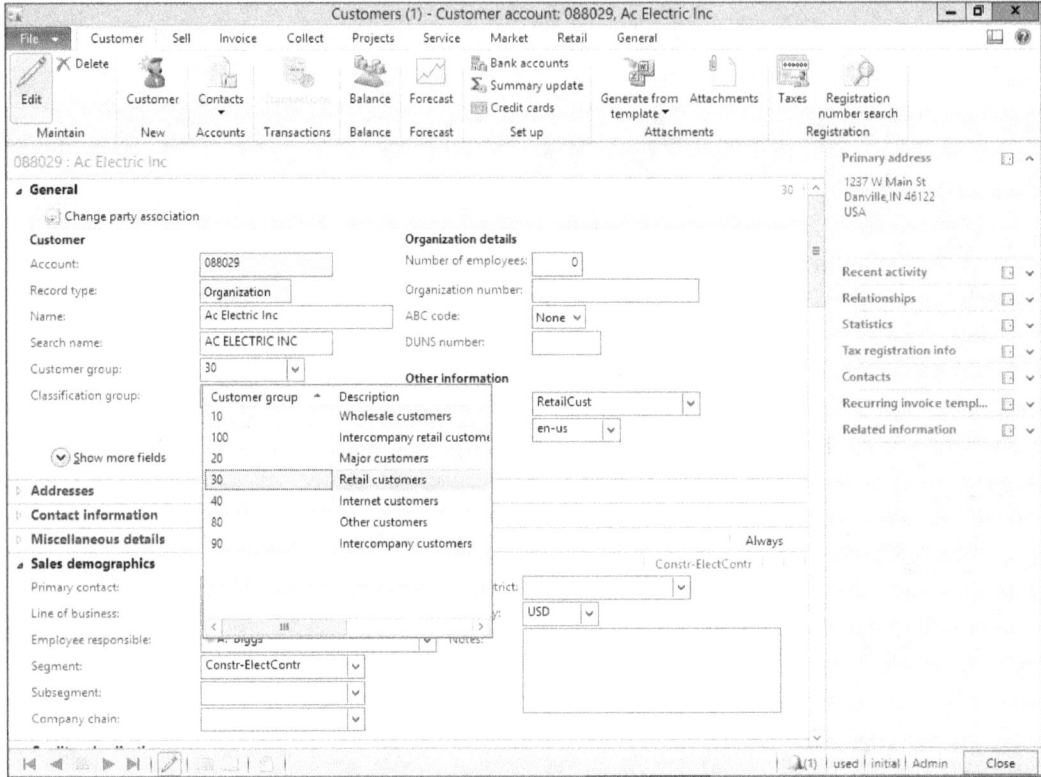

Another feature for Dynamics AX that is incredibly useful is the ability to drill into the related details directly from a form without having to return to the menu and break your process.

For example, here within the Customer maintenance form, we realize that we want to use a new Customer Group that is not currently set up.

Example: Accessing Related Details Mid-Stream

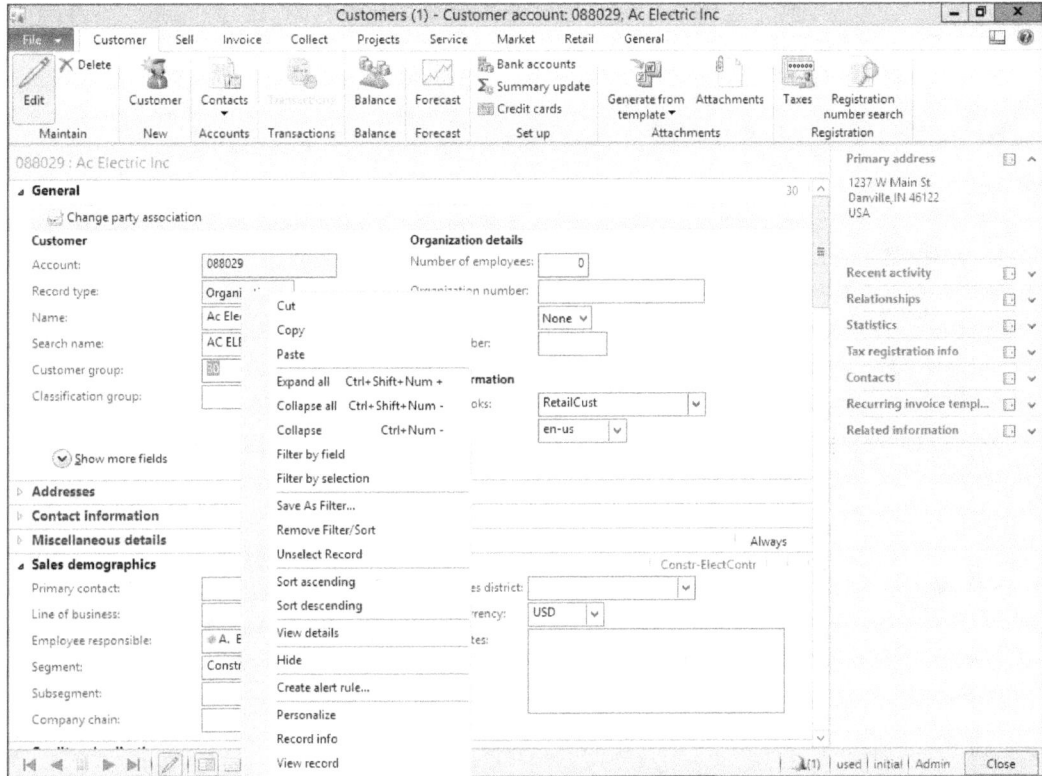

All we have to do is right-mouse-click on the field and select the View Details option.

Example: Accessing Related Details Mid-Stream

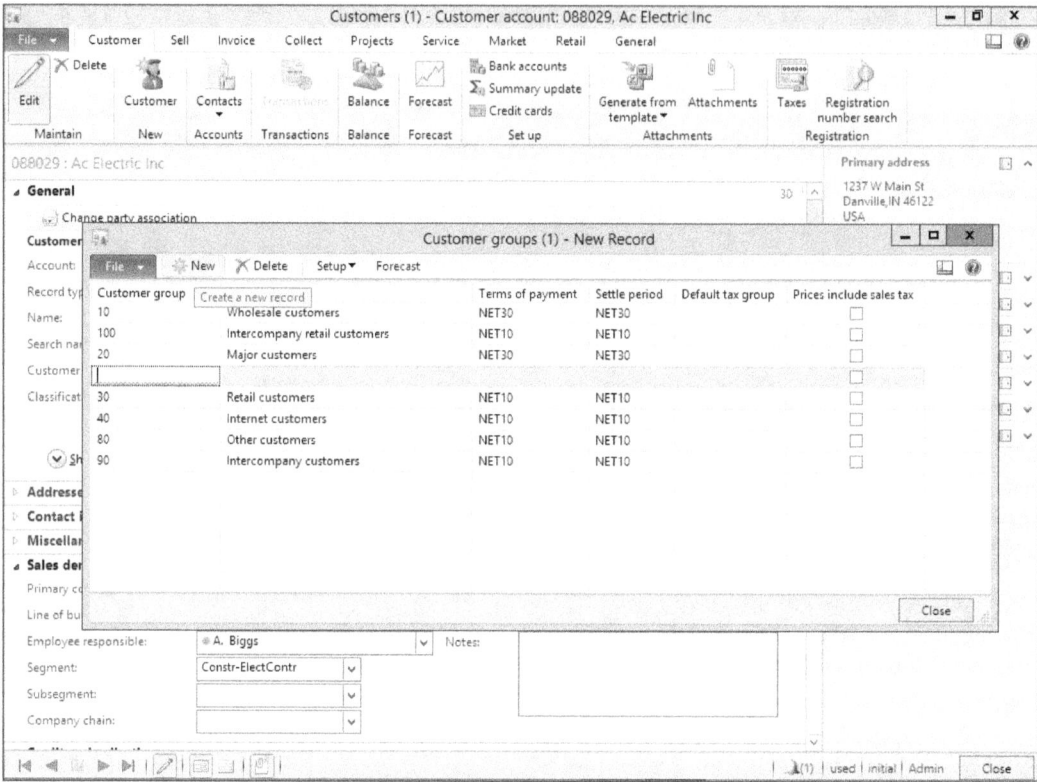

That will open up the Customer Groups maintenance form and we can click on the New button within the menu bar to create a new Customer Group record.

Example: Accessing Related Details Mid-Stream

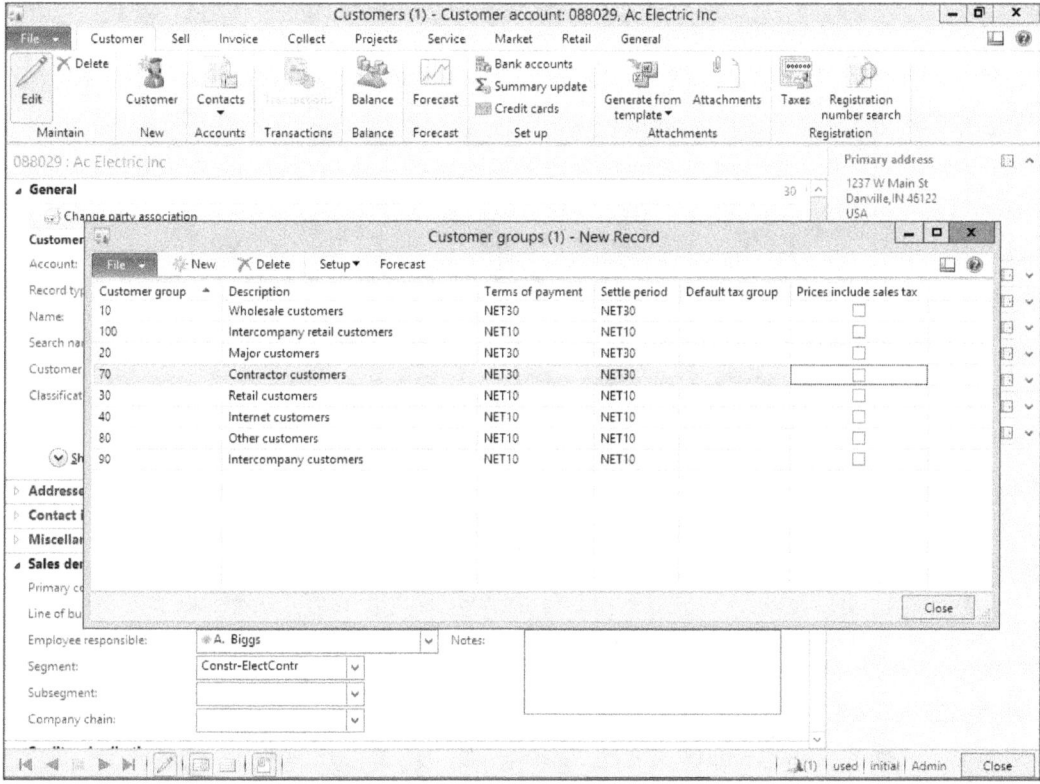

Once we have added our new Customer Group we just need to click the Close button to exit the form.

Example: Accessing Related Details Mid-Stream

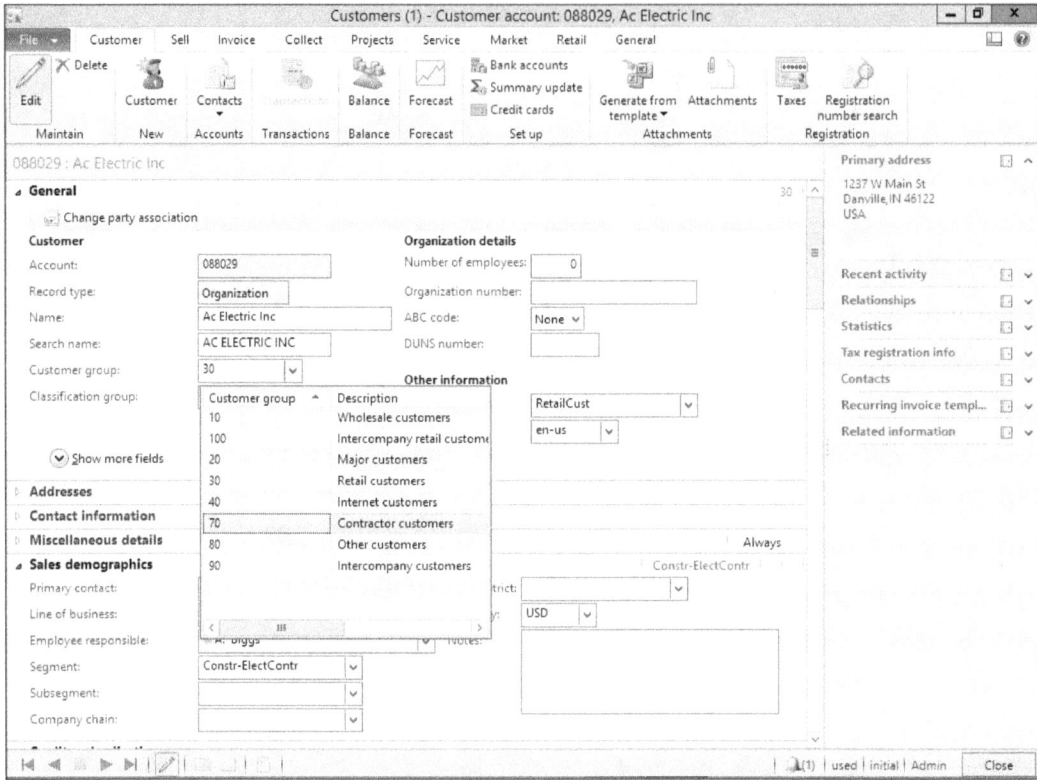

This will return us to the Customer maintenance form, and now when we look up the Customer Group field we will be able to select the new record that we just created.

Example: Drilling In To Record Details Through Hyperlinks

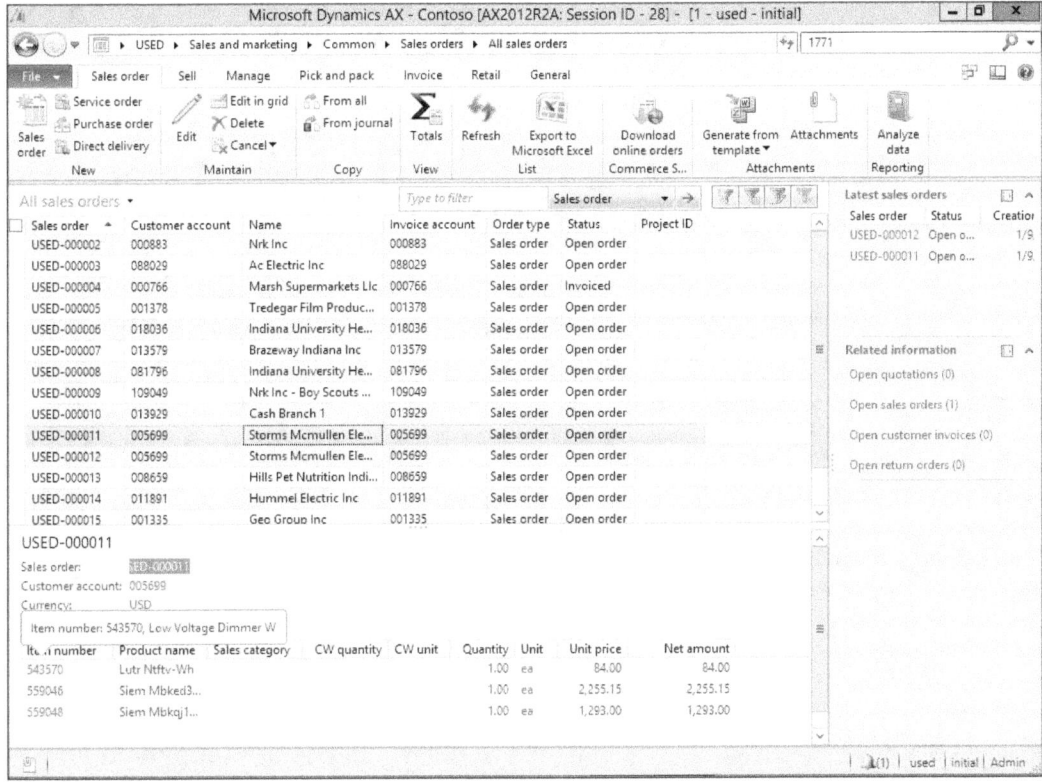

Another feature within Dynamics AX that you may notice is that a lot of the fields (usually codes and master tables) are highlighted as hyperlinks. To access the record that is referenced by the hyperlink, all you need to do is click on it.

Example: Drilling In To Record Details Through Hyperlinks

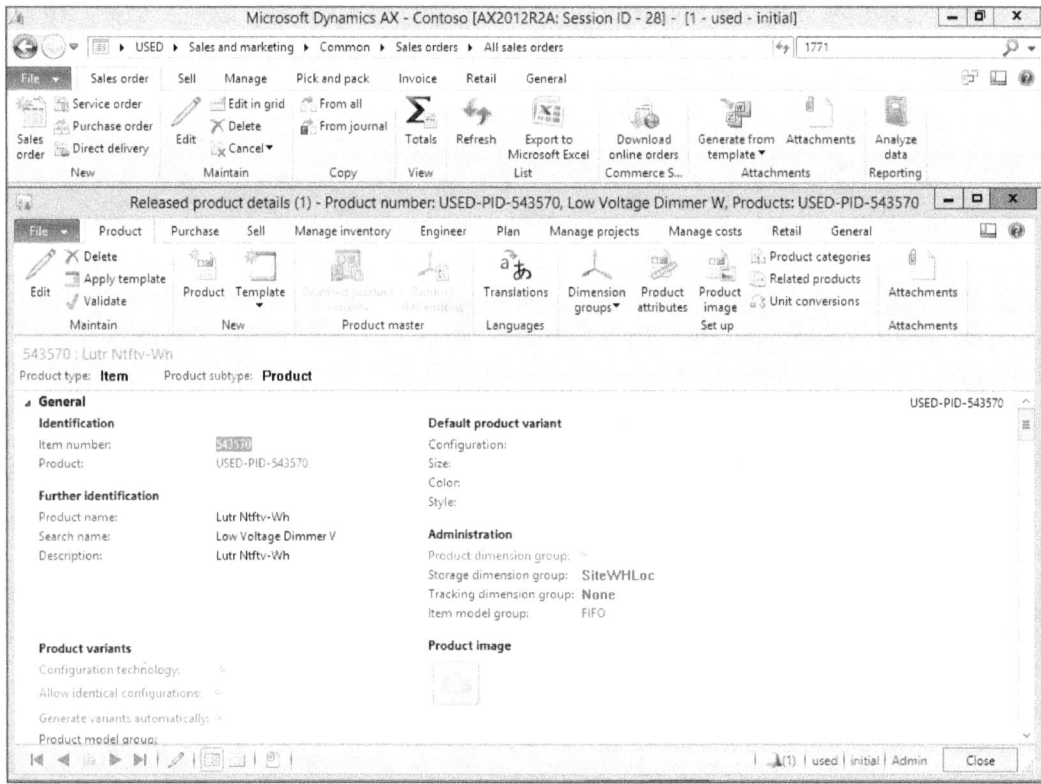

This will open up the maintenance form for that record.

Personalizing Dynamics AX

There is a lot of information that is available within Dynamics AX, and that is a good thing and a bad thing, because you want to have all this information available to you, but maybe not all of it right now.

So the screens and forms within Dynamics AX have been designed to show what everyone probably wants to see. The problem is that there it is more an exception than the rule that all the information that is shown is useful to you and that you have all the information you want.

With other ERP systems, this may be a problem because it may require a developer to make a change to the underlying code in order to show what you want, and then some-one else will be unhappy with what is being presented.

Luckily, as a user, you have the ability to hide any fields that you don't like and also add fields that you may need without getting a developer involved, and this is done without writing a single line of code.

In this section we will show you how you can personalize your views to see exactly what you want.

Example: Hiding Fields That You Don't Want

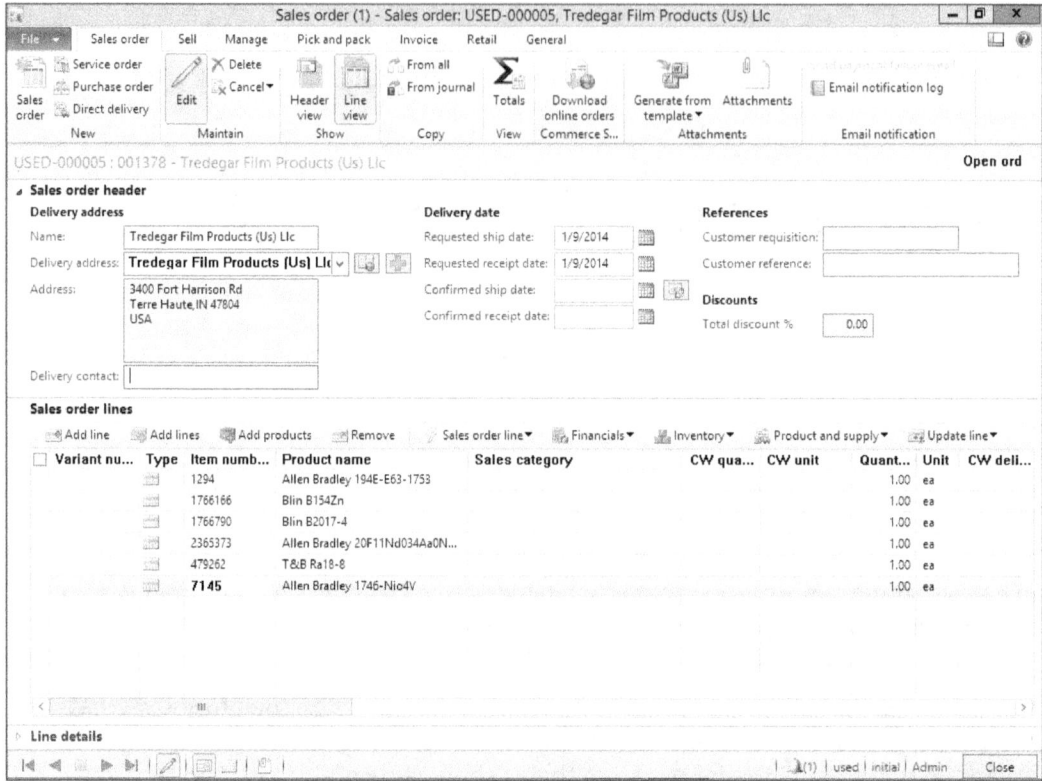

As an example, the standard order entry form within Dynamics AX has a number of fields that I don't really want right now because I am not using Catch weights or Product Variants.

Example: Hiding Fields That You Don't Want

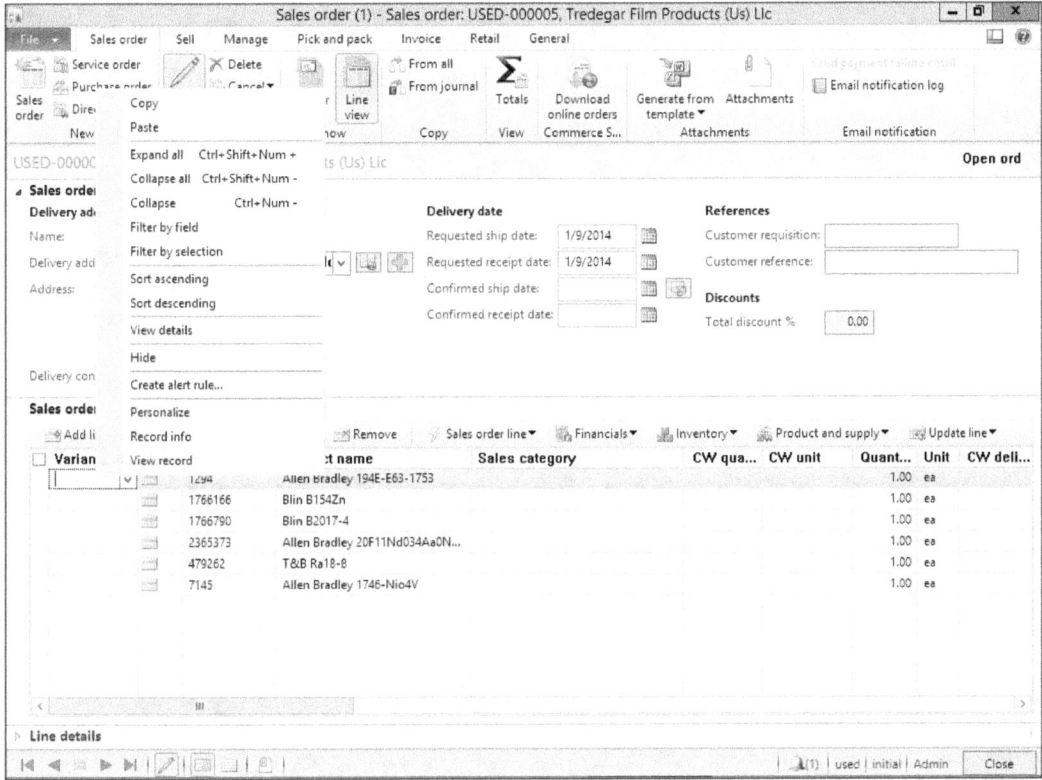

To hide a field, all I need to so is right-mouse-click on the field and select the Hide menu item.

Example: Hiding Fields That You Don't Want

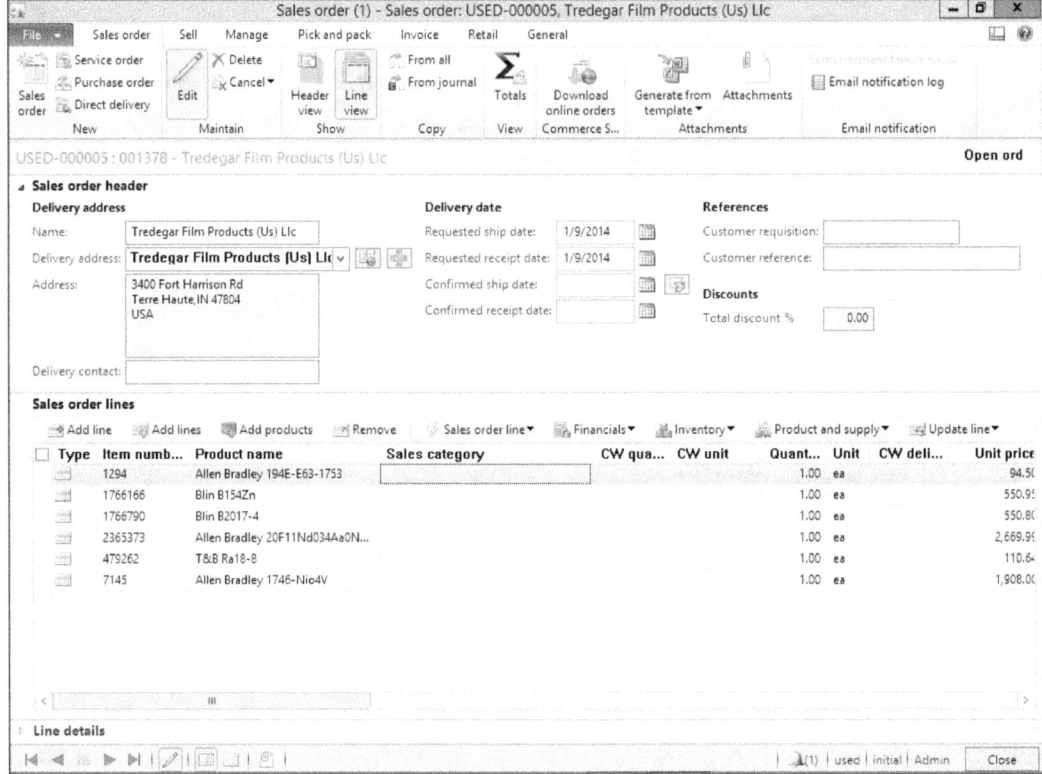

Now it's gone.

Example: Hiding Fields That You Don't Want

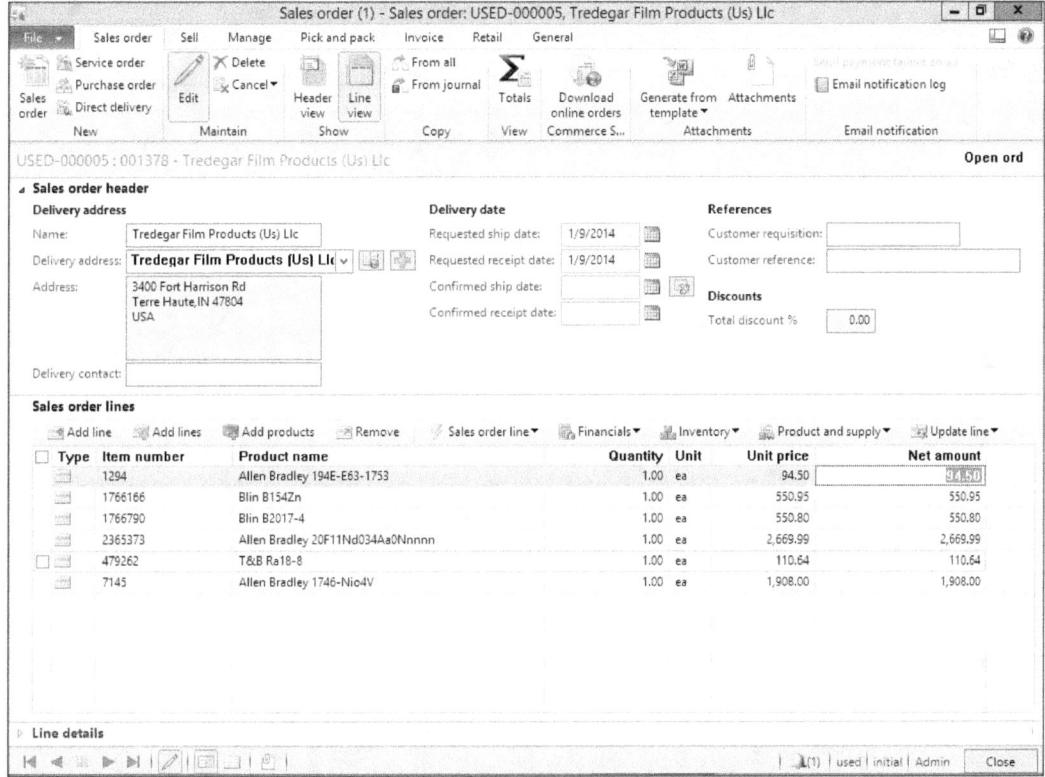

I can continue hiding all of the fields that are not important and now the form is just right for me.

Example: Adding Fields That You Do Need

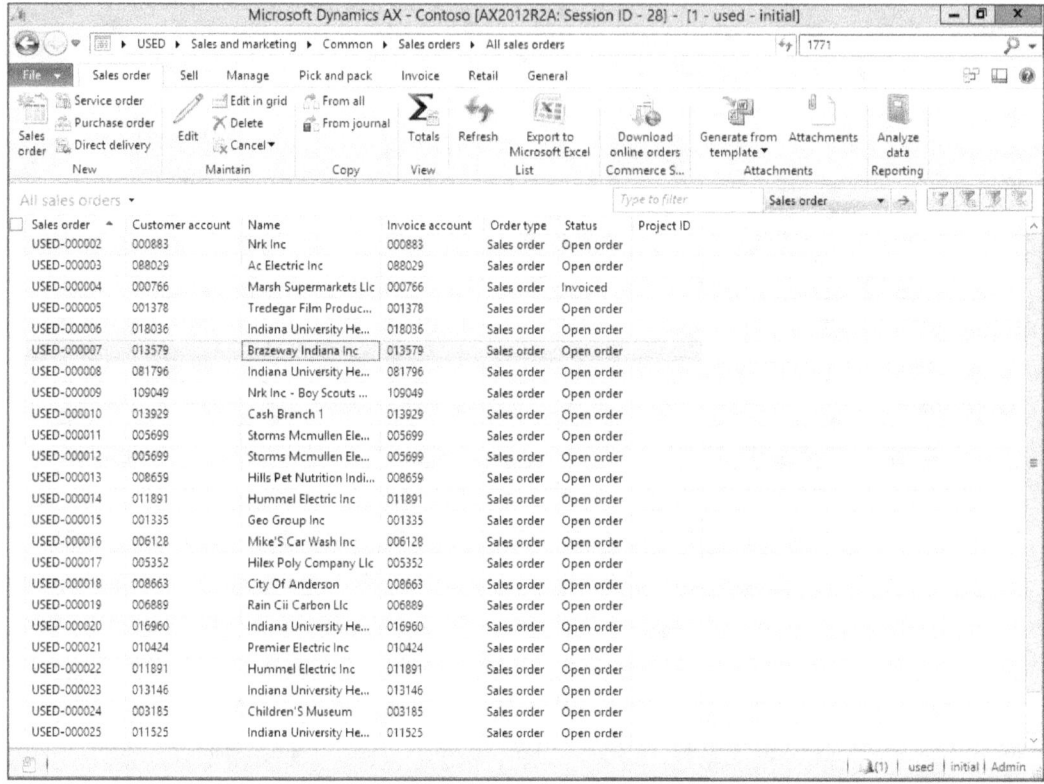

The other side of the coin is that there may be fields that I want to have on a form that are currently not shown. In this example, we are looking at the Sales Orders, and I would like to see all of the Warehouses that are related to the orders.

Example: Adding Fields That You Do Need

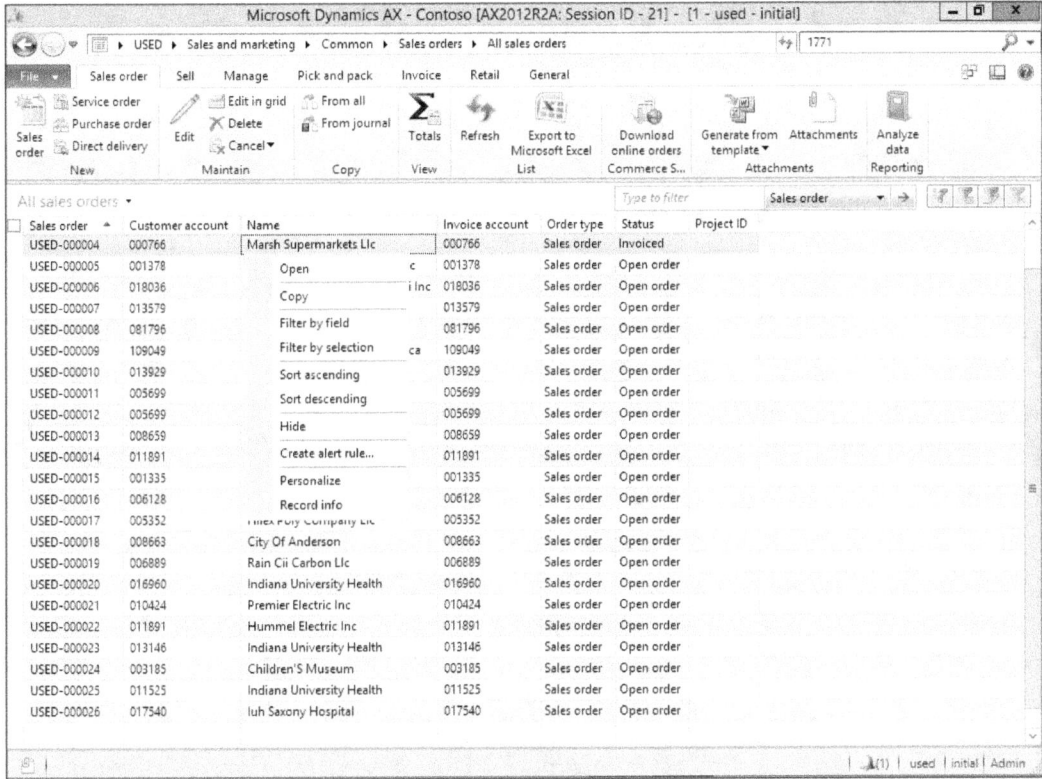

To add a new field to the form, just right-mouse-click anywhere on the form and select the Personalize menu item.

Example: Adding Fields That You Do Need

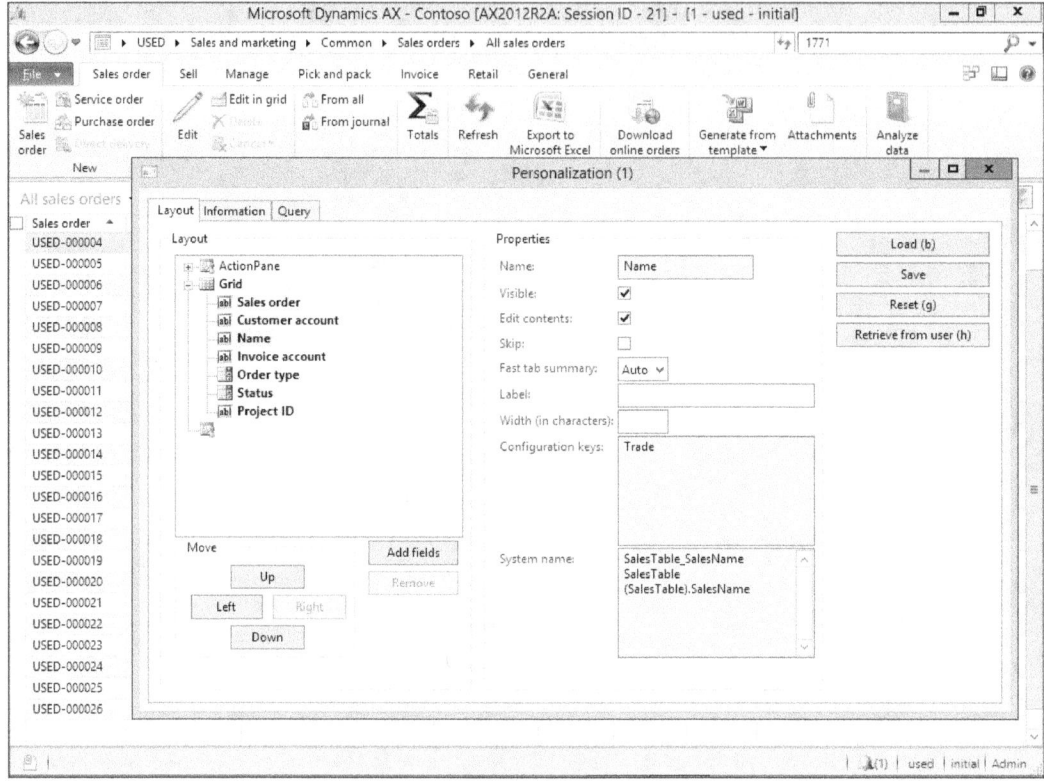

This will open up the Personalization dialog box. If you look at the Layout section you will see all of the fields that were in the list page are listed there.

To add an additional field, you just need to click on the Add Fields button.

Example: Adding Fields That You Do Need

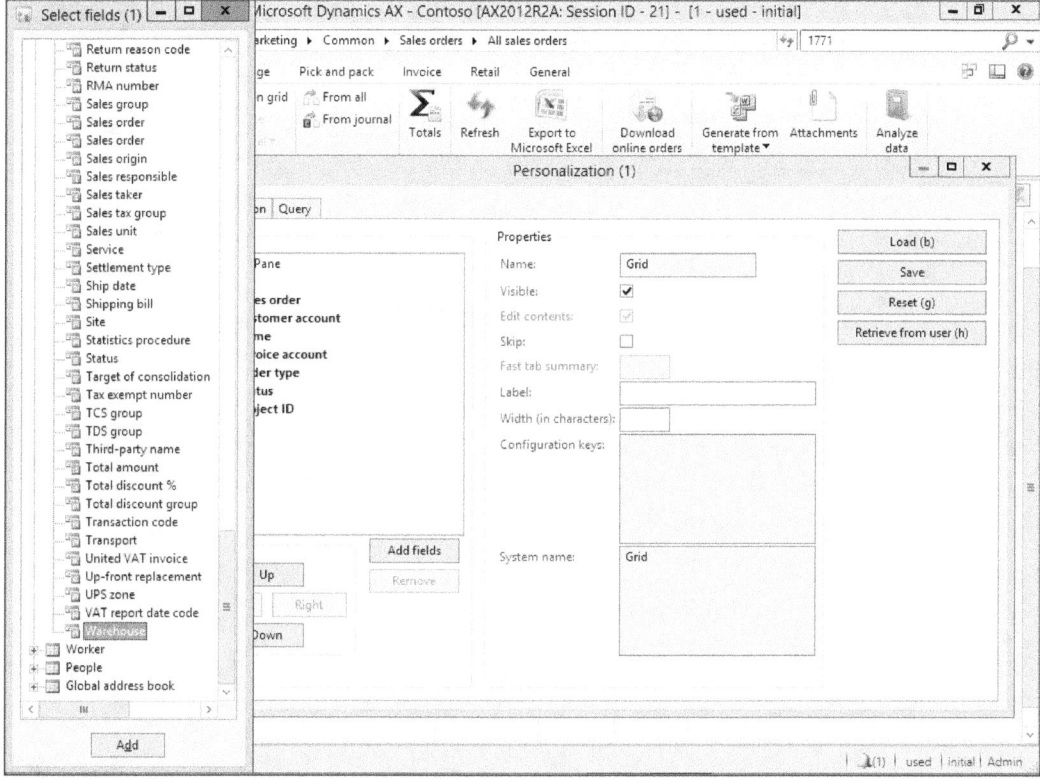

This will open up a list of all the fields that are related to the form (there are a lot to choose from) and we can find the Warehouse field and click the Add button.

Example: Adding Fields That You Do Need

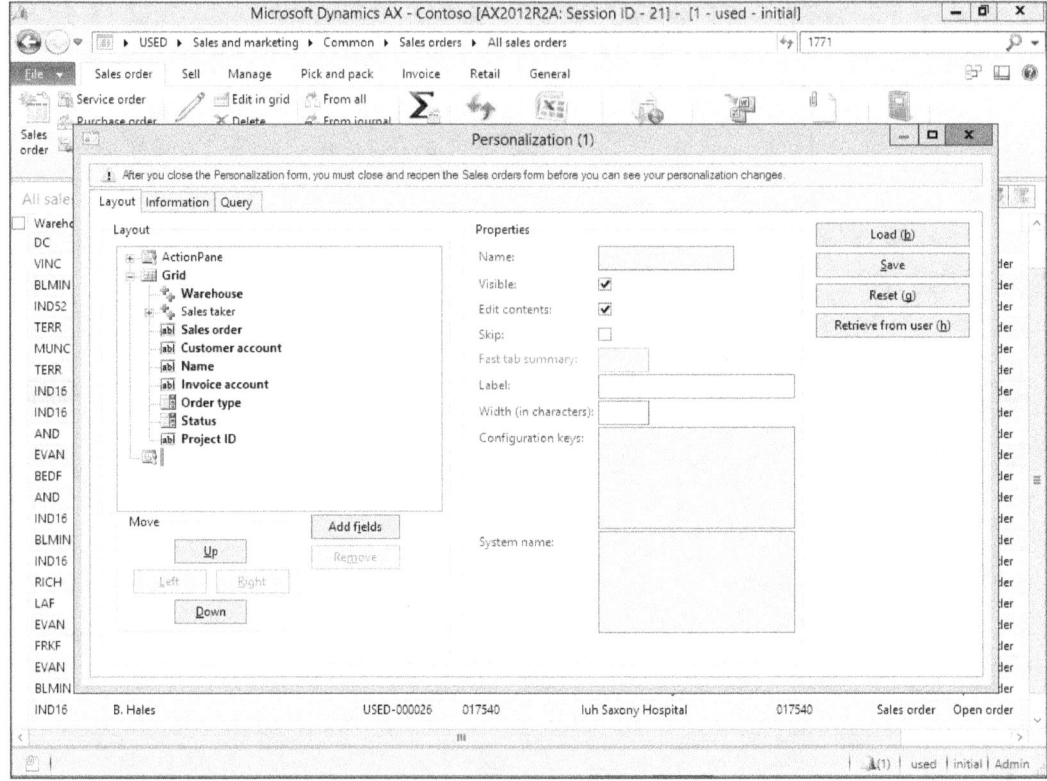

We can add as many additional fields as we like and when we return to the Personalization form we will see that they have been added to the list.

Example: Adding Fields That You Do Need

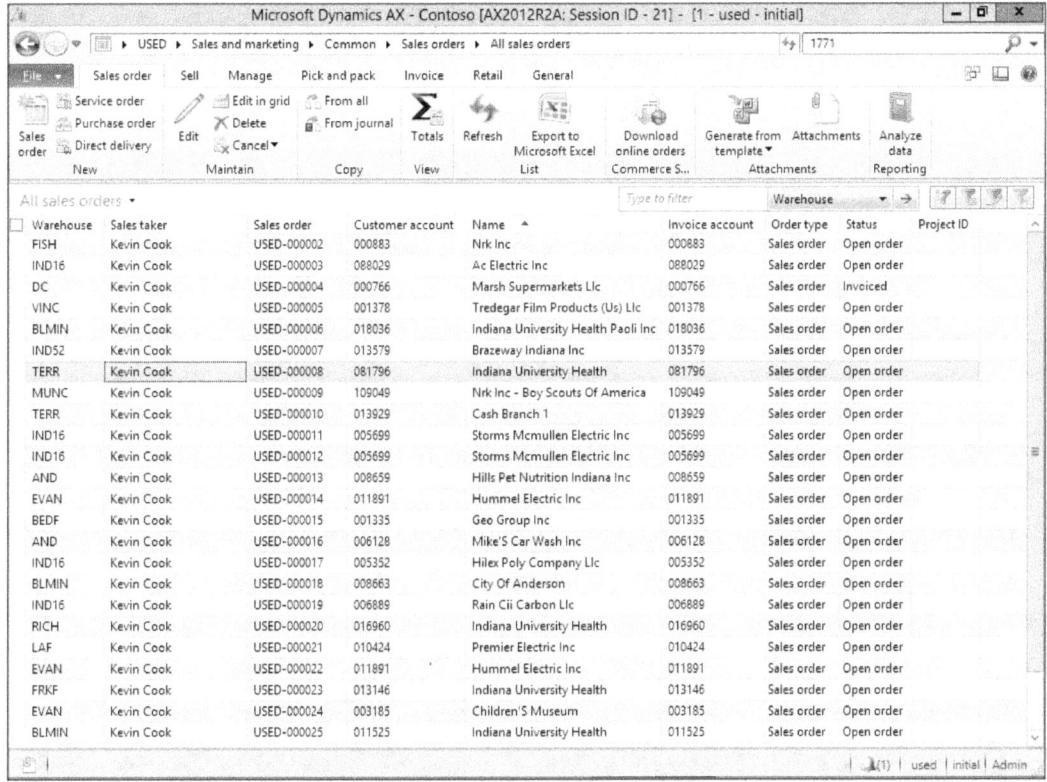

When we close the Personalization form we will see that the Warehouse field and any others that we added are now shown on the form.

Example: Filtering The Data By Selection

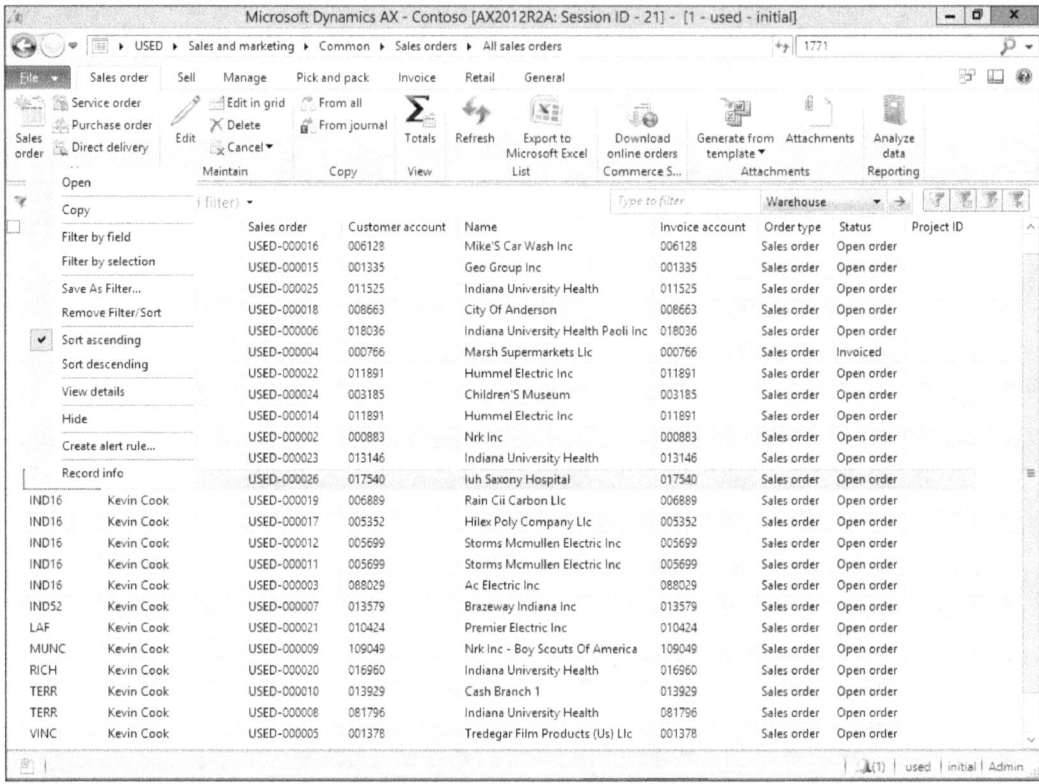

Another way that you can personalize the view is to filter the data to just the information that you are interested in.

A quick way to do this is to select the example field that you would like to filter the data to, right-mouse-click to pull up the context menu, and then select the Filter by Selection option.

Example: Filtering The Data By Selection

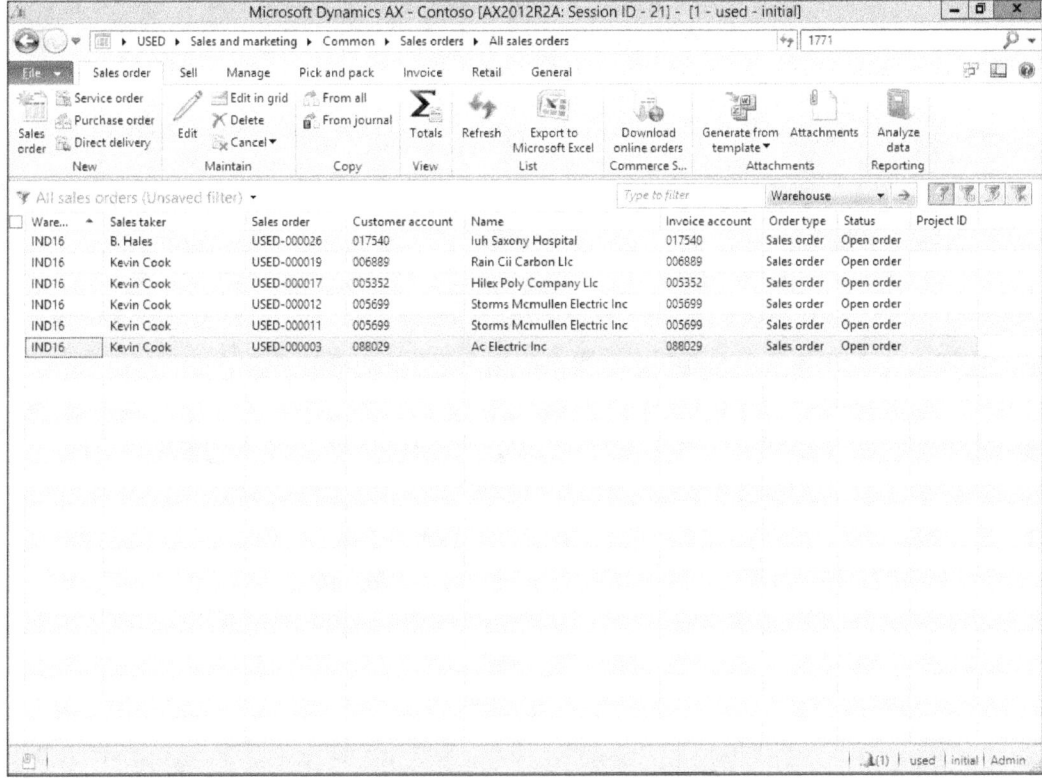

Now you will just see the records that match the field example that you selected.

Example: Saving Filters To Reuse Later On

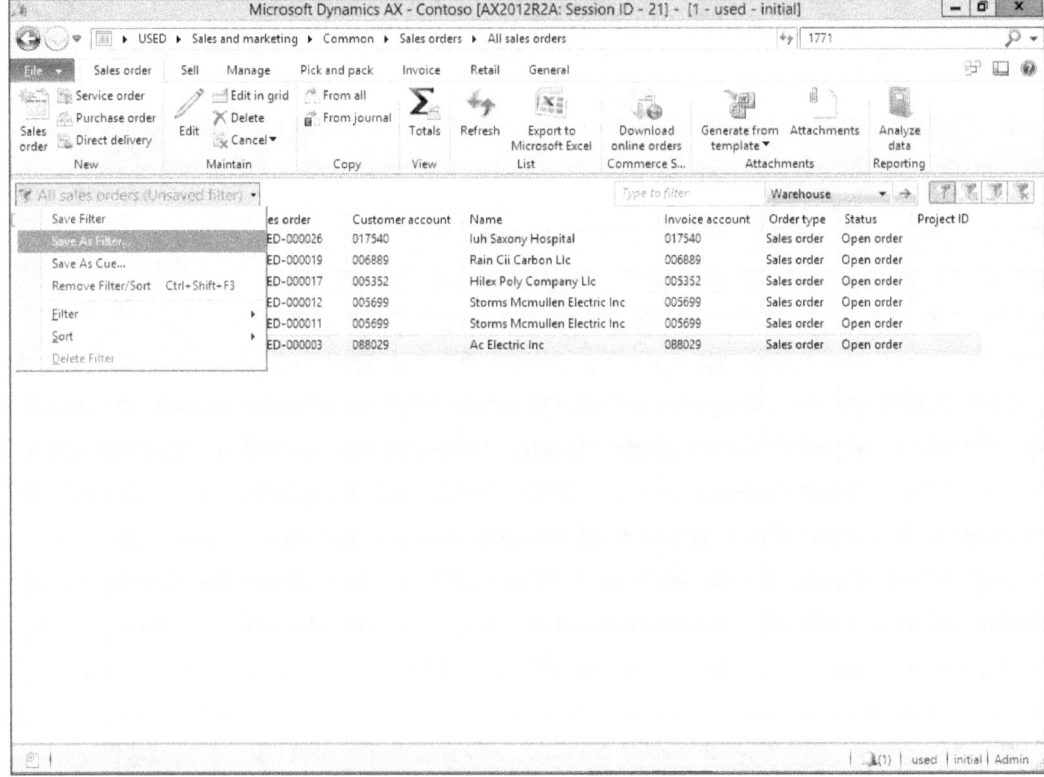

If you always filter the data the same way then you can always save the filtered view and then access it later on.

To do that, you just select the filter drop down from the top of the list page, and select the Save as Filter option.

Example: Saving Filters To Reuse Later On

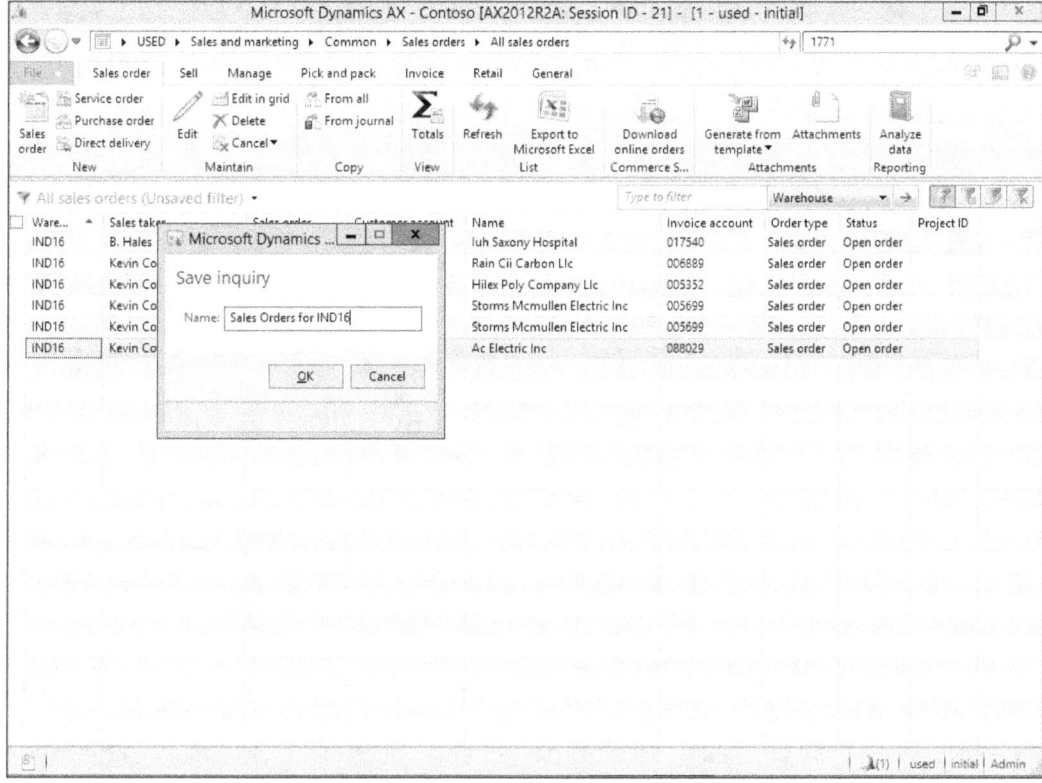

All you need to do is give your filter a Name and then click the OK button.

Example: Saving Filters To Reuse Later On

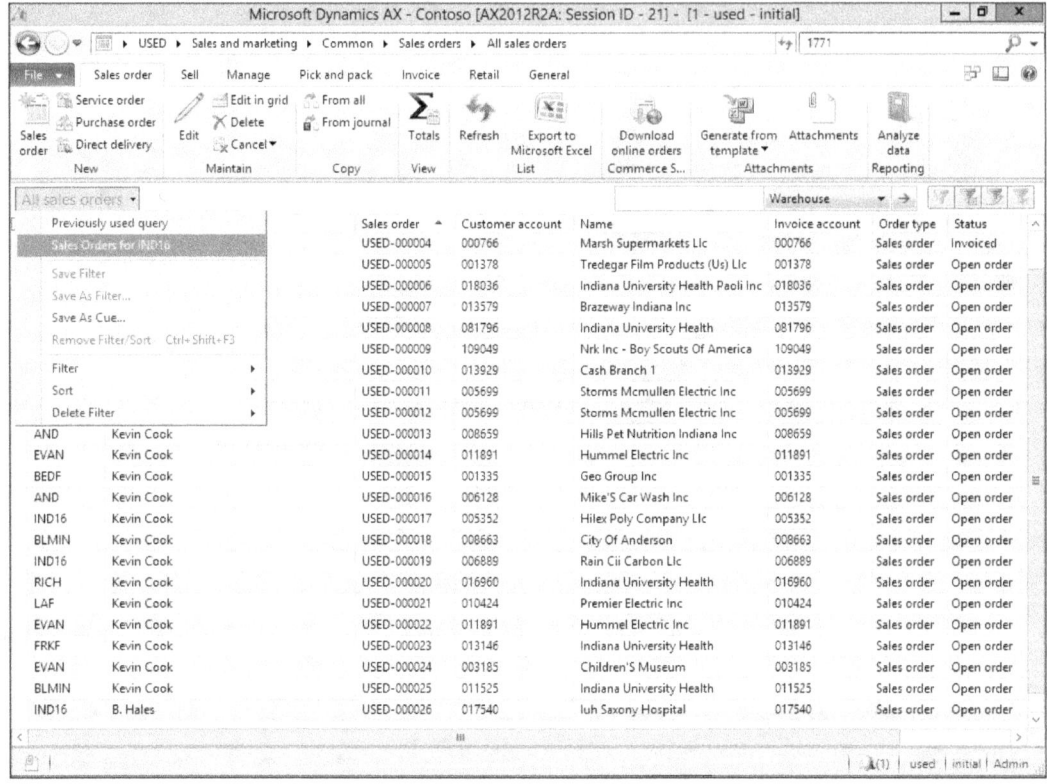

Now when you click on the filter dropdown you will see the filter is saved away and can be re-used.

Example: Saving Filtered Views As Cues

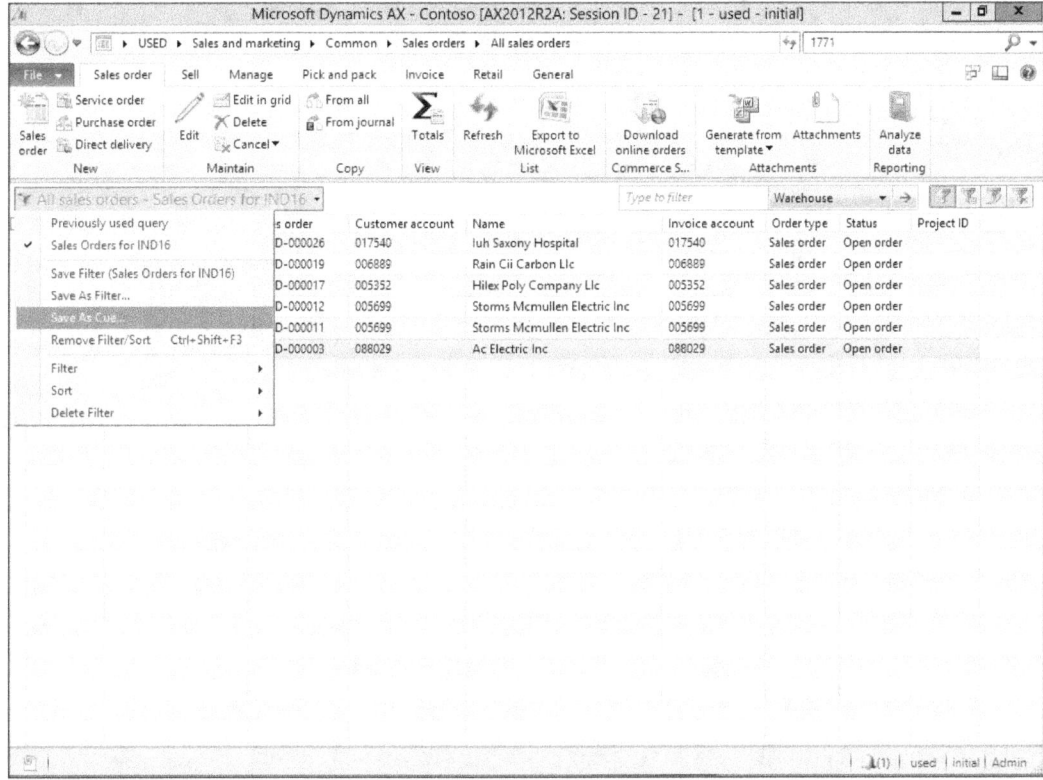

When we were looking at the Role Centers we talked about the Activities and Cues as a way to access data that you want to track. Now we will show how you can create those Cues that then show up on your Role Center.

To create a Cue, filter your data to the information that you are interested in, and then from the Filters dropdown, select the Save As Cue menu item.

Example: Saving Filtered Views As Cues

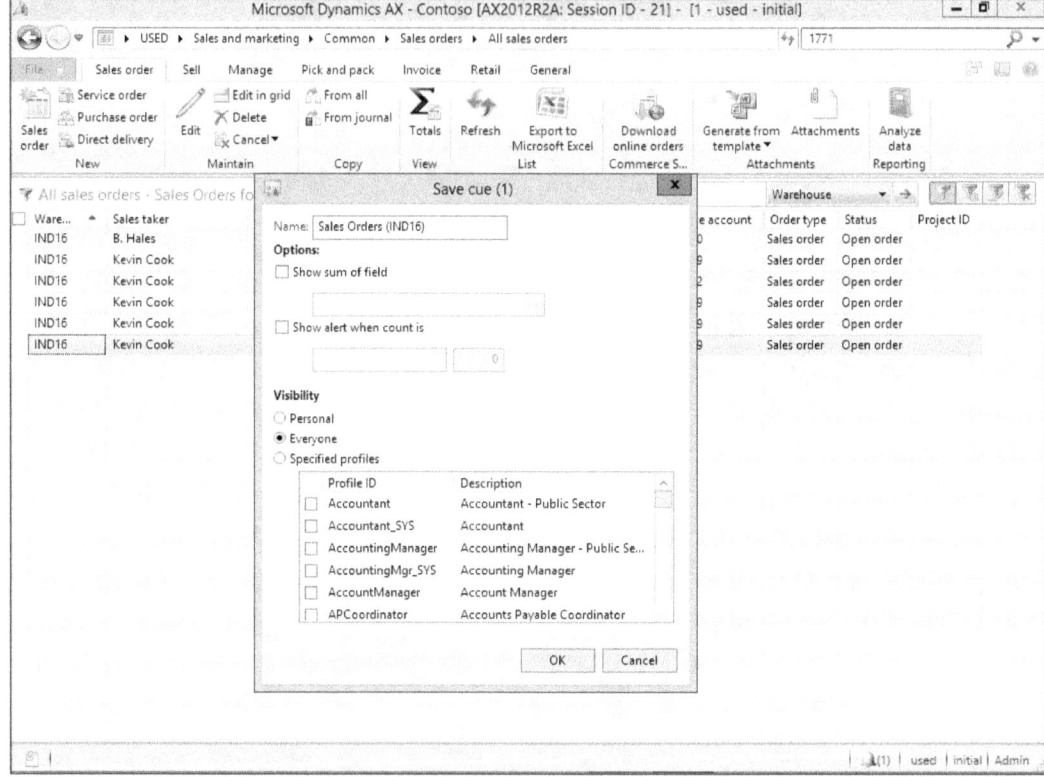

All you need to do is give your Cue an Name and then click the OK button.

Example: Saving Filtered Views As Cues

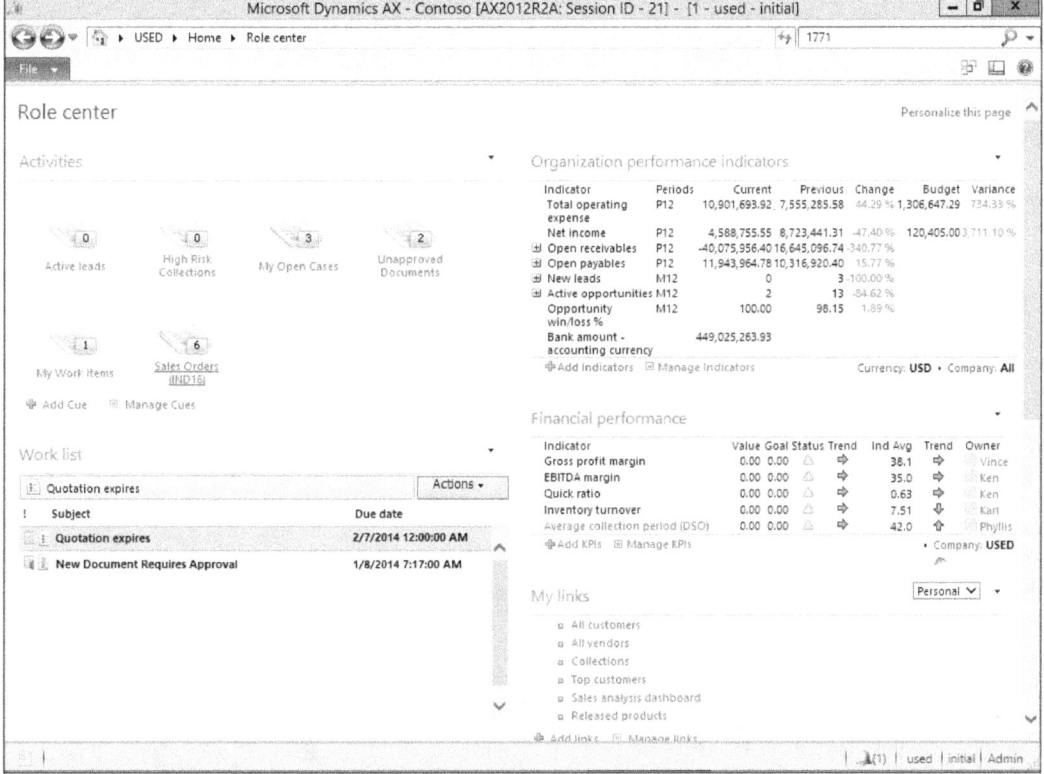

When you return to your Role Center, you will see that there is a new Cue that has been added to the Activities part. If you click on it you will be sent back to the filtered form.

Self Service Reporting and Analysis

There are two main goals that everyone has in mind when they implement a system like Dynamics AX. The first is to track all of the information about the business by entering in data, and the second is to see how the business is doing by getting the information out in reports.

Traditionally the first part is easy because you tell the people to do it, but the second part has been harder because you a developer has usually been required in order to create the reports, and reports take time to build. Everyone puts in their requests for data, the importance of the report is generally directly related to the position of the requestor within the organization, and by the time you get the report, you probably have found other more time consuming ways to get the data out, or it's not quite what you want, or both.

Dynamics AX solves this problem by giving the users a whole slew of different ways that they can get the information out themselves without having to bother a developer in most cases.

In this section we will show some of the different options for reporting that are available.

Example: Analyzing Through PowerView Directly From The Forms

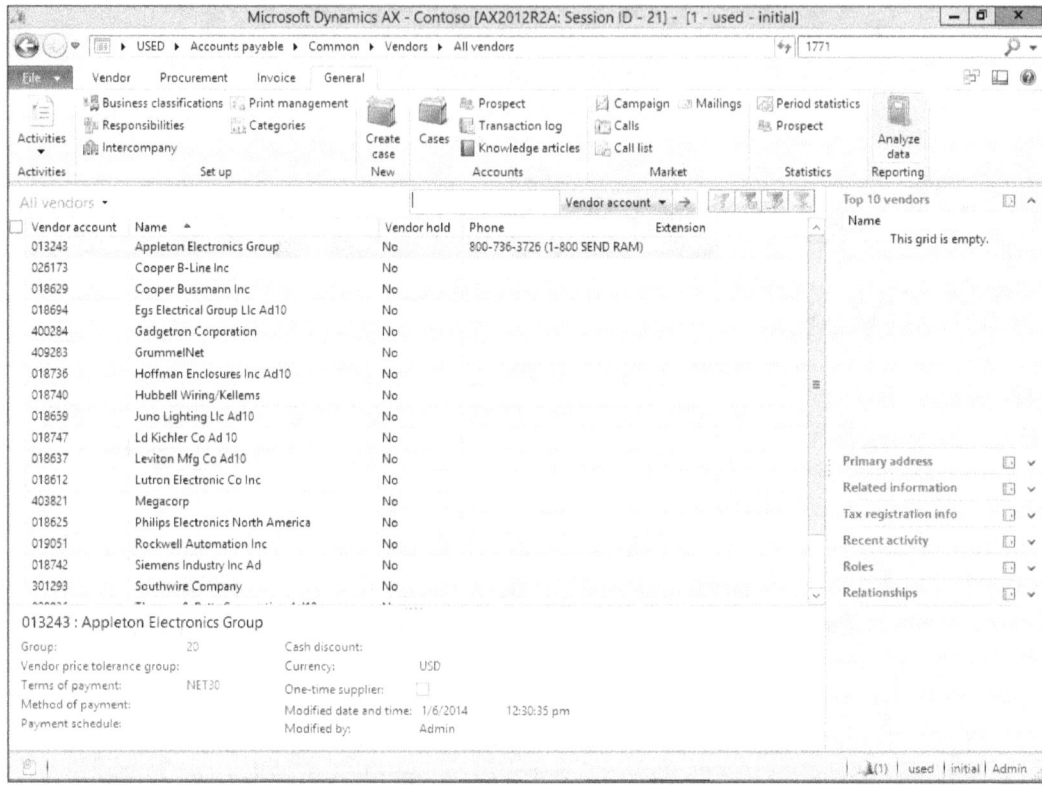

The easiest way to create your own dashboard or report is to do it directly from the Dynamics AX forms by clicking on the Analyze Data button that you can find on most of the main forms.

Example: Analyzing Through PowerView Directly From The Forms

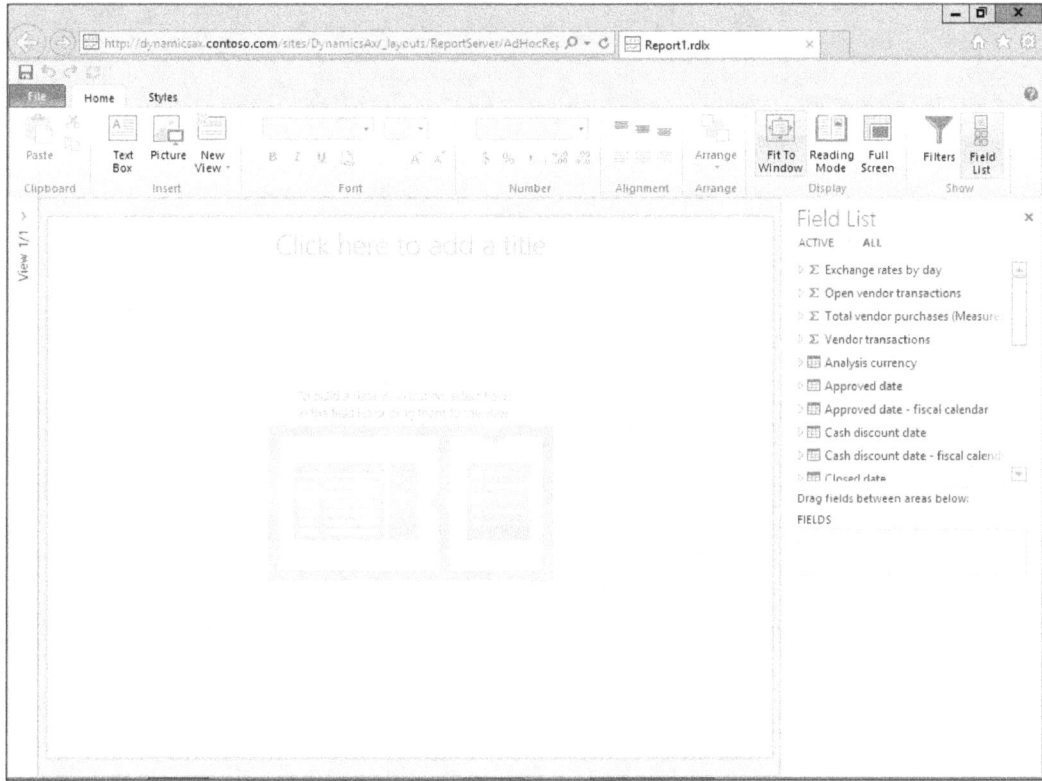

This will open up a PowerView canvas with all of the things that you can report off showing up in the Field List to the right. This information has been simplified down so that there are no table names or cryptic fields that you have to decipher in order to create your reports.

Example: Analyzing Through PowerView Directly From The Forms

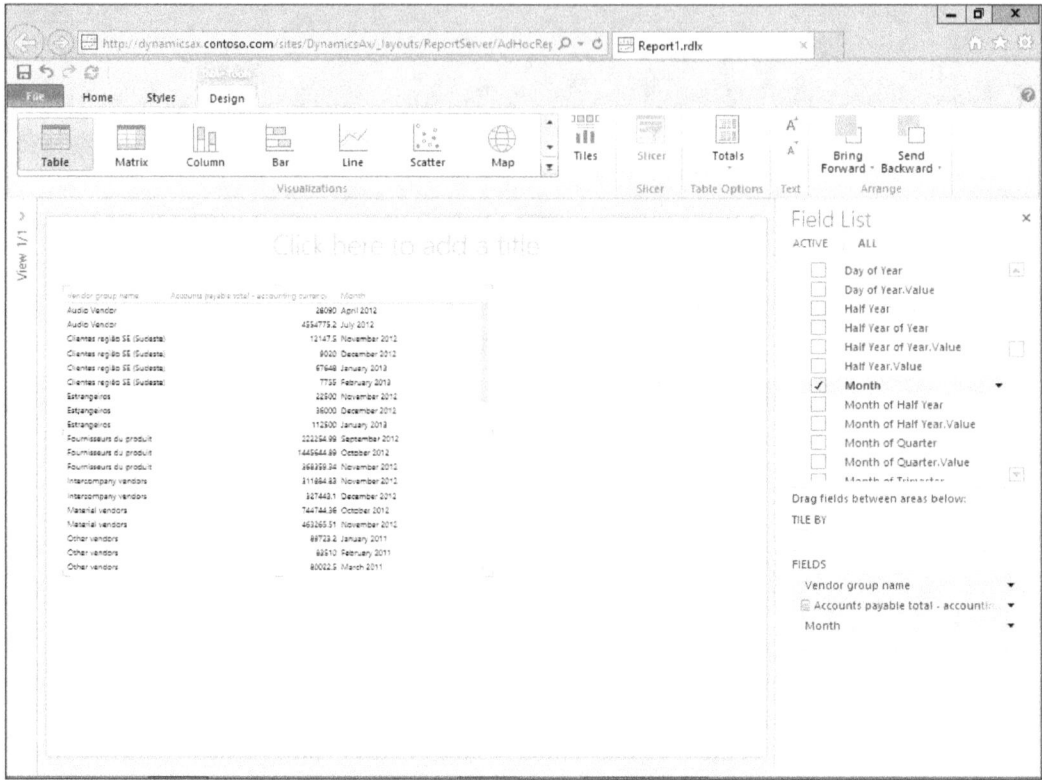

All you have to do is select the fields that you want to report off and they will be added to the reporting canvas.

Example: Analyzing Through PowerView Directly From The Forms

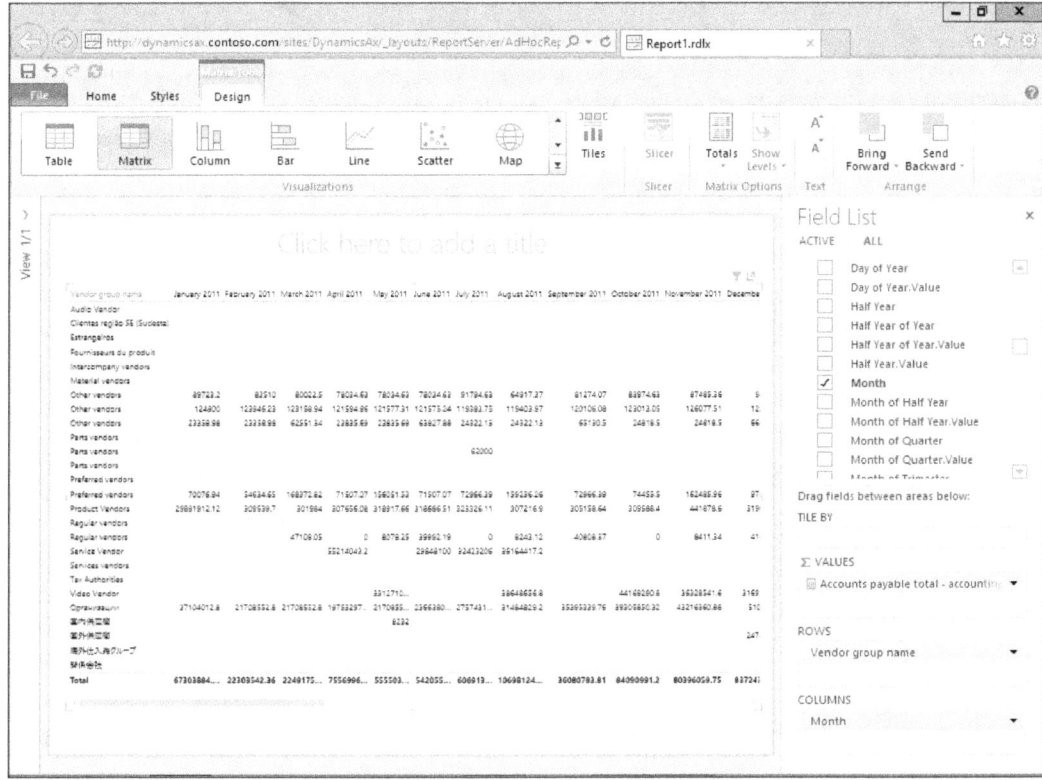

You can tweak the view to convert it to a tabular matrix view and change the columns to match what you are trying to report off.

Example: Analyzing Through PowerView Directly From The Forms

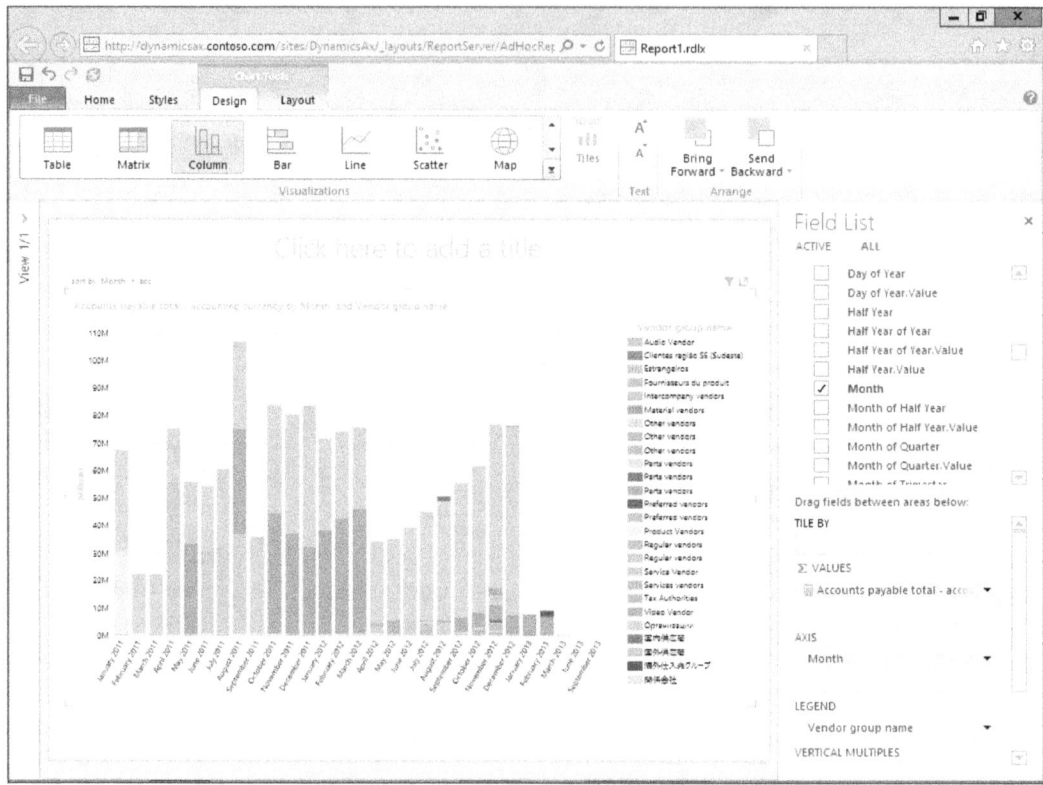

You can then convert the data into charts and graphs to make the view more visual.

Example: Saving Your Dashboards To Use Later On

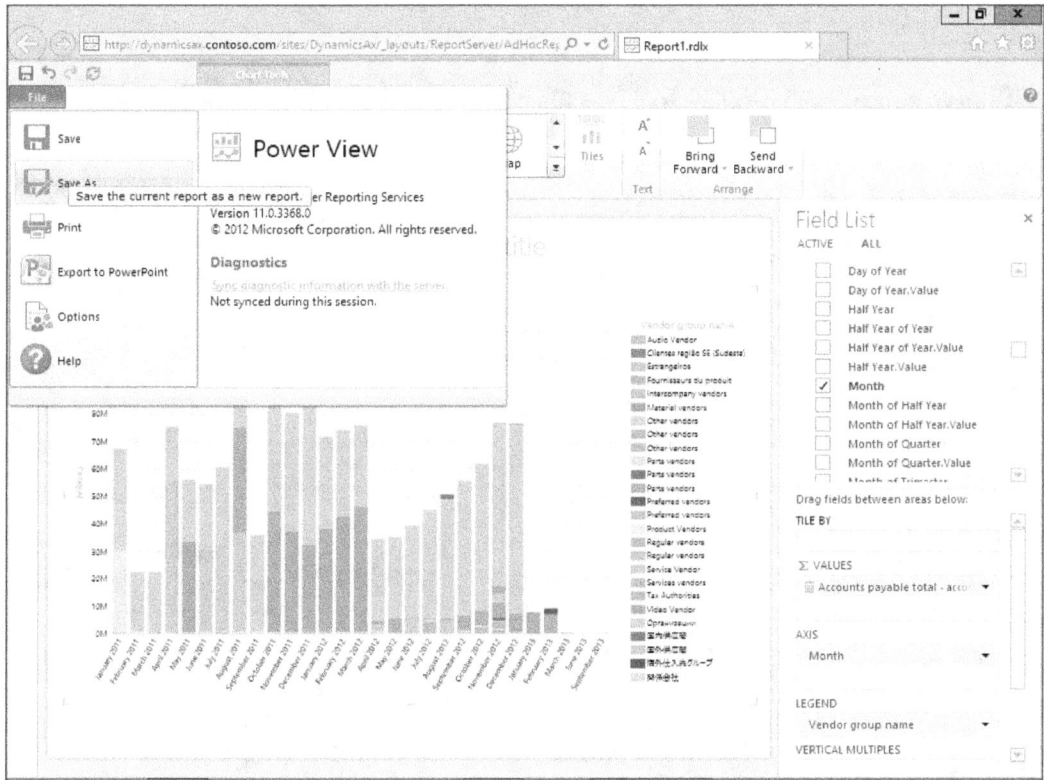

Once you create a dashboard or report, you may want to store it away so that you can use it later on.

To do that, just click on the File menu and select the Save As button.

Example: Saving Your Dashboards To Use Later On

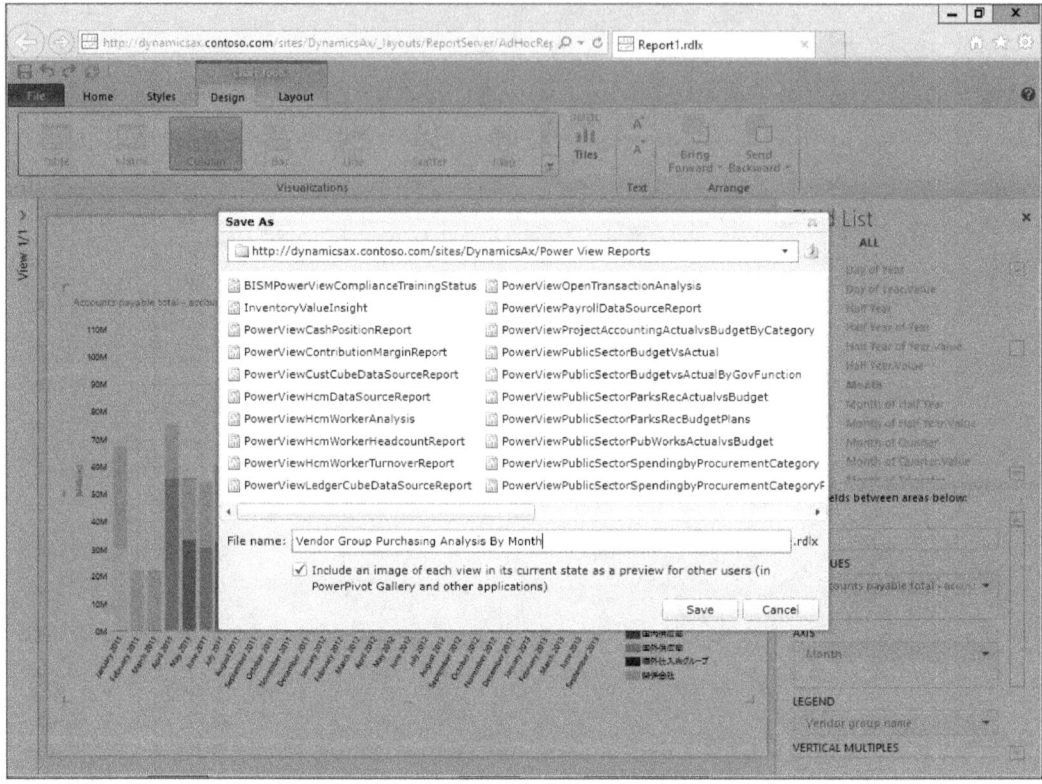

Then give your report a name and click the Save Button.

Example: Exporting To PowerPoint To Create Dynamics Slideshows

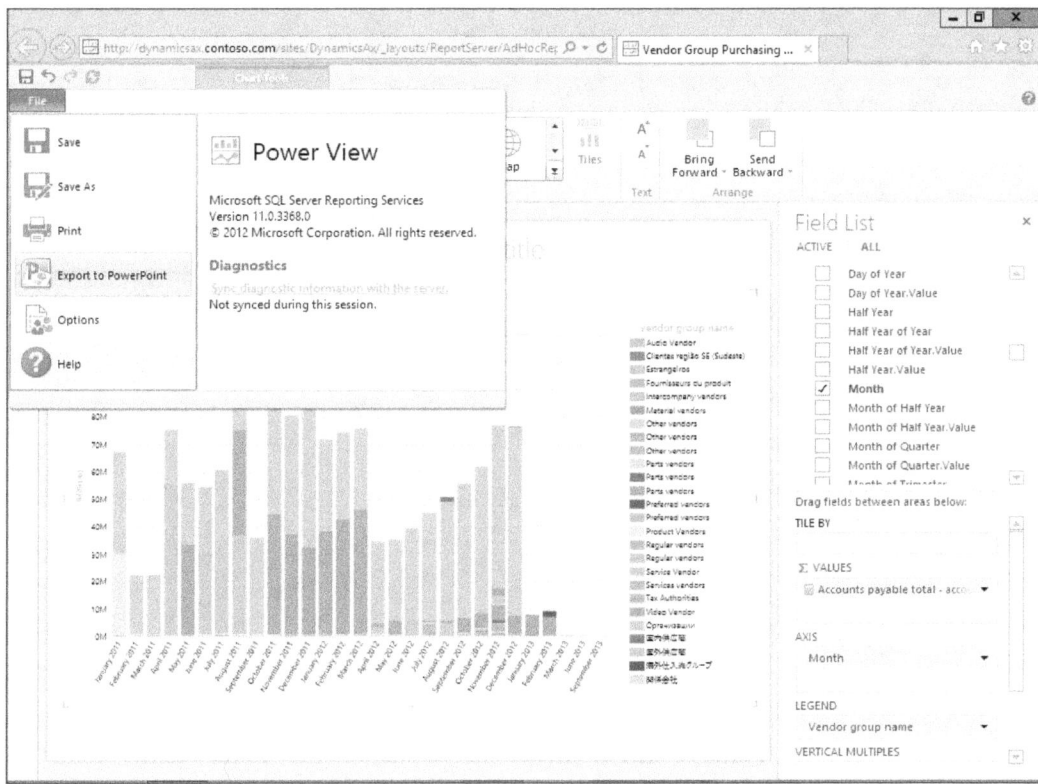

One reason why you may be creating the dashboards or reports is because you want to use them in a presentation. In the past you may have done this through Excel and then cut and pasted the chart into PowerPoint. The only downside of this is that the next time you want to update the chart you have to go through the process again. When you have dozens of charts, then this can be time consuming.

PowerView has an added benefit in that once you create the dashboard, you can tell it to create an embedded version in PowerPoint that will refresh itself.

To do that, click on the File menu item and select the Export to PowerPoint option.

Example: Exporting To PowerPoint To Create Dynamics Slideshows

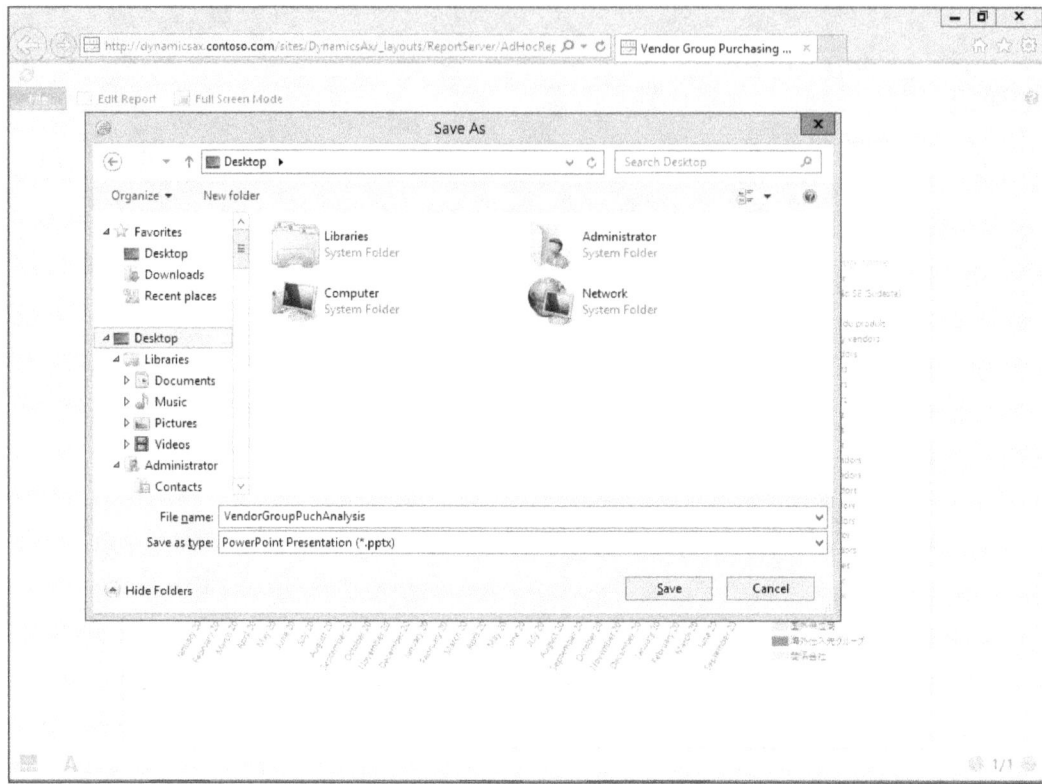

Now specify the name of the PowerPoint that you are creating and click the Save button.

Example: Exporting To PowerPoint To Create Dynamics Slideshows

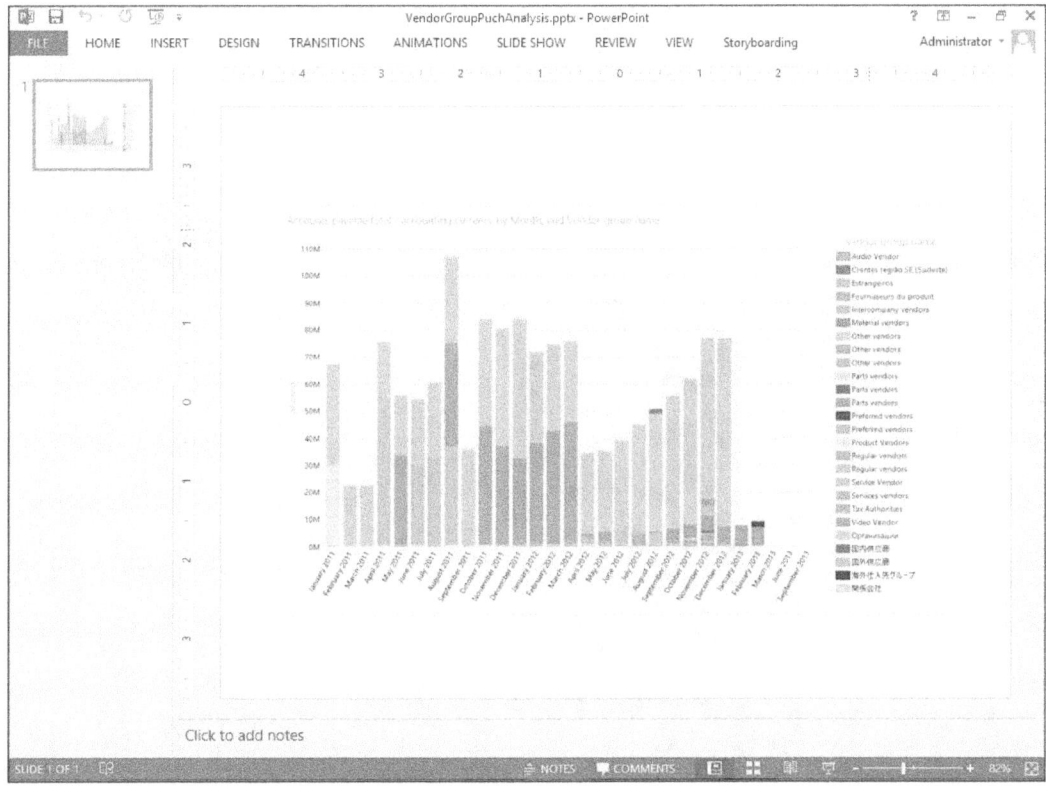

When you open up the PowerPoint, you will see that the report is embedded in the slide.

Example: Exporting To PowerPoint To Create Dynamics Slideshows

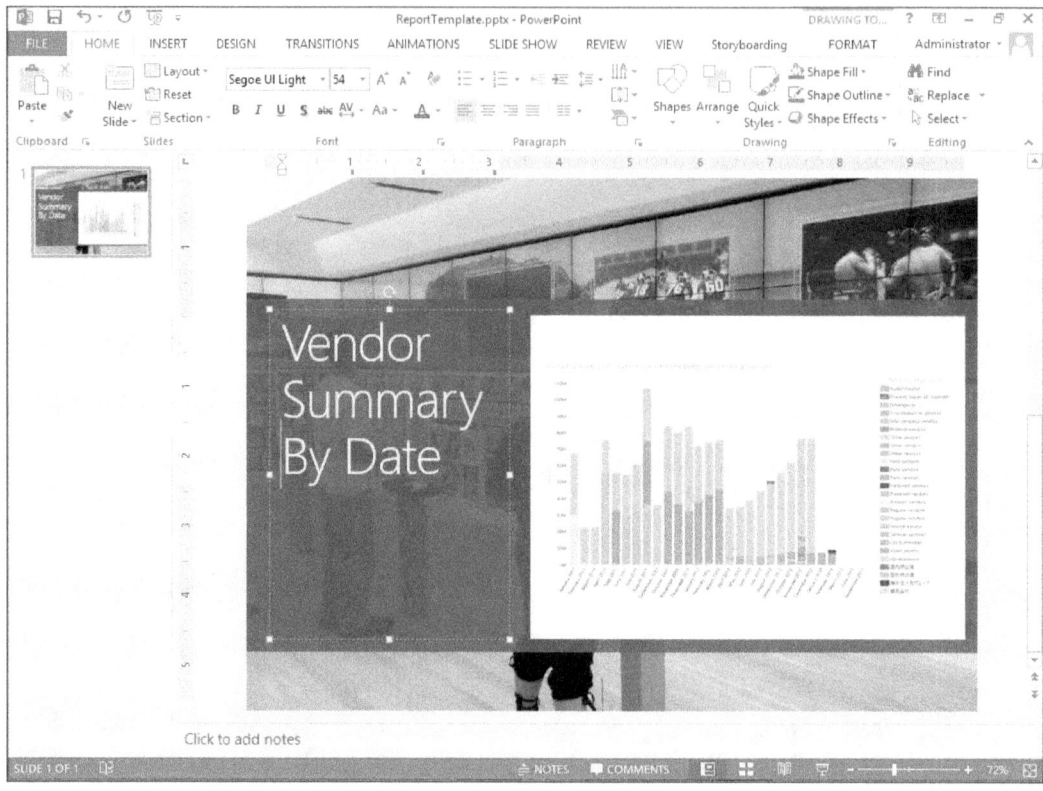

All you need to do is add a little bit of style and panache to the slide.

Example: Exporting To PowerPoint To Create Dynamics Slideshows

When you open up the presentation in SlideShow mode, it will initially show the cached view of the chart, but to see something cool, just click on the Interact link in the bottom right of the dashboard.

Example: Exporting To PowerPoint To Create Dynamics Slideshows

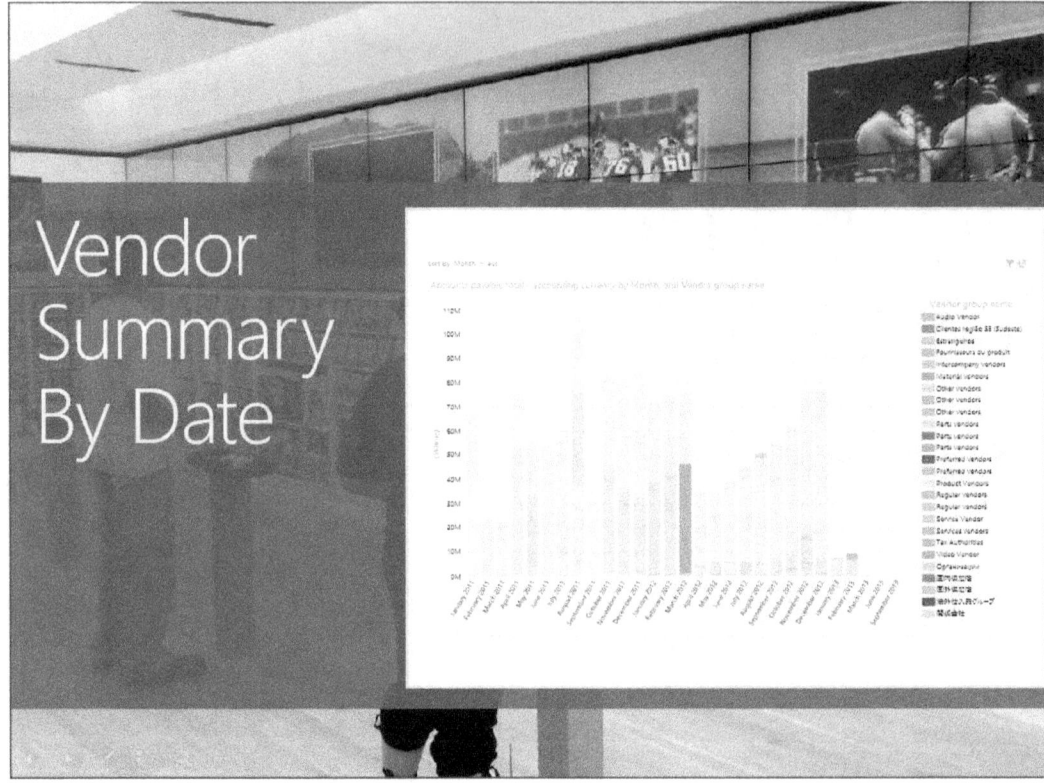

That will then fetch all of the current data from Dynamics AX and you can even drill into the information interactively through the PowerPoint presentation.

How cool is that!

Example: Exporting Linked Data Directly To Excel

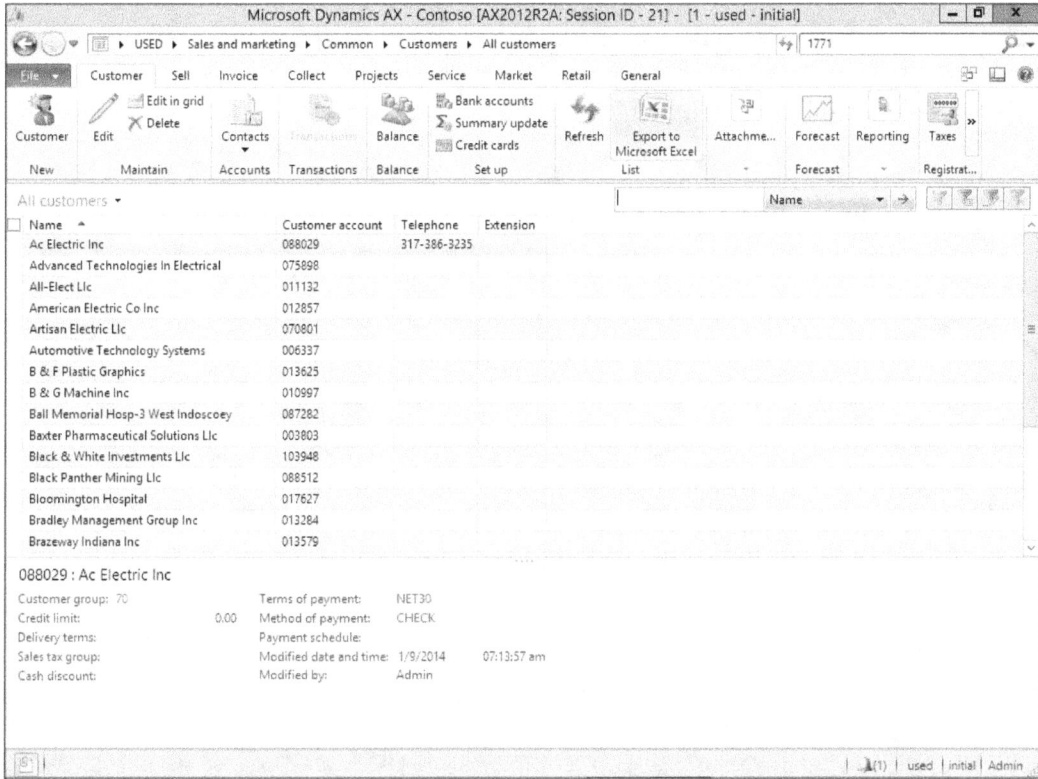

Another way that you can report off the data within Dynamics AX is to use Excel – which is really the most widely used reporting tool out there.

The difference in the way that Dynamics AX does this is that rather then just doing a cut and paste from the form to Excel, which disconnects the data, the data that is exported to Excel is still linked to Dynamics AX, and will refresh each time that you refresh the spreadsheet.

All you need to do to create a report from Dynamics AX within Excel is click on eth Export to Microsoft Excel button within the ribbon bar.

Example: Exporting Linked Data Directly To Excel

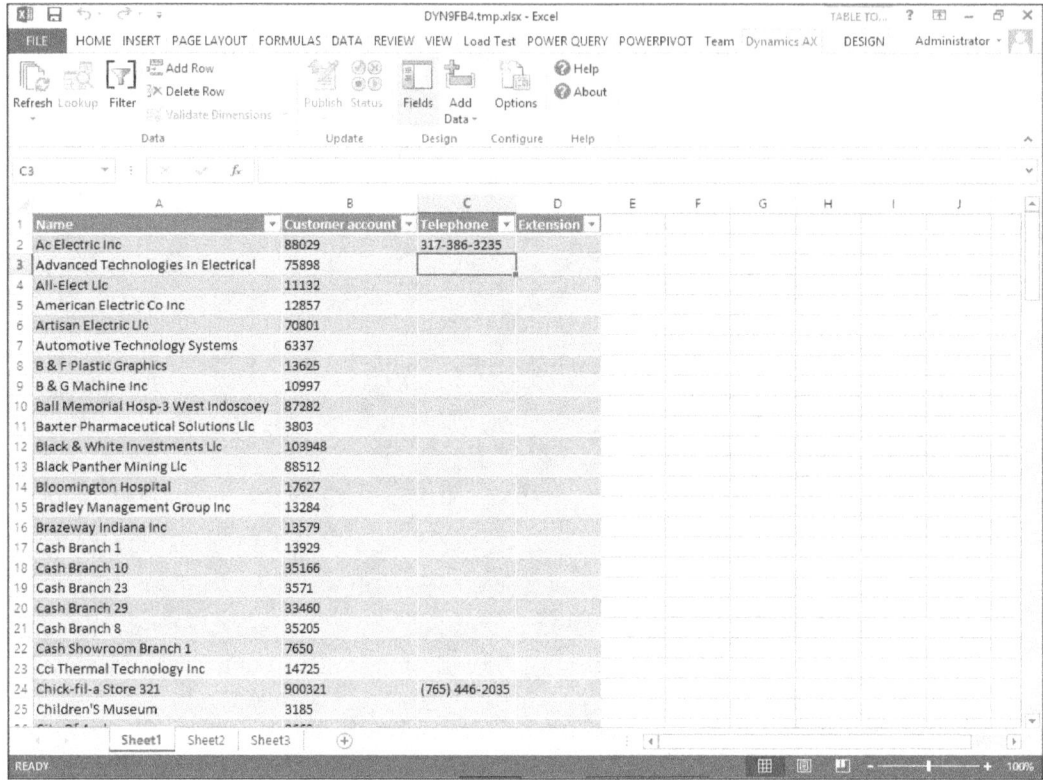

This will open up Excel and all of the data that was in the list page will be there.

Example: Adding Additional Fields To Linked Excel Spreadsheets

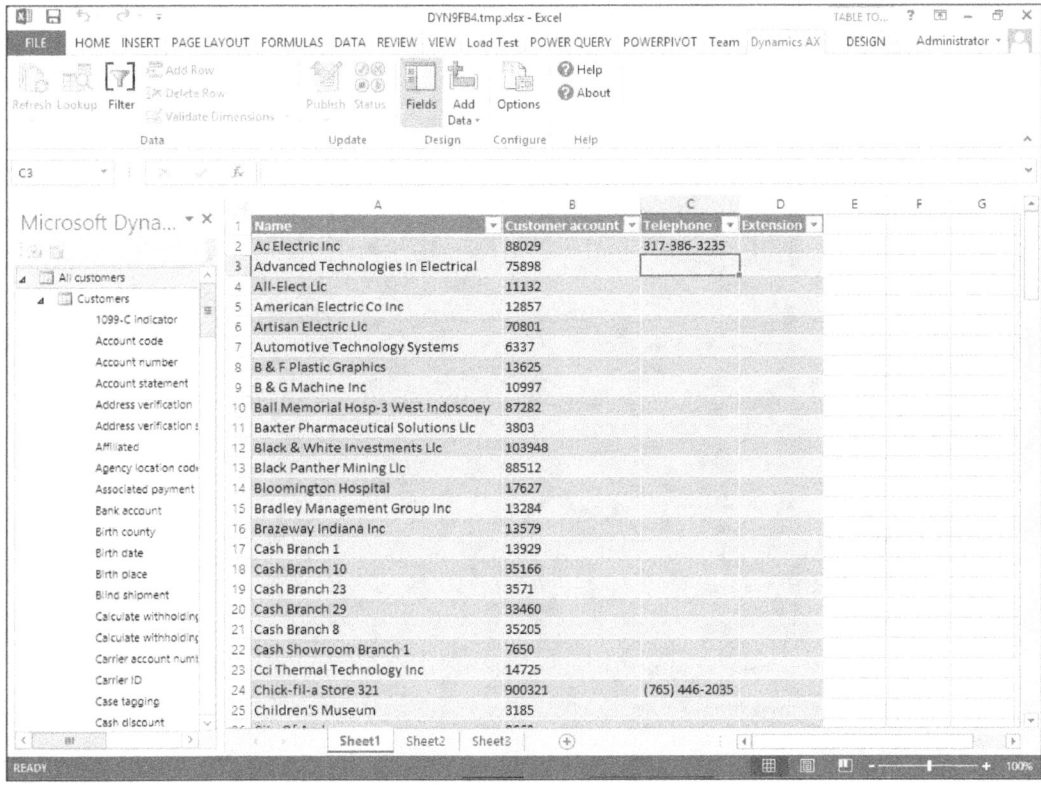

Another benefit of the linked Excel spreadsheets is that you have access to all of the additional fields within Dynamics AX, and can add them to your Excel spreadsheet at any time.

To view the additional fields, just click on the Fields button within the Dynamics AX ribbon bar. This will open up the field browser on the left hand side.

Example: Adding Additional Fields To Linked Excel Spreadsheets

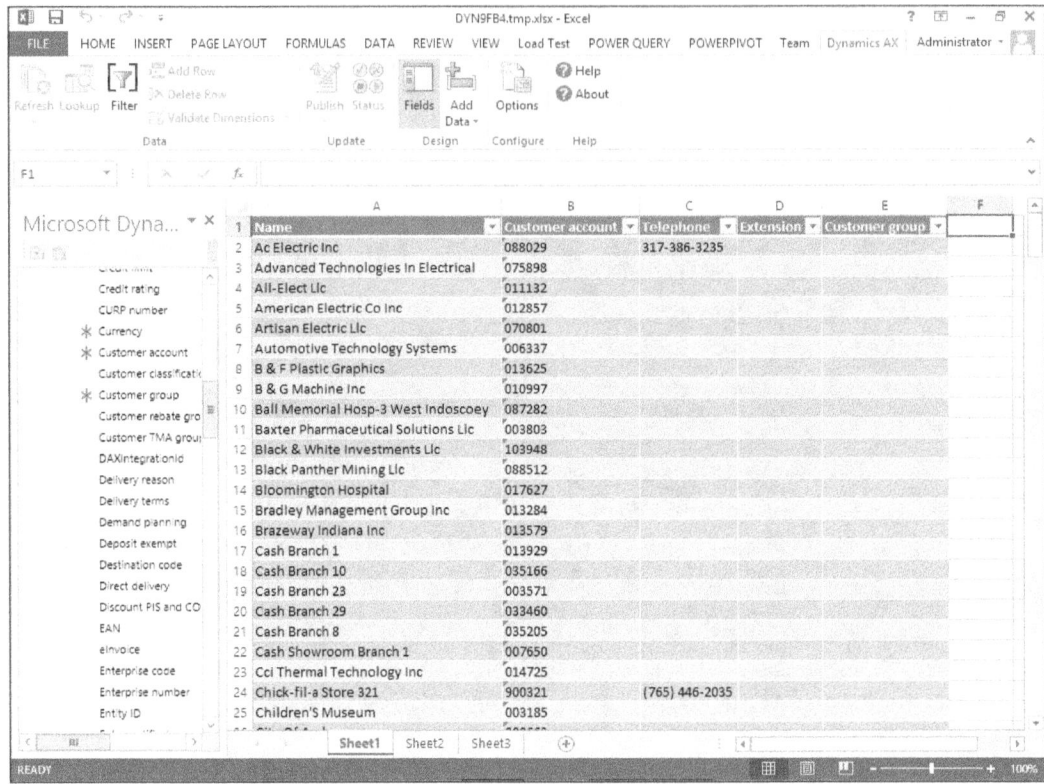

To add a field to the spreadsheet just drag it from the browser over to an adjacent column.

Example: Adding Additional Fields To Linked Excel Spreadsheets

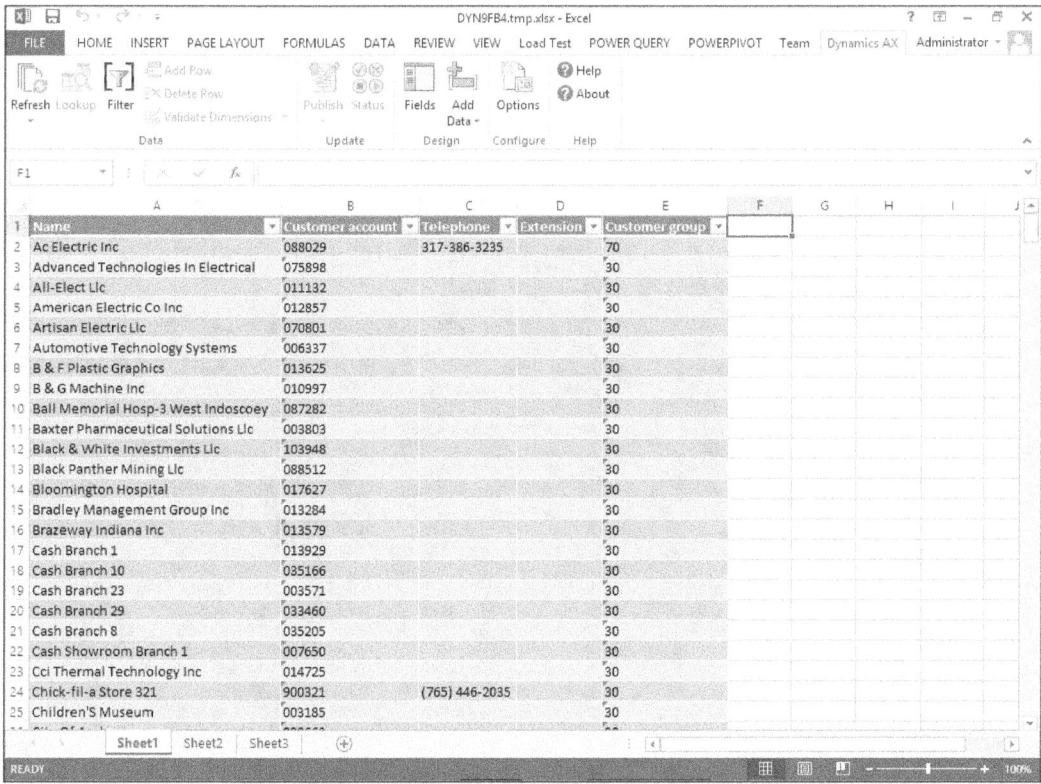

When you have finished adding your fields to the spreadsheet, click on the Fields button again to exit the design mode, and then click on the Refresh button to get all of the data, including the new field data that you added.

Example: Creating Dashboards Within Excel Using PowerView

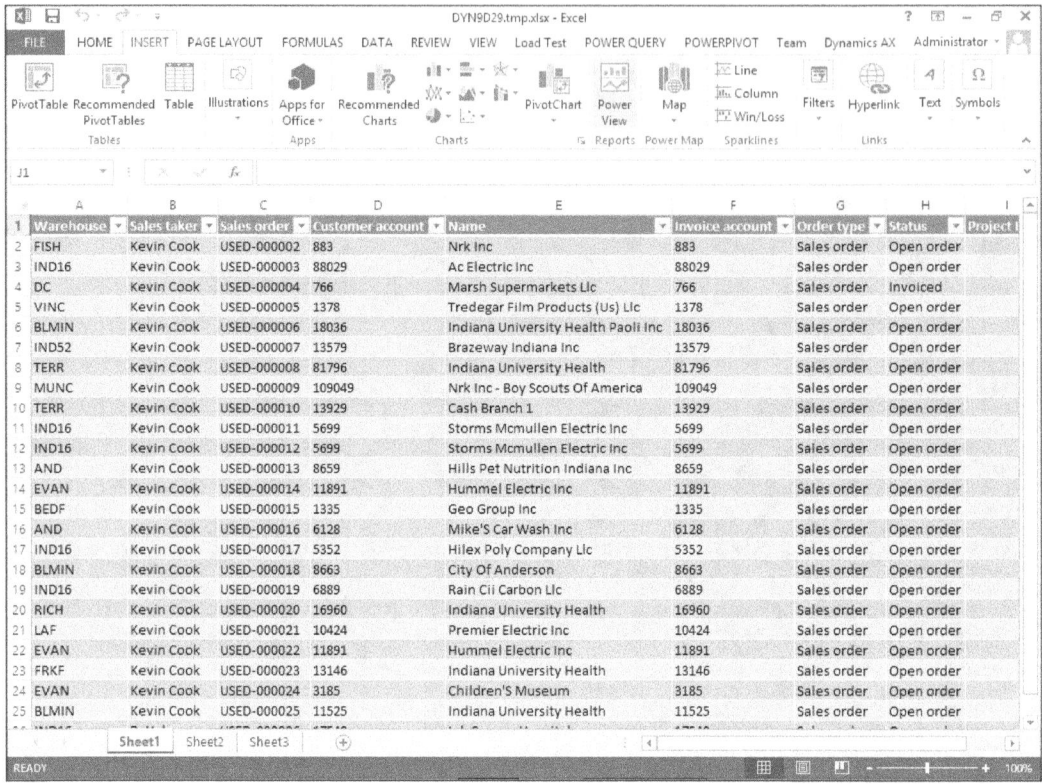

Once you have the data within Excel, you can then take advantage of all the reporting capabilities that it offers as well. You can create charts, graphs, pivot tables etc. But with Office 2013 you can also create PowerView Dashboards.

To do this, just export some data from Dynamics AX to Excel, and then click on the PowerView button within the Insert ribbon bar.

Example: Creating Dashboards Within Excel Using PowerView

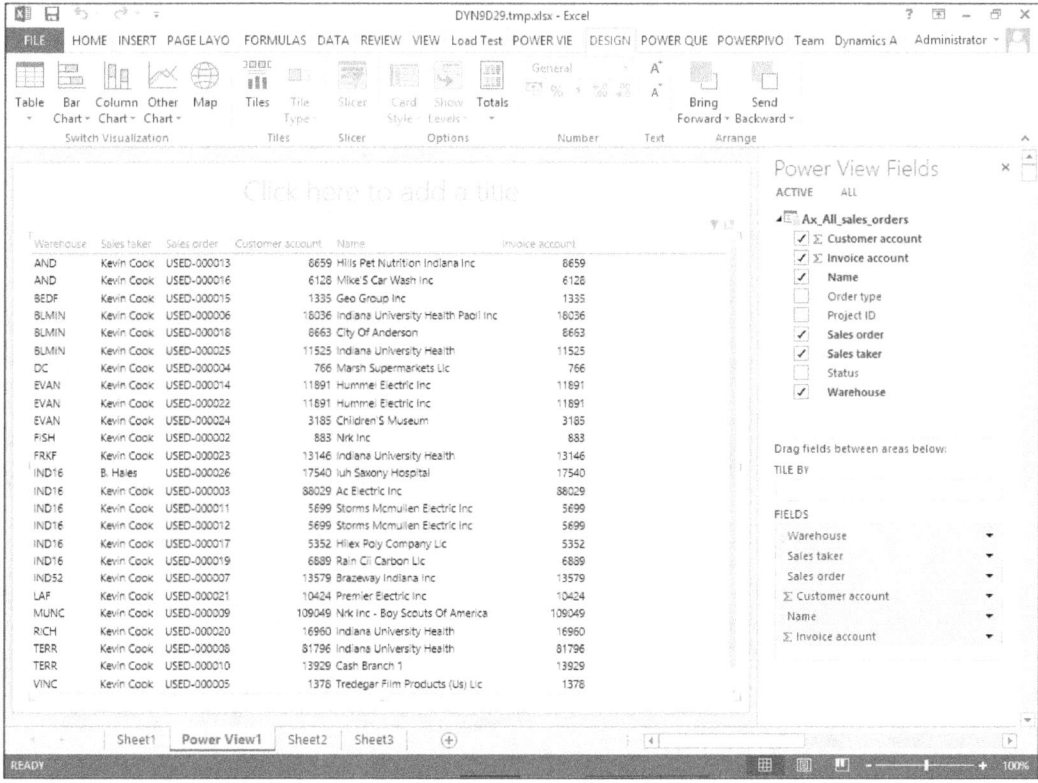

This will create a PowerView reporting canvas within Excel and pre-populate it with some of the data from the excel spreadsheet for you.

Example: Creating Dashboards Within Excel Using PowerView

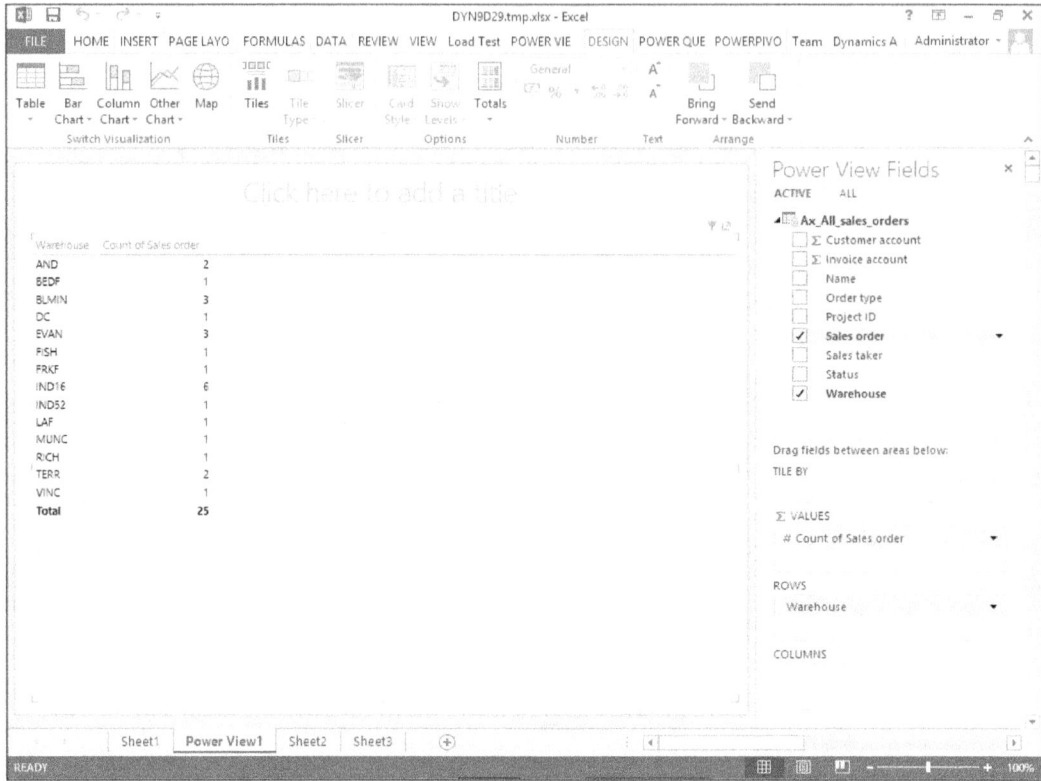

All you need to do is clean up the fields to just the information that you want to report off.

Example: Creating Dashboards Within Excel Using PowerView

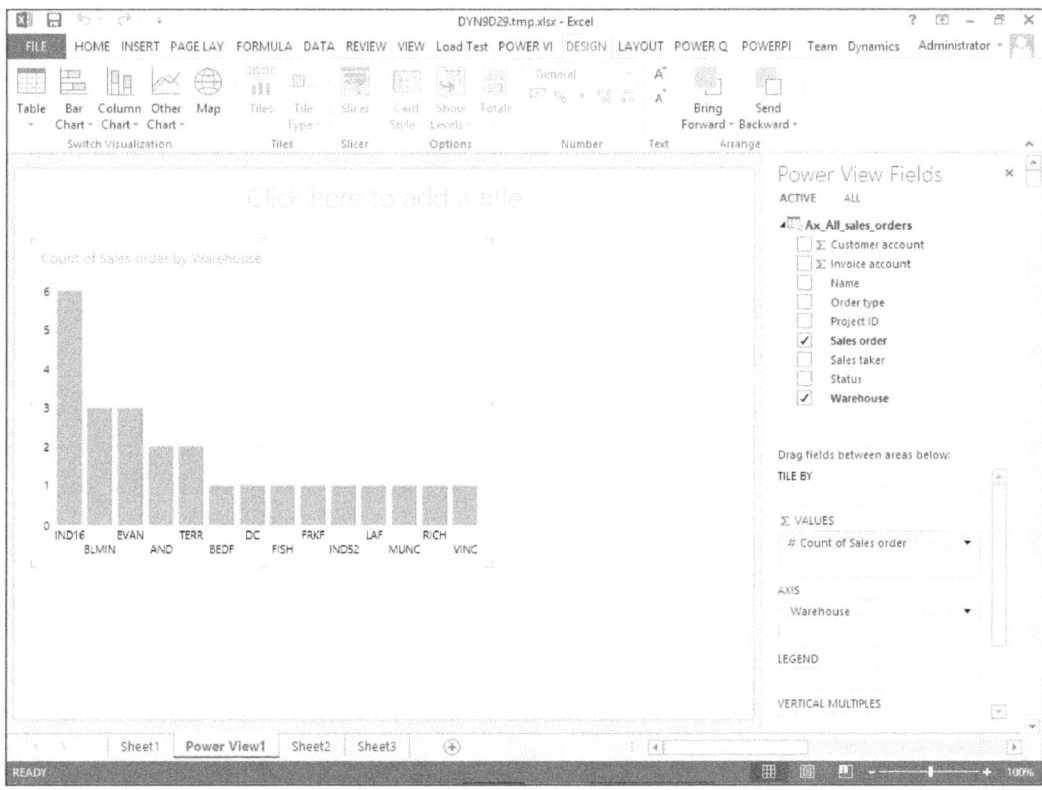

You can then convert the data into a chart if you like.

Example: Creating Dashboards Within Excel Using PowerView

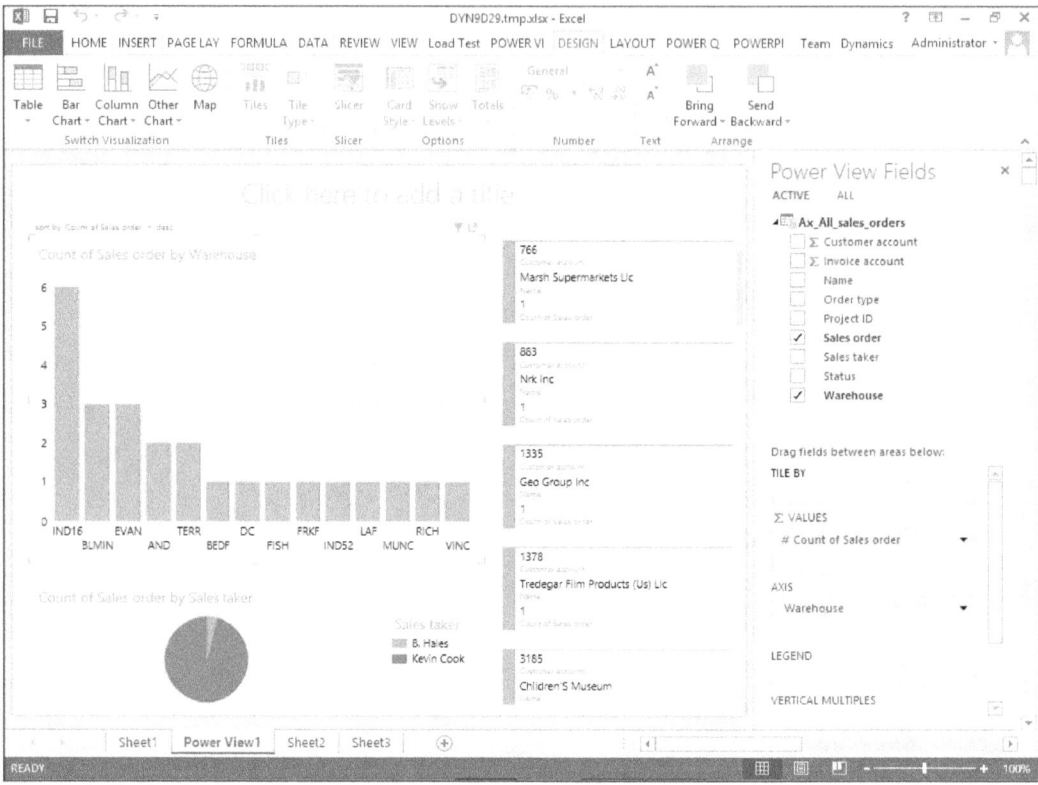

And even create multiple panels in the PowerView dashboard showing different diced reporting values.

You can then save this spreadsheet and access it any time you like.

Example: Asking For Reports Using PowerBI Q&A

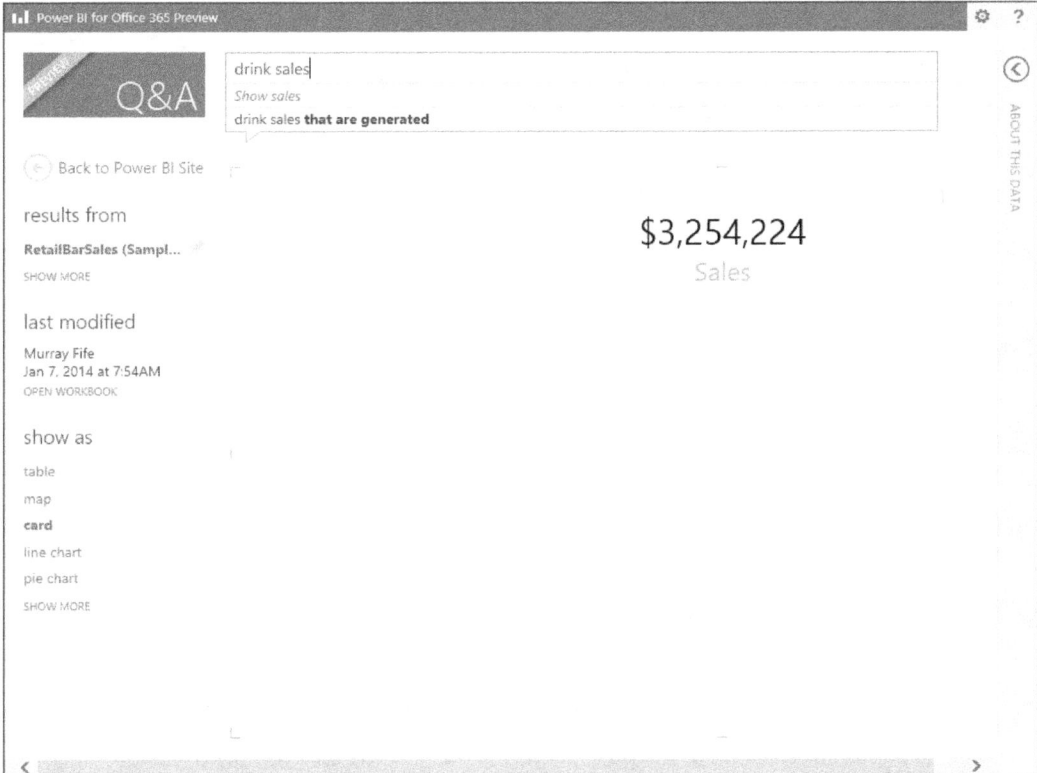

PowerView is part of the PowerBI suite of reporting tools that are being delivered by Microsoft. There is an additional product that you may want to try out which is called Q&A that is part of that suite. It allows you to publish your Excel datasets that you create up to PowerBI in Office 365, and allows you to do something incredibly cool.

All you need to do to create a report is ask Q&A a question about the data.

Example: Asking For Reports Using PowerBI Q&A

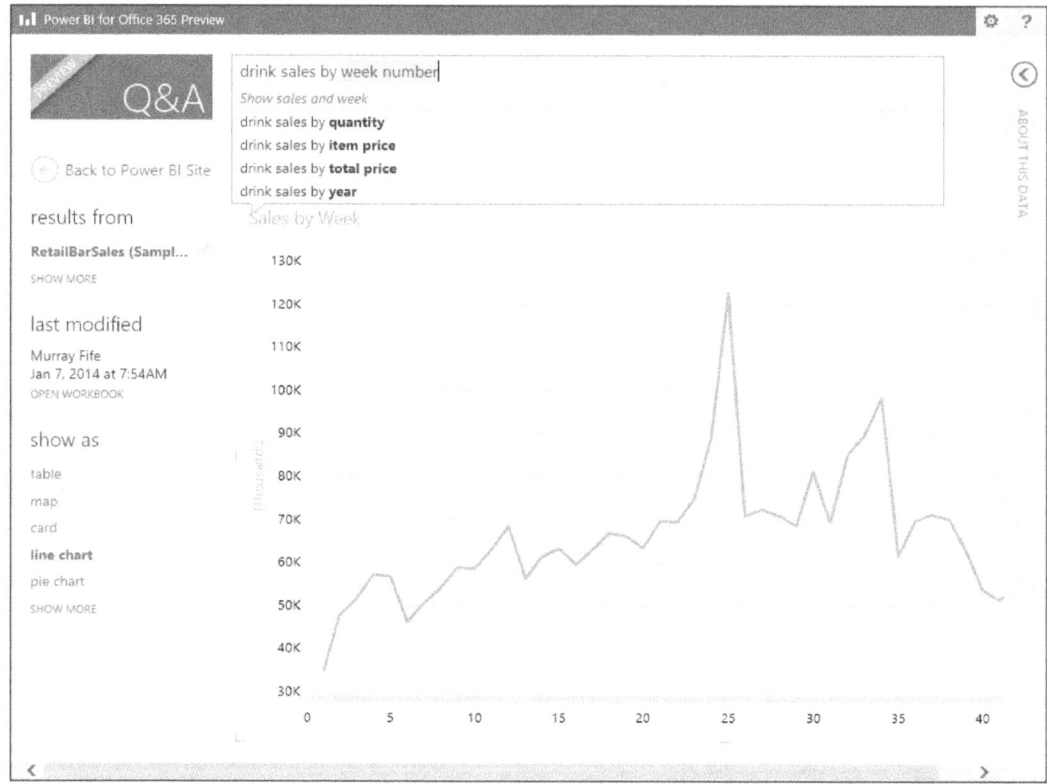

If you ask it with a time dimension then it will turn it into a line chart automatically.

Example: Asking For Reports Using PowerBI Q&A

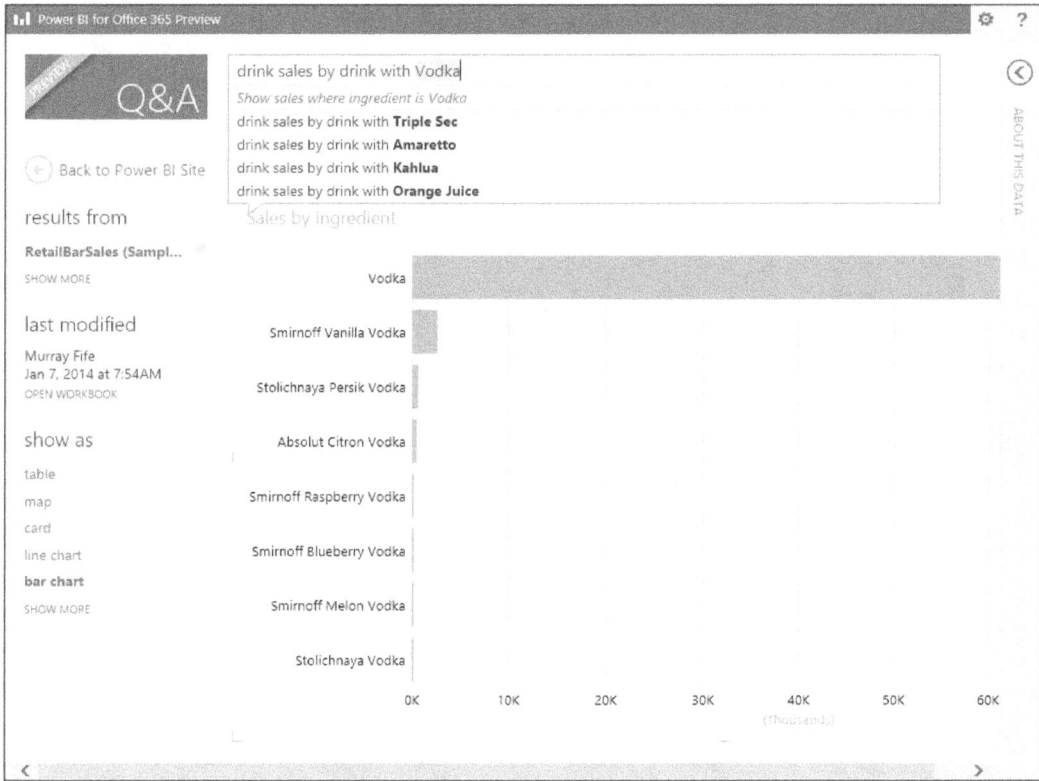

If you ask it a question that is quantitative, then it will show the information as bar charts.

You don't even have to think about how you want to report your data any more.

Using Office With Dynamics AX

Since Dynamics AX is a Microsoft product, then it just makes sense that it leverages a lot of the other Microsoft products to make the product even better. And Office is no exception. In the previous sections we have shown how you can use Excel as a reporting tool, but that is not the extent of what you can do.

You can also use Excel to import and update data, which makes it a great tool for maintenance of the data, and you can also use Word to create templates that are driven off the Dynamics AX data making it a simple reporting tool as well for all of your power users.

In this section we will show some of the other ways that you can use the Microsoft Office products to make your life just a little easier.

Example: Updating Dynamics AX Data Through Excel

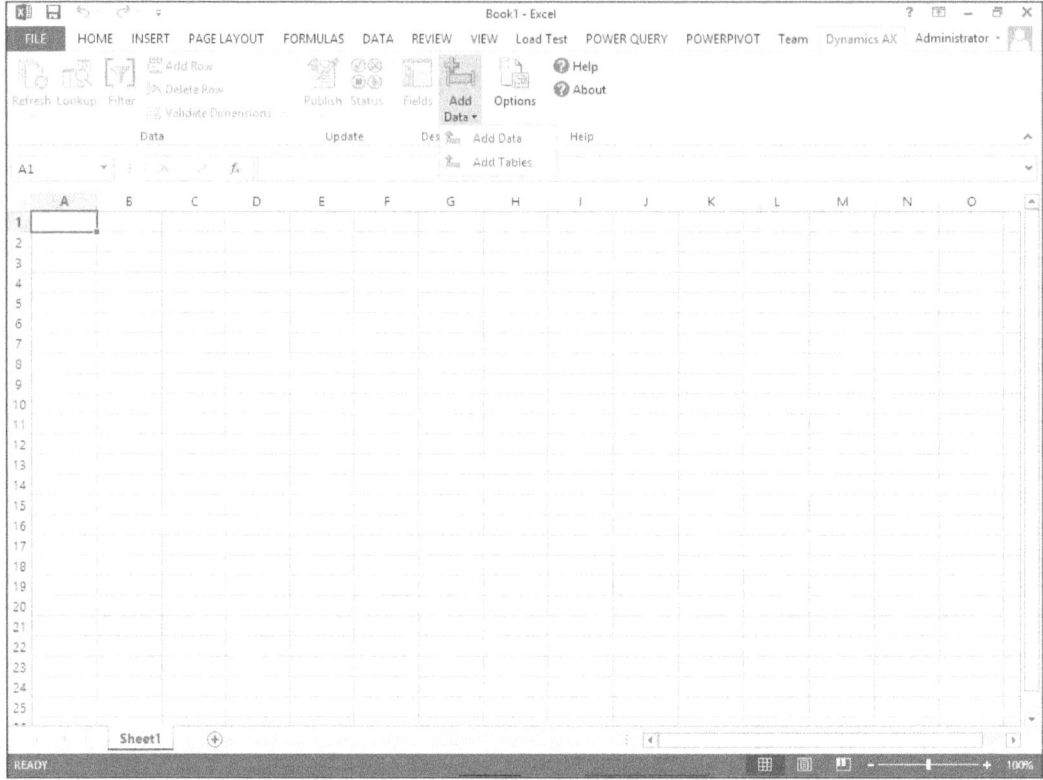

The Integration with Excel is not just a one-way street that allows Dynamics AX to push information down to it, it also has the ability to publish information back up to Dynamics AX.

This is especially useful when you have a lot of data that you need to either import or update, like the updating of standard price lists, or the rearrangement of sales territories, because you probably have all of this information within Excel somewhere, and it's a lot easier to cut and paste rather than key in the data individually.

To create an data update spreadsheet, all you need to do is click on the Add Data button within the Dynamics AX tab of Excel and then select the Add Tables option.

Example: Updating Dynamics AX Data Through Excel

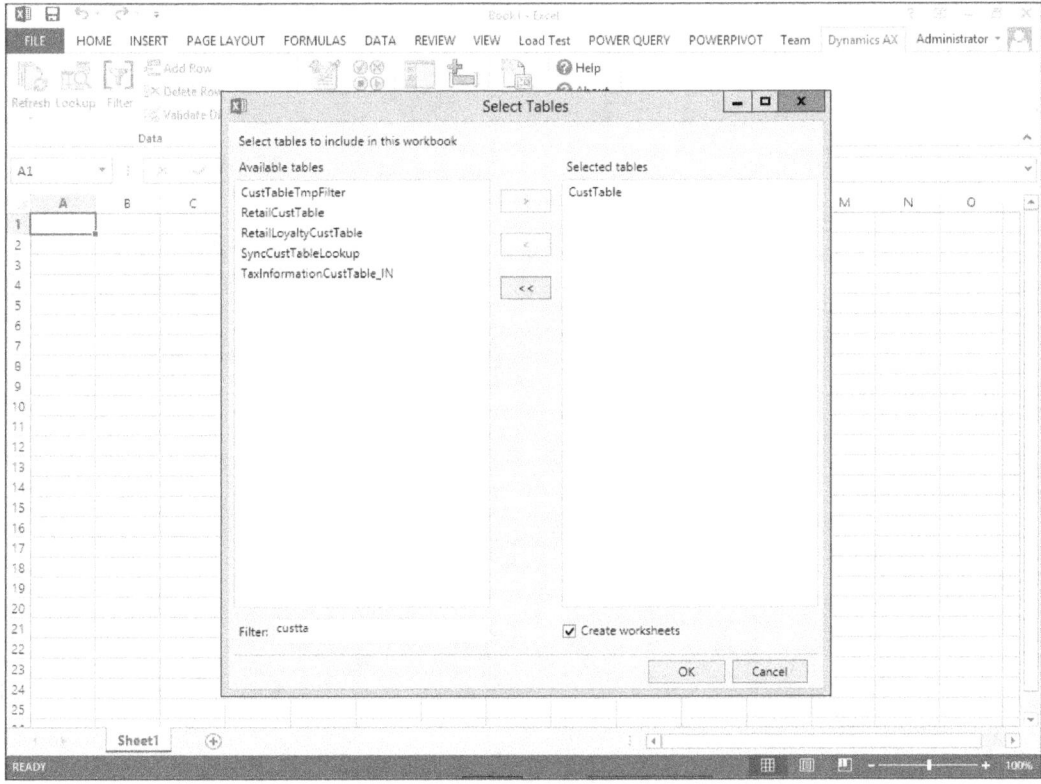

When the Select Tables dialog box is displayed, you just find the table that you want to update, add it to the selected tables, and then click the OK button.

Example: Updating Dynamics AX Data Through Excel

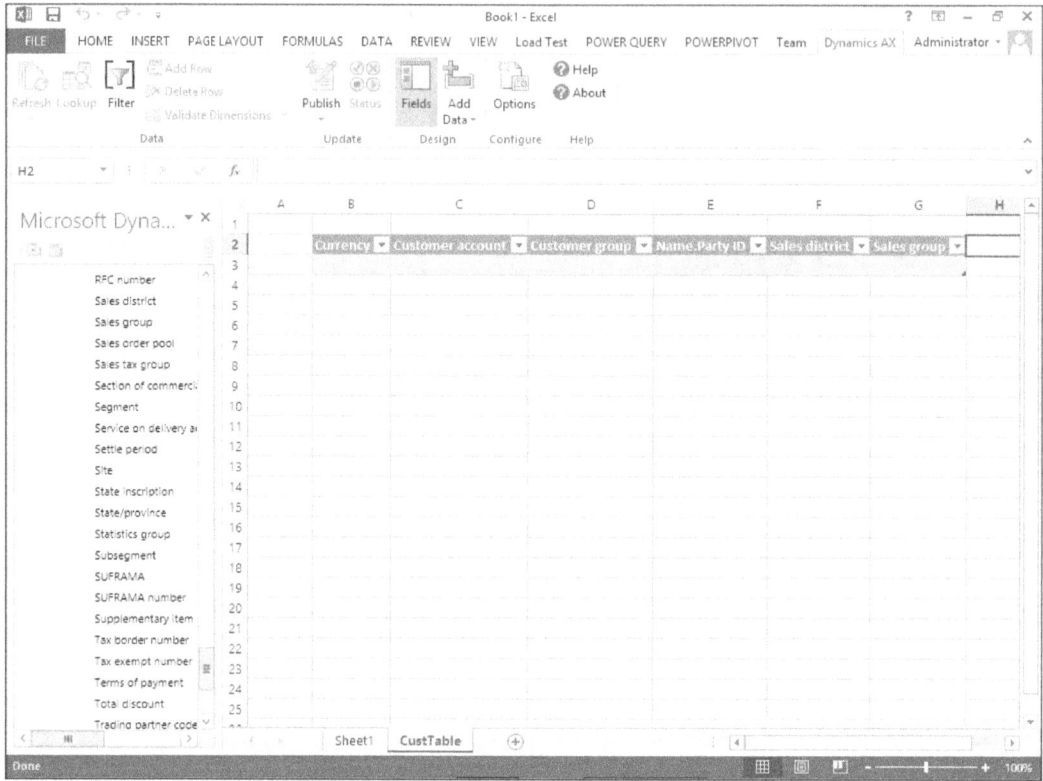

This will create a new worksheet for you with the key fields already populated on the form, and all of the available fields showing in the field browser. You can drag and drop additional fields over to the spreadsheet as well.

When you have finished designing the import template, just click on the Fields button in the Dynamics AX ribbon bar.

Example: Updating Dynamics AX Data Through Excel

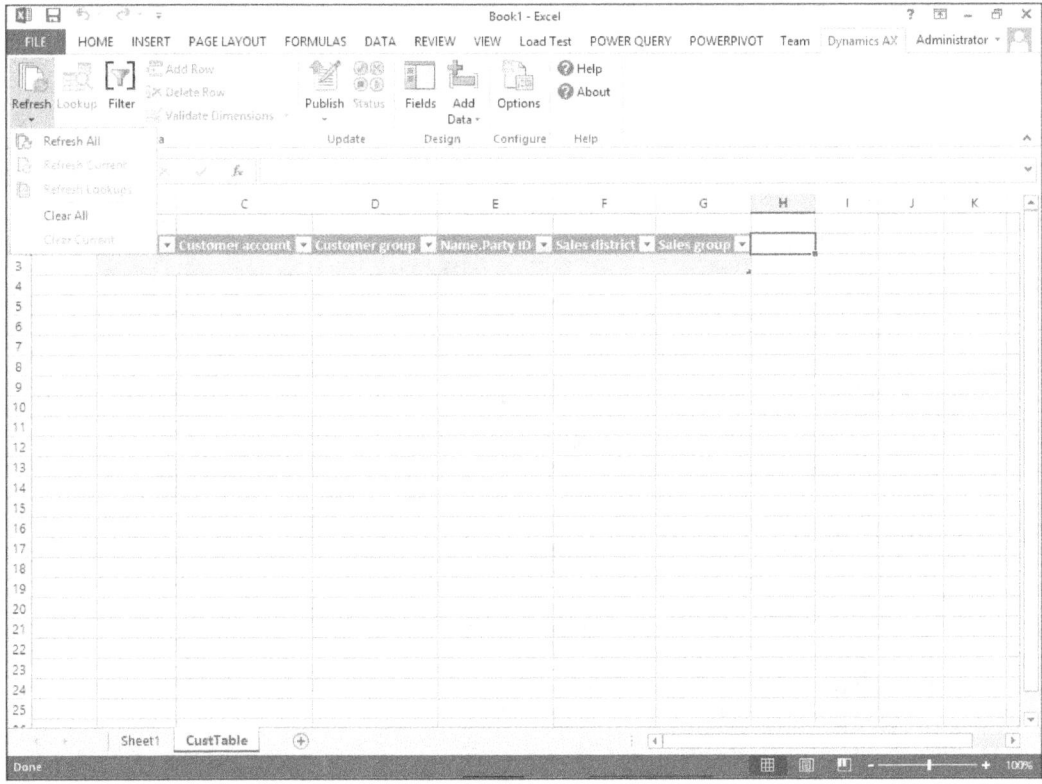

To populate all of the data in the spreadsheet, just click the Refresh button in the Dynamics AX ribbon bar.

Example: Updating Dynamics AX Data Through Excel

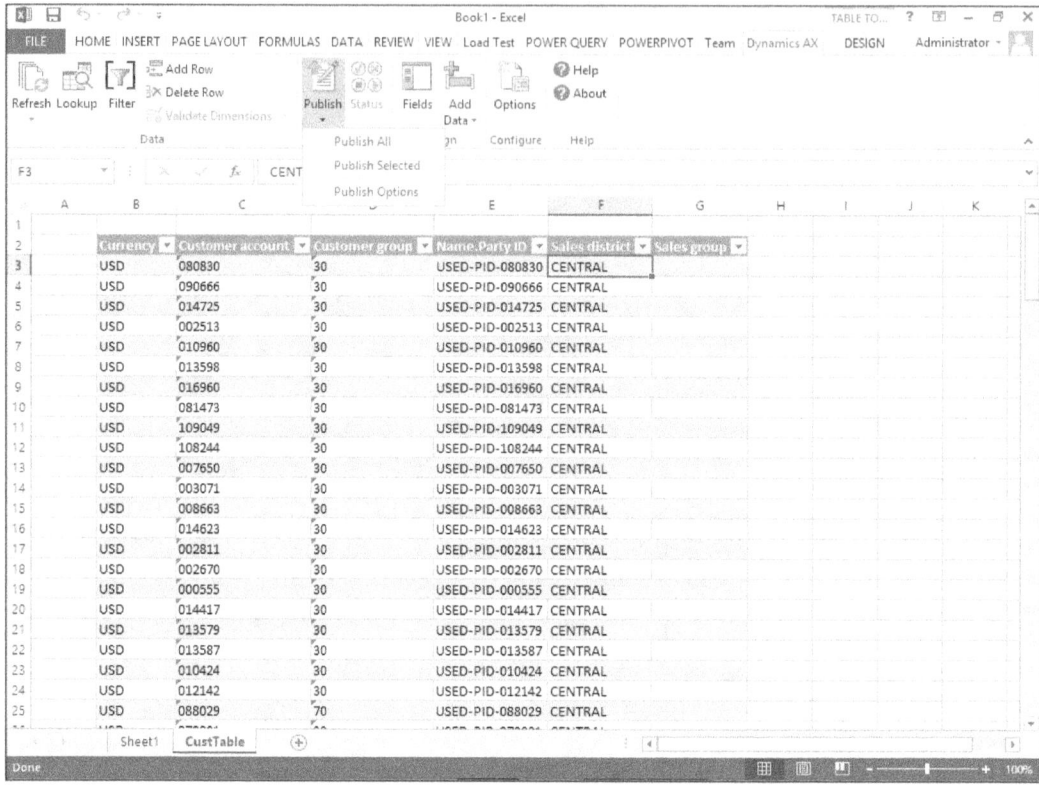

Now you can update any of the fields within the spreadsheet, and when you want to update Dynamics AX, just click on the Publish button, and select the Publish All option.

Example: Updating Dynamics AX Data Through Excel

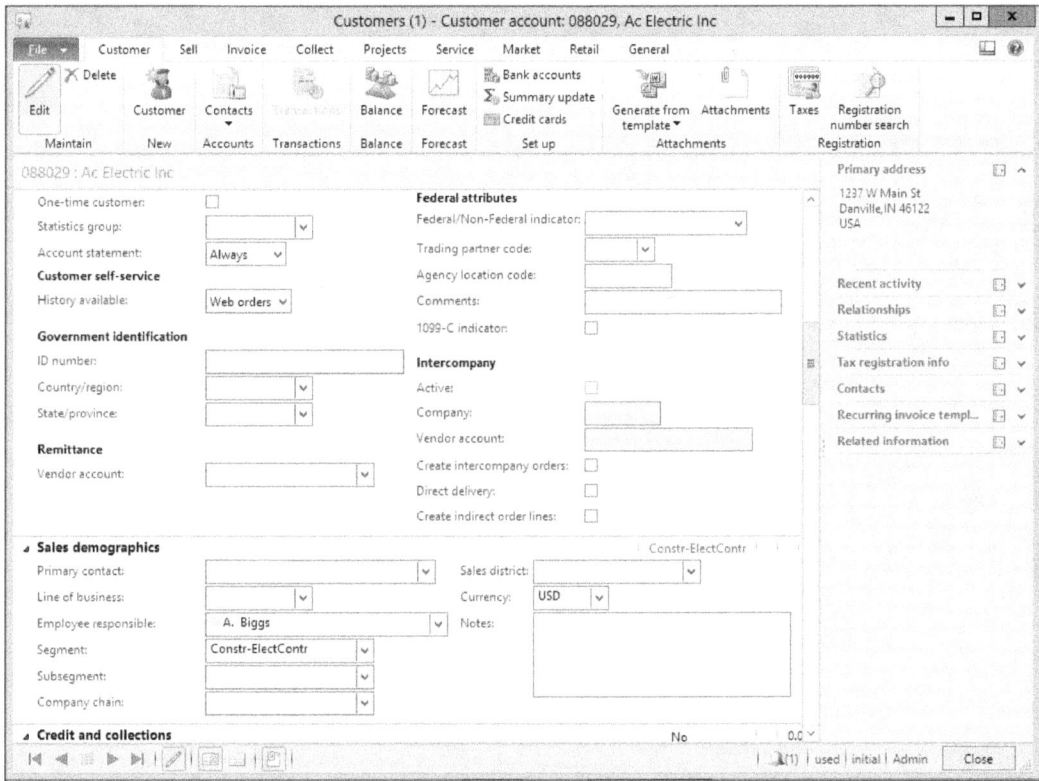

This was the data before the update...

Example: Updating Dynamics AX Data Through Excel

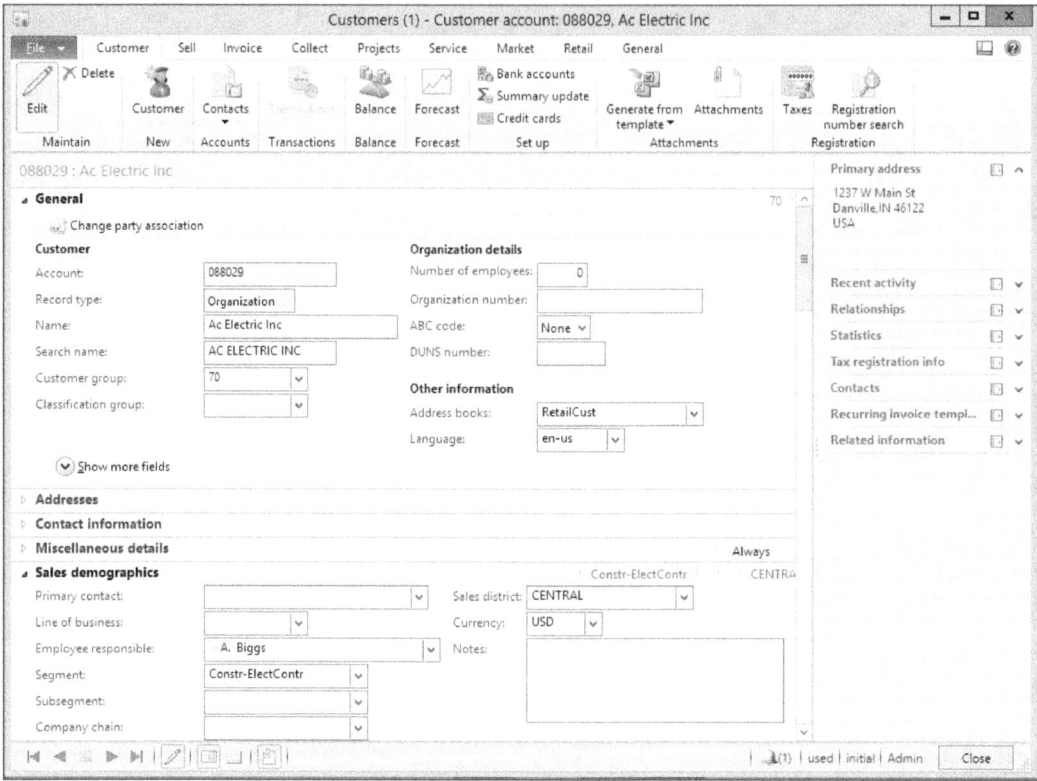

And here is the data after the update…

Example: Using Word To Create Form Letters

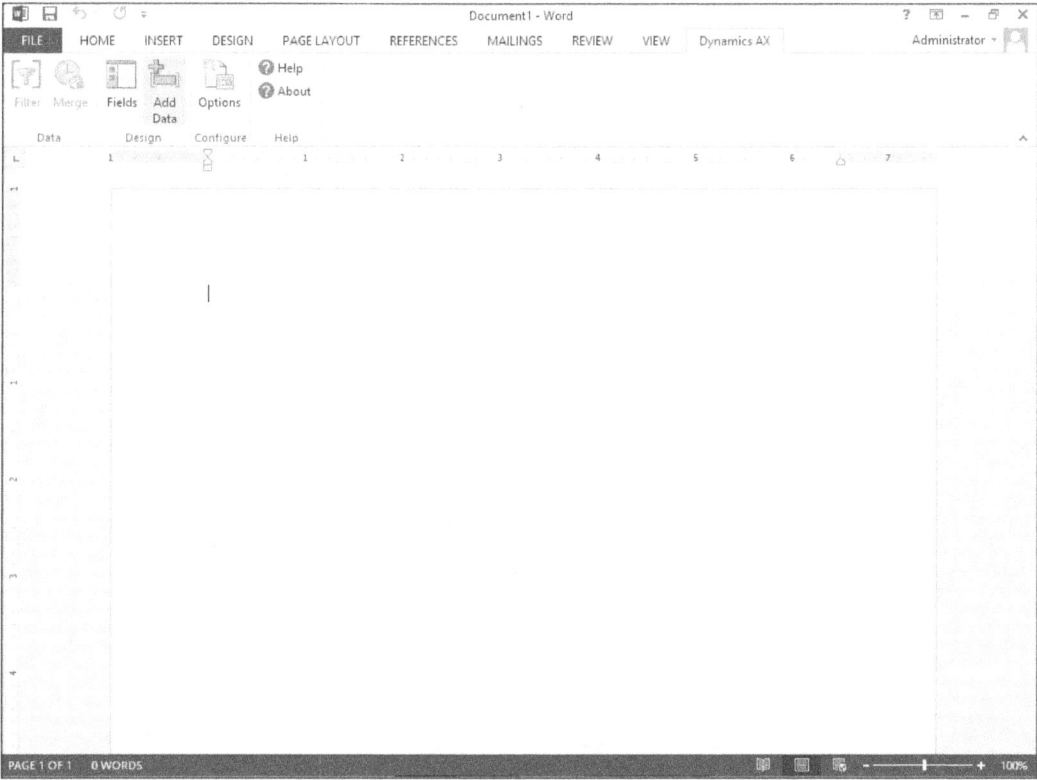

Excel does not have a monopoly over the Office integration with Dynamics AX. You can also access Dynamics AX data within Word and use it to create mail merge style documents that are populated from Dynamics AX.

To do this, all you need to do is open up Word, and then click on the Add Data button within the Dynamics AX ribbon bar.

Example: Using Word To Create Form Letters

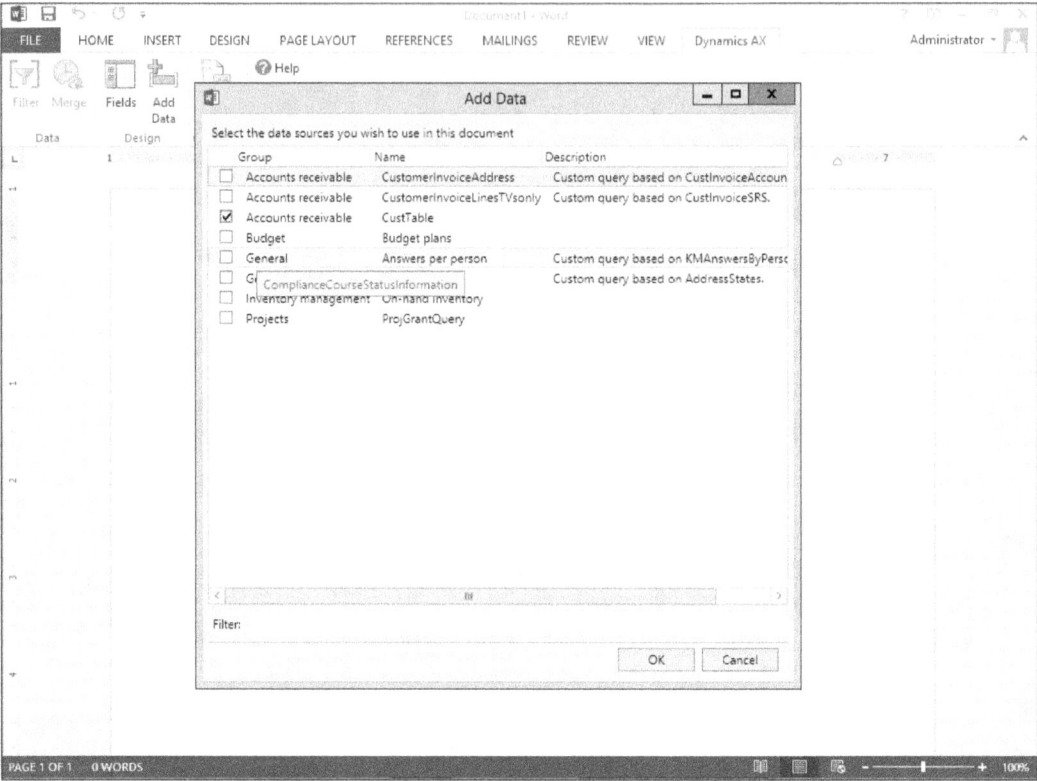

This will open up a dialog box that shows you all of the data within Dynamics AX that has been published and is available to Word. All you need to do is select the data source and then click the OK button.

Example: Using Word To Create Form Letters

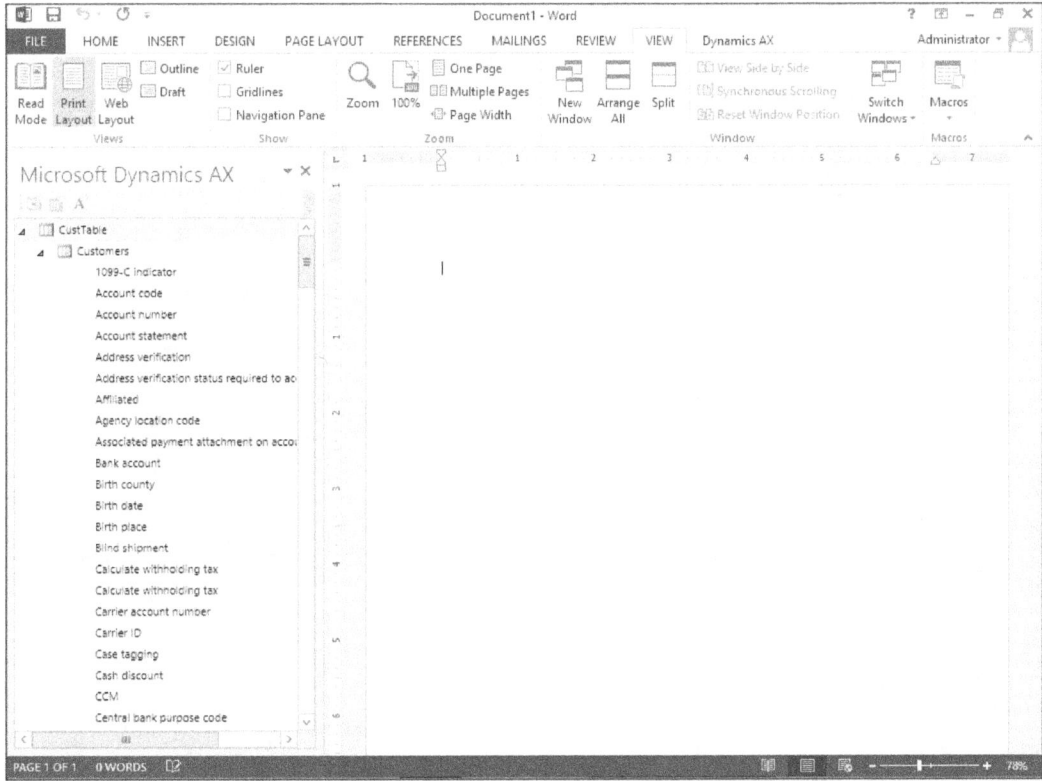

This will open up the same field browser that we have been using within Excel showing all of the merge fields that we can add into out document.

Example: Using Word To Create Form Letters

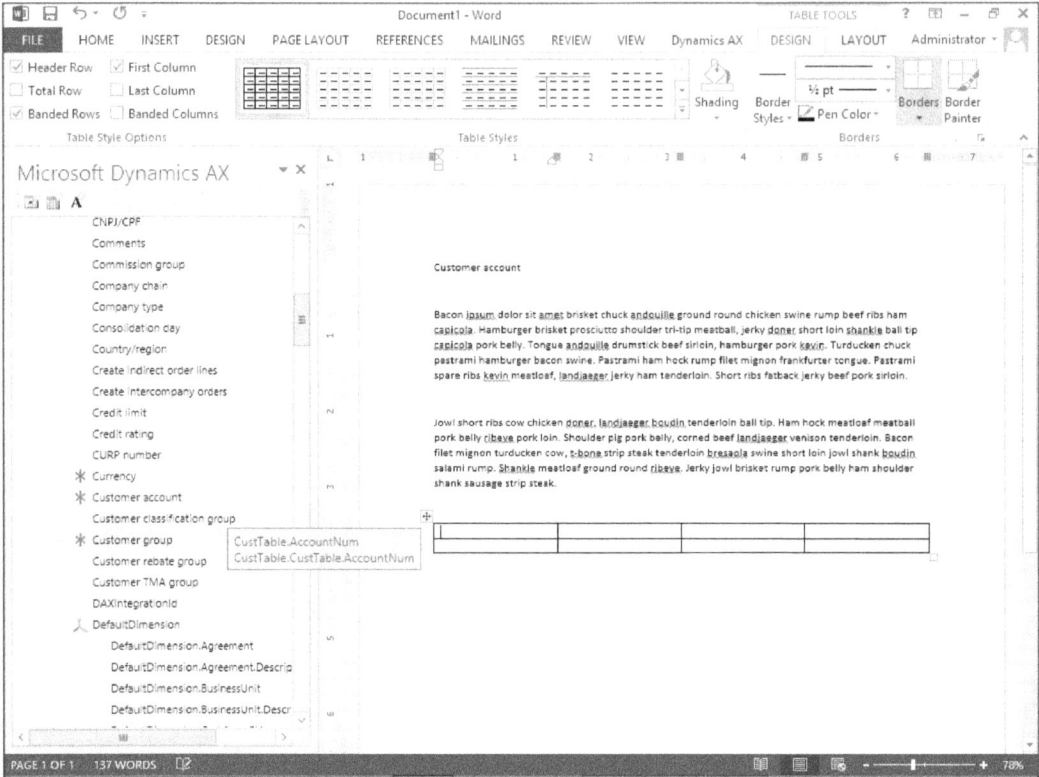

All we need to do to add a field is drag it over into the Word document.

We can then add any other verbiage that we may want in the document.

If we have tabular information that we want to show, then we can create a table to format the data.

Example: Using Word To Create Form Letters

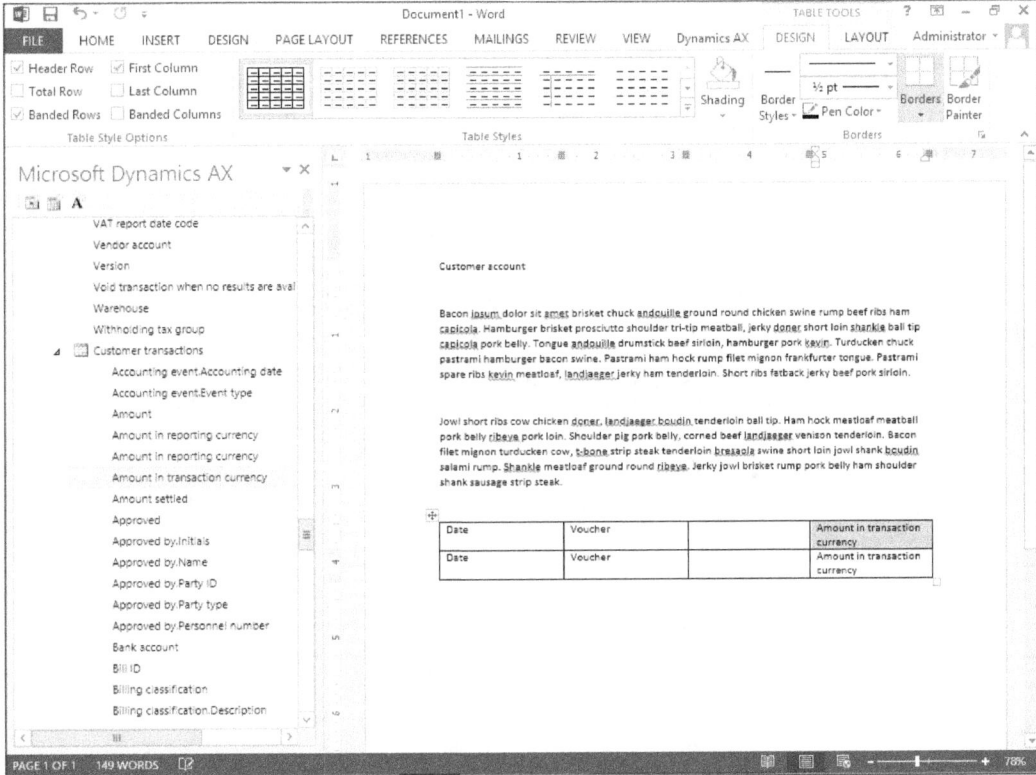

Then when we drag and drop any fields over to the table it will automatically add a heading label directly from Dynamics AX.

Example: Turning Word Templates Into Dynamics AX Templates

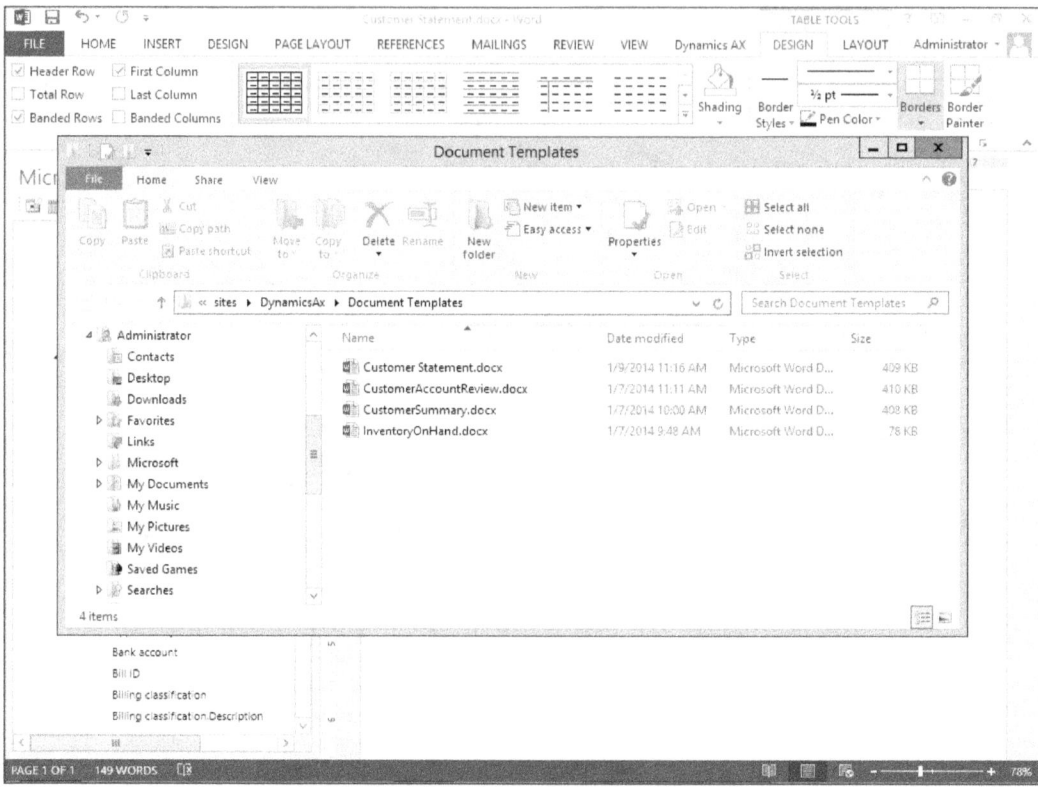

Once you have created a Word template that is linked to Dynamics AX, then you can register it with Dynamics AX so that it becomes available through the client.

To do this all you need to do is save the template that you created to the templates library for Dynamics AX.

Example: Turning Word Templates Into Dynamics AX Templates

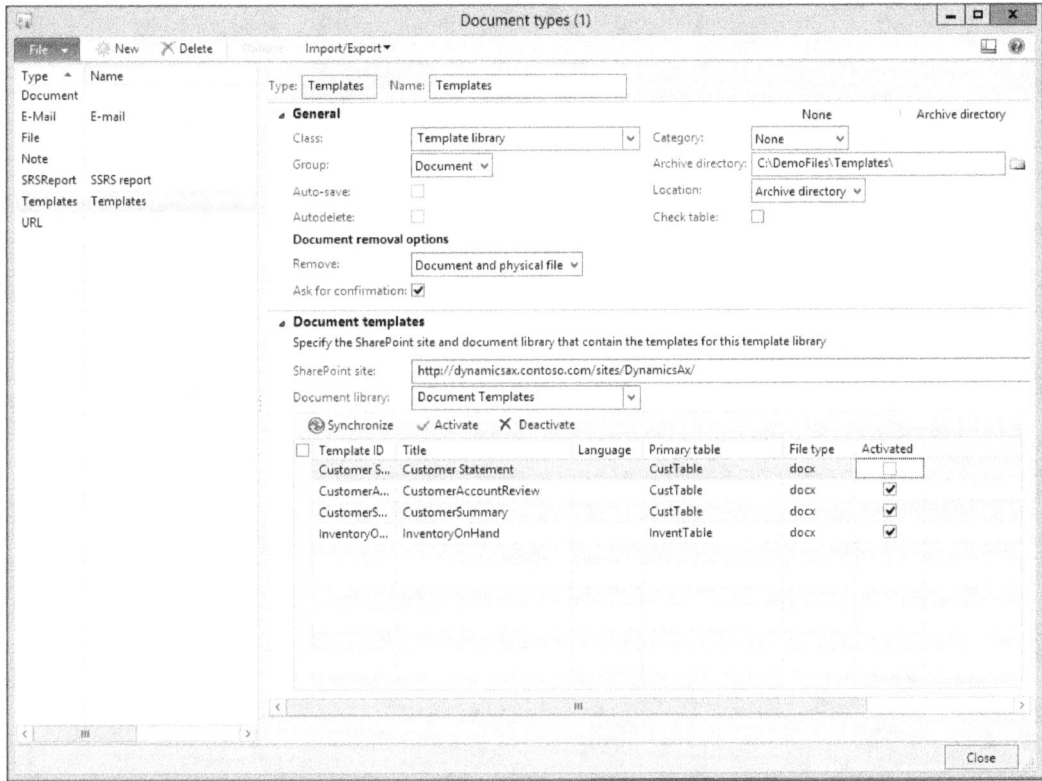

Once it is there, Dynamics AX will be able to discover the document template and you can activate it.

Example: Turning Word Templates Into Dynamics AX Templates

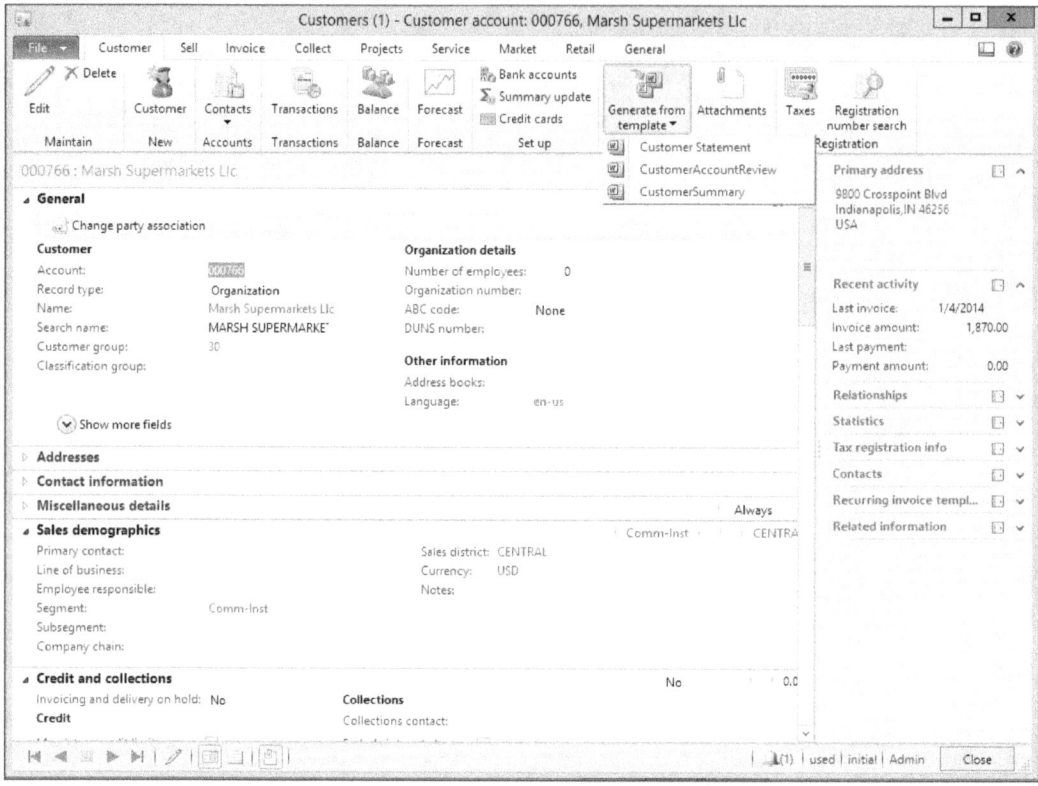

Now when you go to the master forms you will be able to see the document within the Generate From Template selector.

Example: Turning Word Templates Into Dynamics AX Templates

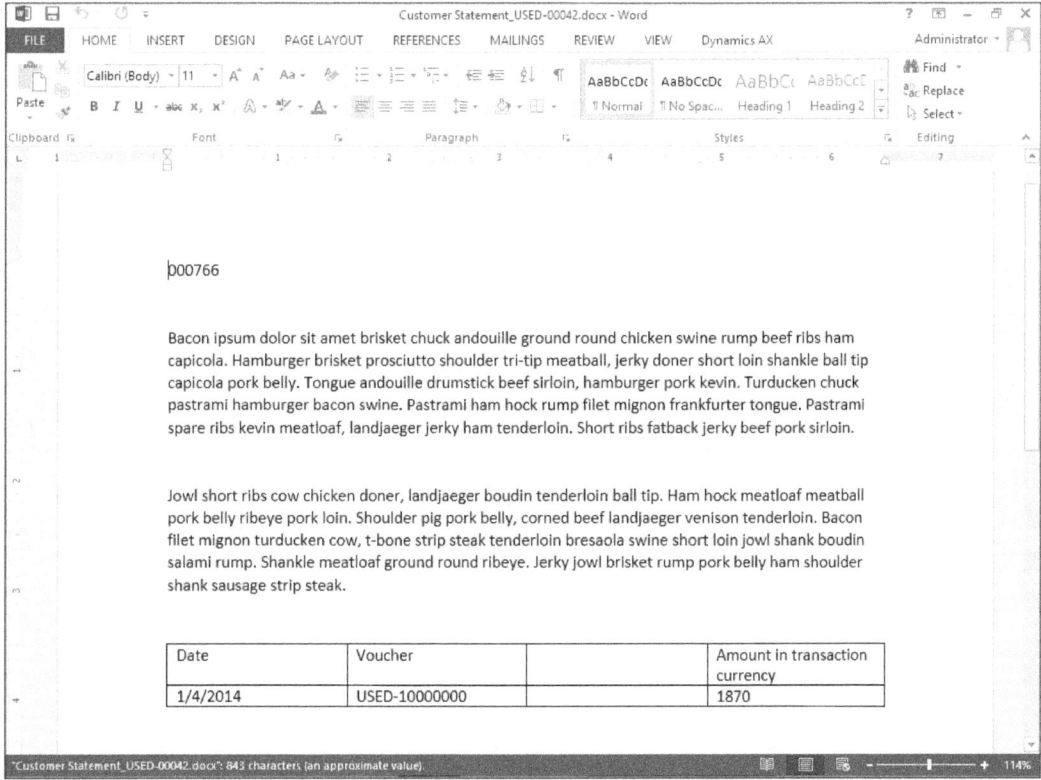

If you click on the template that you created, then Word will open, and it will populate all of the data saving you all the time that it would normally take to create the form letter by hand.

The Lifecycle Management Tools

One of the struggles that everyone has when they implement an ERP system is the management of the entire lifecycle of the project. As you are implementing the system, you need to document how the system works, and also you need to build in a mechanism for passing along training information to the new users that will be introduced to the system.

This process becomes a lot easier with the Lifecycle Services tools that are delivered along with Dynamics AX, because they provide a way that you can easily document all of your business processes directly through Dynamics AX, and then you can access them through the Lifecycle Services portal so that everyone has access to them for retraining, and also business process documentation.

In this section we will look at some of the tools that you can use to help you manage your Dynamics AX project lifecycle.

Example: Using The Task Recorder To Create Training Documents And Videos

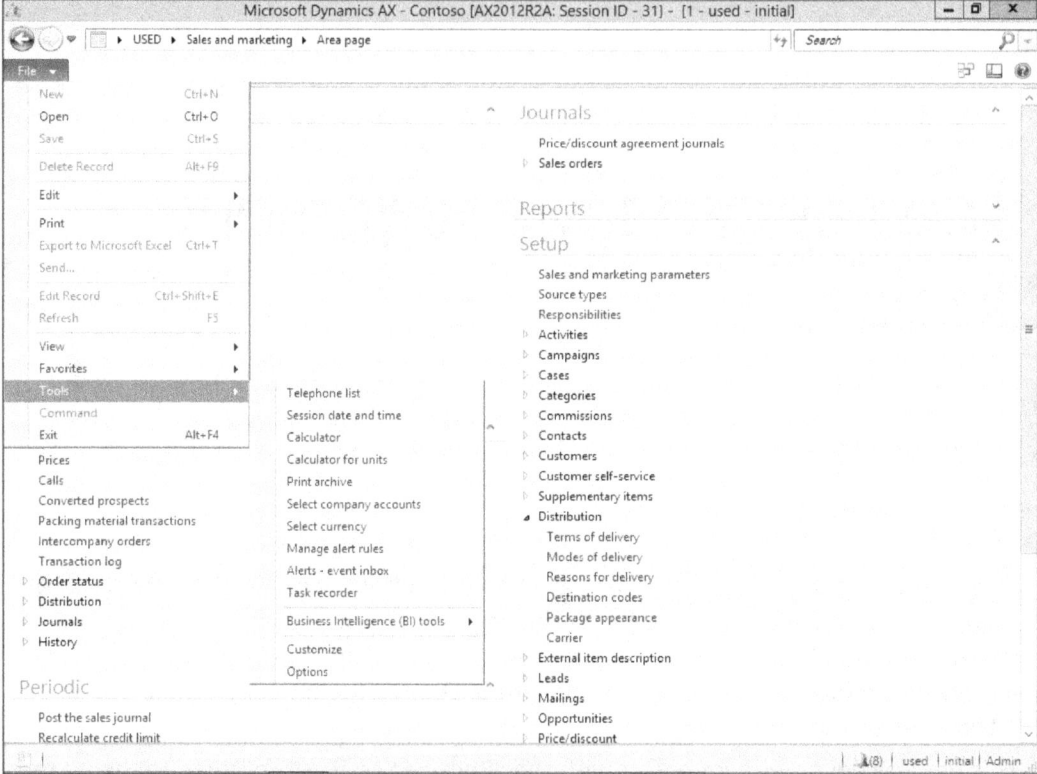

The Task Recorder is a tool that is built into Dynamics AX that records everything that you do while you are doing it within Dynamics AX. This makes the generation of training martial, and reference videos a breeze.

To use it click on the Files menu, select the Tools menu item, and select the Task Recorder submenu.

Example: Using The Task Recorder To Create Training Documents And Videos

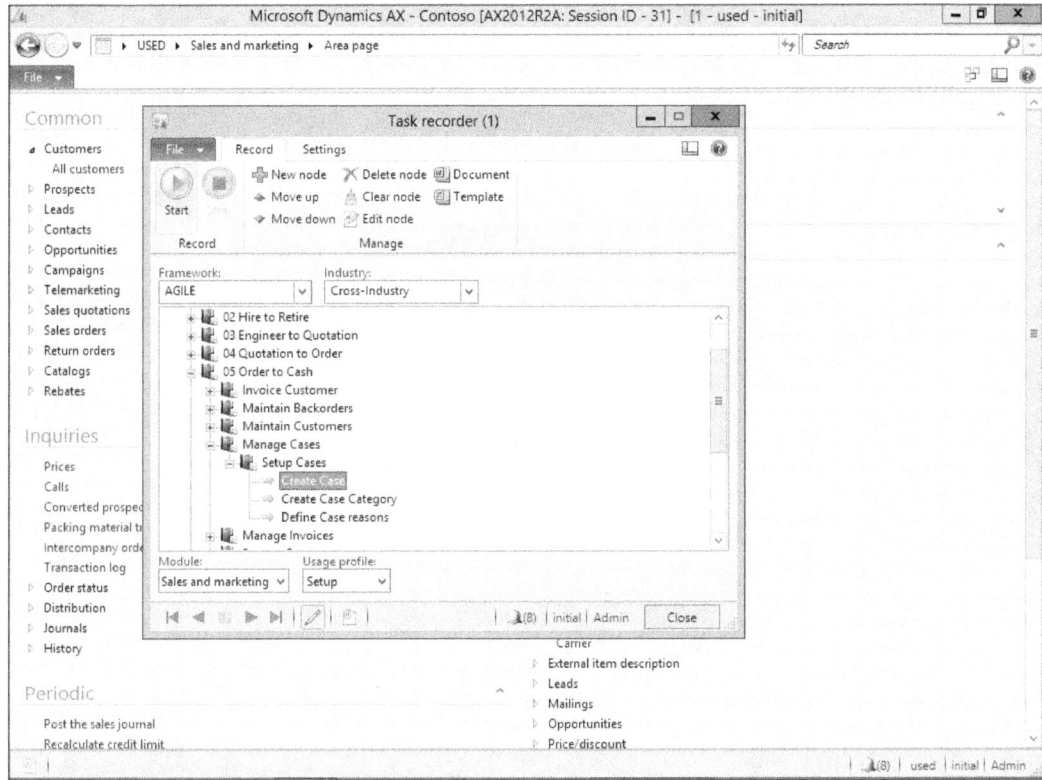

When the Task Recorder opens, select the node in your Framework Hierarchy that you want to record the training material for, and click on the Start button within the Record group of the Record ribbon bar.

Example: Using The Task Recorder To Create Training Documents And Videos

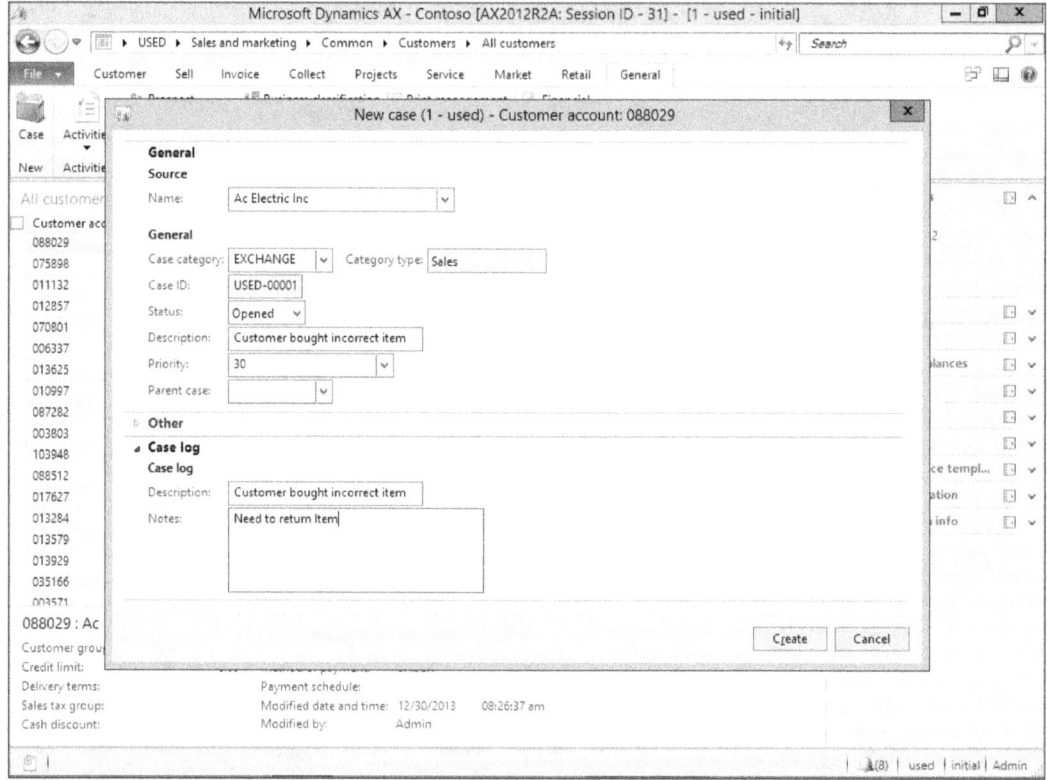

Then perform the task.

Example: Using The Task Recorder To Create Training Documents And Videos

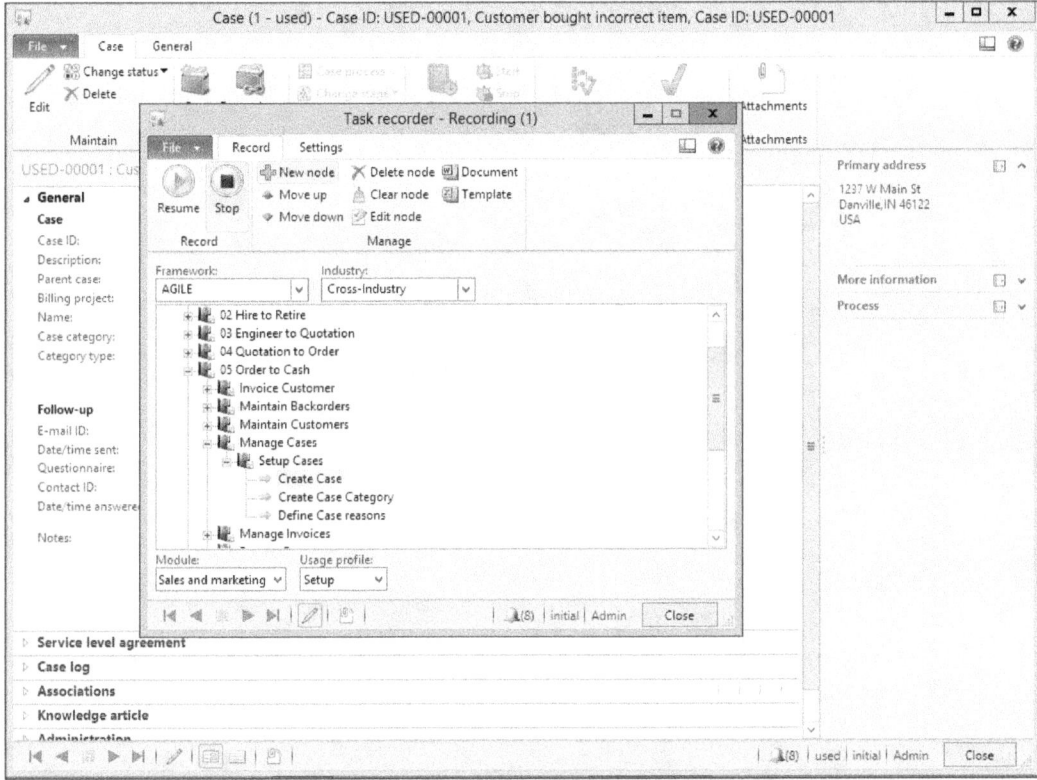

When you have finished the task, return to the Task Recorder and click the Stop button within the Record group of the Record ribbon bar.

Example: Using The Task Recorder To Create Training Documents And Videos

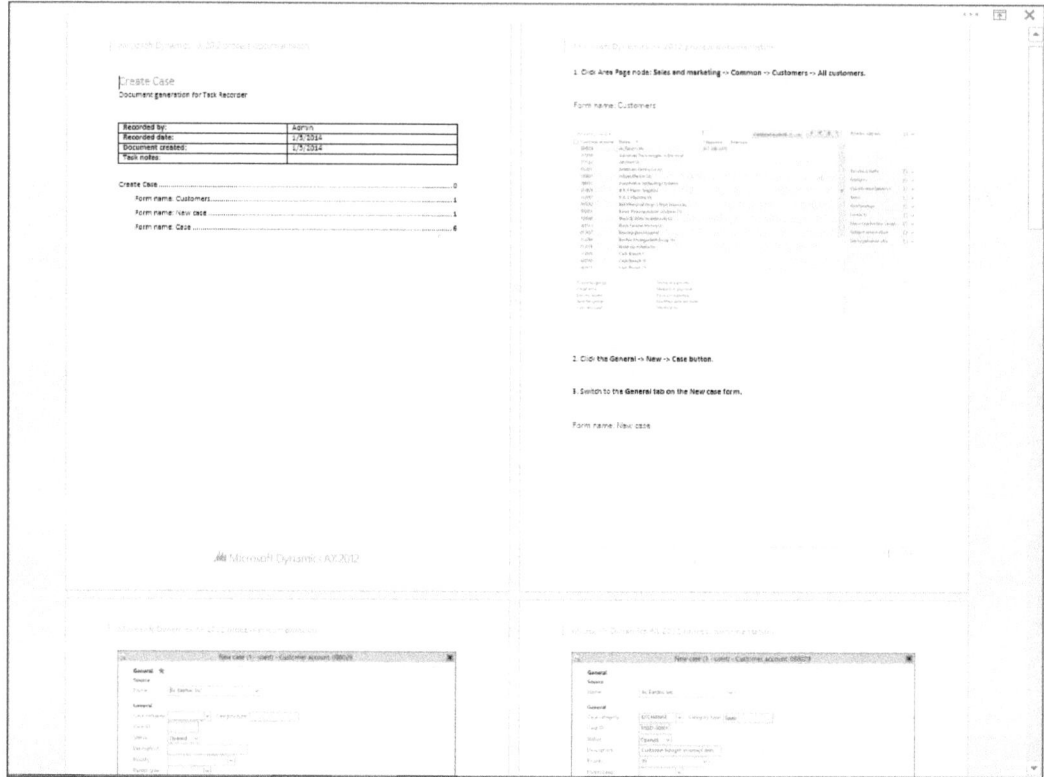

The Task Recorder automatically created a Word transcript of the task recording.

Example: Using The Task Recorder To Create Training Documents And Videos

It also creates a .wmv version that allows you to see everything that you did in real time.

Example: Accessing Business Processes Through Lifecycle Services

As you record all of your processes using the Task Recorder, you can export them to the Dynamics Lifecycle Services Portal, to register them as your standard business processes.

When the task recordings are available through the Lifecycle Services, they become even more useful.

You can browse on-line to see what business processes you have documented, and also see if there are business processes available to view.

Example: Accessing Business Processes Through Lifecycle Services

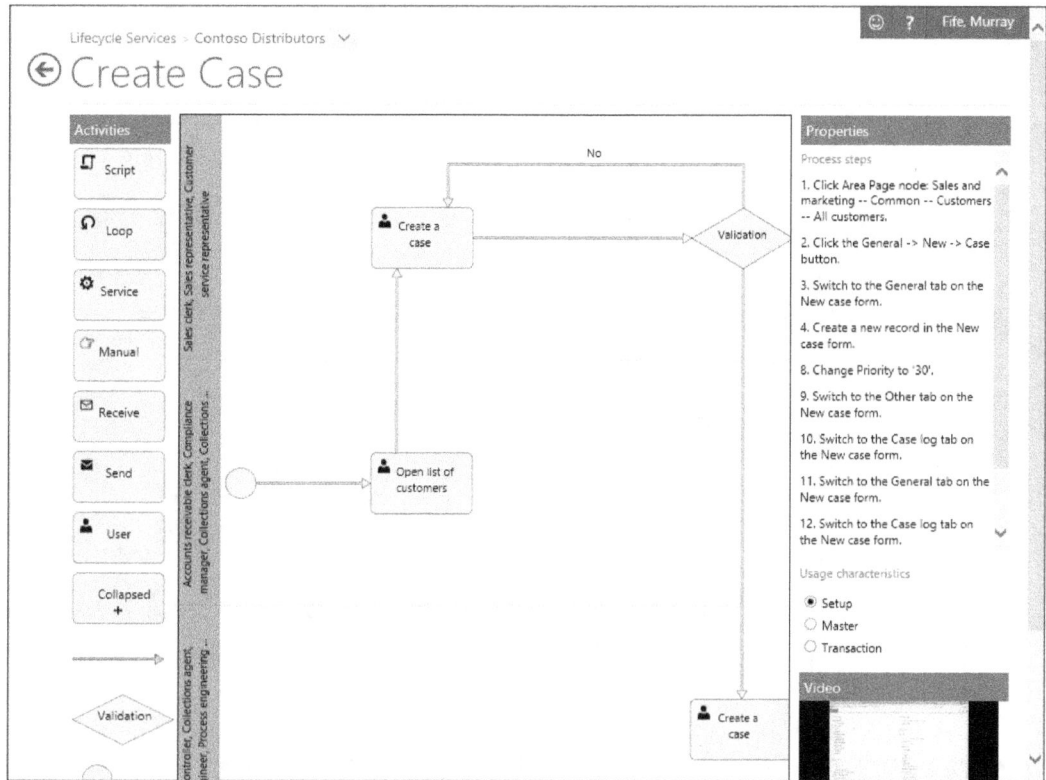

If you drill into a business process through Lifecycle Services then you will be able to see the business flow, as a swim-lane diagram, as a narrative, and also as a video that you can view at any time.

Example: Accessing Business Processes Through Lifecycle Services

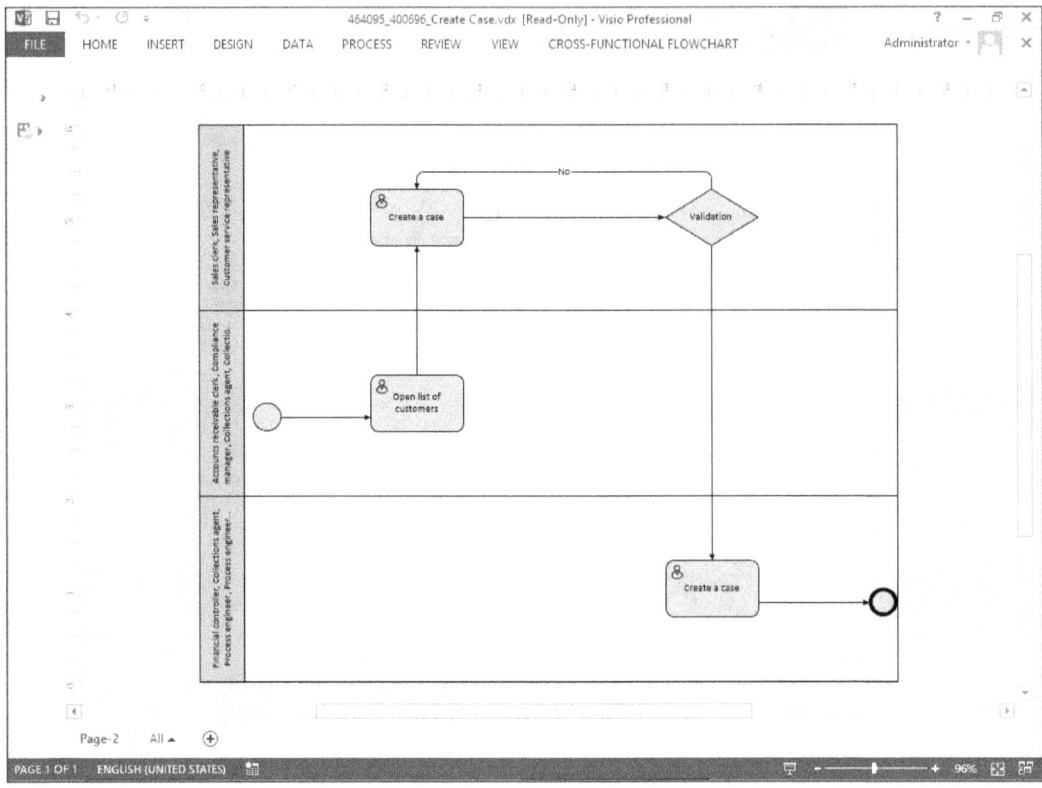

Additionally you can export out your process flow at any time to create Visio documentation of any business process.

You will never have to build a business process by hand ever again.

PART II: DYNAMICS AX OVERVIEW

Dynamics AX is such a full featured product, it is hard to illustrate all of the things that it is capable of tracking and managing without creating a textbook style book. Even then, it is hard to piece everything together with all of the detail that is provided, and even then, you probably are not interested in most of the detail.

A better starting point for you as you are discovering an exploring Dynamics AX is to get a more holistic view of the application showing all of the different general features that are available. Knowing that something is possible within Dynamics AX is 90% the battle, learning how it does it is a relatively simple after that.

This companion for Dynamics AX is designed to do just that. It is a high level reference that you can use to see what you can do if you want to leverage the many features within the system.

Product Management

The first area that we will look at within Dynamics AX is the Product Management area where all of the product details are maintained. A lot of the setup that you will perform here will be leveraged by the other areas within Dynamics AX, so it's a good place to start.

Master Data Management
Product Details

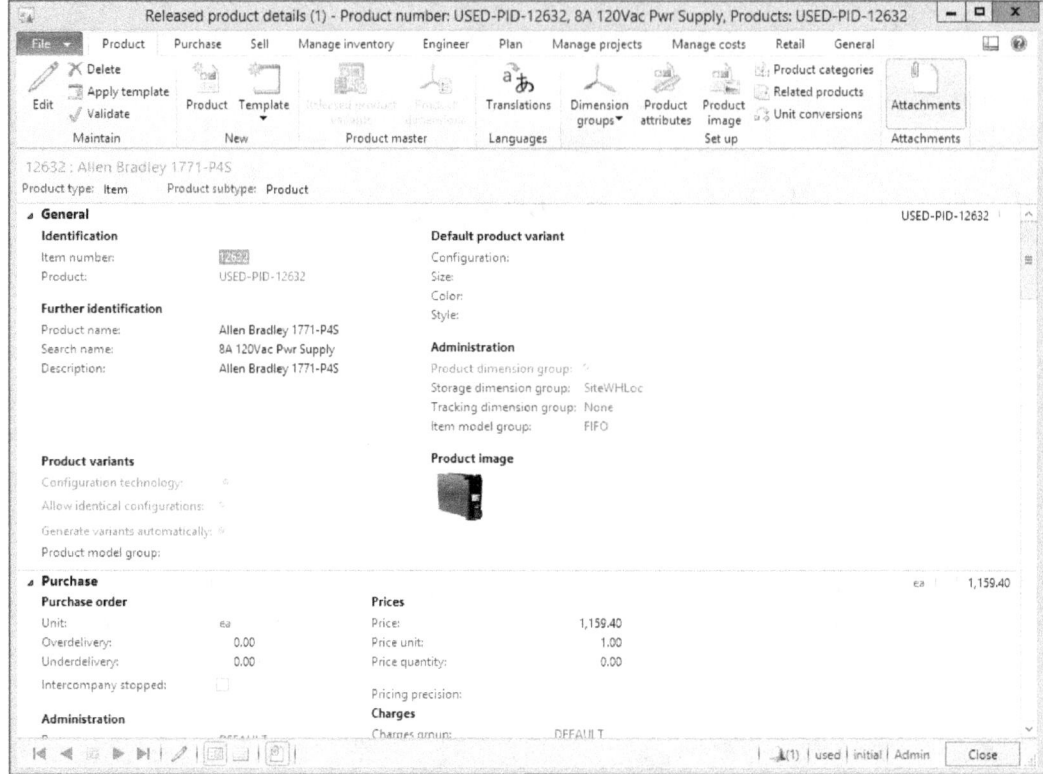

Key Features

- Product Templates for easy record creation

- Unlimited number of Attachments

- Unlimited length Detailed Description

- Product Images

Master Data Management
External Codes

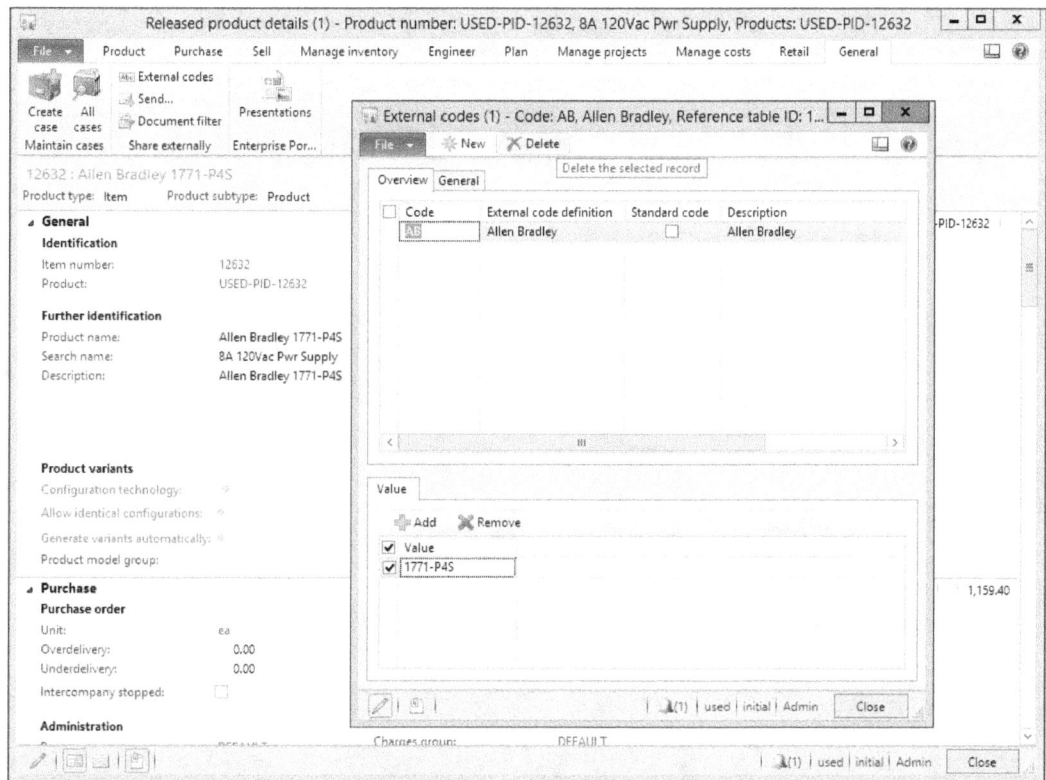

Key Features

- External item numbers and descriptions

- External codes and descriptions

Master Data Management
Alternate Products

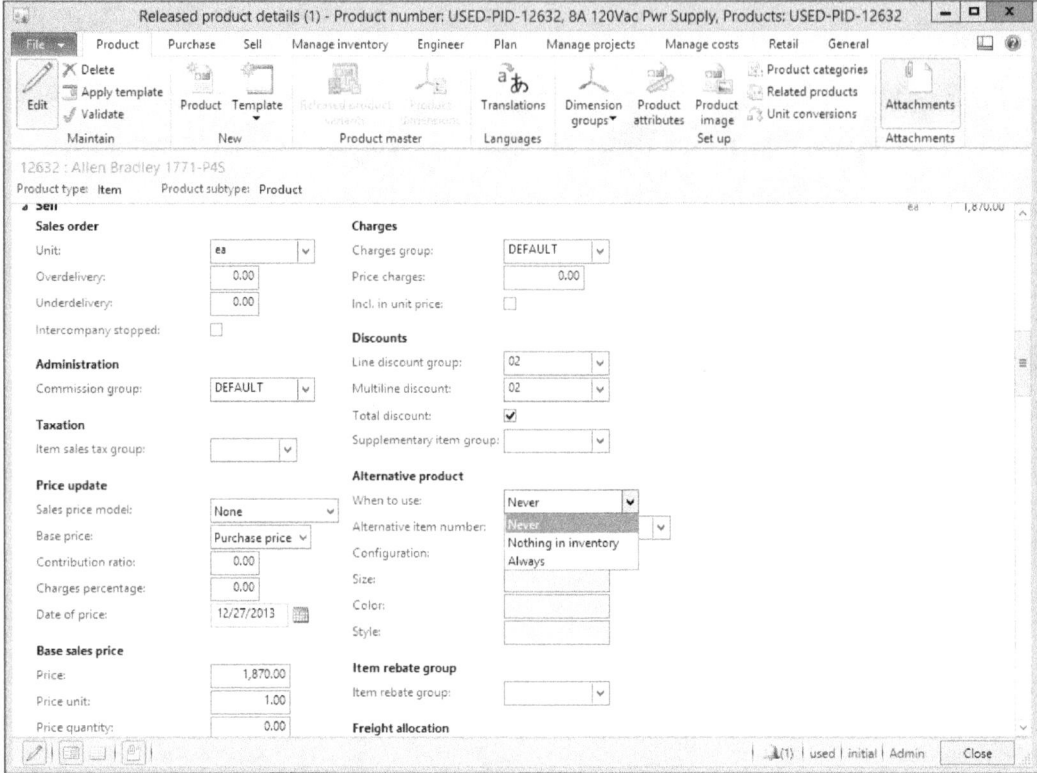

Key Features

- Enable/Disable products for Sale, Purchase, & Inventory

- Alternative Parts When Inventory Depleted

Master Data Management
Category Hierarchies

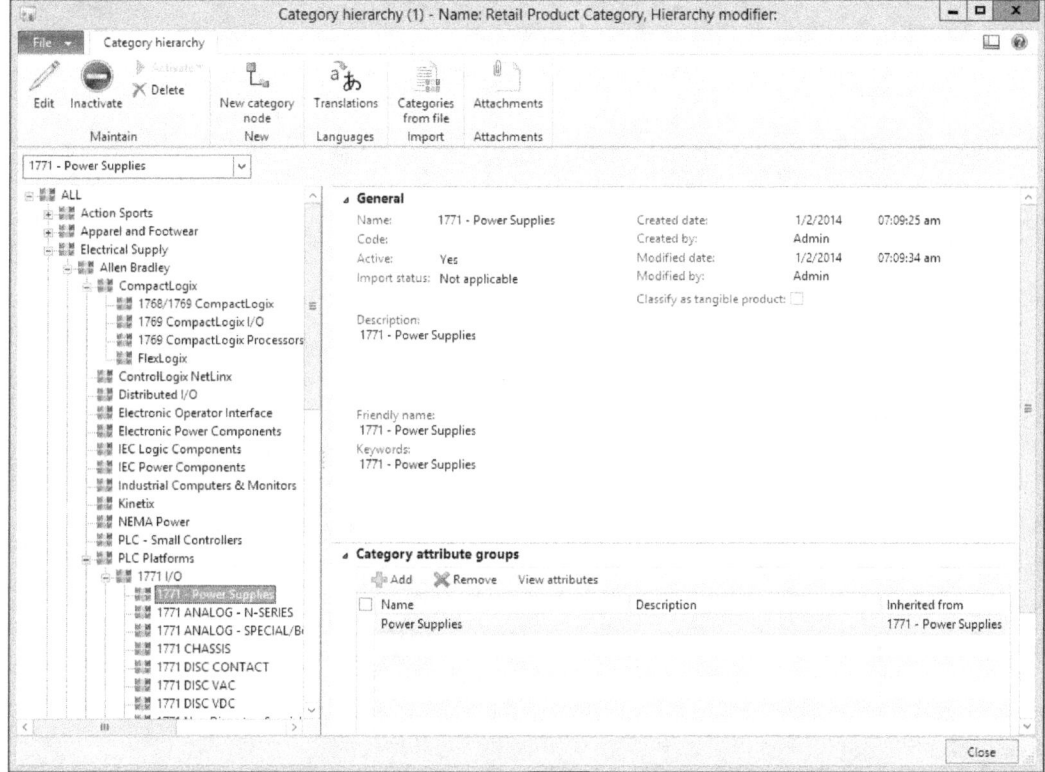

Master Data Management
Product Attributes

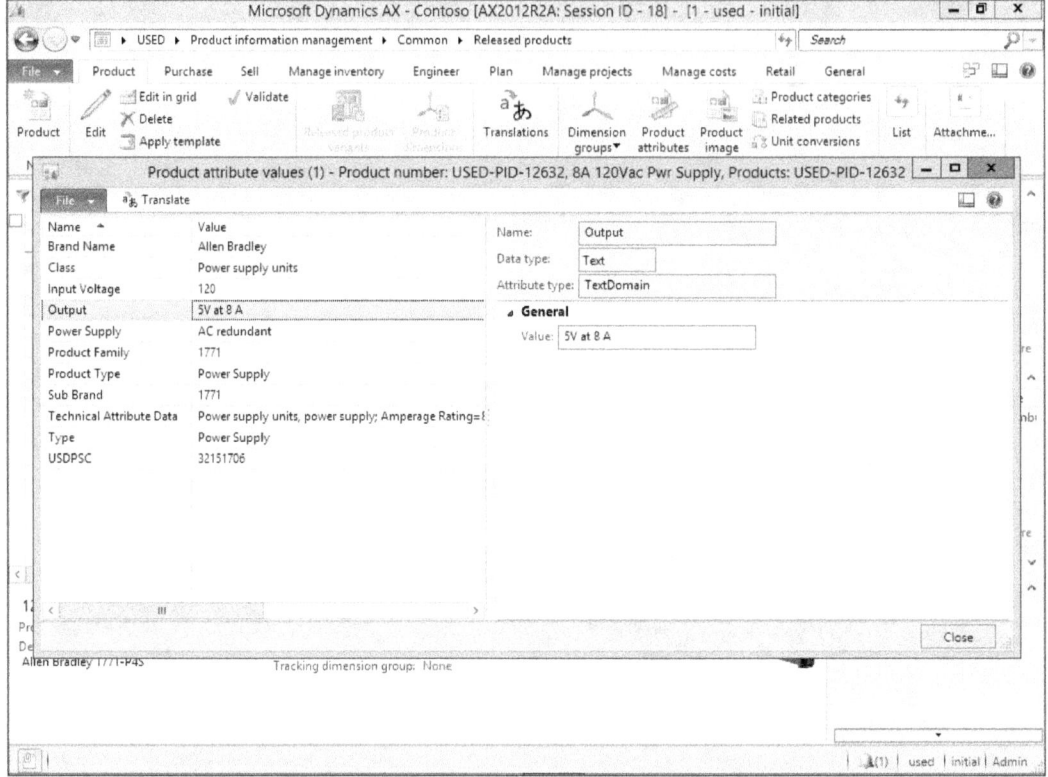

Master Data Management
Product Configurations

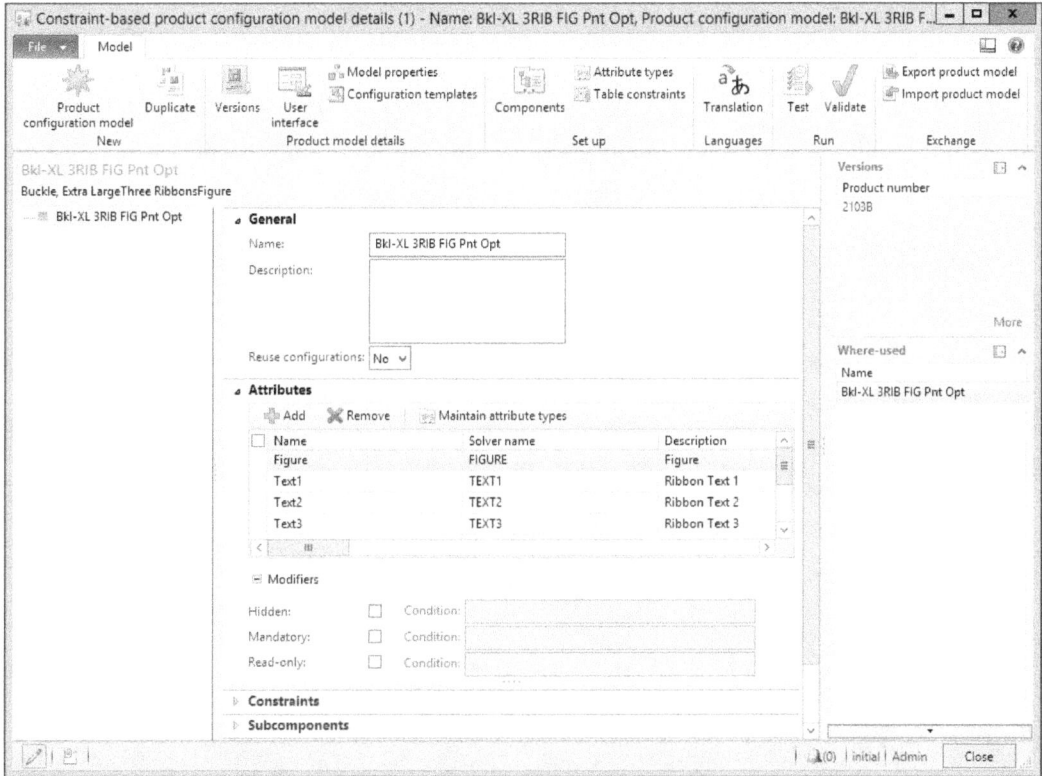

Key Features

- Reusable configuration components

- Attributes can be hard coded or dynamically created from table data

- Dynamic price calculation

Order To Cash

The Order To Cash process within Dynamics AX includes a number of different areas including Customer & Pricing Management, Orders, Fulfillment, Receivable, and Collections.

In this section we will show the highlights of the process and also a number of the capabilities that are included in the product to help manage the customer buying process.

Master Data Management
Customers

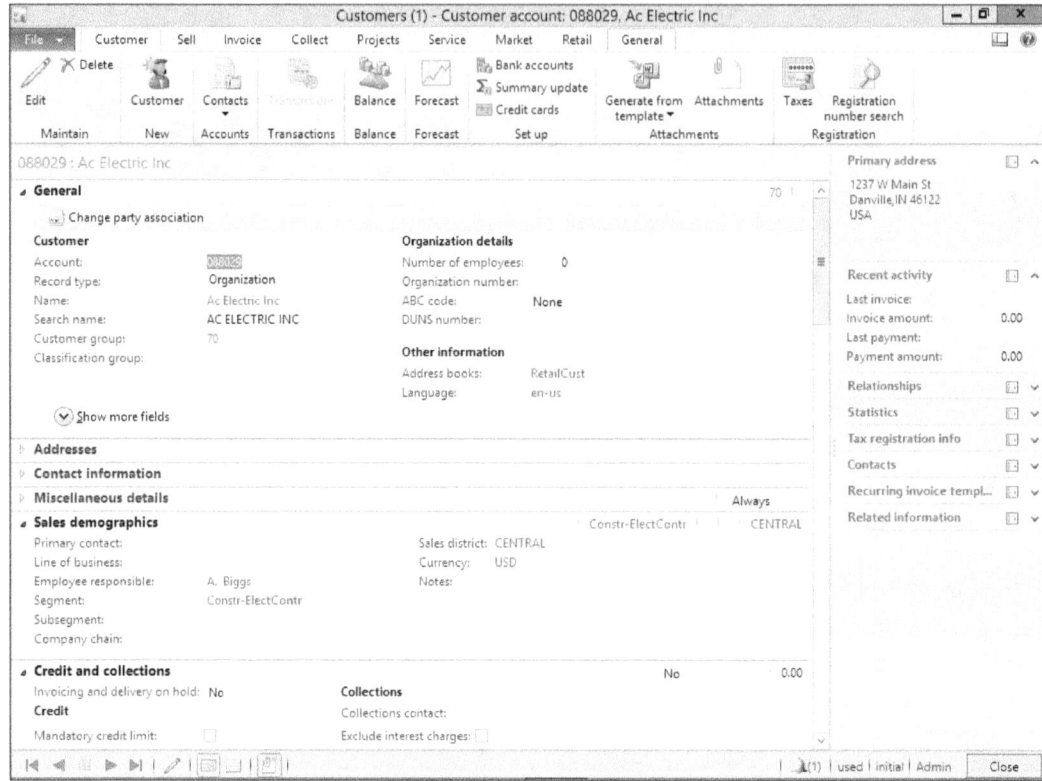

Key Features

- Access to Customer Contact Information

- Multiple Addresses with Purpose definition

- Contact Preferences for e-mail and phone

- National Account Chain

- Invoice Accounts for Parent/Child Relationships

- Access to Customer Transaction History

Master Data Management
Contacts

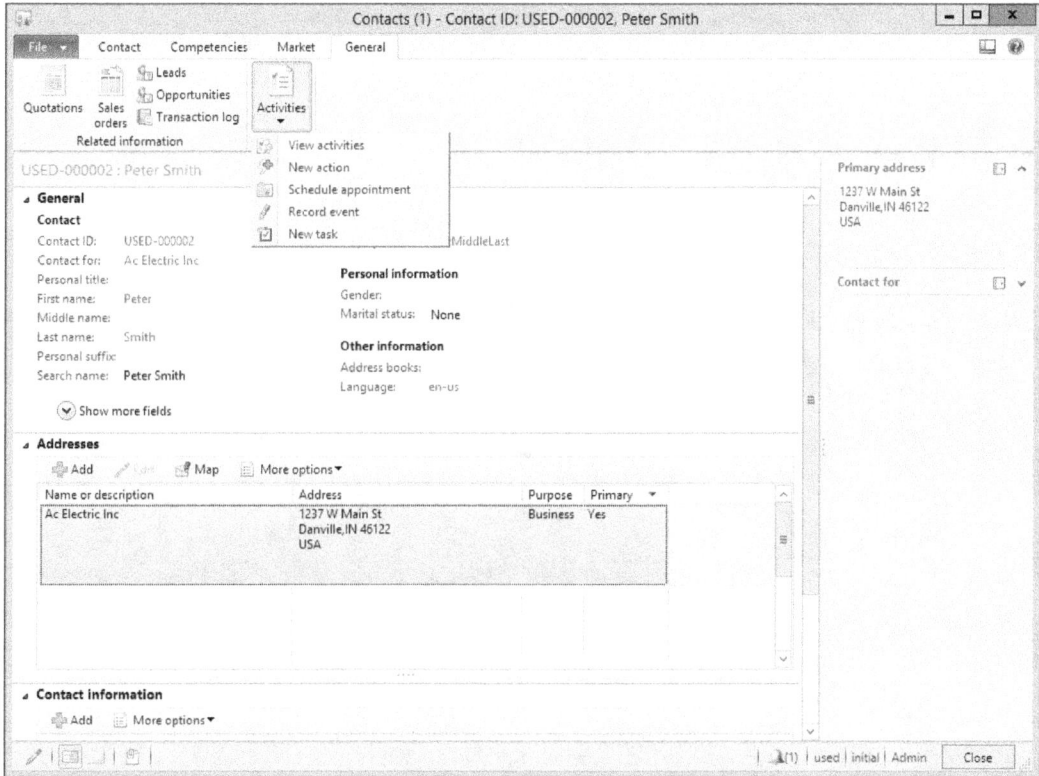

Key Features

- Contacts attached to Customers, Vendors & Competitors

- Track activity against a contact

- Integrated Case Management tools for Contacts and Parties

- Attach documents and filed to Contact Record

Price & Discount Management
Price Agreements

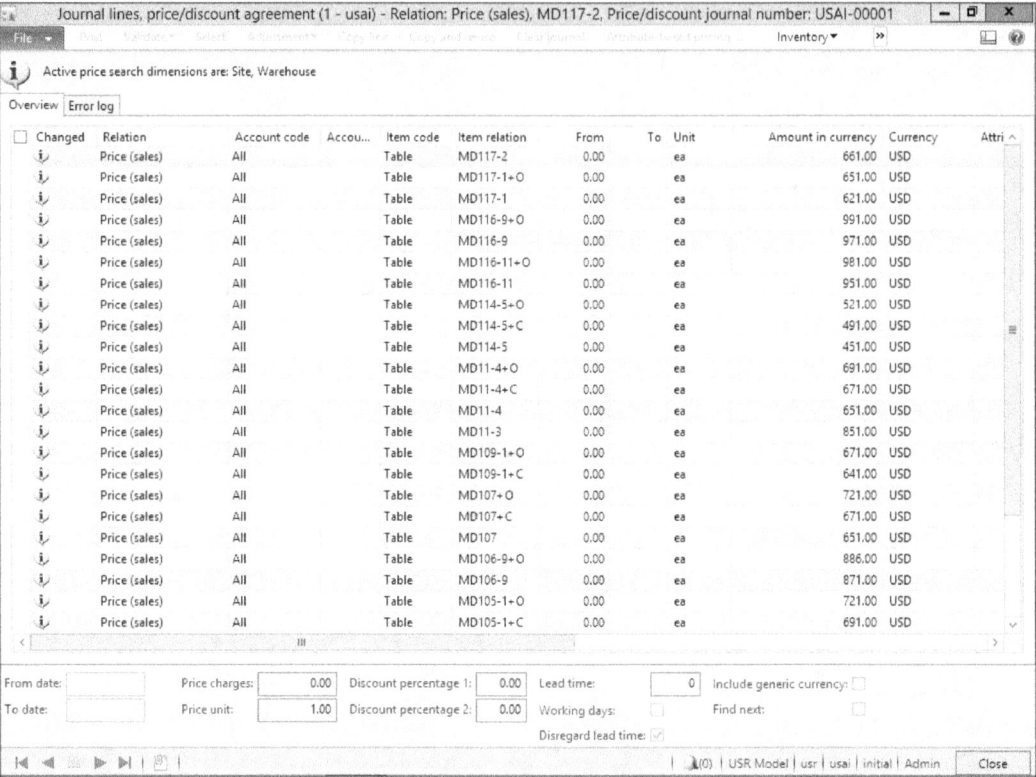

Key Features

- Price Lists defined as Journals

- Import Pricing directly from Excel

Price & Discount Management
Discount Agreements

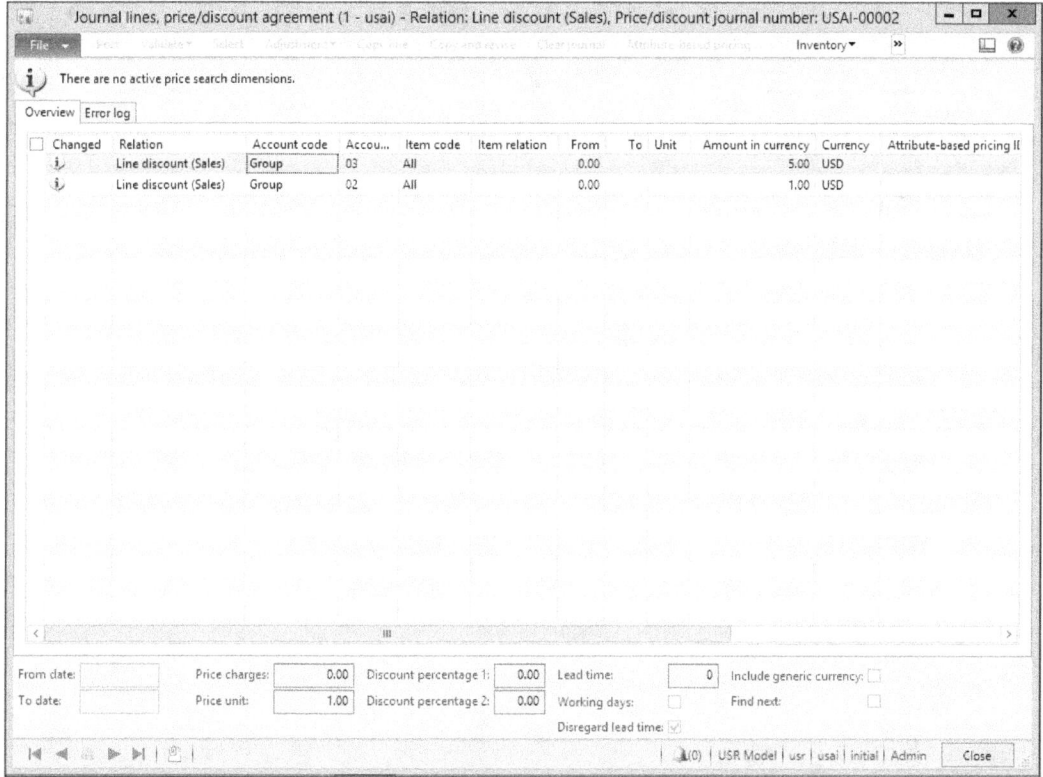

Key Features

- Date Ranges on Discounts

- Automatic Pricing at time of Order Entry

- Quantity breaks on pricing and discounts

Order Management
Order Placement

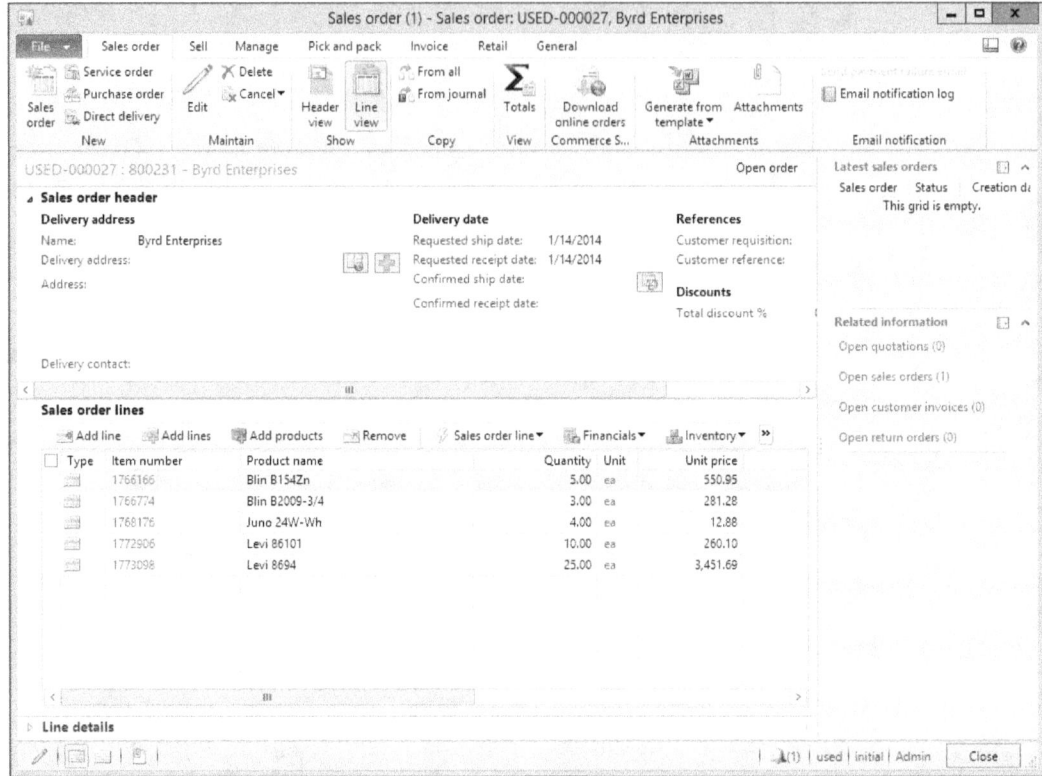

Key Features

- Drop Ships and Direct Delivery from Order Entry

- Delivery and Billing Addresses from Customer Master

- Create lines through based on inventory availability

- Customer Transaction History Fact Boxes

- Multiple Dates tracked against Order

- Inventory and Available To Promise

Order Management
Pricing & Discounting Inquiry

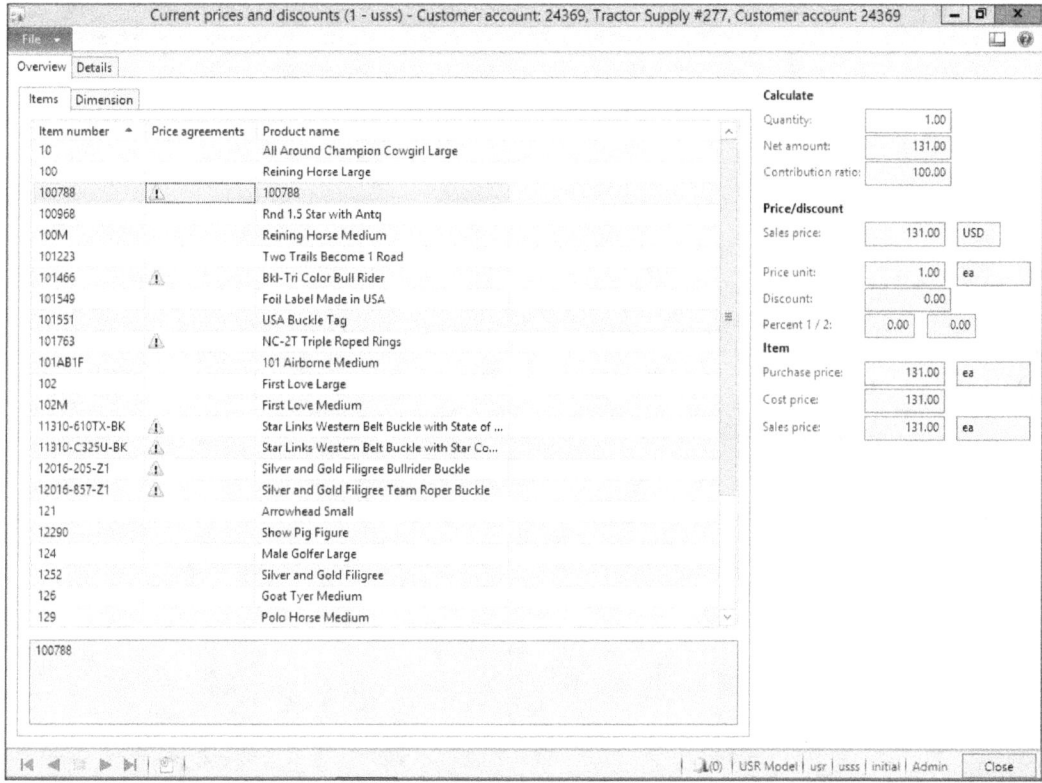

Key Features

- Access to pricing and discounting at Order Entry

- Ability to view effective pricing and promotions

- Effectivity Dates on pricing and discounts

- Multiple pricing structures

Order Management
Real Time Availability

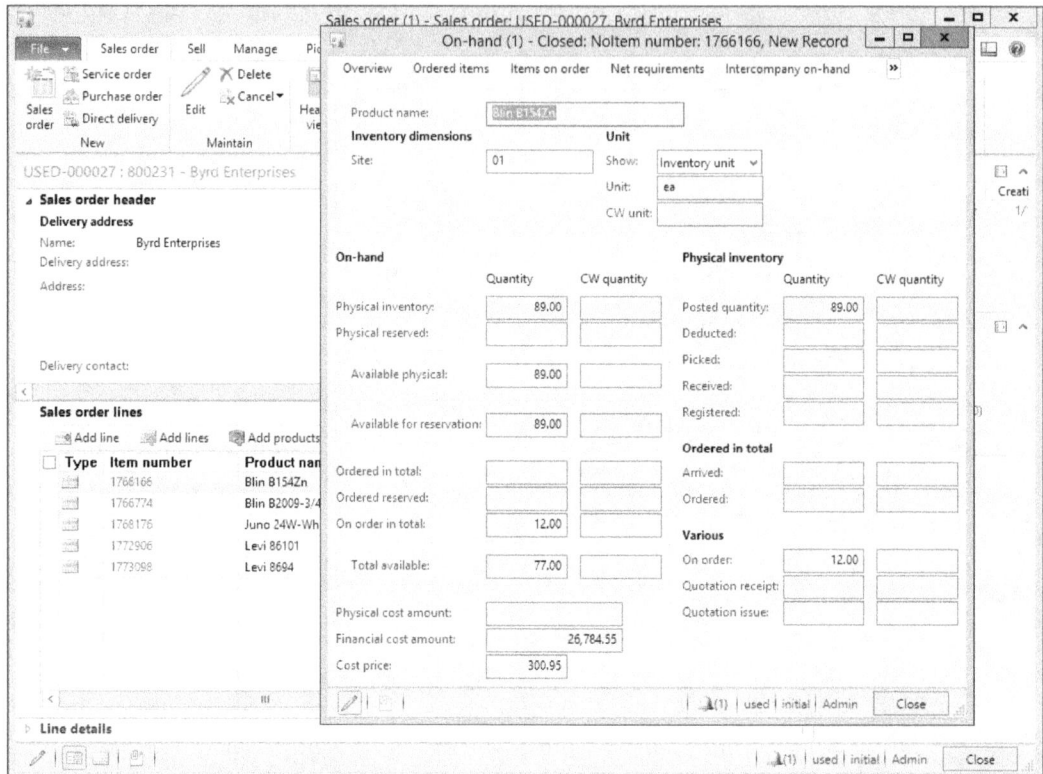

Key Features

- Availability Inquiry directly from Order Entry

Order Management
Kitted Products

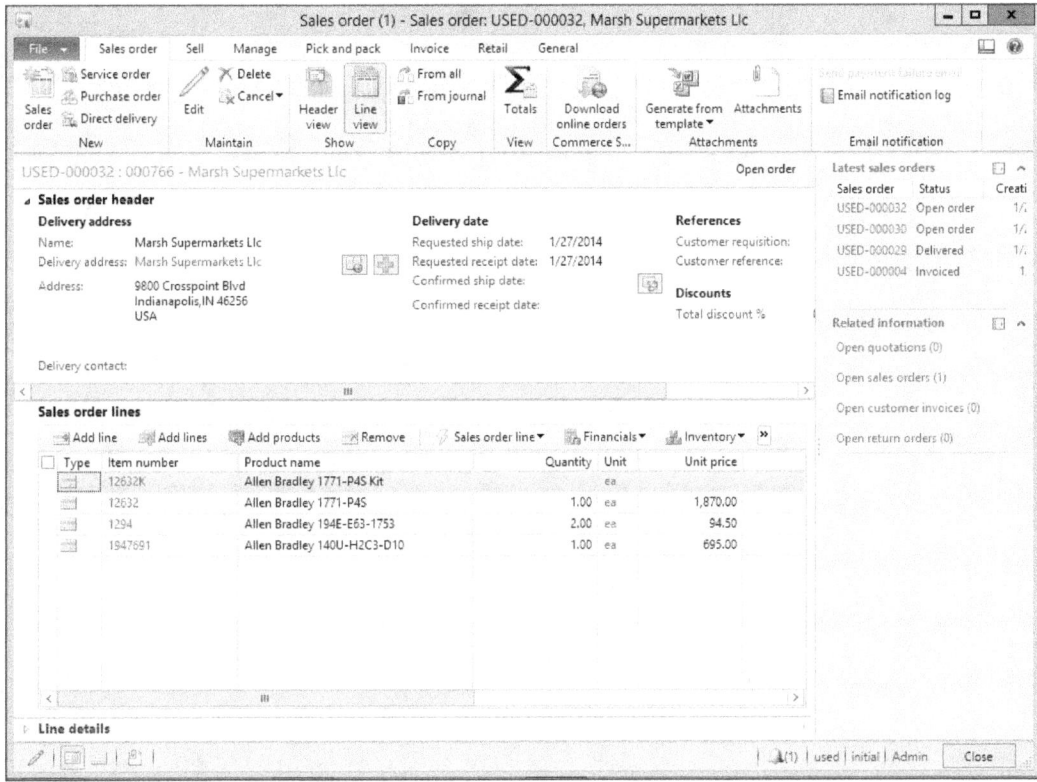

Order Management
Credit Card Processing

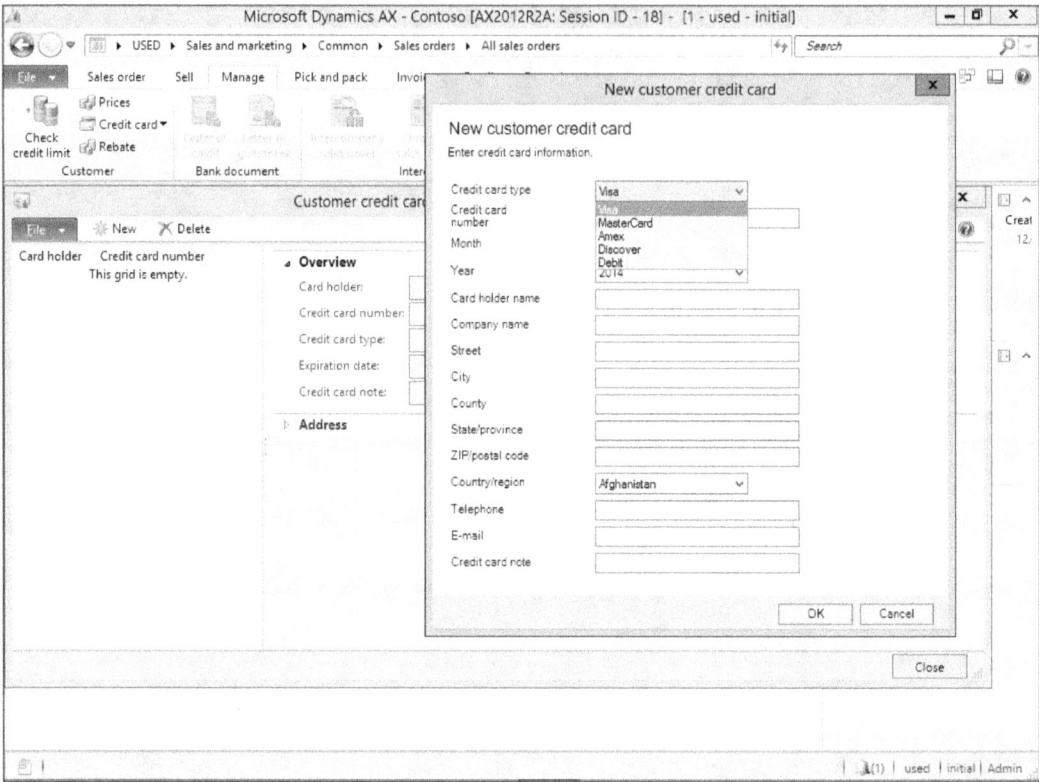

Key Features

- Credit Card processing directly from Orders

- Fully PCI Compliant

- Address verification built into Credit Card interface

Order Management
Product Configuration

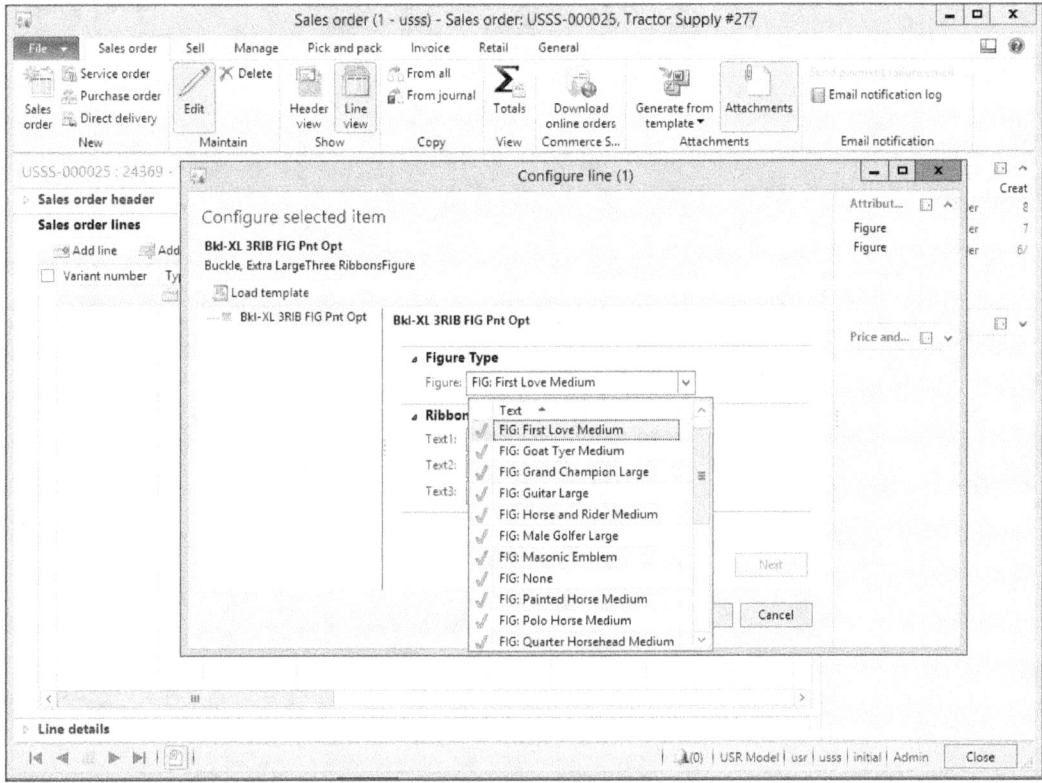

Key Features

- Configure order lines from Order Entry

Order Management
Ship Date Calculation

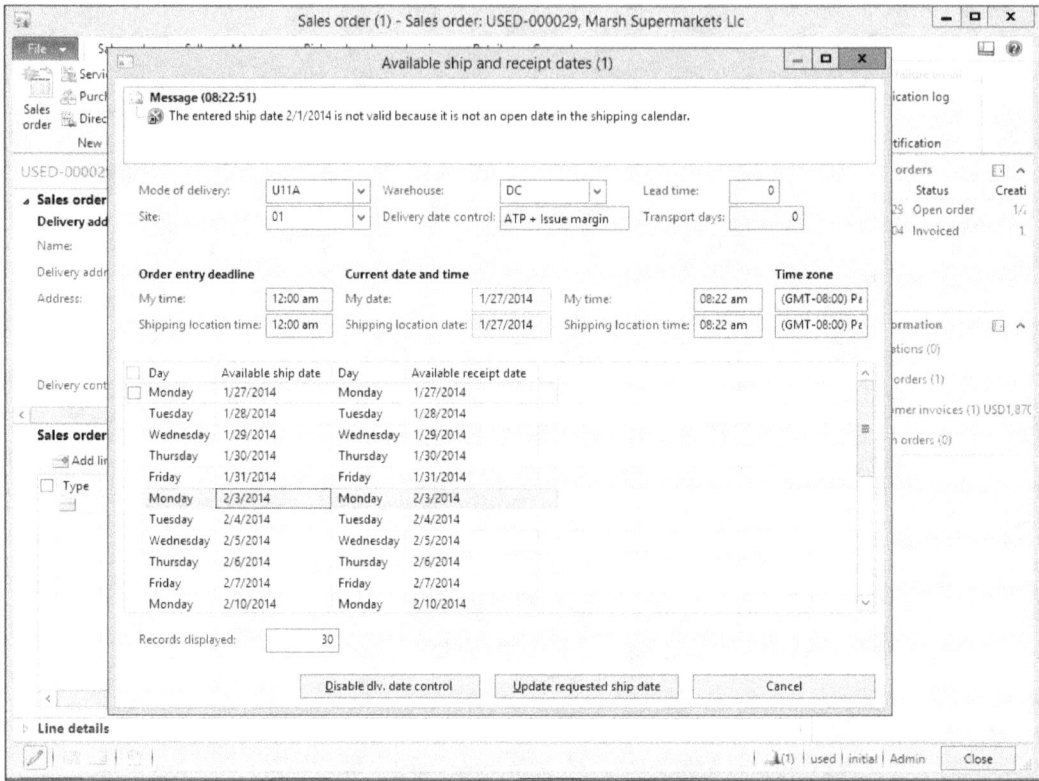

Key Features

- Calendar identifies non-shipping days

Order Management
Releasing Order To Production

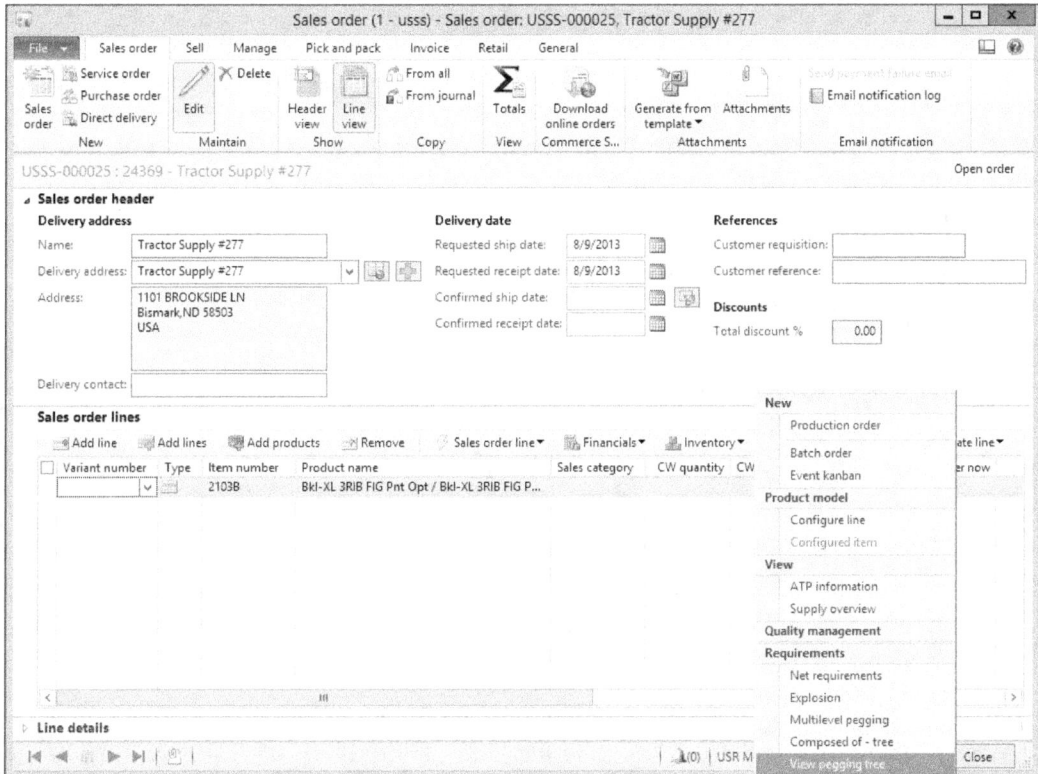

Key Features

- Generation of Kanban events

- Release order directly from order screen

Quotation Management
Sales & Project Quotations

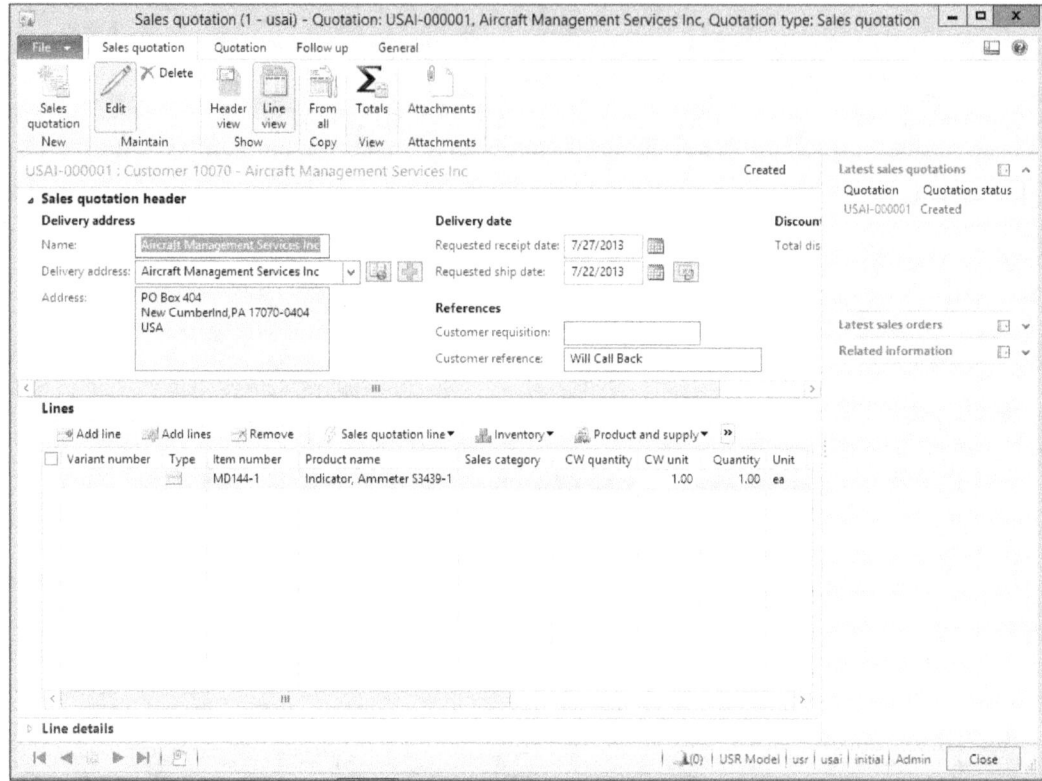

Key Features

- Sales Quotations

- Same form used to generate Project Quotations

- Convert Quotation directly to Order

- Expiration dates for Quotations

- Attach an unlimited number of documents

- Copy from other Quotation

Pick & Pack Management
Picking

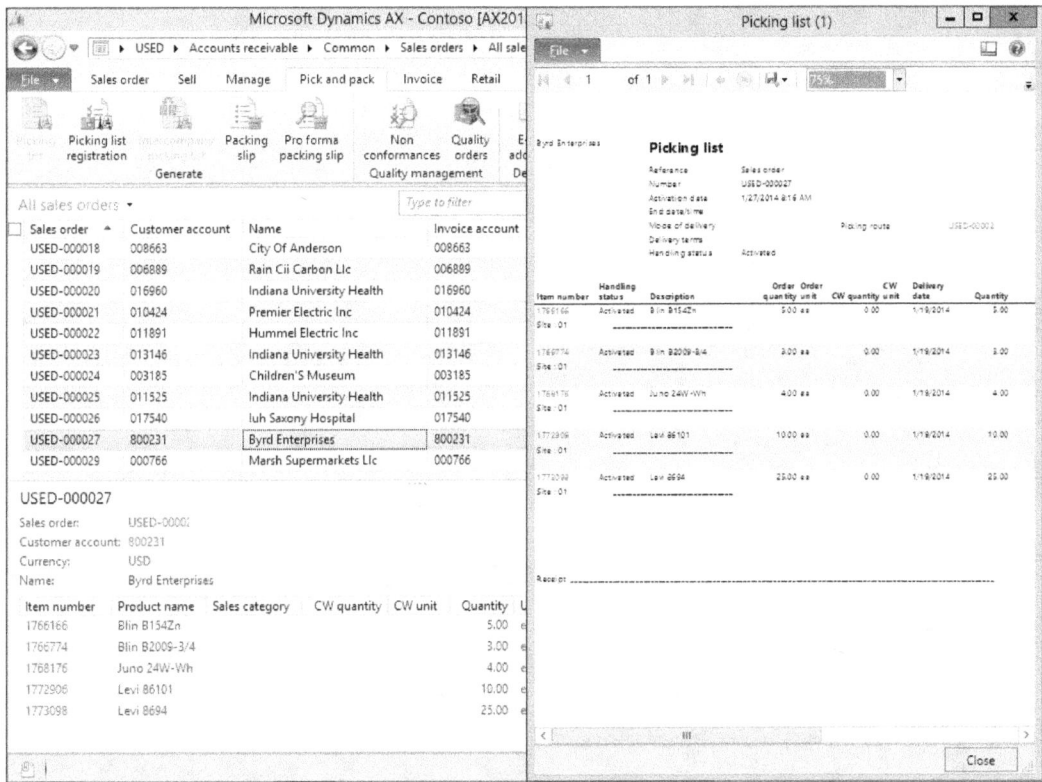

Key Features

- Estimated Delivery Date

Pick & Pack Management
Pick Registration

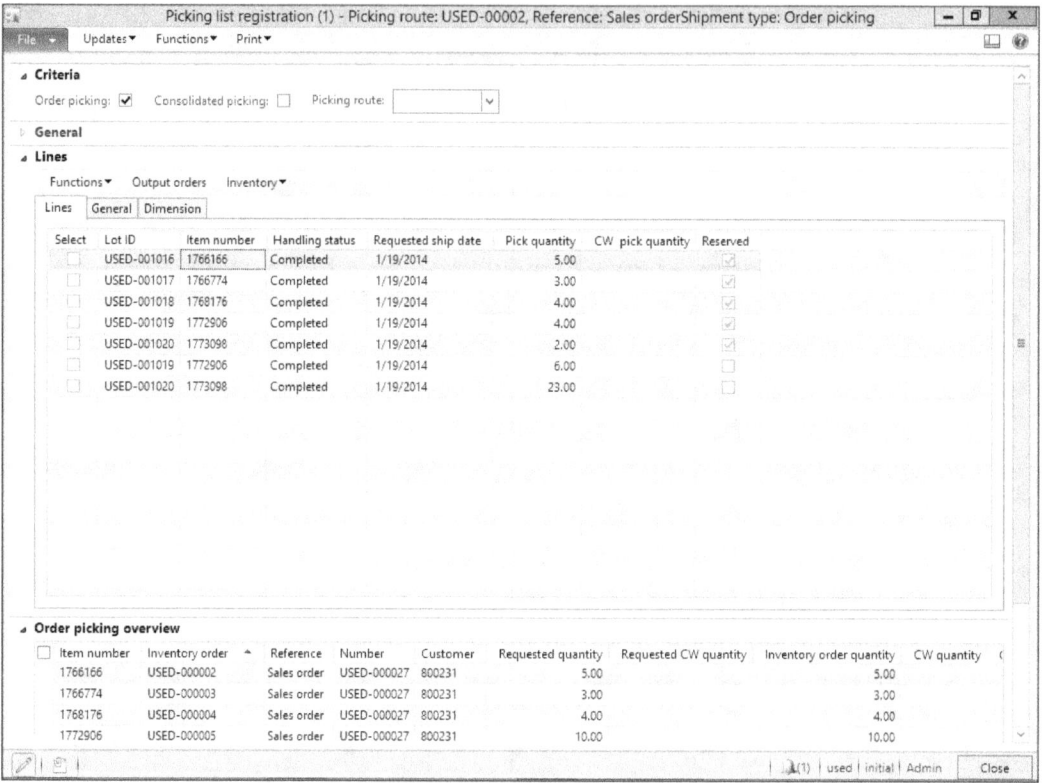

Key Features

- Picking List Approval and Update

- Can add, delete, change Pick List Lines

- Picking List Activation

- Picking List generation

- Consolidated Picking

- Picking Routes

Pick & Pack Management
Packing

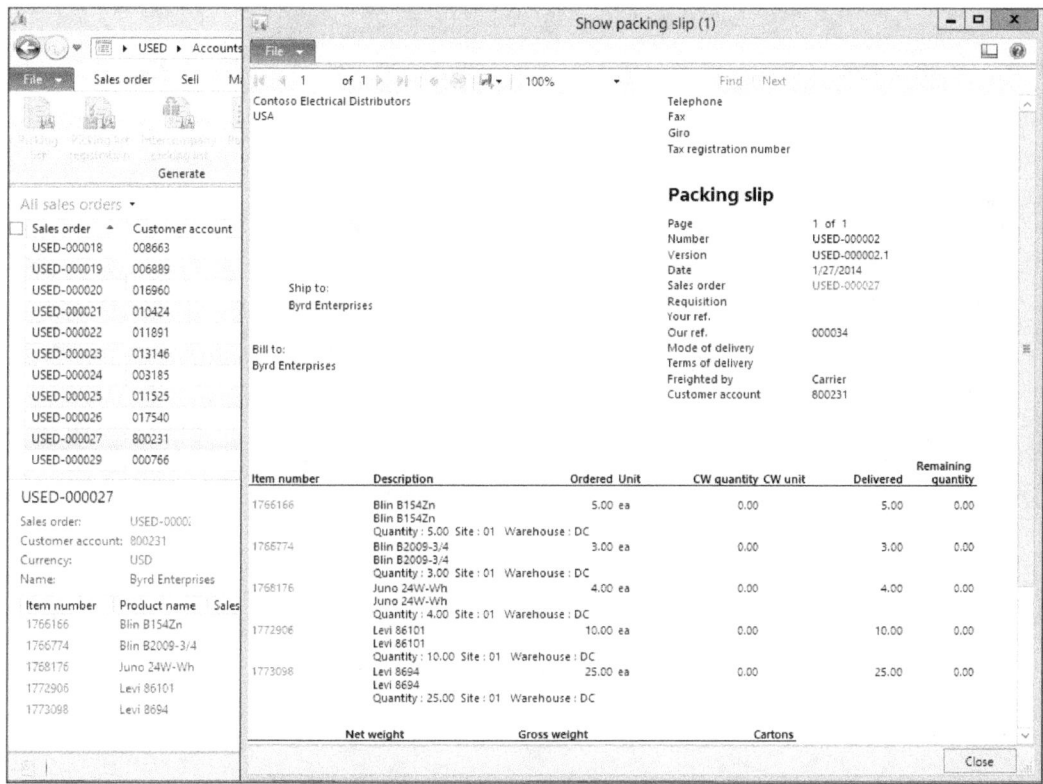

Pick & Pack Management
Shipper Tracking

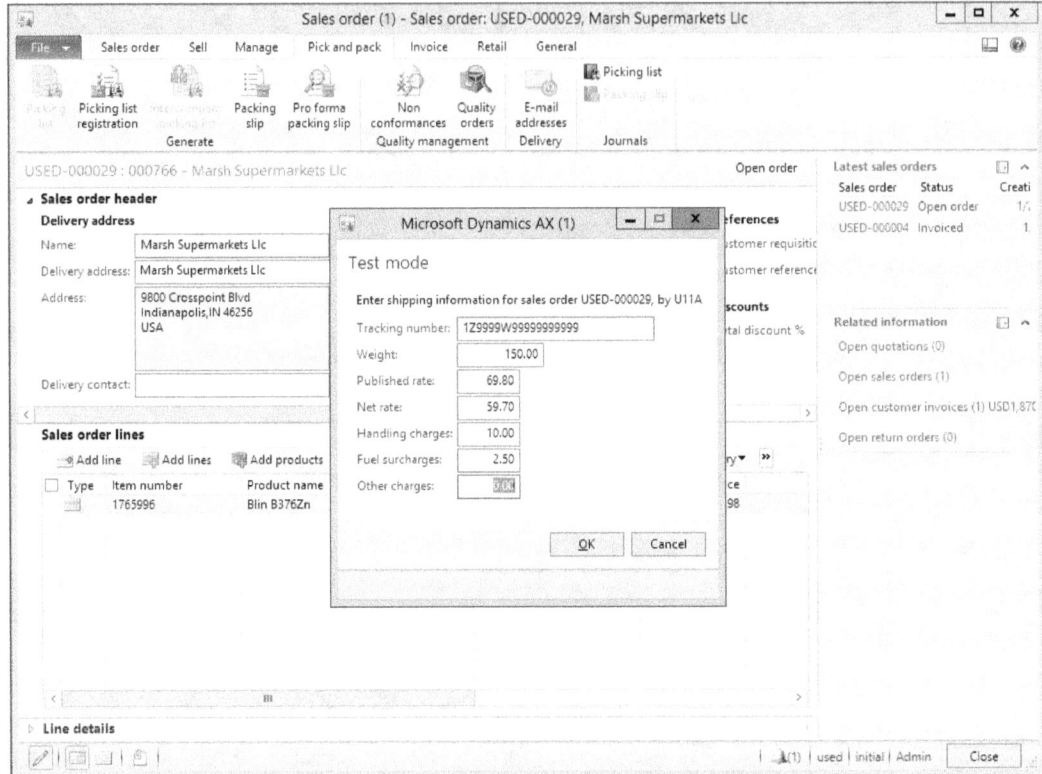

Key Features

- Standard Integration into Carrier Interfaces

- Shipping Interfaces calculate freight at Order Entry

Invoice Management
Invoicing

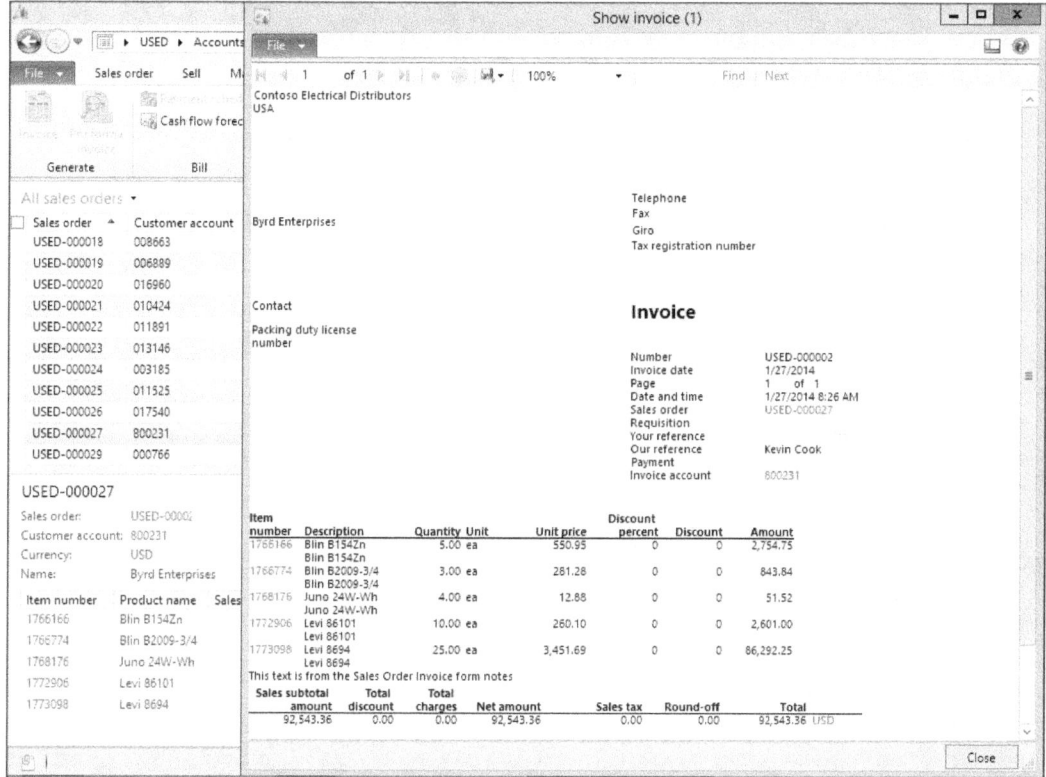

Key Features

- Non-stock invoice generation

- $0 line items still tracked

- Automatically send documents through email and fax through Print Controls

Invoice Management Statements

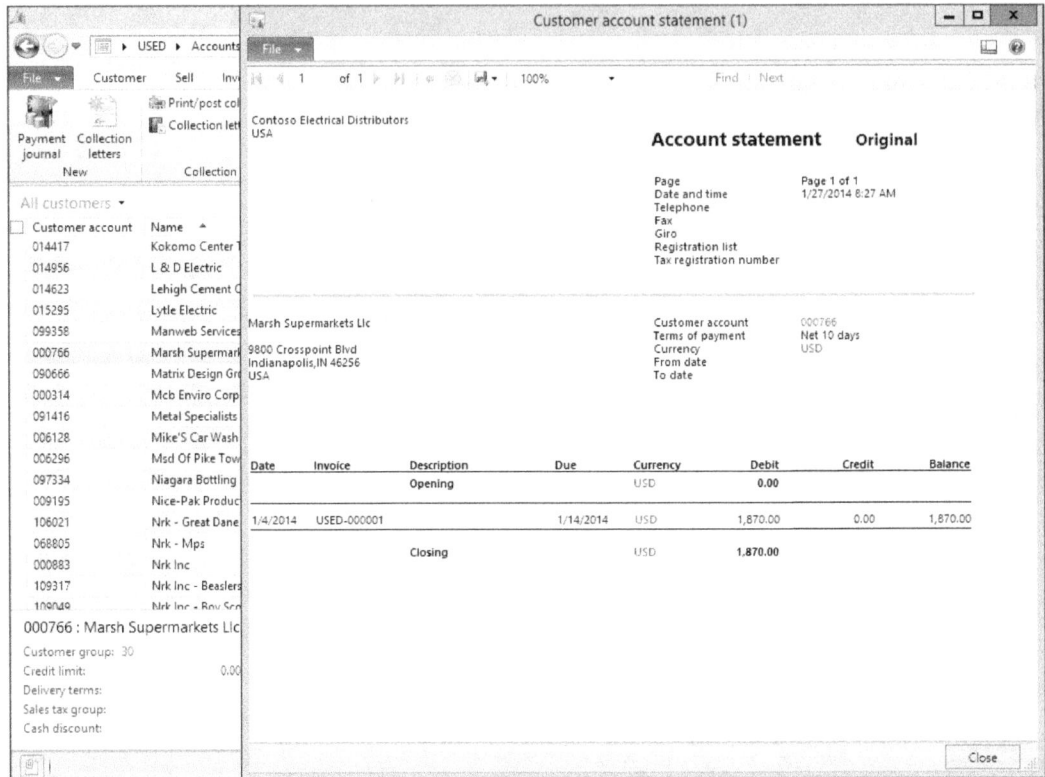

Key Features

- Account Statement Generation

Returns Management
Returns, Credits & Voids

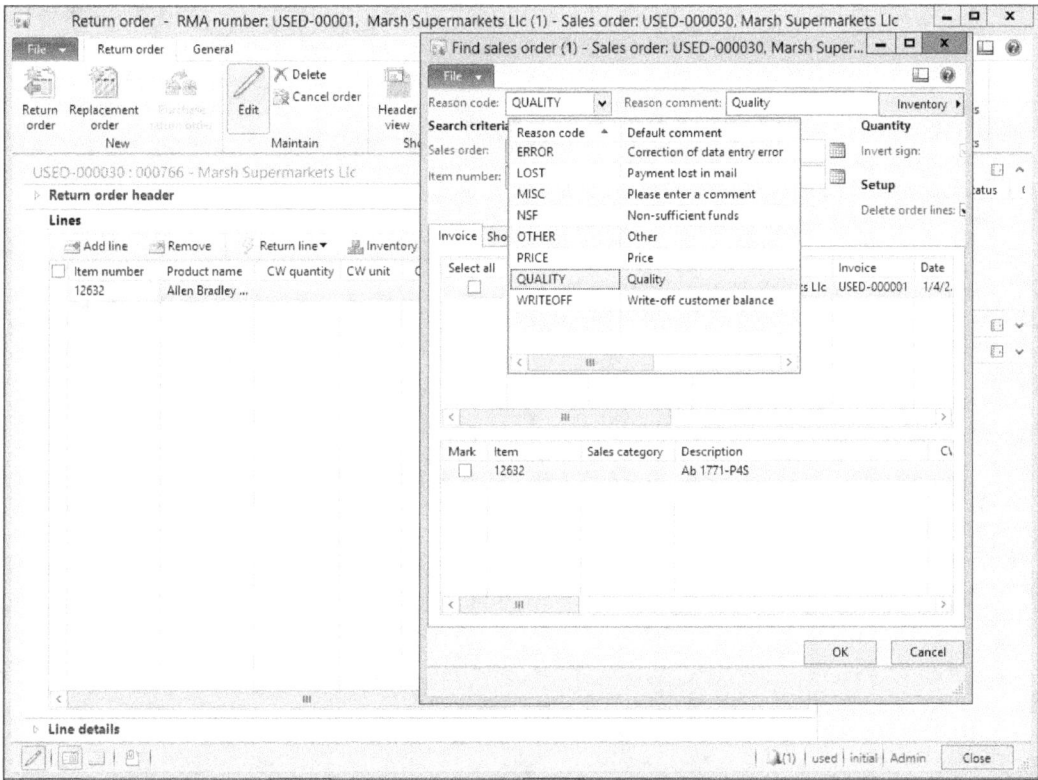

Key Features

- RMA generation from Invoices and Sales Orders

- Automatically retrieves actual Invoice price & extended value

Returns Management
Returns, Credits & Voids

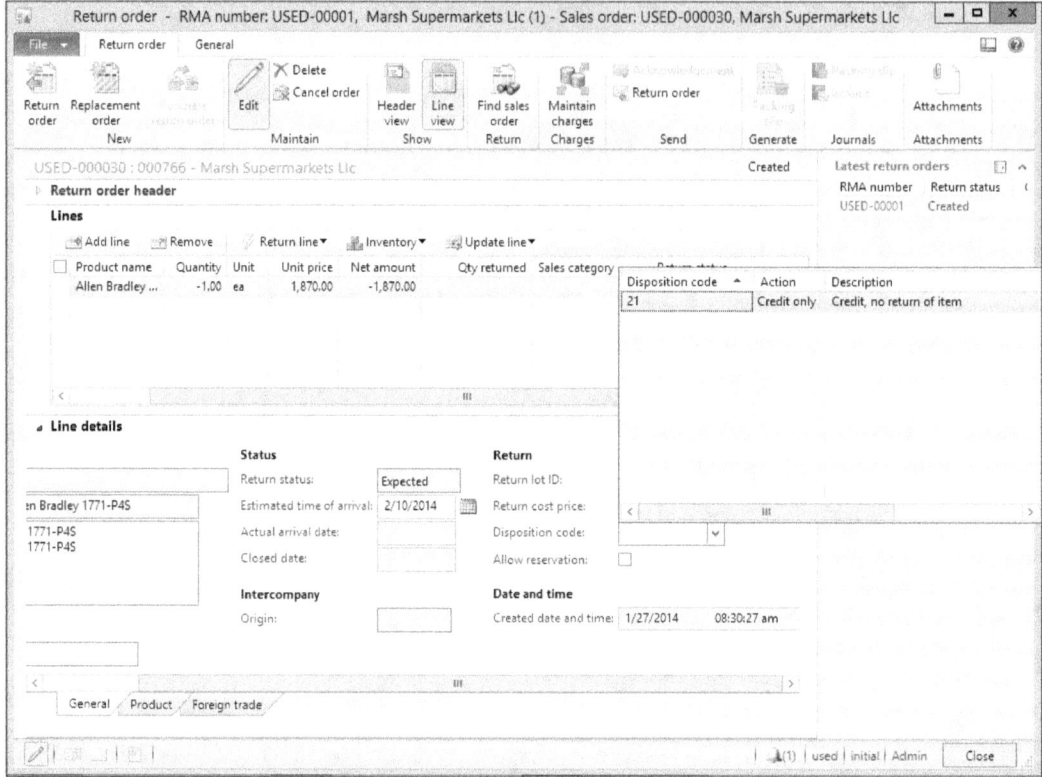

Key Features

- Return Reason codes

- Customer Contact for return

- Disposition code for return

- Create Replacement Orders

Credit Management
Credit Hold

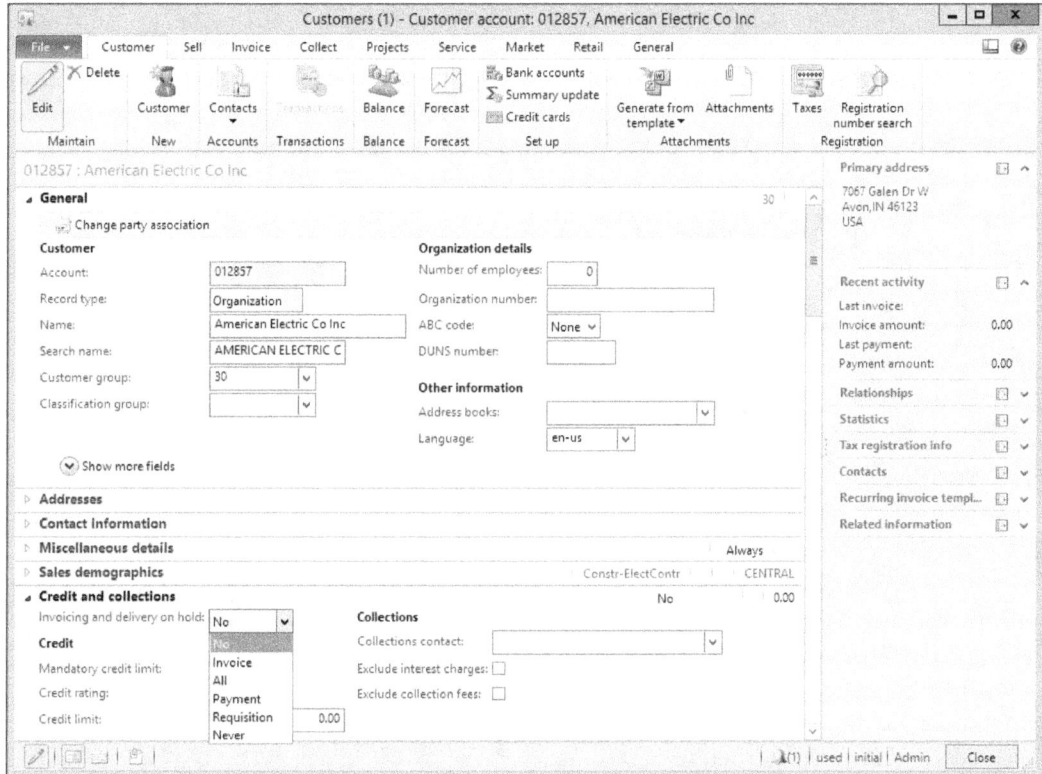

Key Features

- Multiple credit hold rules

Credit Management
Aging & Collections

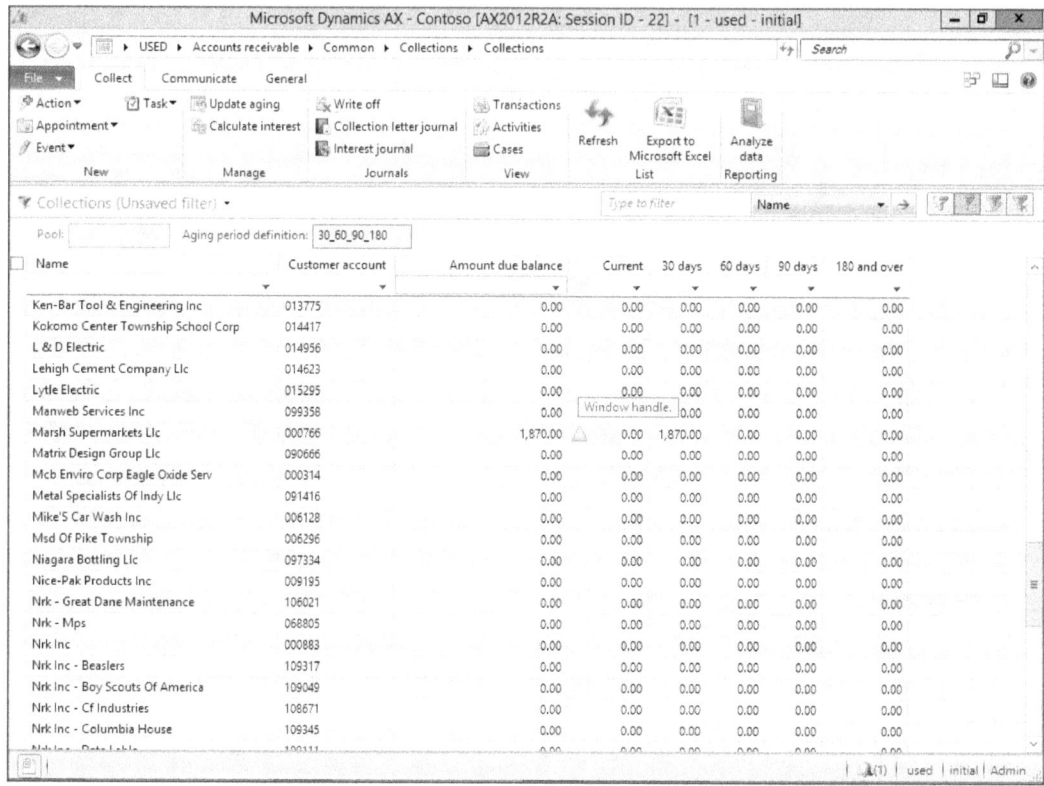

Key Features

- User defined ageing buckets

- Case Management Integrated into Collections

- Unlimited number of search fields through personalization

- Ad-hoc reporting from Collections Interface

- Export to Excel

- Collection Letters generated directly from Collection

Credit Management
Finance Charges & Dunning

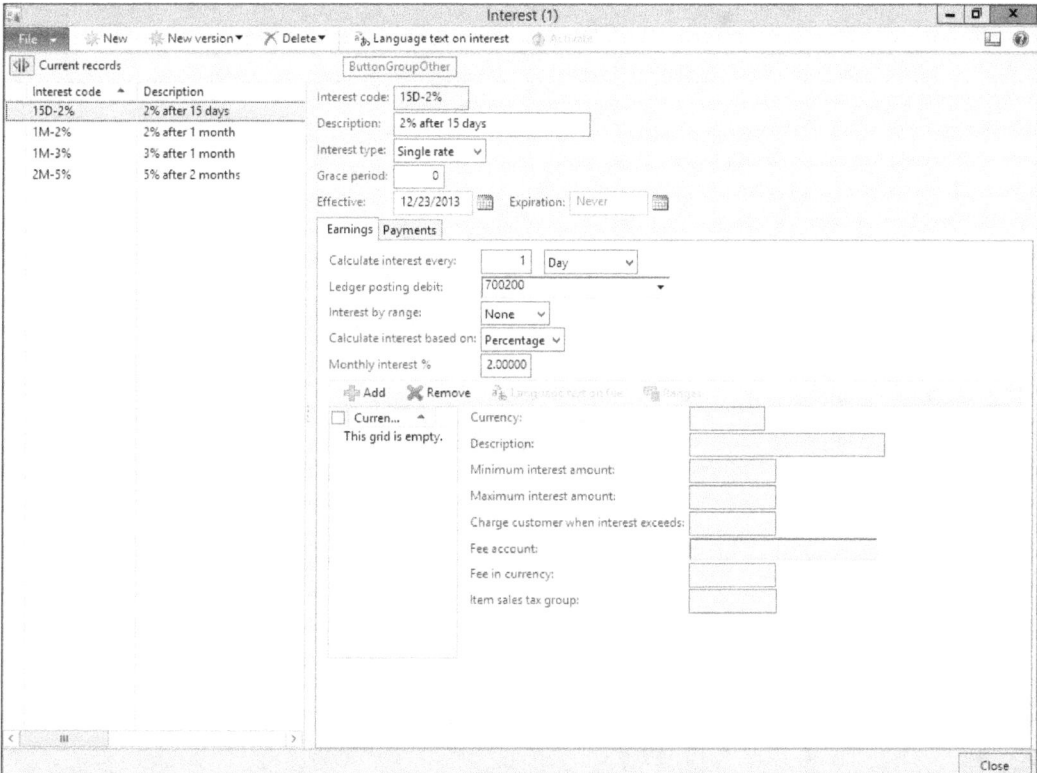

Key Features

- Finance Charges and Dunning Calculation from within Collections

- User defined interest calculations

- Monthly, Daily & Yearly interest calculations

Credit Management
Collections Letters & Notifications

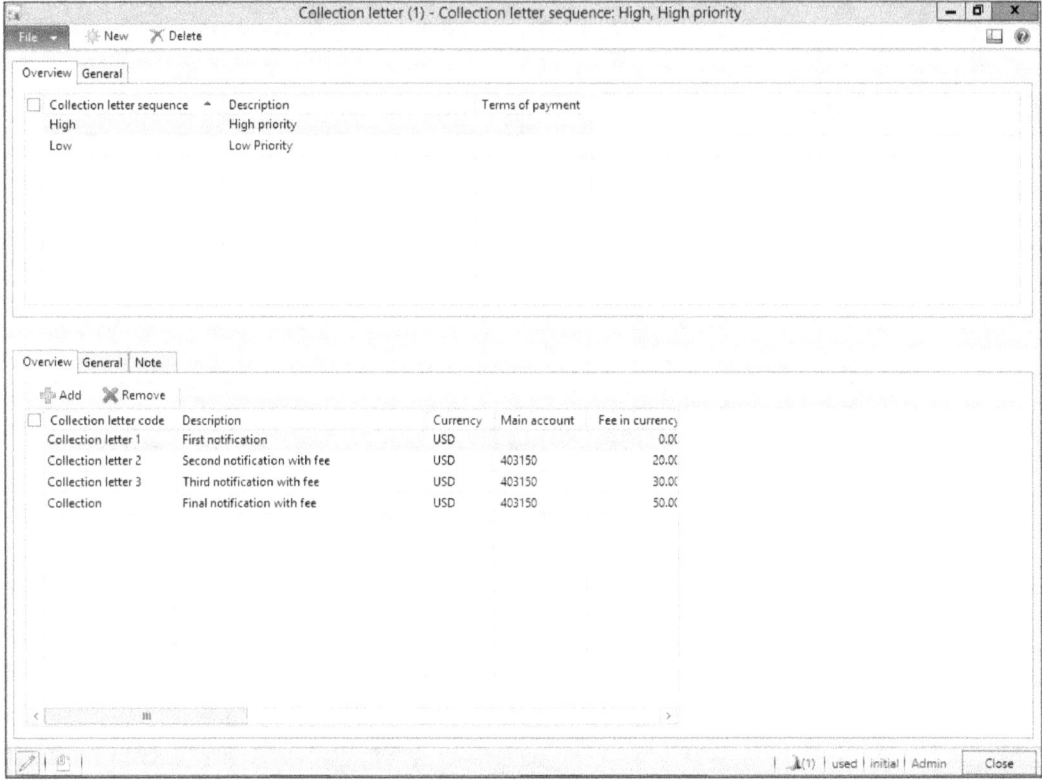

Receivables
Cash Receipts

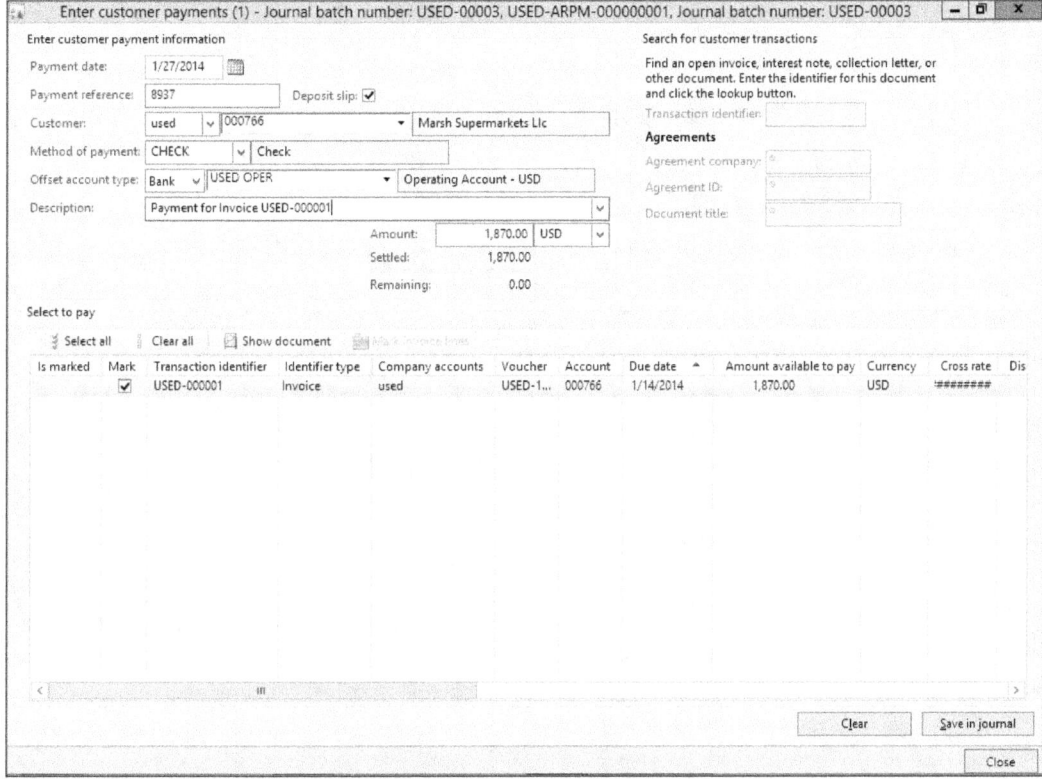

Tax Management
Sales Tax

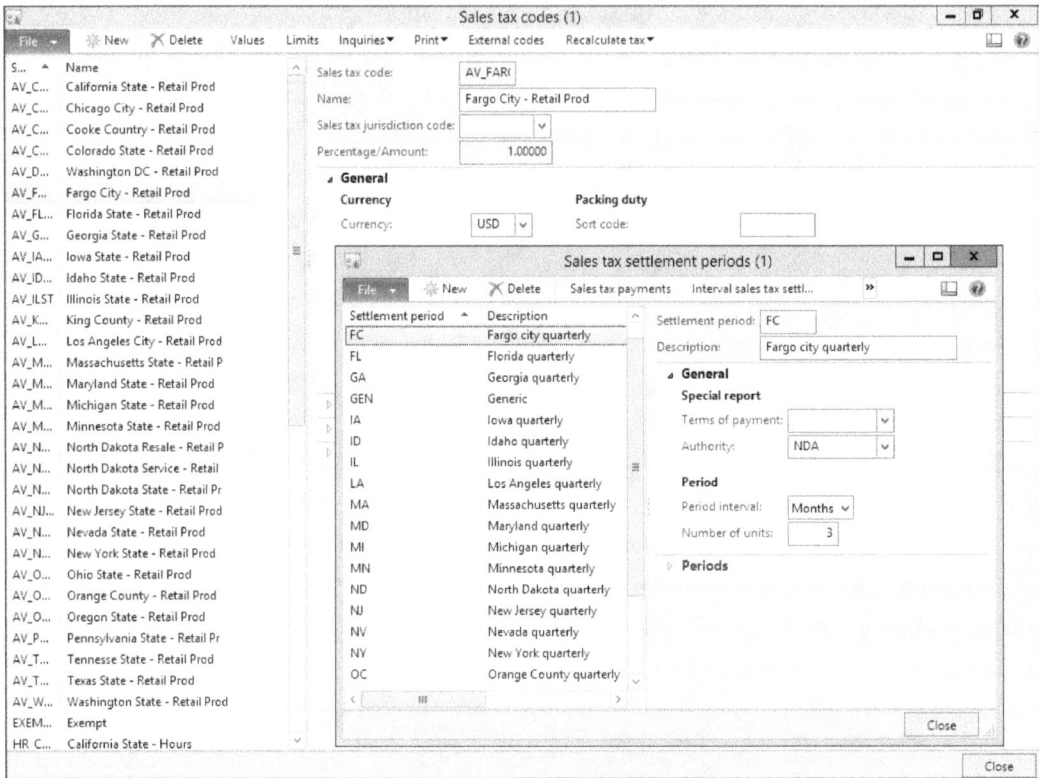

Key Features

- Multiple Sales Tax Codes, Authorities and Groups

- Update Tax Rules manually or Import from Tax Rule Providers

- Address Information can drive Tax Calculations

Sales Reporting
Ad-Hoc Analysis

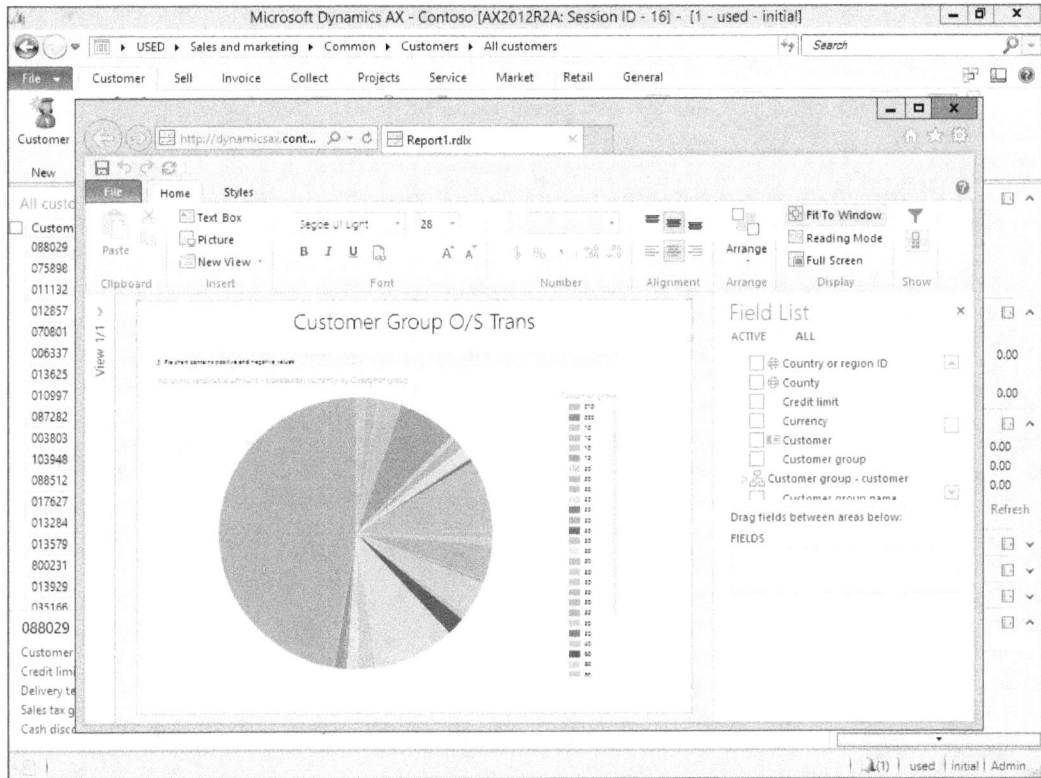

Key Features

- User reporting available through Dashboards

- Access Reporting from Transactional Screens

Document Management
Document Attachments

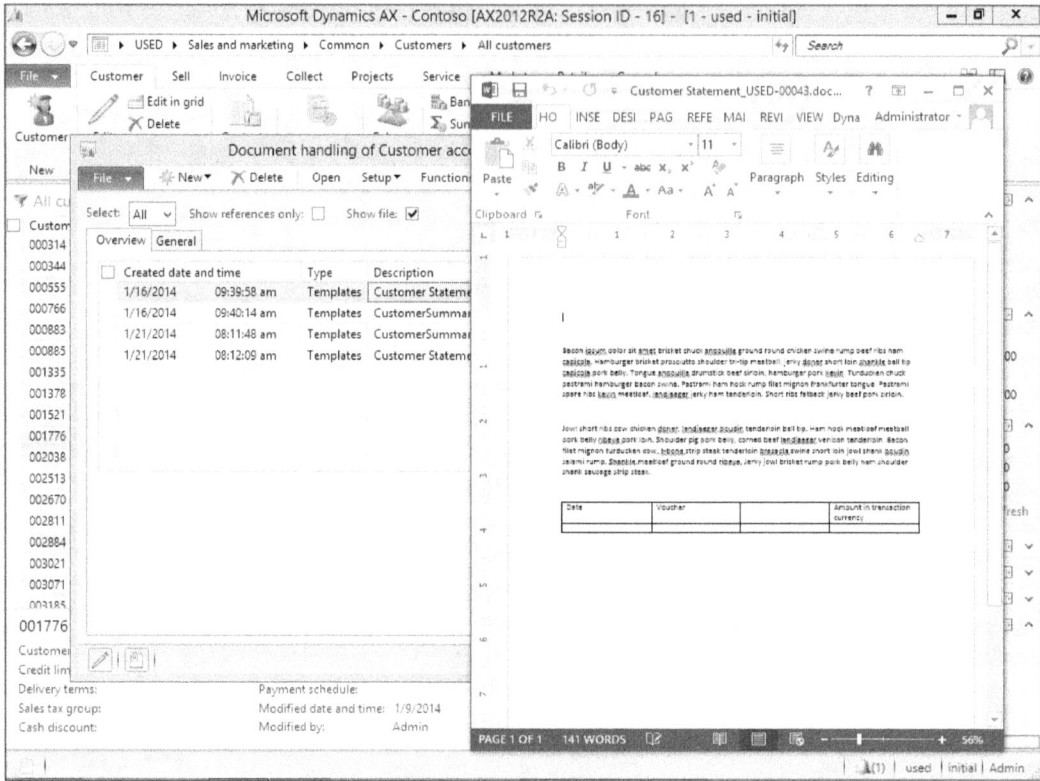

Key Features

- Attachments can be associated with any record in the system

- Archived reports and documents available

- Unlimited number of documents and attachments

Portals
Customer Self Service

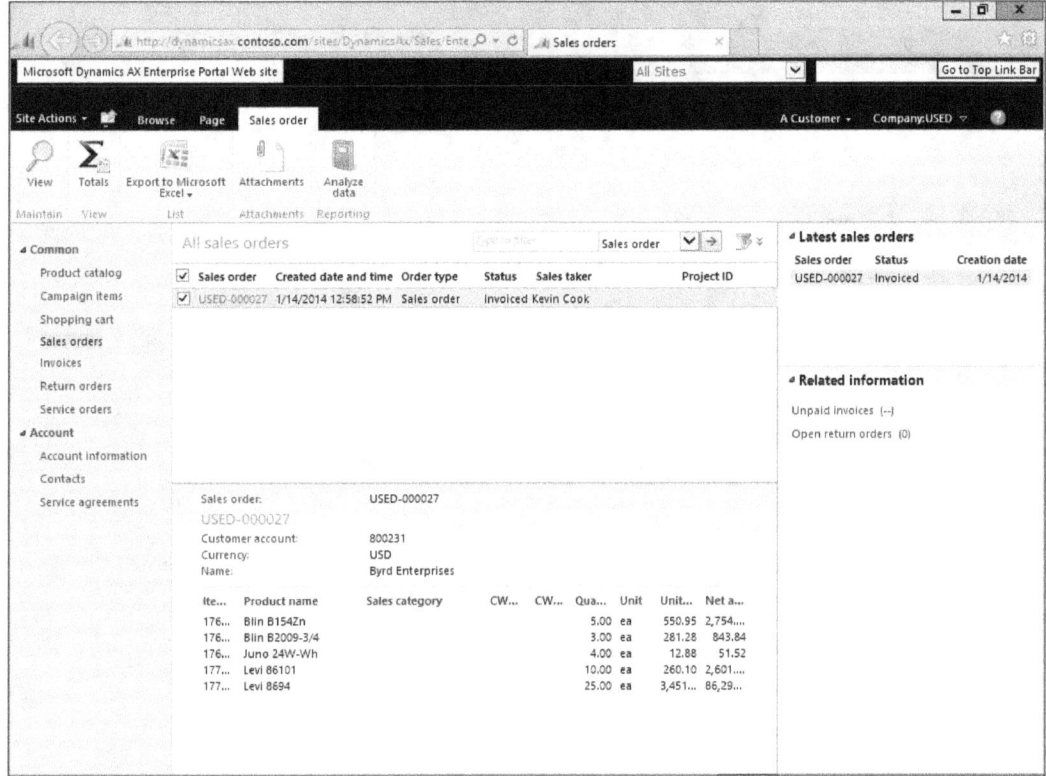

Key Features

- Customer Portal provides external access to Customer Accounts

- No additional user license for External Customers

- Access to same detailed information that is available in Rich Client

Portals
Sales Portal

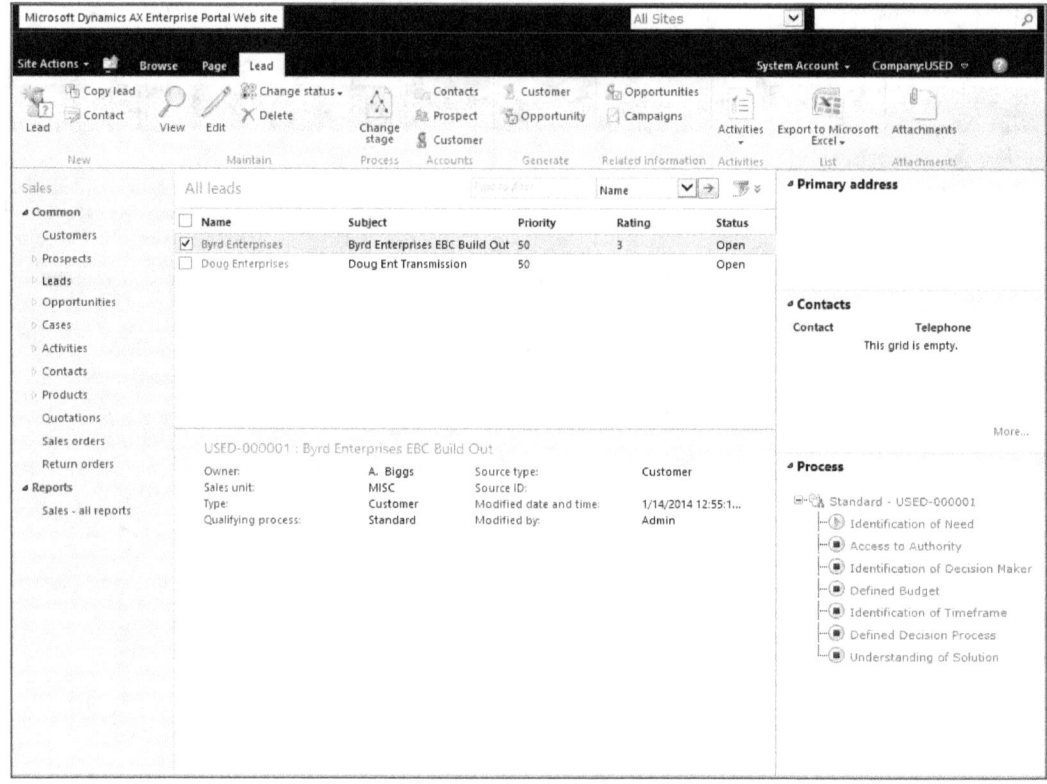

Portals
eCommerce Portal

Key Features

- Native eCommerce Retail site for B2C

- All product information refreshed from master data

Retail Management
Point Of Sale Registers

Key Features

- Helps employees better serve customers in a timely manner

- POS on standard POS terminals & tablets

Sales & Marketing

The Sales & Marketing module within Dynamics AX is a completely integrated CRM module for the management of Customers, Prospects, Leads, Opportunities, Campaigns and more.

Additionally, all of the information that you maintain through the Sales & Marketing module is available throughout the rest of the application, allowing you to track activities, tasks, appointments and cases from virtually everywhere.

Also, even though CRM modules traditionally only apply to customers, since all contacts including vendors and workers are tracked within the same structure, then all of CRM functions are also available for vendor campaigns and even employee notifications.

In the following section we will show some of the key features of the Sales & Marketing module.

Sales Management
Sales Units & Hierarchies

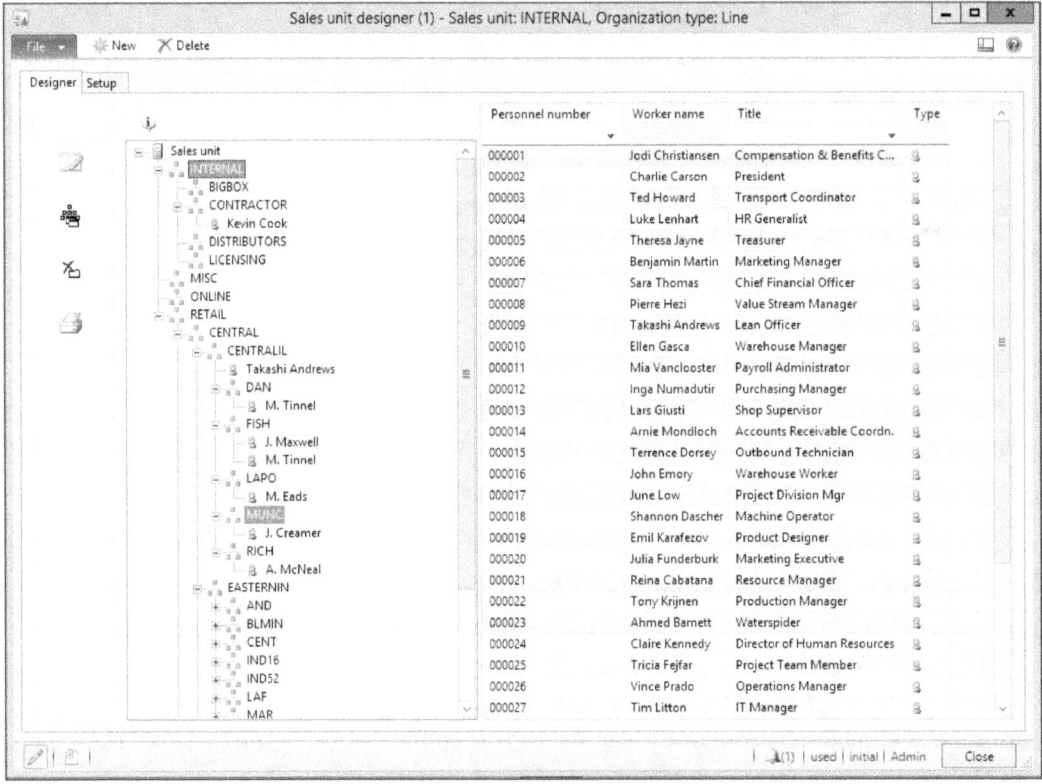

Sales Management
Leads

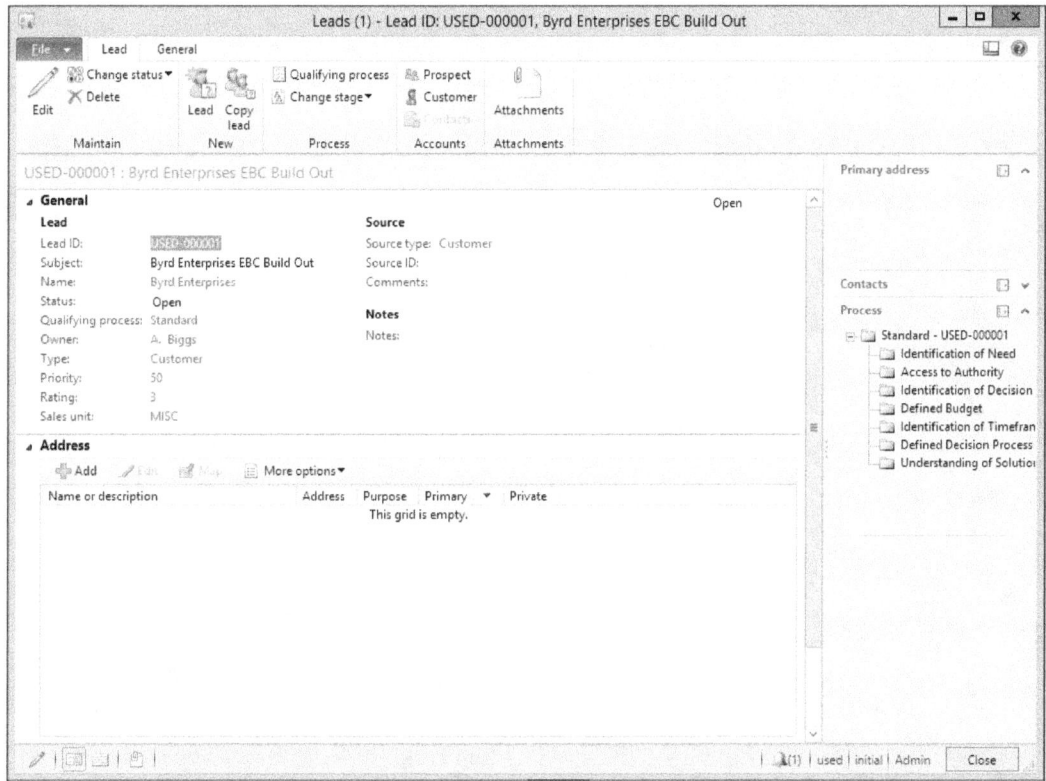

Sales Management
Prospects

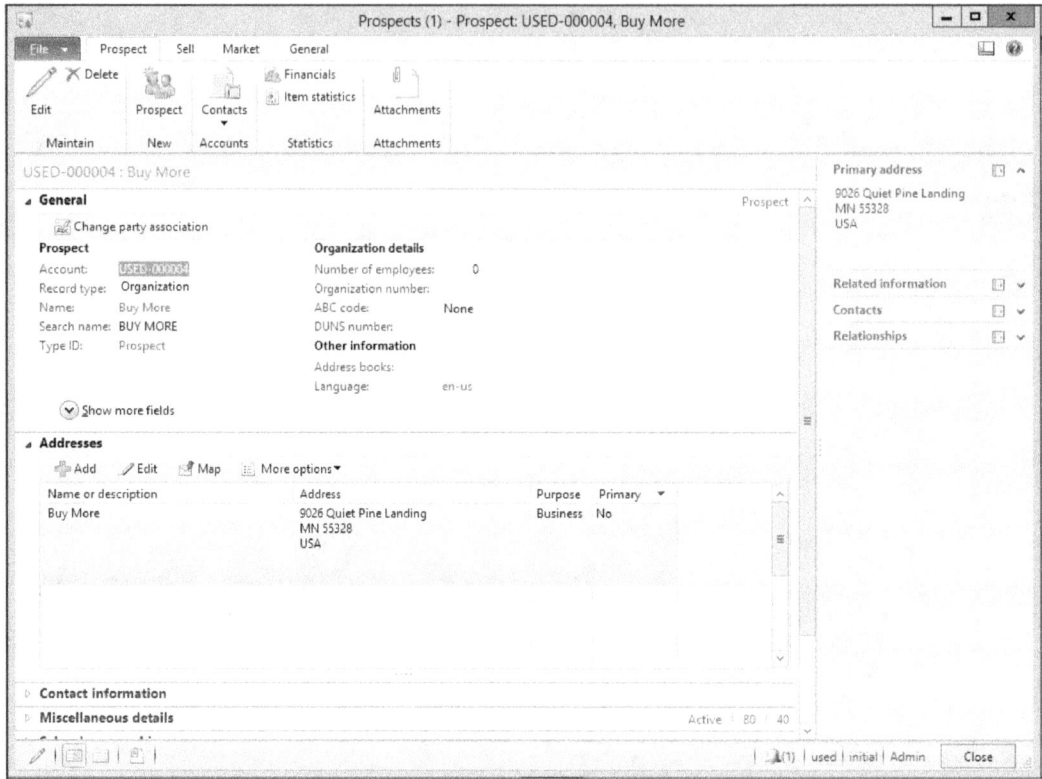

Sales Management
Opportunities

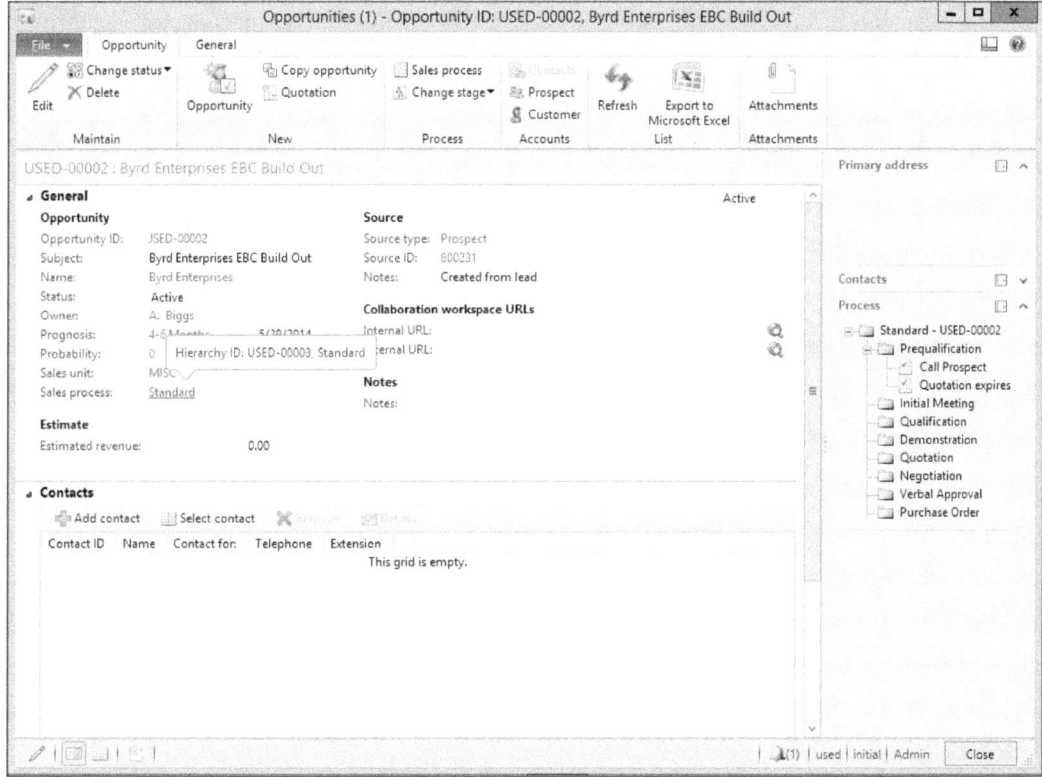

Activity Tracking
Activities

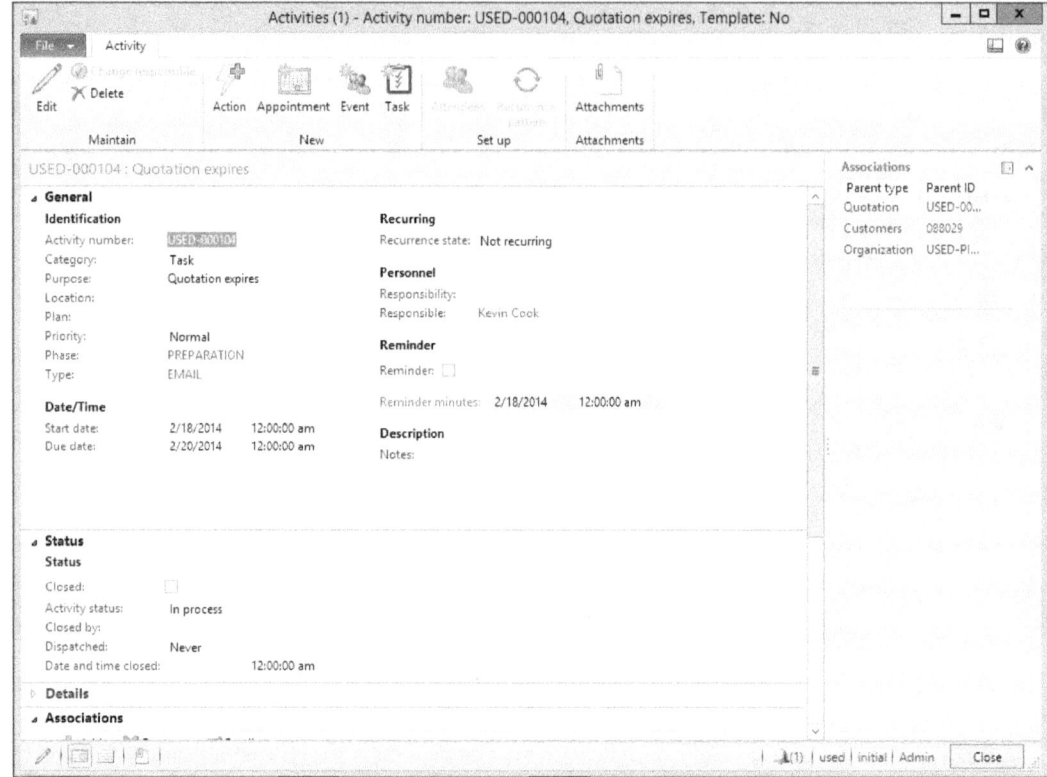

Activity Tracking
Case Management

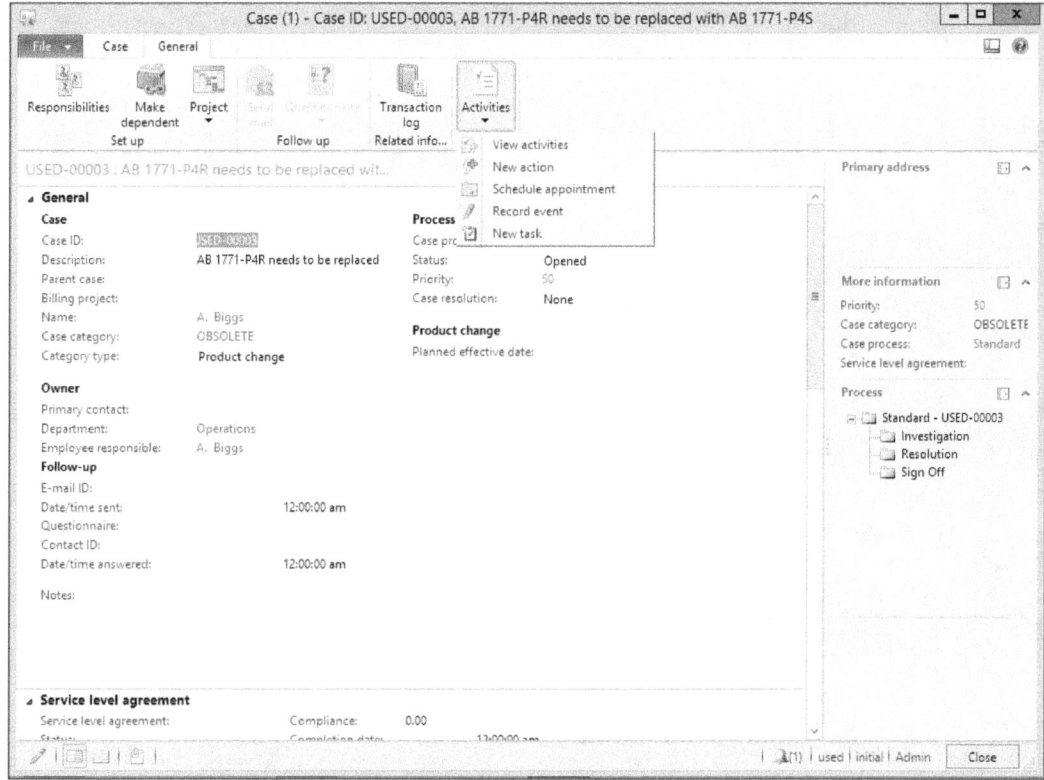

Marketing Campaigns

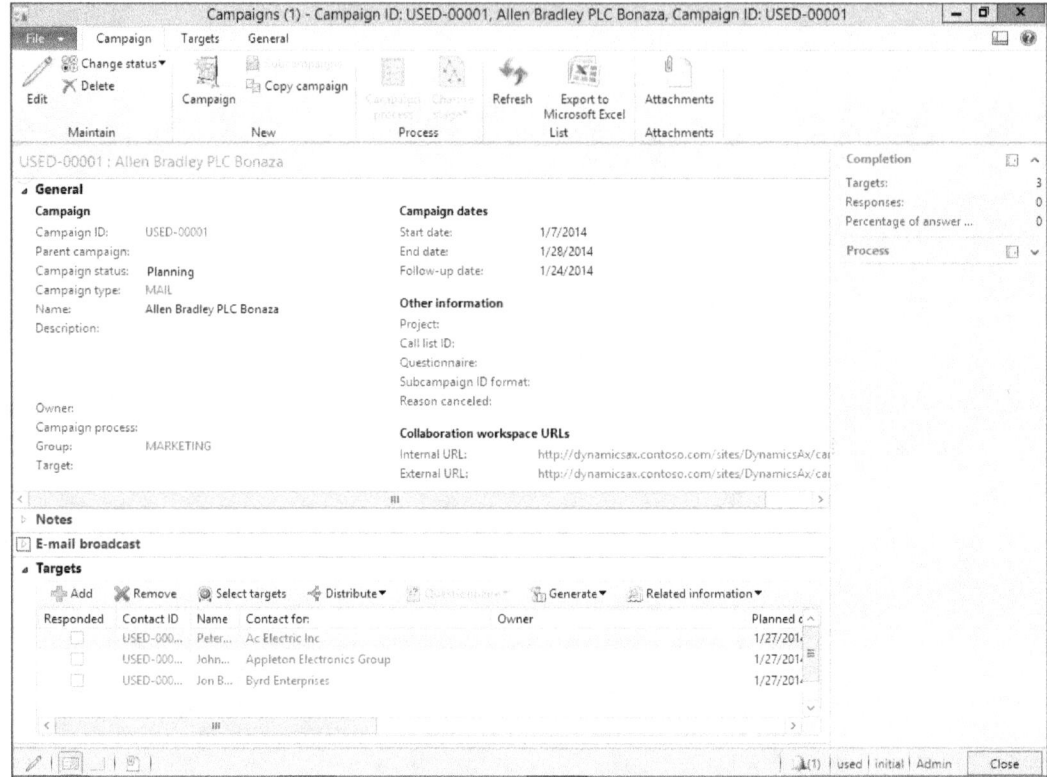

Call Center Management
Call Lists

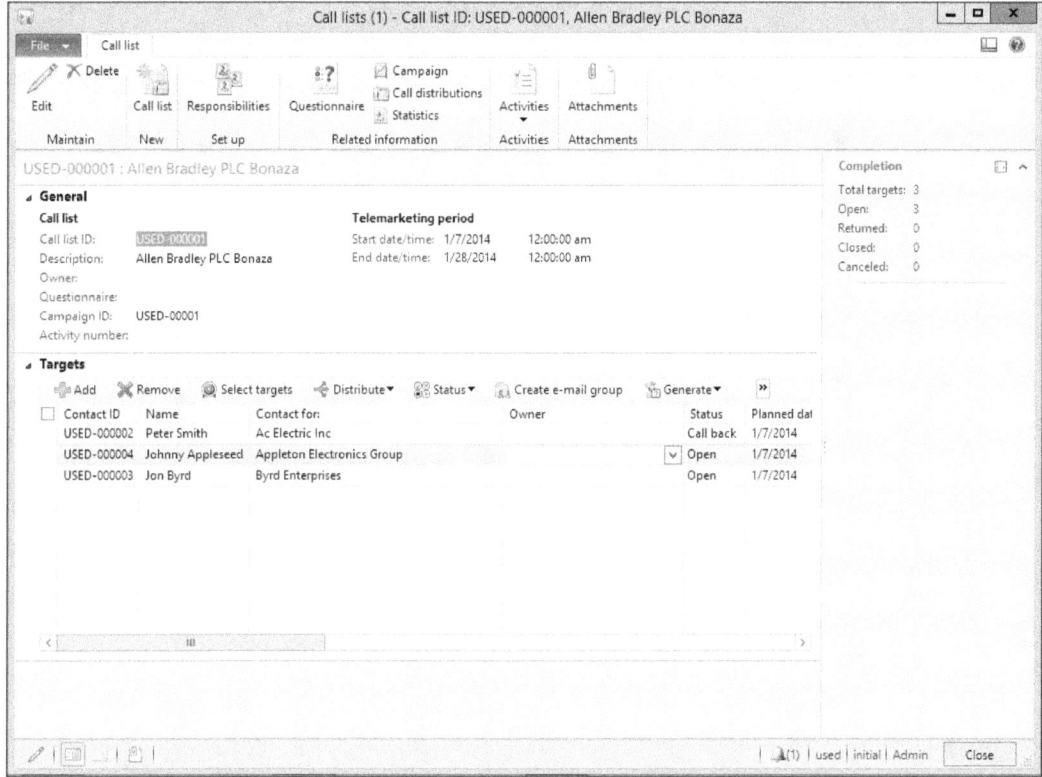

Telephony
TAPI Integration

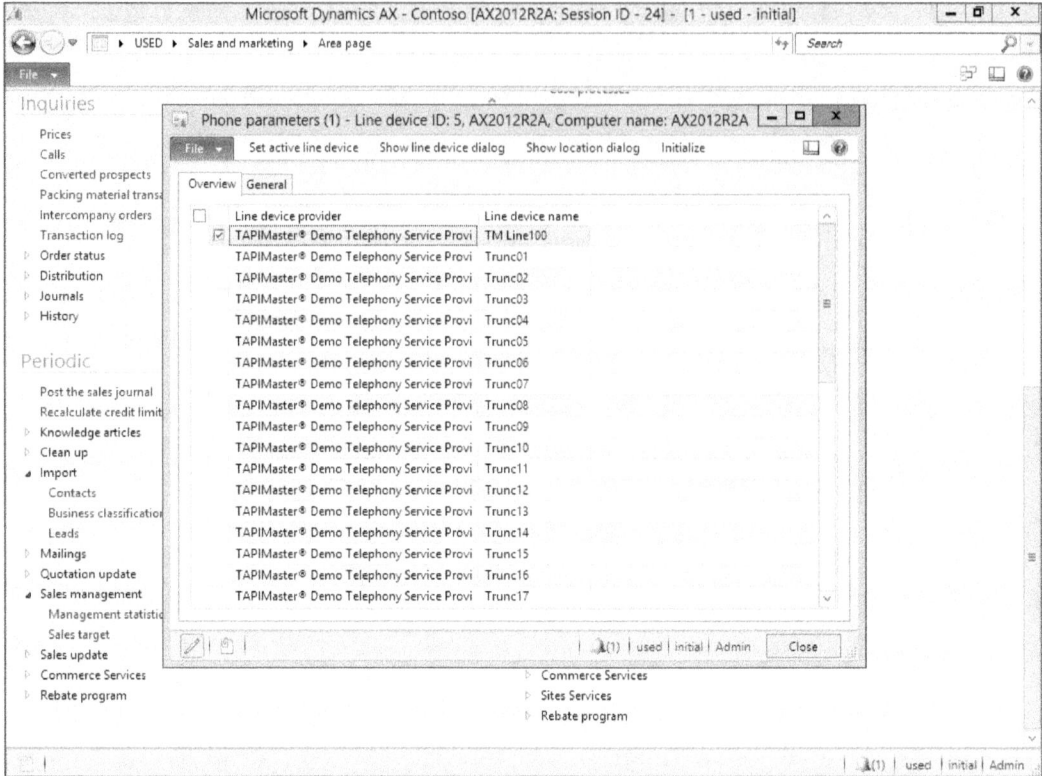

Operations

The Operations modules within Dynamics AX span Inventory Control, and Production and allow you to manage all of the inventory and also perform light to heavy manufacturing jobs directly from the system.

Within the inventory control module, you are able to define by product individual rules and constraints, tracking them at multiple levels including batch and serial, and also track multiple dimensions against a product allowing you to aggregate up and down to different levels for inventory management.

The manufacturing module within Dynamics AX gives you the flexibility to perform any level of light assembly to complex manufacturing, discrete or process formula based manufacturing orders, and even traditional, lean, or mixed mode manufacturing.

In this section we will uncover some of the features that would be useful to your Operations group.

Master Data Management
Inventory Master

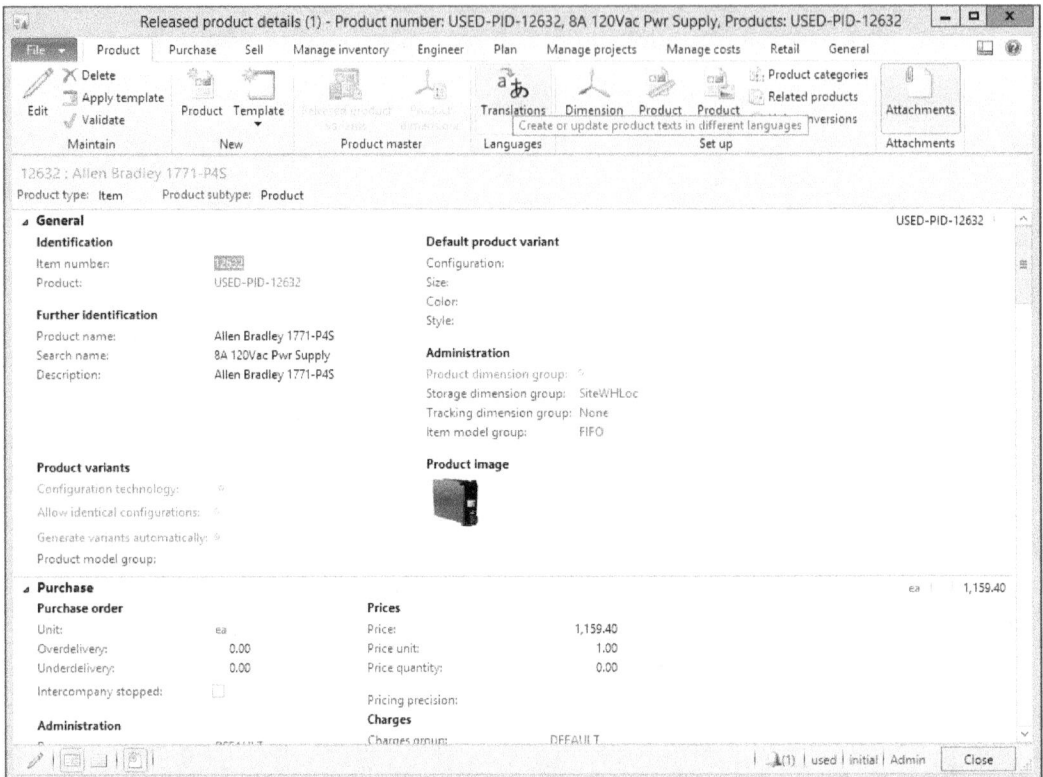

Key Features

- Detailed Description of Product

- Product dimensions and tracking Codes

- Unlimited number of product attributes

- Product Image associated with Product Record

Master Data Management
Warehouse & Location Configuration

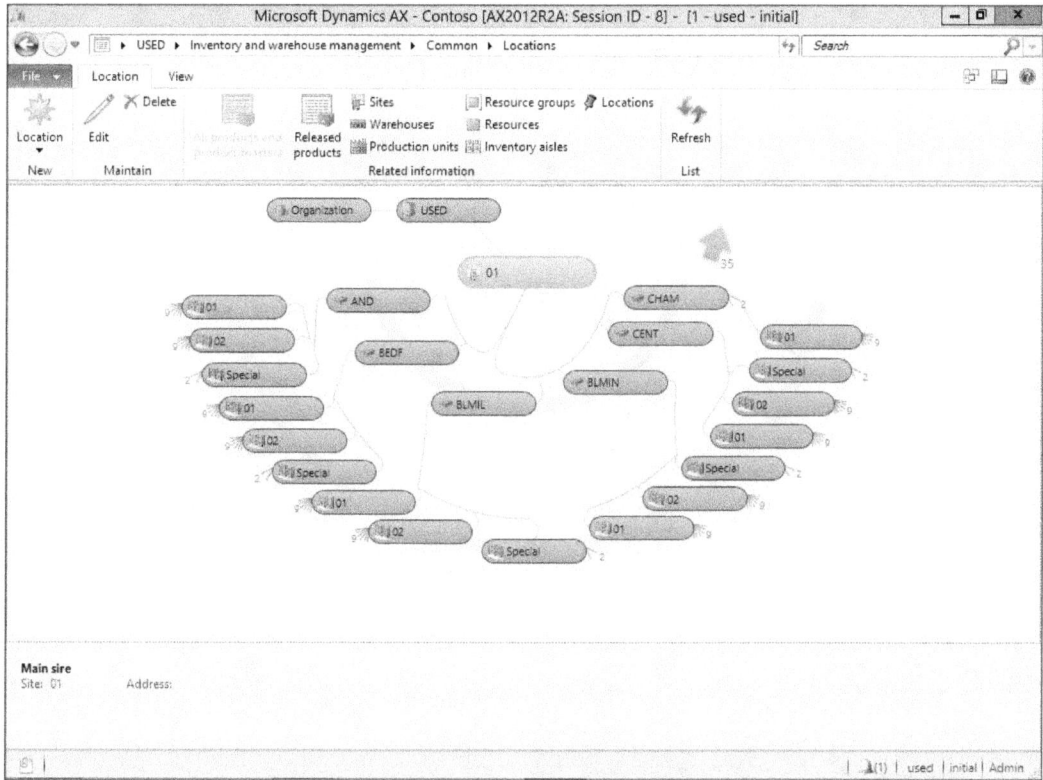

Key Features

- Site, Warehouse, Aisle, Rack hierarchy

Inventory Management
Inventory Visibility

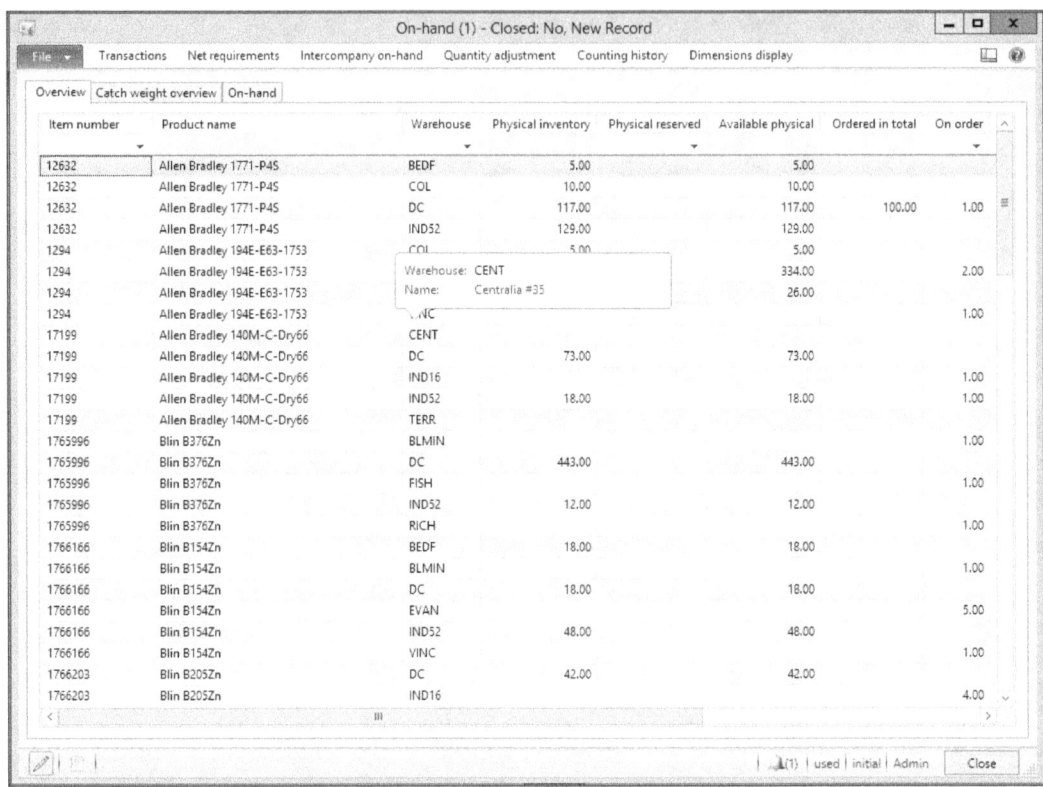

Key Features

- Aggregate inventory to any level required

Inventory Management
Cycle Counting

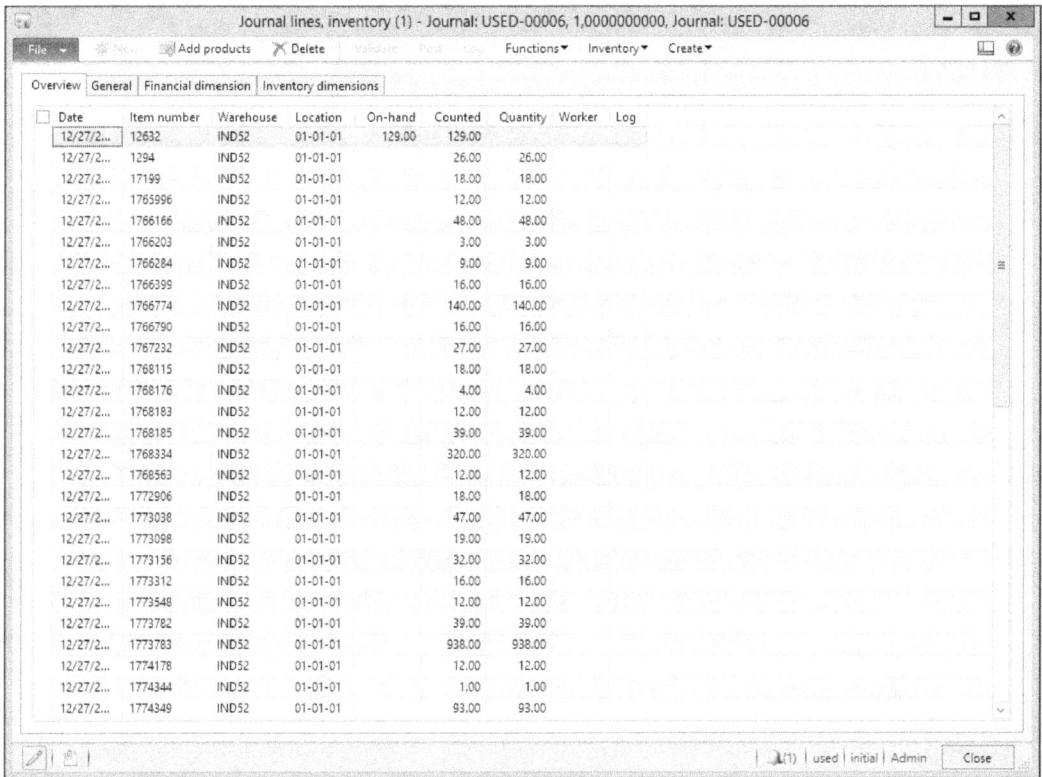

Key Features

- User defined Counting Journal creation

- Generate count sheets based on inventory codes, locations, and last count date

Inventory Management
Count Analysis

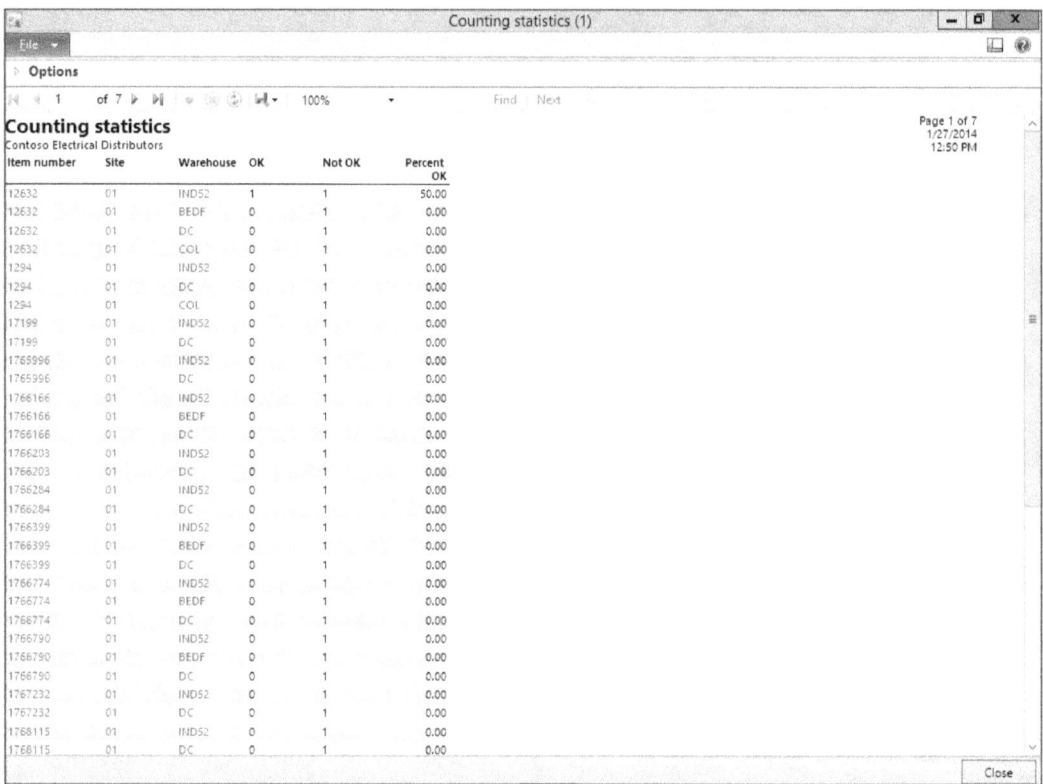

Key Features

- Count accuracy statistic reporting

- Reports link back to original transactions

Engineering Management
BOM/Kit Specification

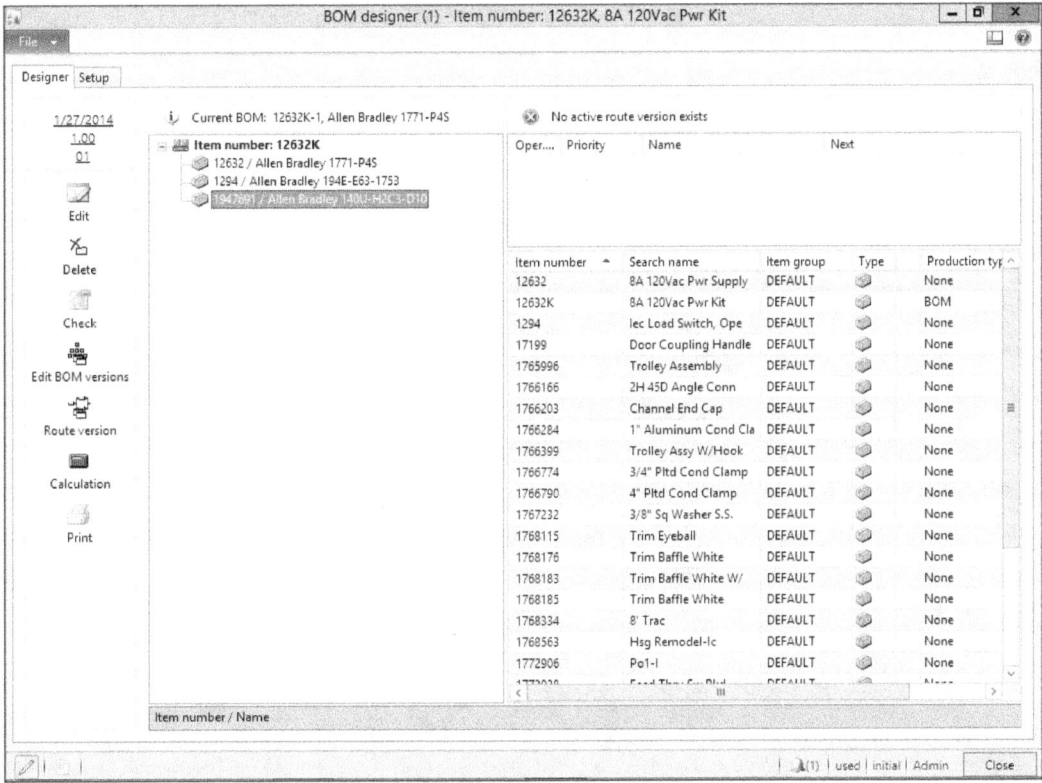

Key Features

- Effectivity Dates

- Unlimited number of versions and components lines

- Activation & Approval

- Unlimited number of subcomponent levels

Engineering Management
Product Change Management

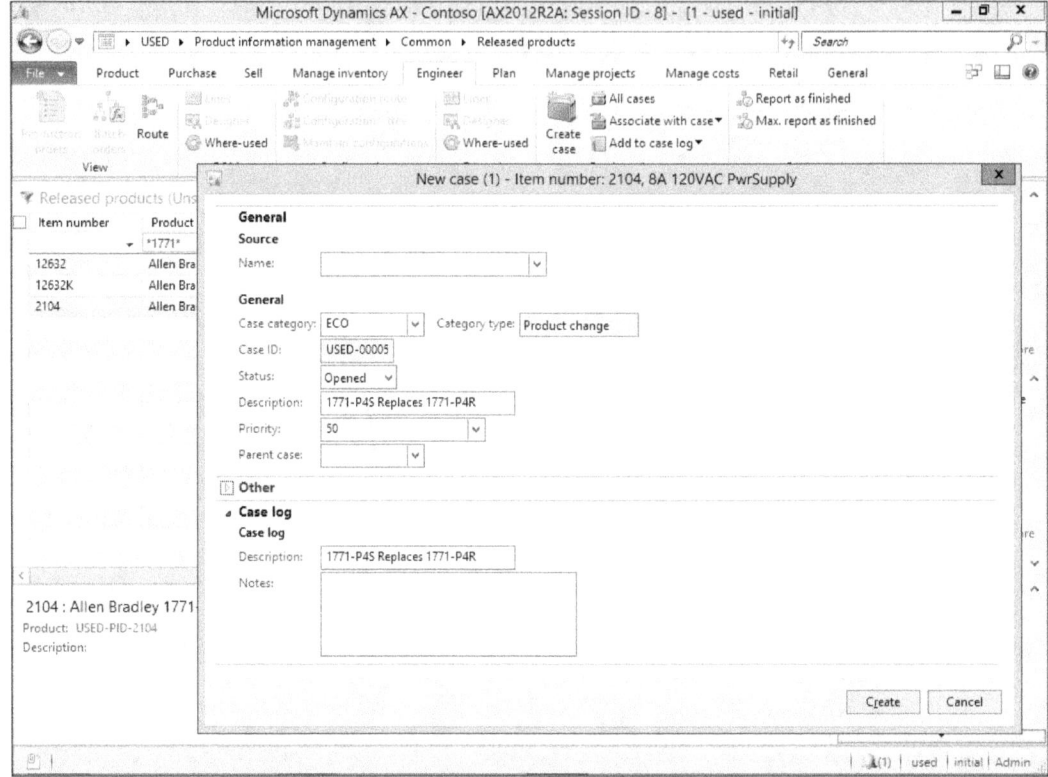

Engineering Management
Where Used Analysis

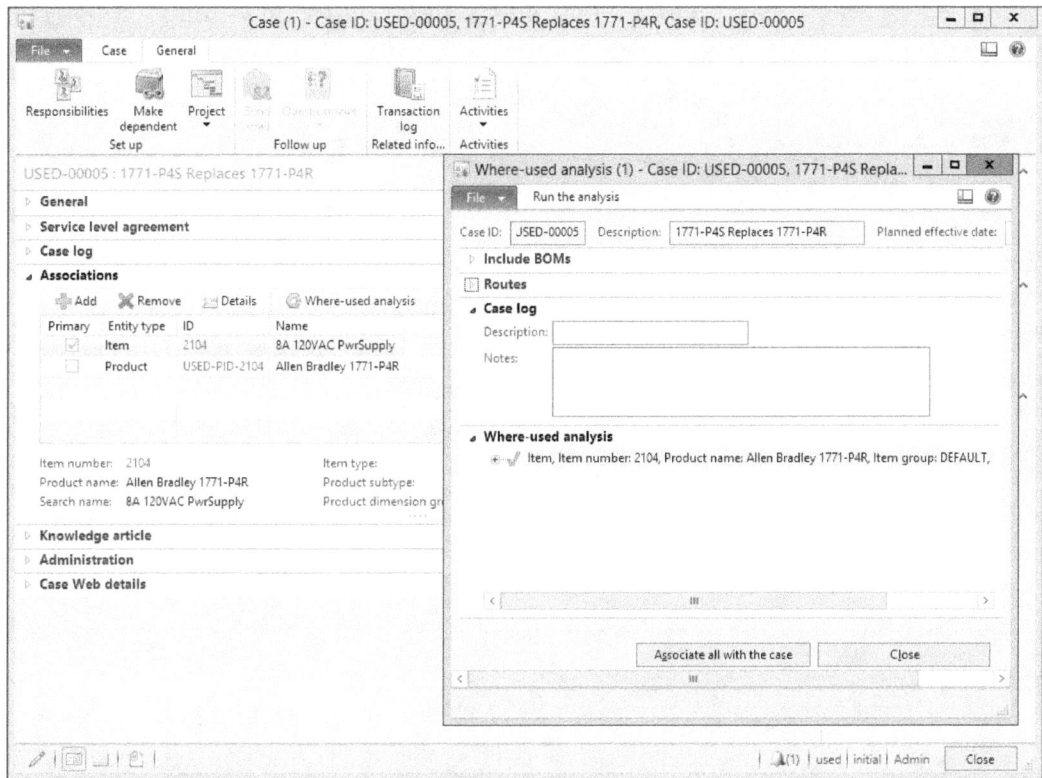

Key Features

- Flexible search and Where Used selection

- Mass update of BOM lines

Engineering Management
Route Configuration

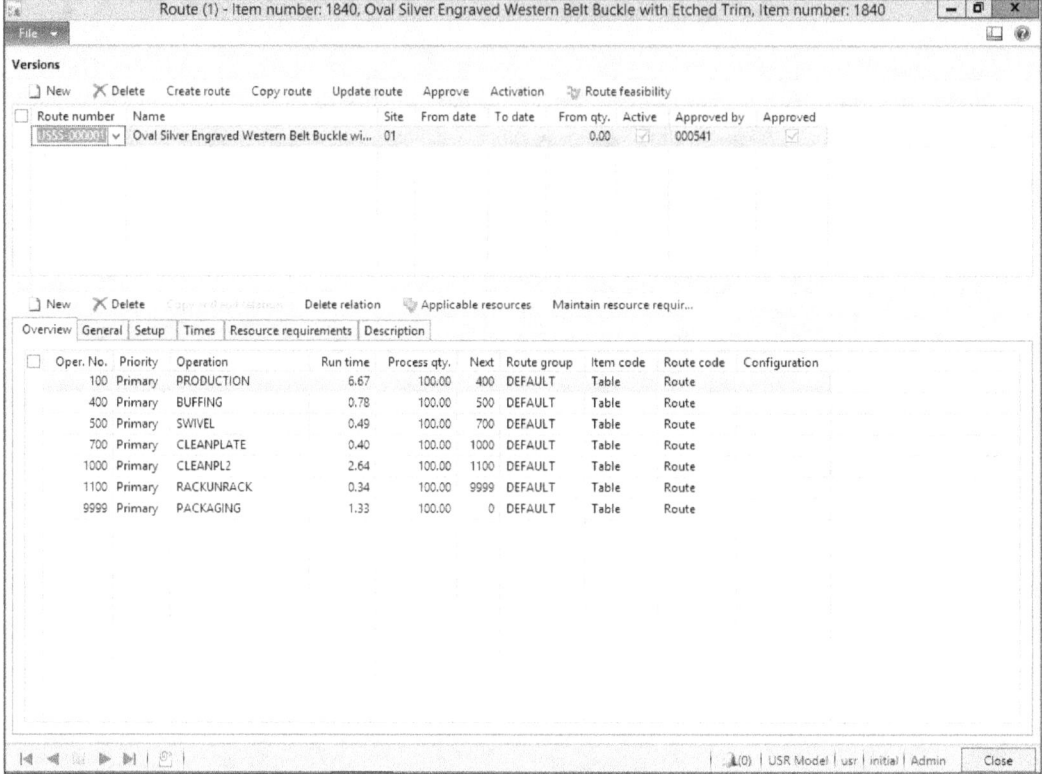

Key Features

- Route Effectivity dates

- Route sequencing

- Multiple active Routes

- Route Approval can require new versions for updates

Engineering Management
Subcontracting Steps

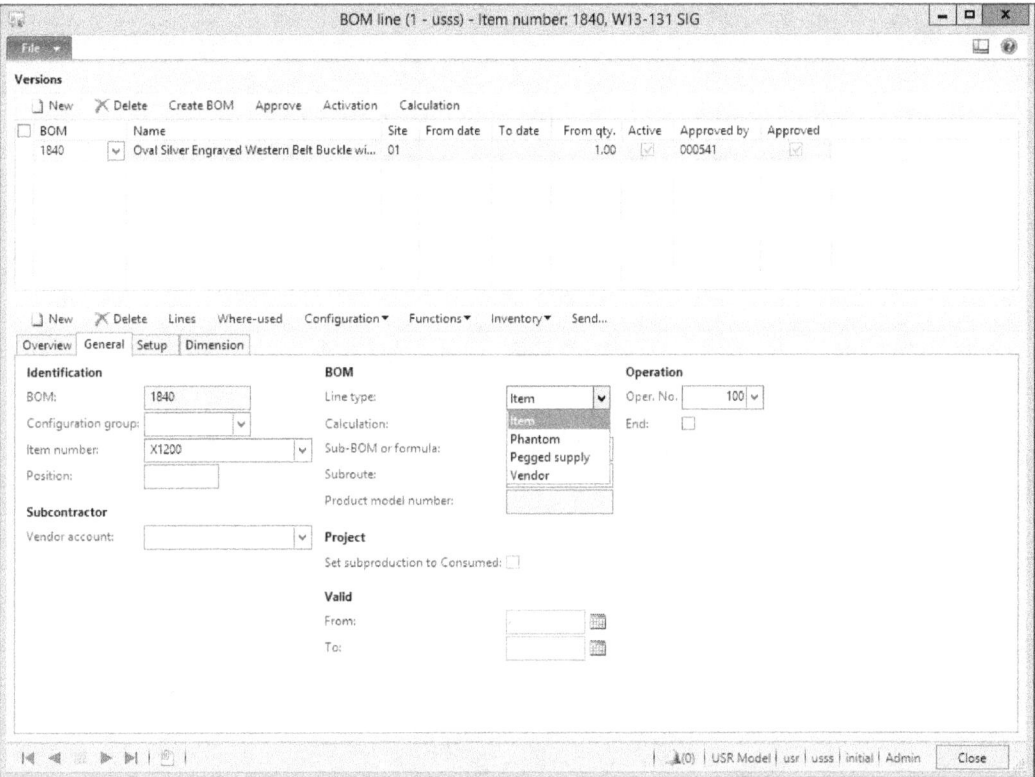

Key Features

- Route Lines can be in-house, or sub-contracted

- Built in analytics for reporting Route efficiency

- Purchase Orders automatically generated for sub-contracted jobs

- Shipments automatically scheduled for sub-contracting operations

Engineering Management
Subcontracting Resources

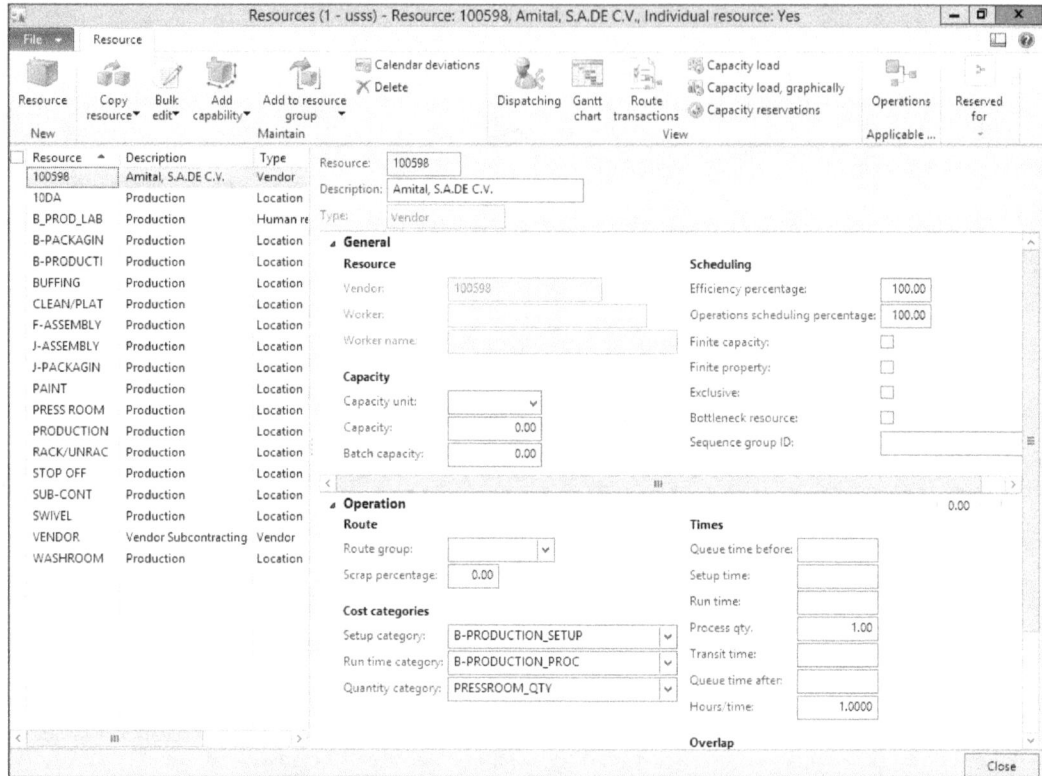

Key Features

- Subcontractors defined as resourced

- Capacity planning and scheduling of sub-contracting steps

Costing
Product Cost Calculation

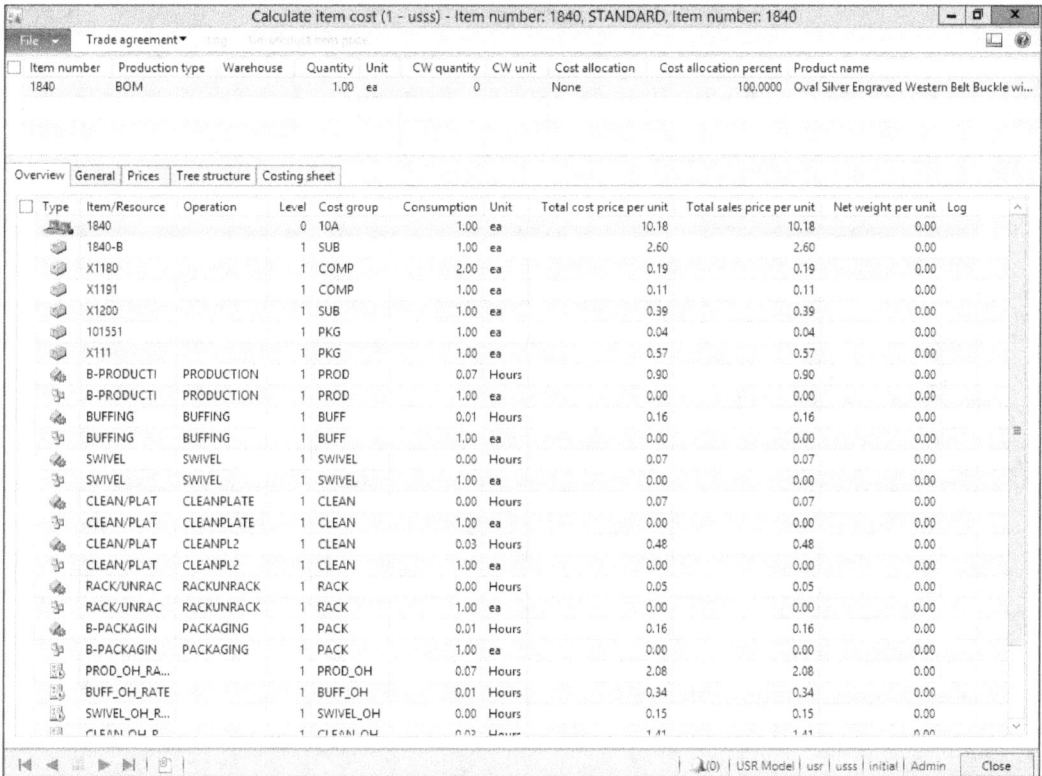

Key Features

- No limit to cost categories tracked

- Multiple work center costs and overheads

- Costs rolled up into cost categories

Costing
Labor & Overhead Costing

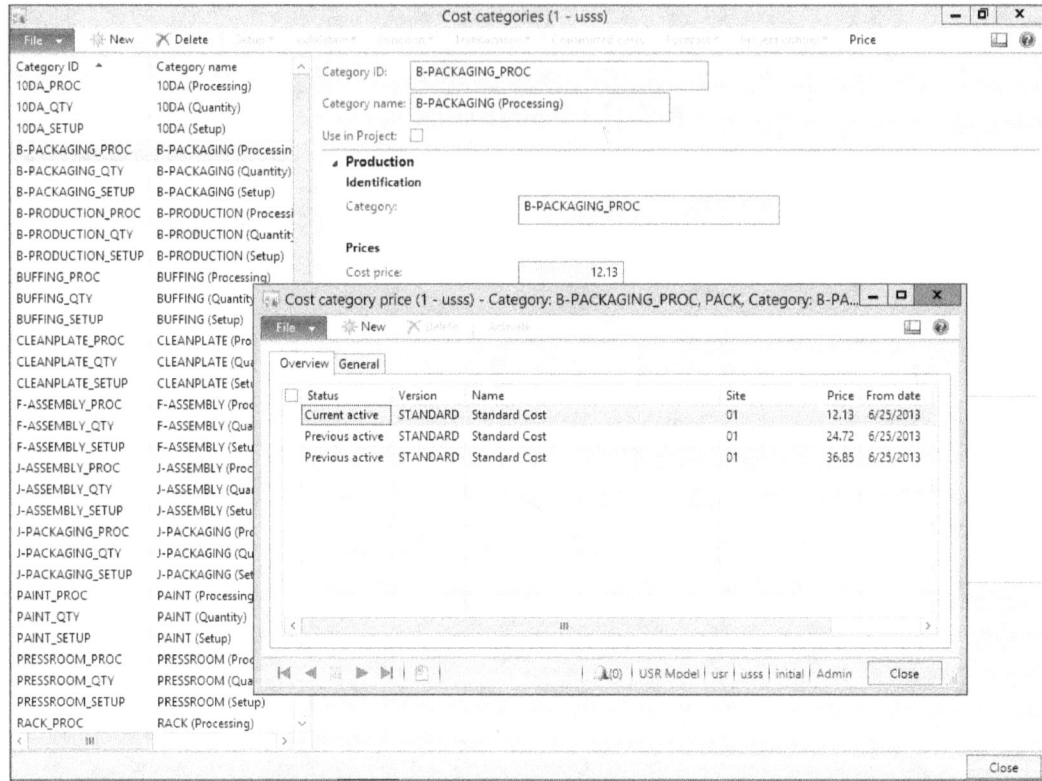

Key Features

- Labor costs tracked by work center

- Multiple costing versions supported

- Multiple labor costs with effectivity dates

Costing
Cost Sheet Configuration

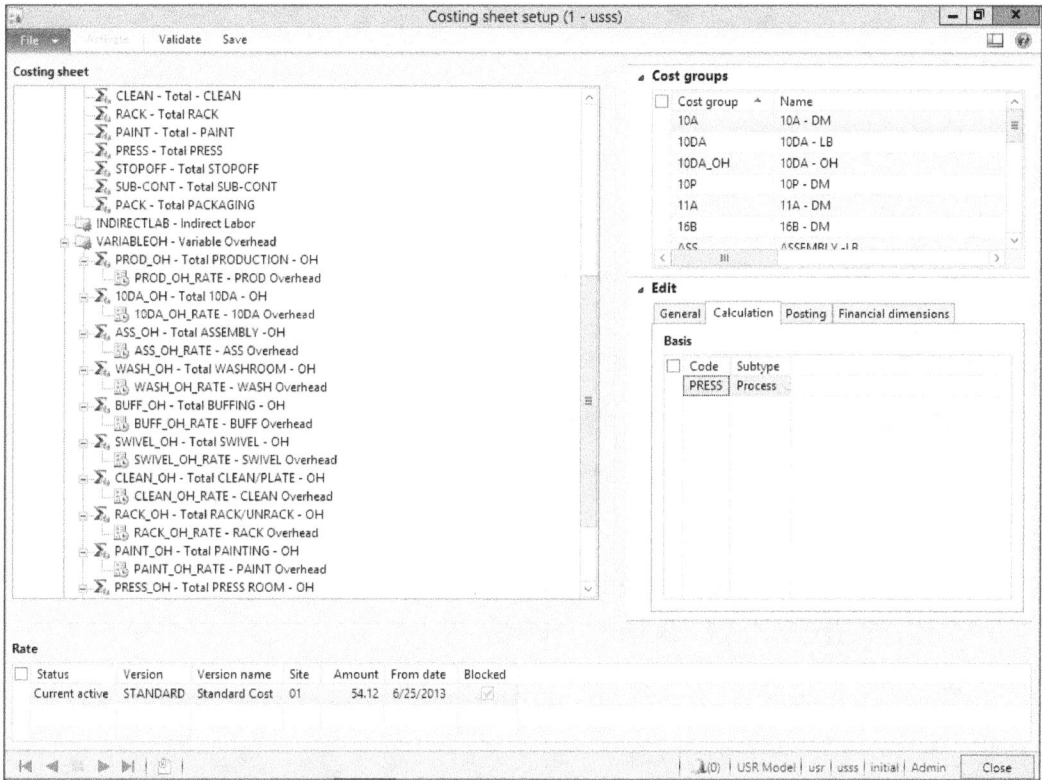

Key Features

- Overhead surcharges calculated by time and unit

- Surcharges linked to Route Steps

Costing
Cost Sheets

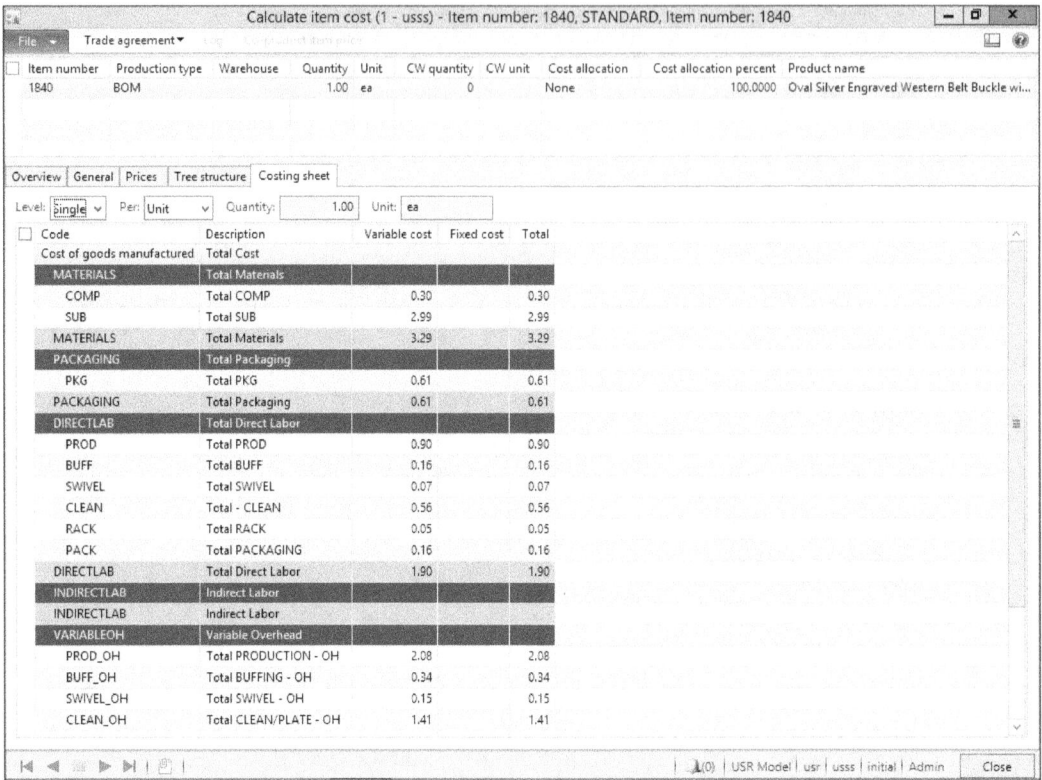

Key Features

- Single and Multi-level roll ups for costs

- User defined Costing Sheet for Analysis

Production Management
Production Scheduling

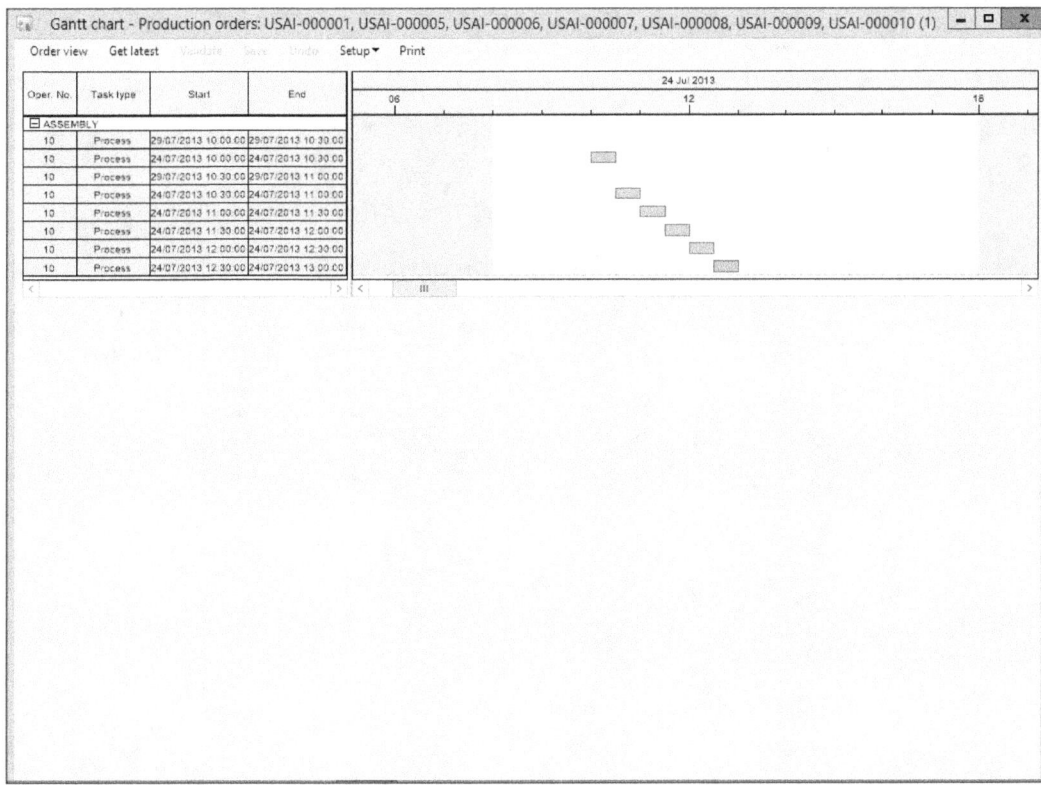

Key Features

- Graphical Scheduling

- Drag and drop rescheduling

- Thumbnail view of scheduling World View

- Can toggle between work center and order view

Production Management
Job Execution

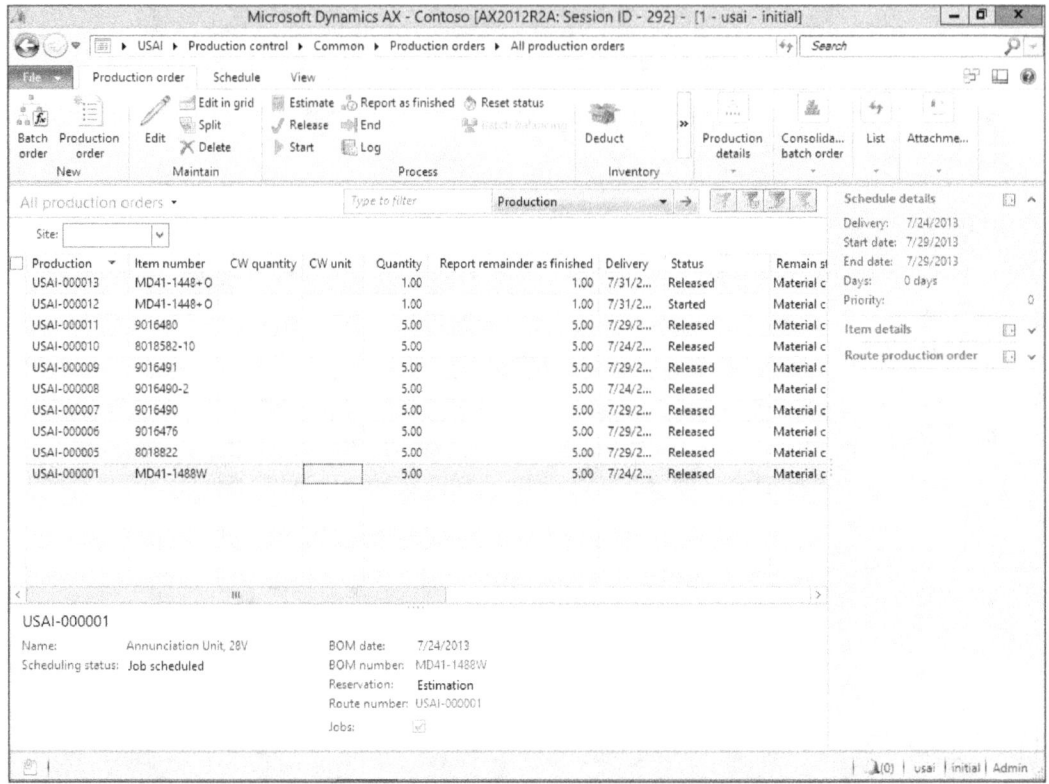

Key Features

- Multiple release statuses for production orders

- Capacity planning on Jobs

- Job-BOM and Job-Routes allow for changes to running jobs

Production Management
Labor Tracking

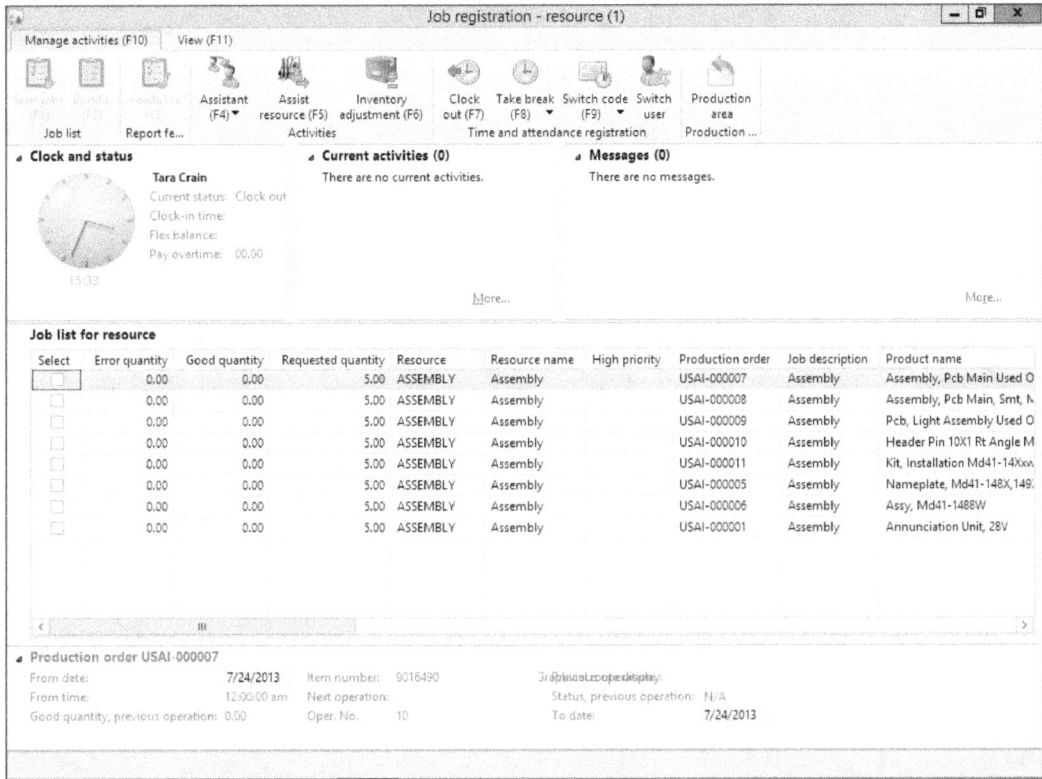

Key Features

- Job Registration touchscreen for work center reporting

- View currently released jobs

- Worker Check In and Check Out

Production Management
Material Issues & Usage

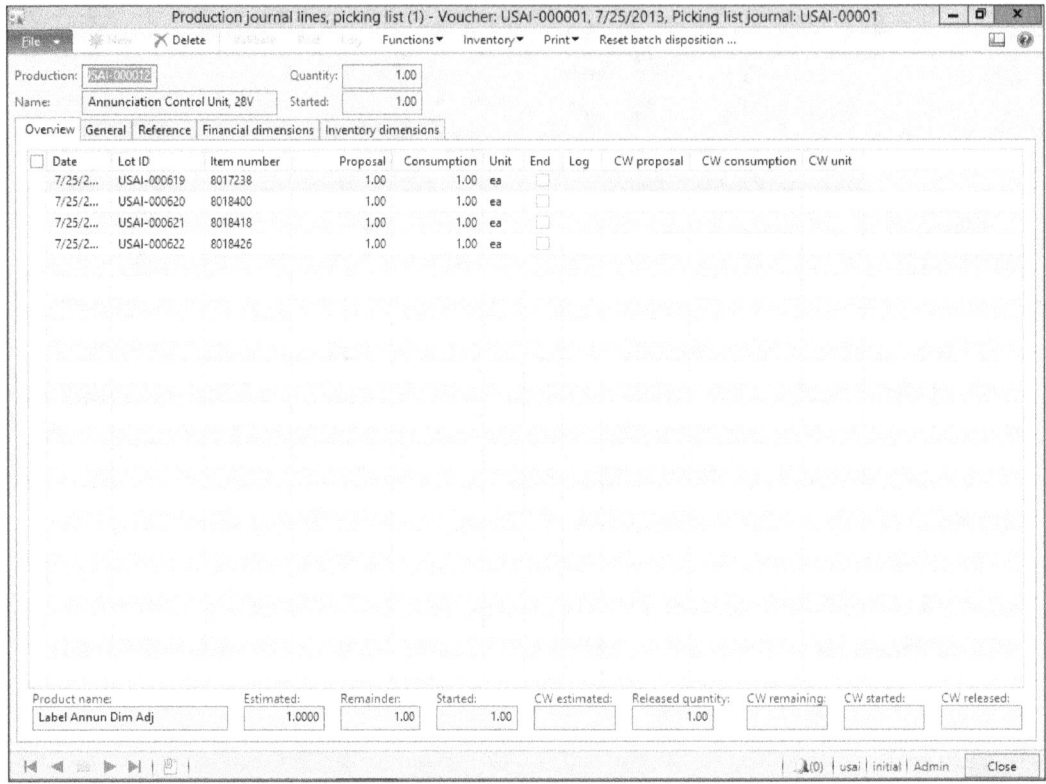

Key Features

- Pick List and Route Card access from Job Maintenance

- Actual issues and usage reporting

Production Management
Kanban Scheduling Board

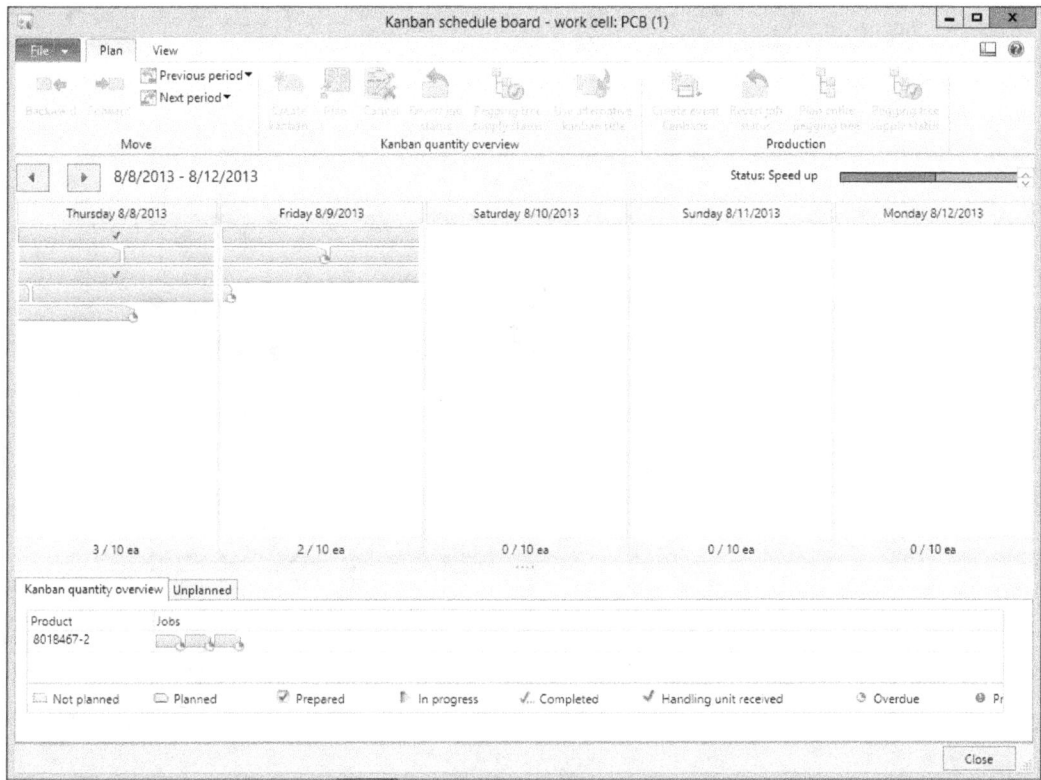

Key Features

- Schedule

- Capacity – Loaded/Total

- Kanban quantity Overview

- Cycle time performance indicator

- Job status symbols legend

- Lean schedule group: colors

Production Costing
Job Costing

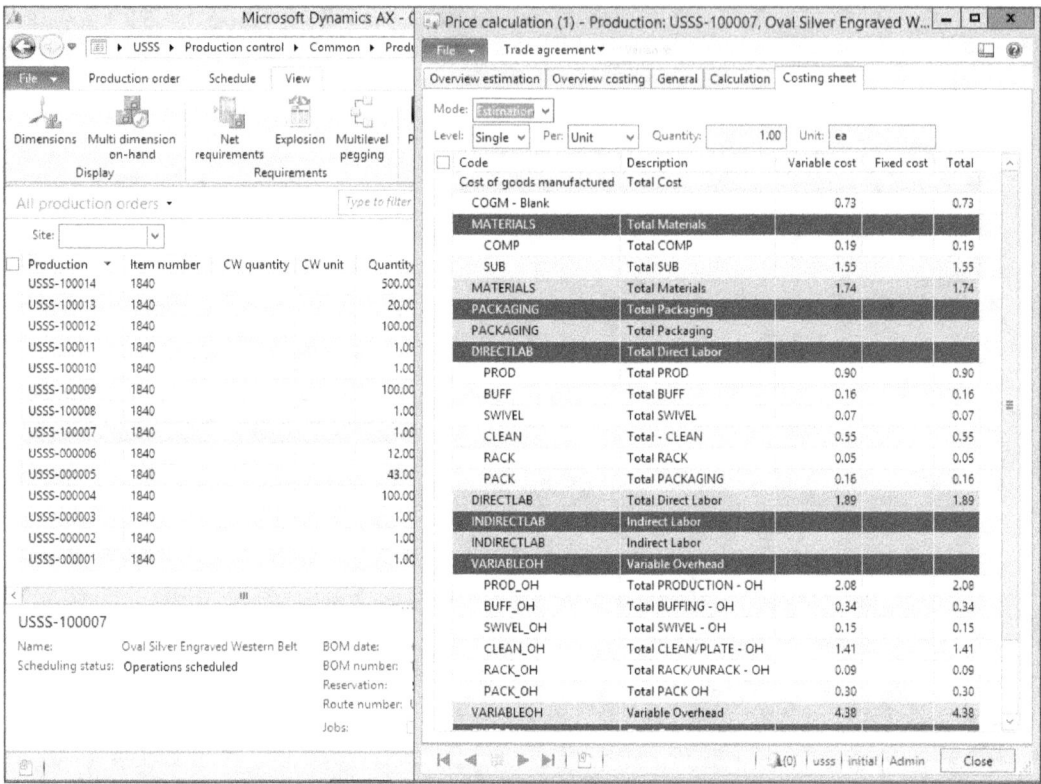

Key Features

- Costing Sheet provides job variance reporting at Cost Category level

Production Costing
Job Costing

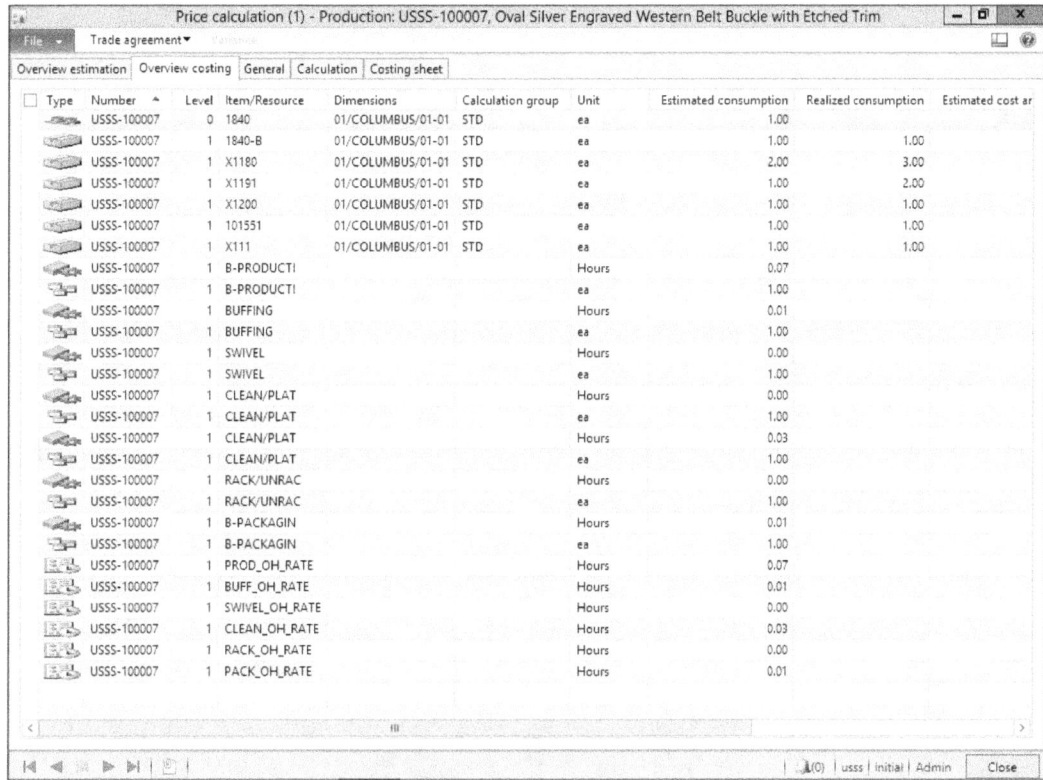

Key Features

- Detailed job cost variances by material, work center etc.

Planning & Forecasting

The Planning and Forecasting areas within Dynamics AX allow you to model your demand based for products by item, group, and also customer and then use the forecasts to create planned requirements and suggest replenishment and production. Once the master plans are created you can adjust the then firm up the plans with just a click of a button.

In this section we will show some of the planning and forecasting functions that are available within Dynamics AX,

Master Data Management
Inventory Policies

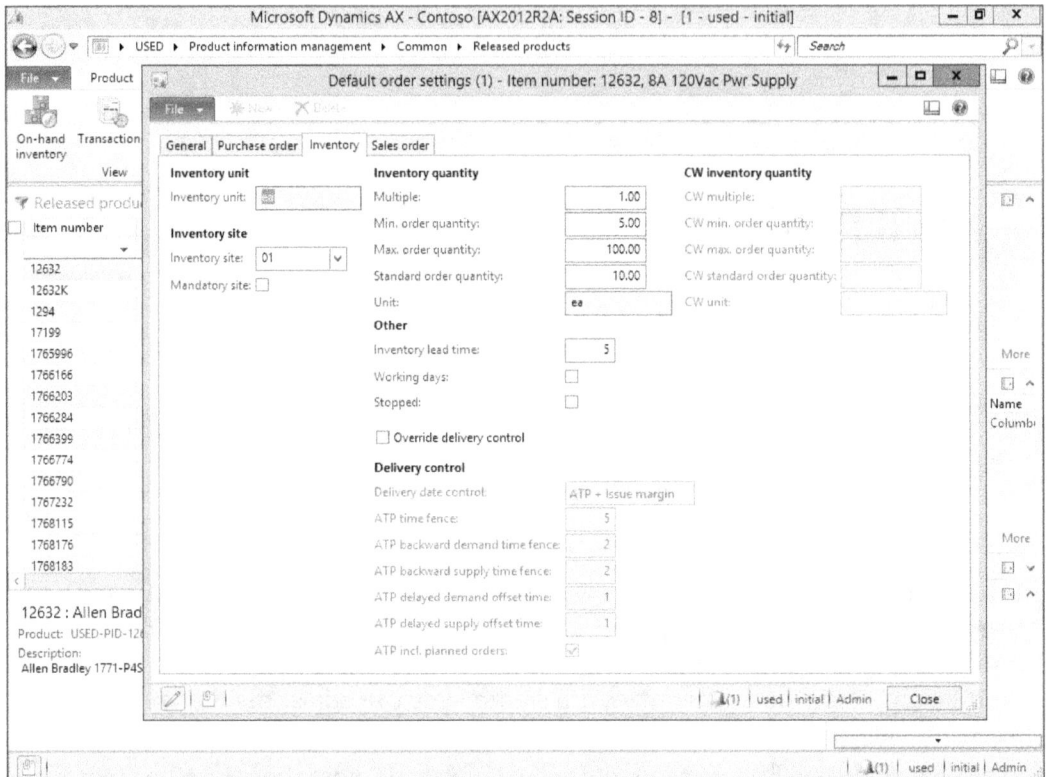

Key Features

- Inventory policies defined by product

Master Data Management
Safety Stock & Coverage Groups

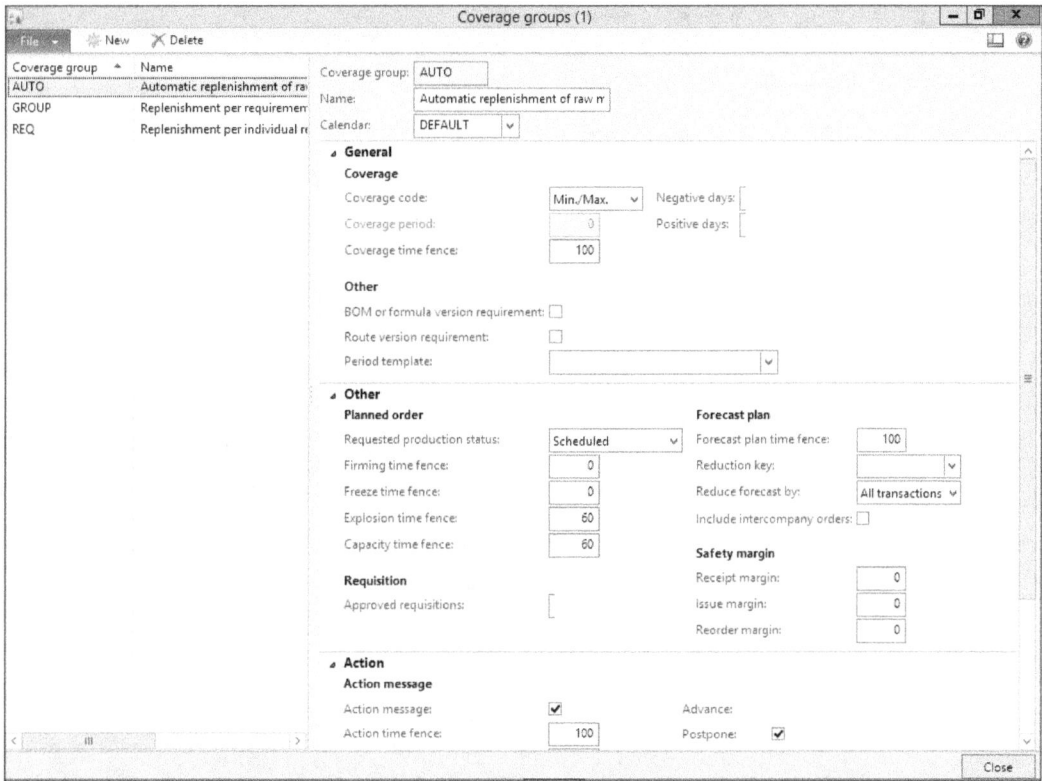

Key Features

- Min/Max & Period Coverage Groups

- Coverage groups by Product

Master Data Management
Calendars

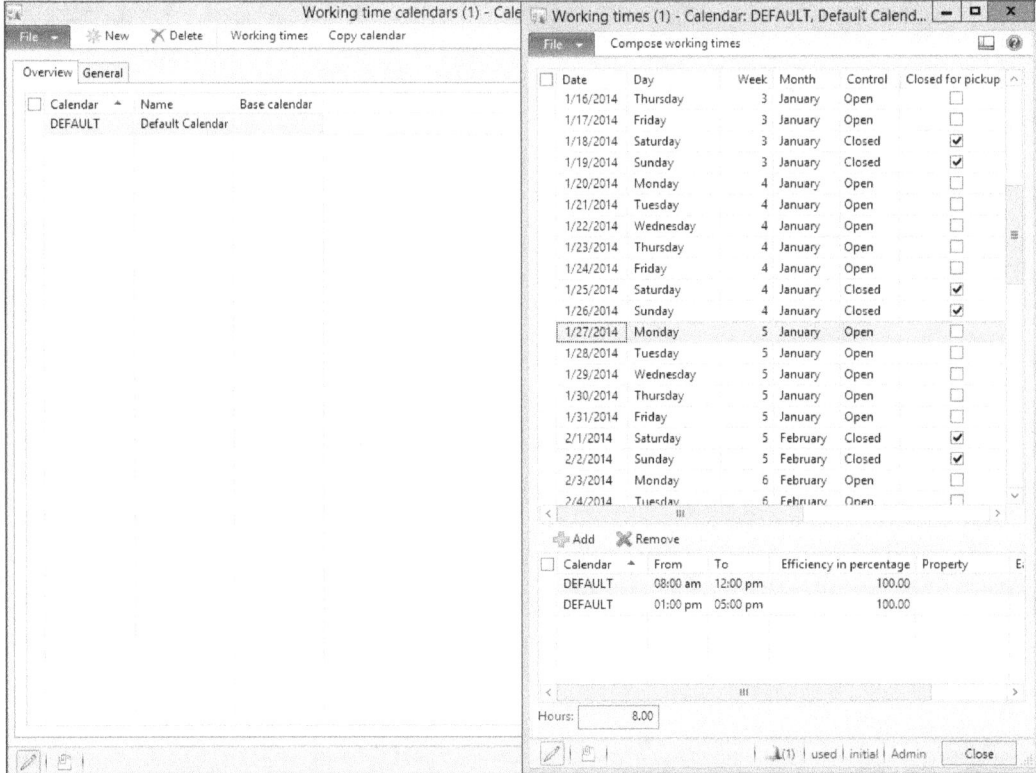

Key Features

- Multiple calendars defined

- Calendars inherited from base calendars

- Closed days

- Working times defined by calendar day

Master Data Management
Refilling Warehouses

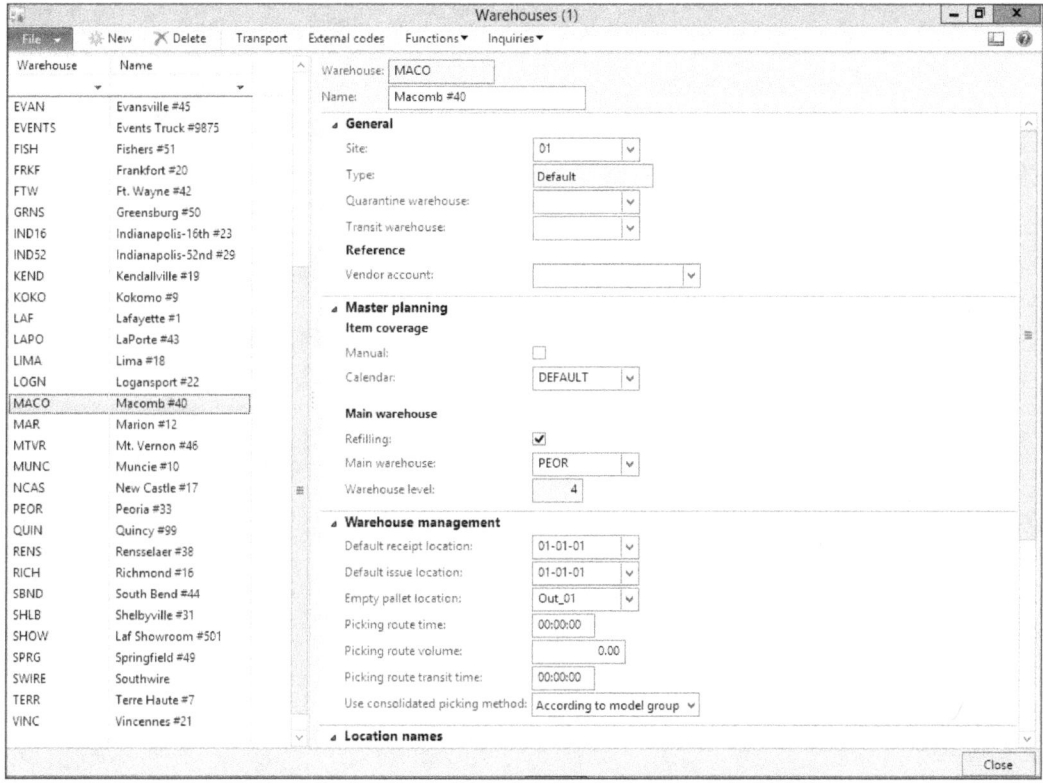

Forecast Management
Forecast Entry

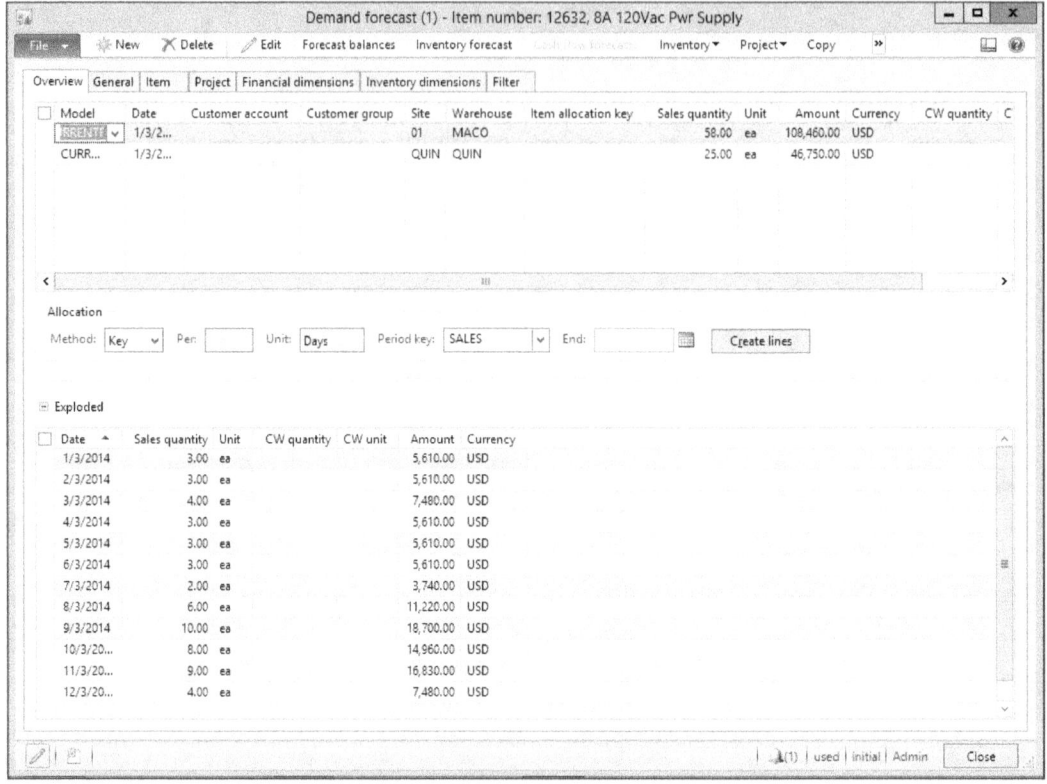

Master Planning
Suggested Requirements

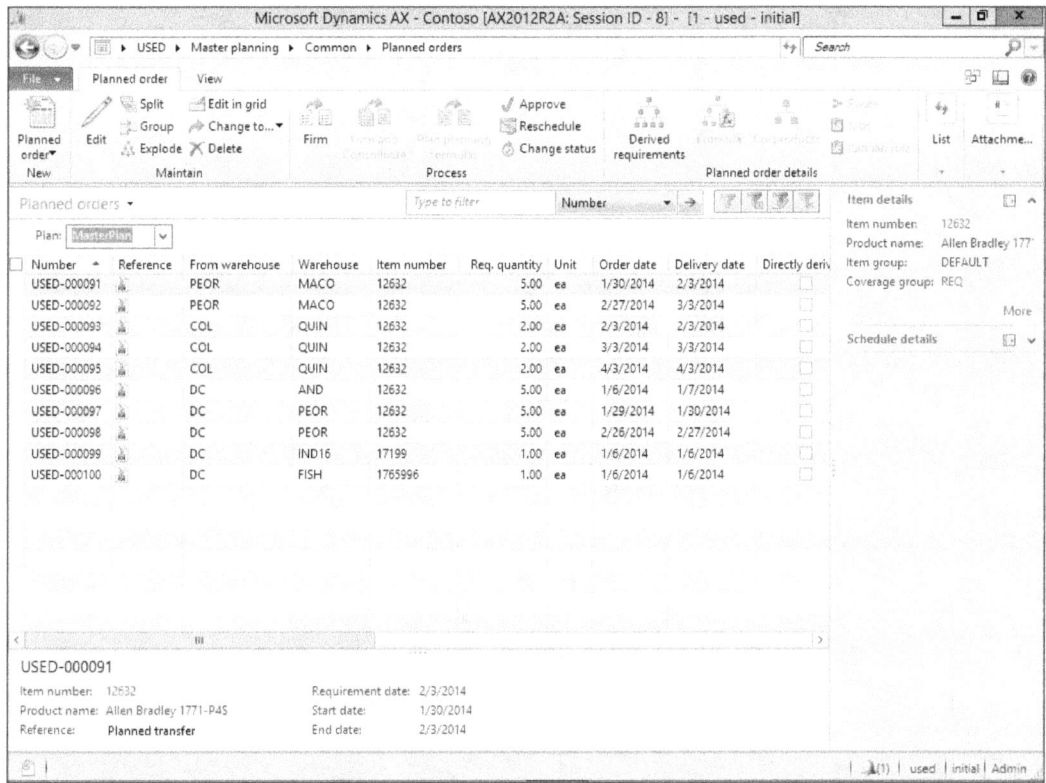

Key Features

- Multiple forecast Plans

- Suggested Purchase Orders Based On Live Sales

- Firm up suggestions to live purchases and jobs

- Split/Group suggestions

Master Planning
Supply Schedule

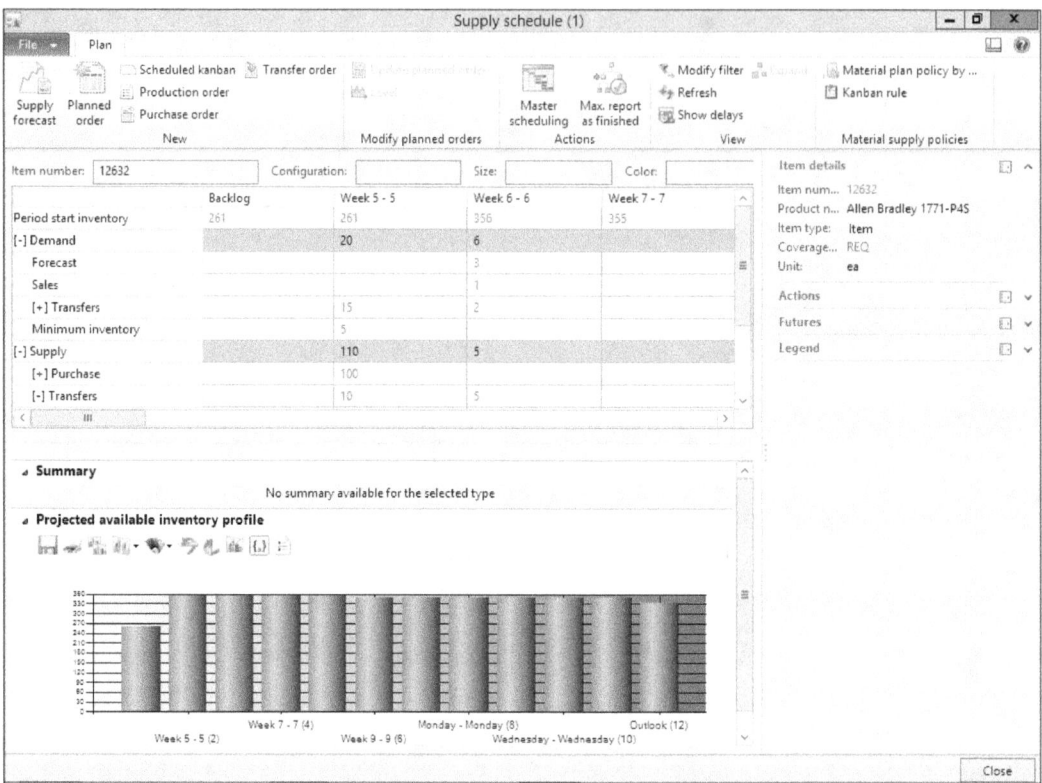

Key Features

- Period Based Inventory Overview

INTRODUCTION TO DYNAMICS AX

289

Procure To Pay

The Procure to Pay process within Dynamics AX includes functions from areas including the Purchasing, and Accounts Payable modules, and includes capabilities such as Requisitioning, Bid Management, Purchase Orders, Invoice and Payment.

Additional features that are included in the Procure To Pay features are Vendor Onboarding, and also Vendor Rating, allowing you to manage the entire lifecycle of the Vendors.

In this section we will show some of the key areas within the Procure To Pay Process.

Master Data Management
Vendor Details

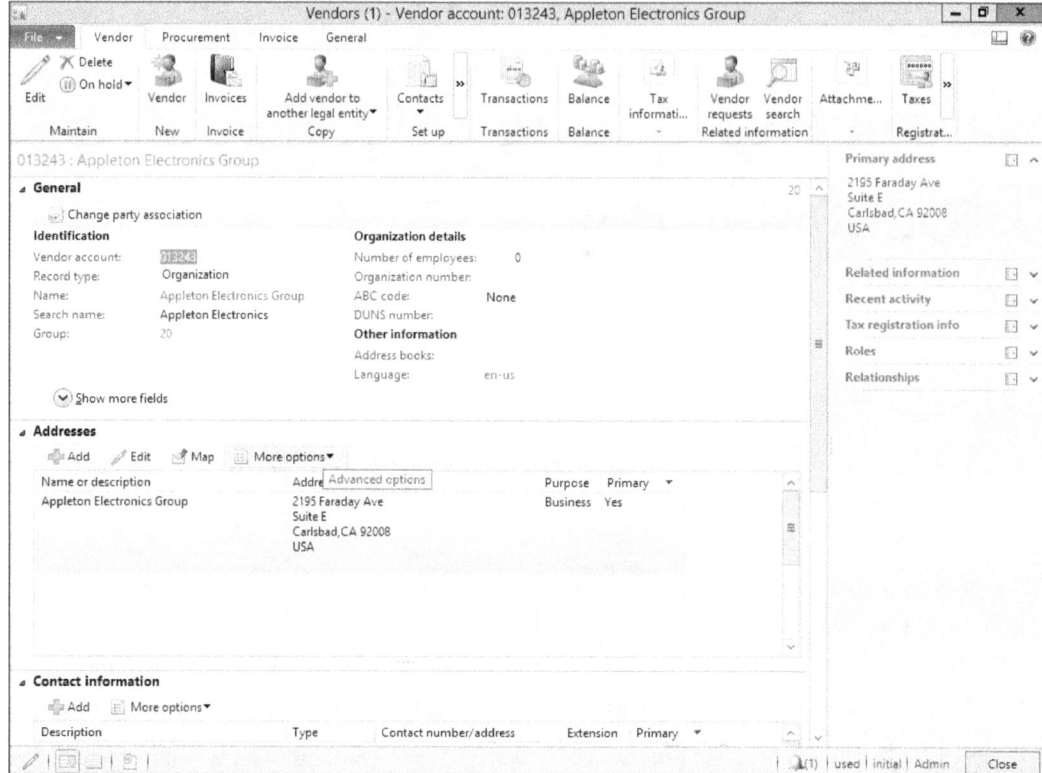

Key Features

- Vendor contact information

- Vendor contact information such as email, URL, fax, phone

- Multiple addresses

- Contact Management

Requisition Management
Online Requisition Submission

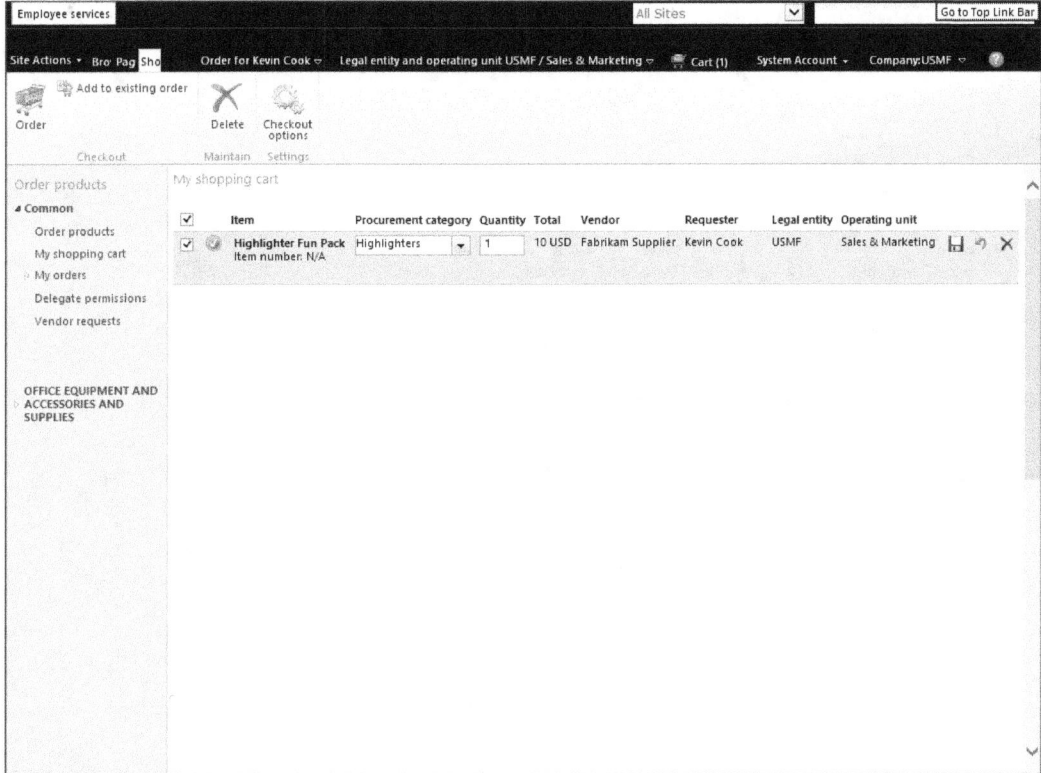

Key Features

- Requisition created through Employee Self Service Portal

Requisition Management
Requisitions

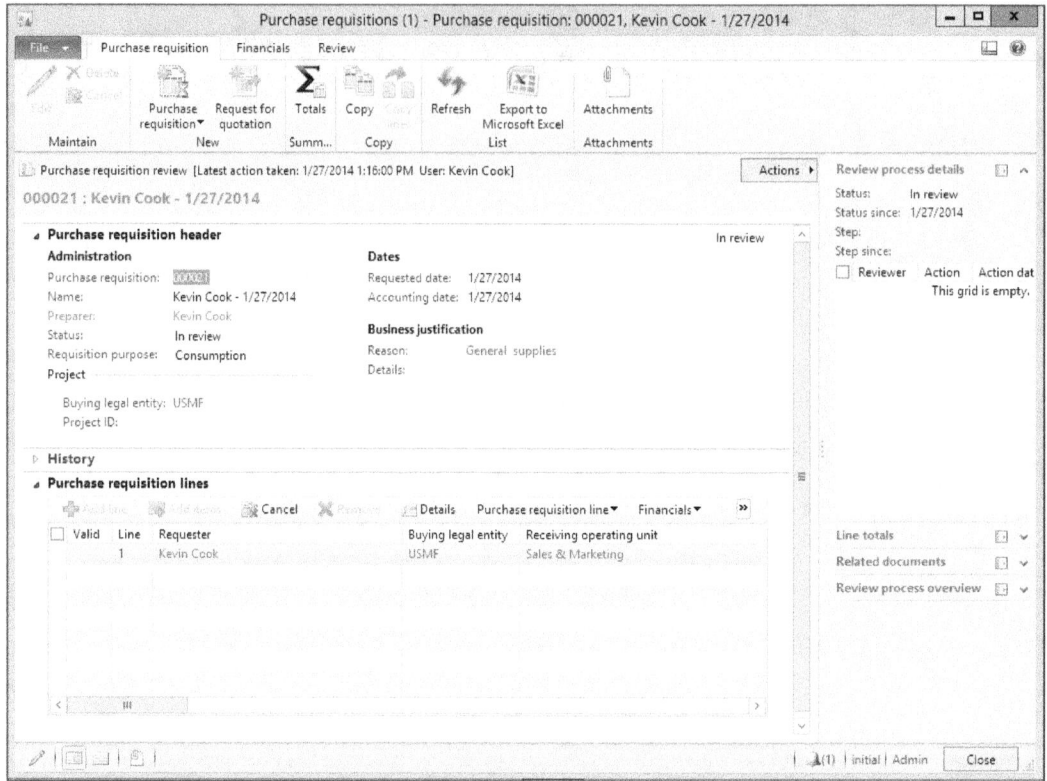

Key Features

- Requisitions generated through Rich Client

Requisition Management
Requisition Approval Workflow

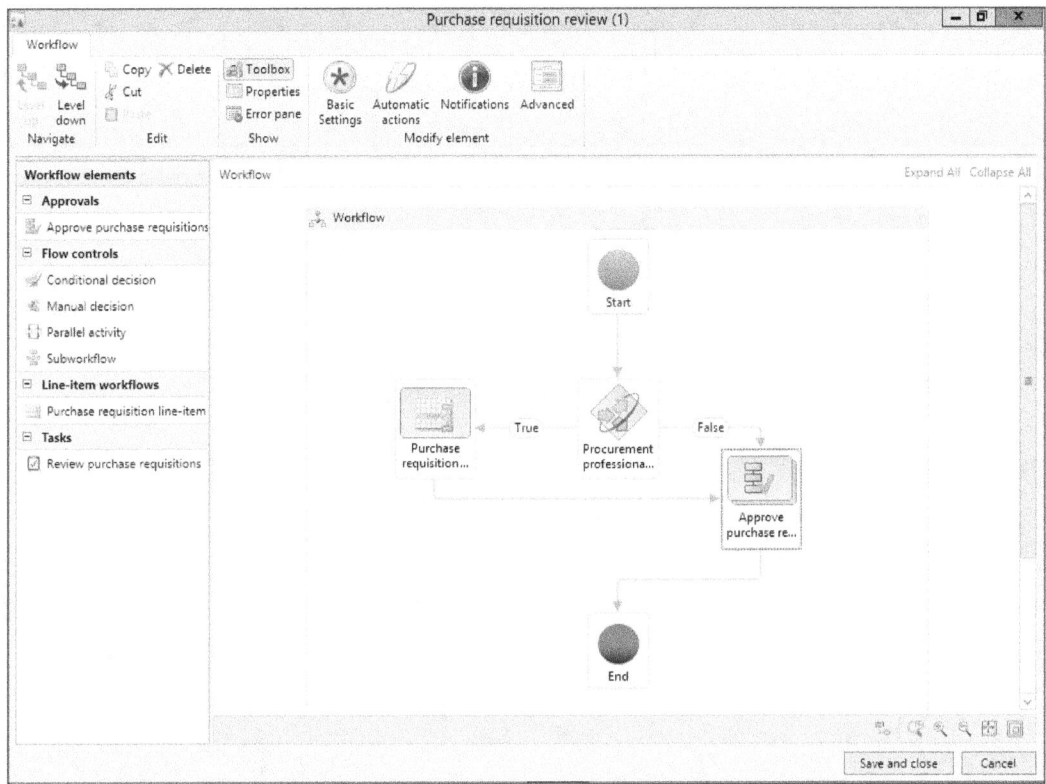

Bid Management
Request For Quotation Management

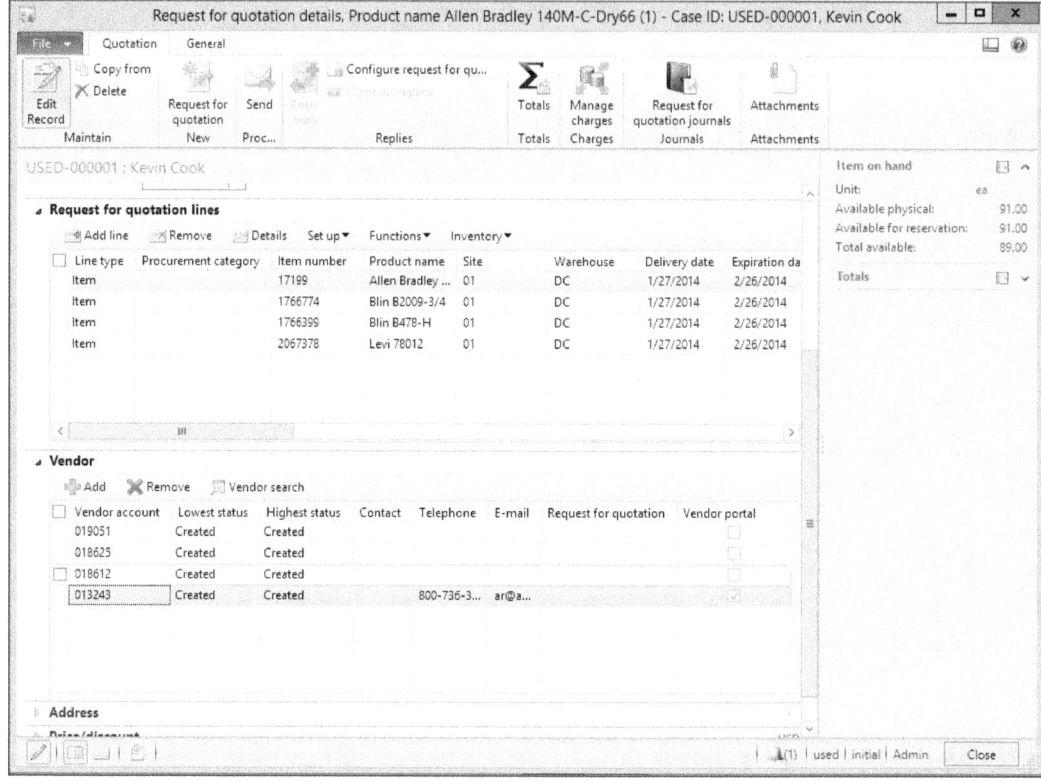

Bid Management
Online Vendor Response

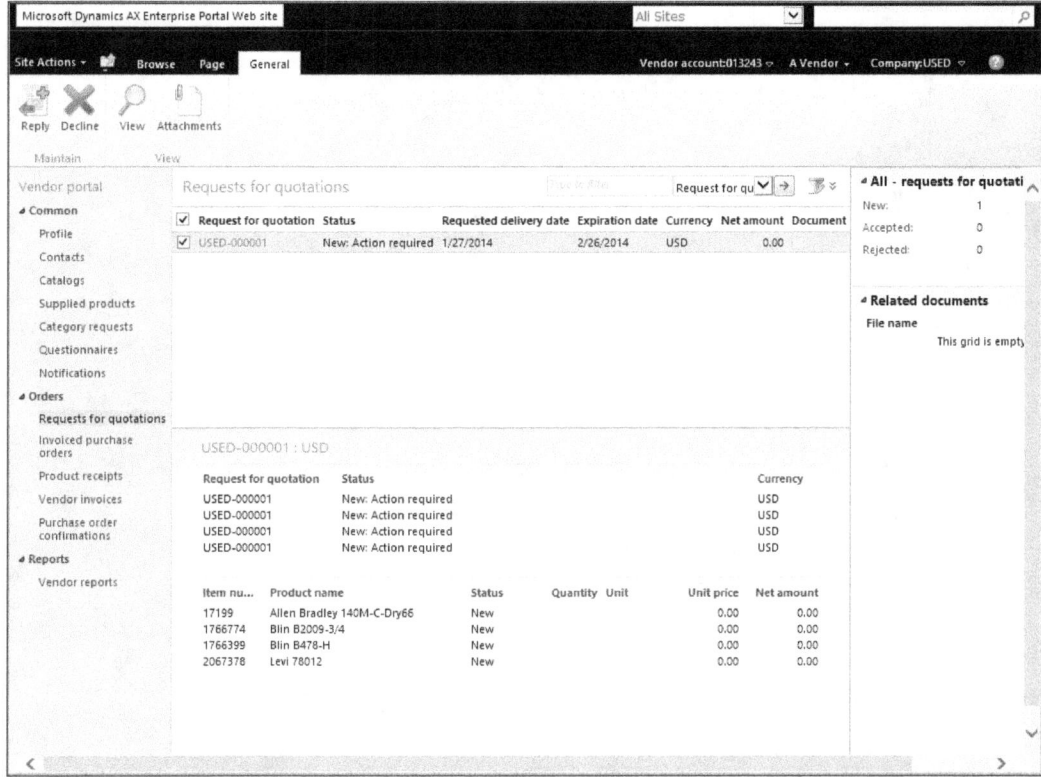

Purchase Order Management
Purchase Orders Creation

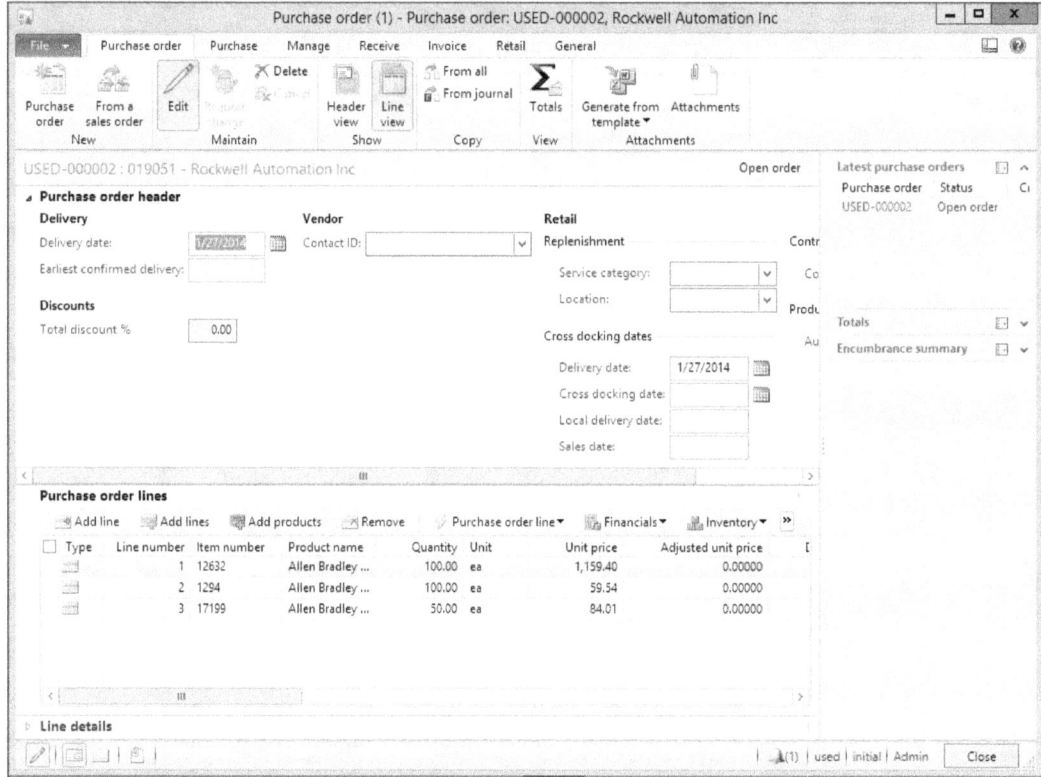

Key Features

- Inventoried and Non-inventoried purchases

- Multiple dates associated with PO

- Automatic pricing from pricing agreements

Purchase Order Management
Purchase Orders Creation

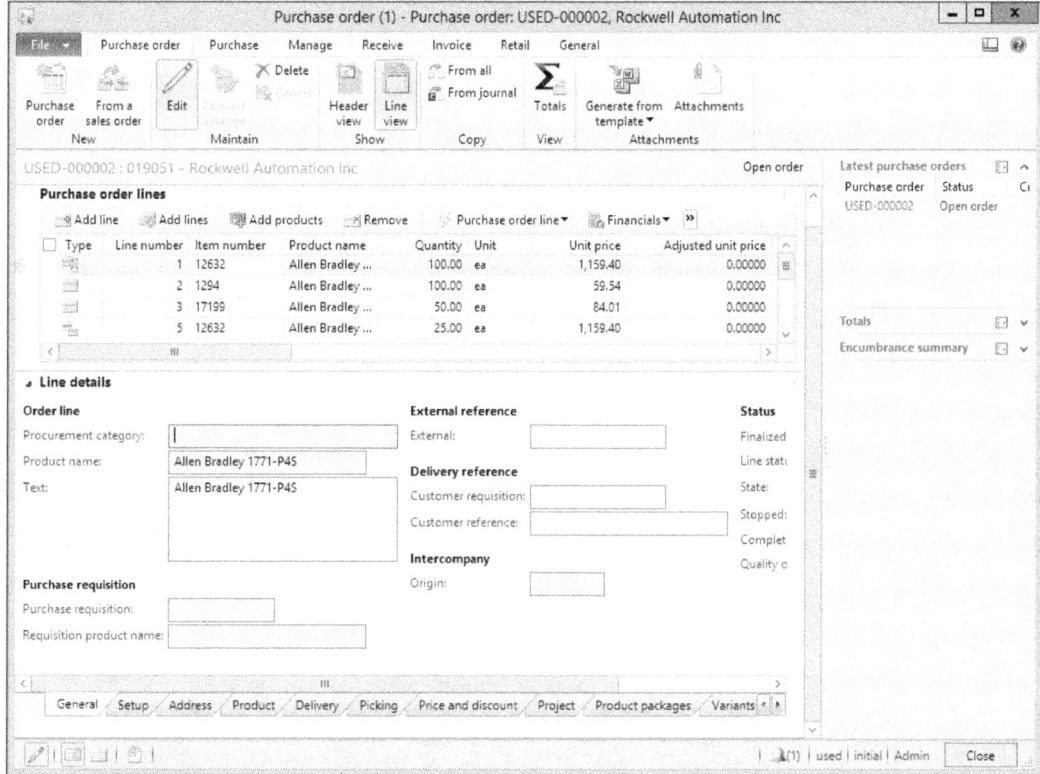

Key Features

- Detailed product description

Purchase Order Management
Blanket Orders

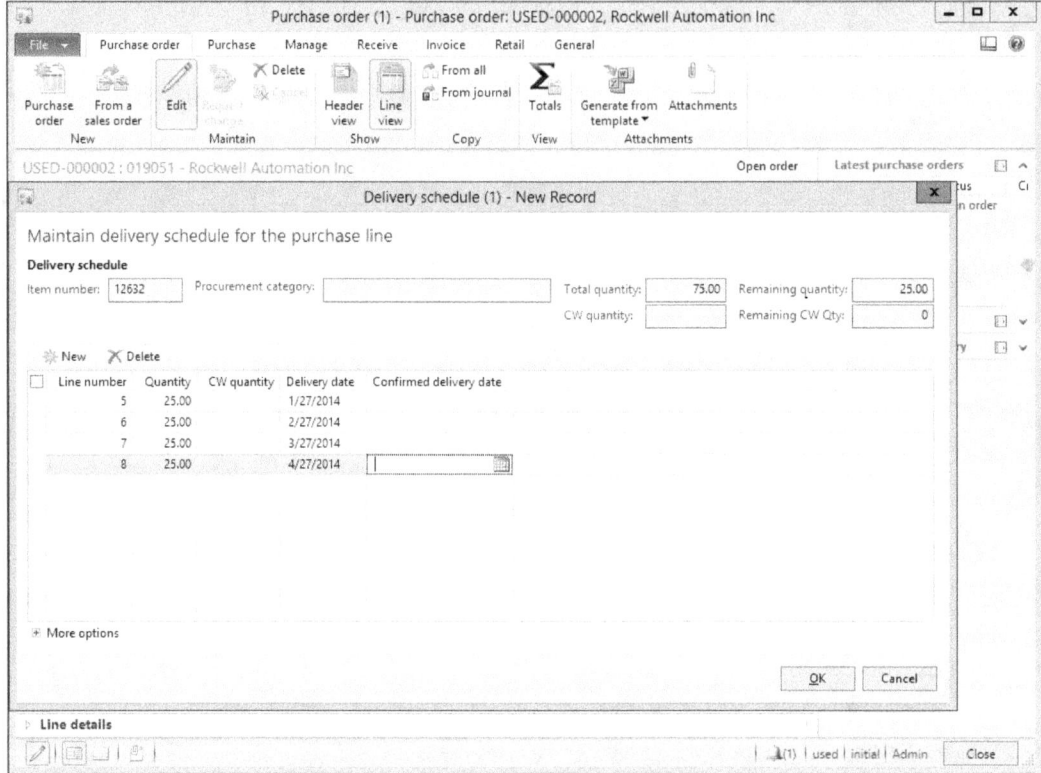

Key Features

- Multiple release dates by line

Receiving
Receipt Tracking

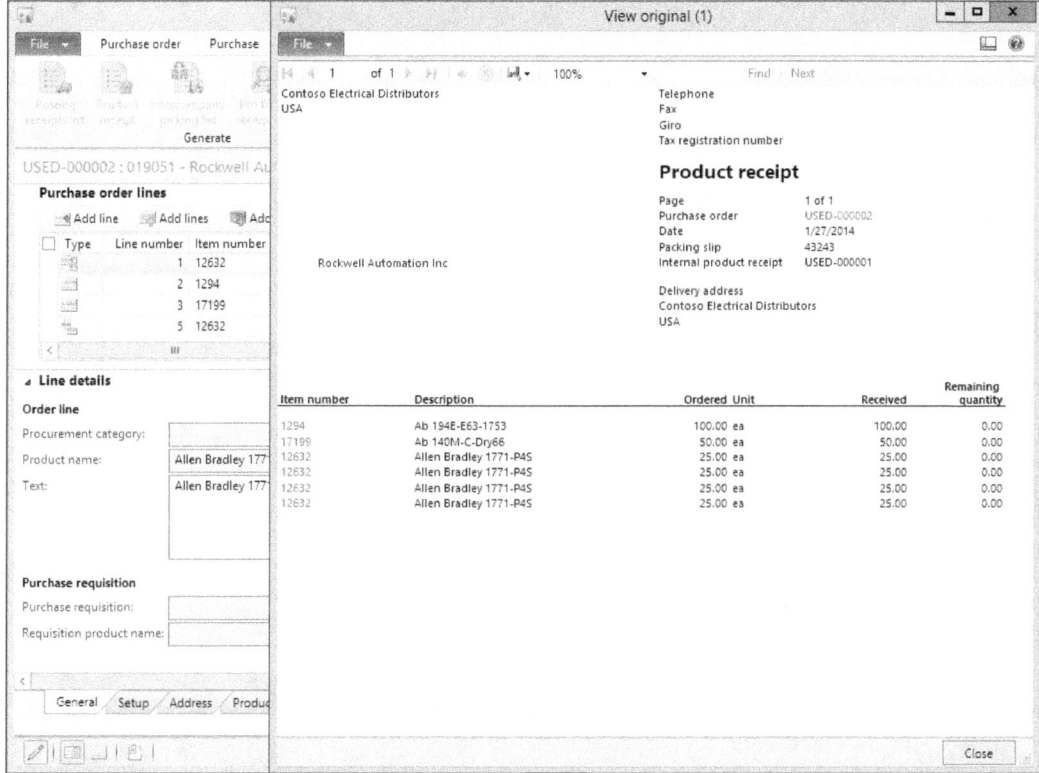

Key Features

- Receipts List Generation

- Quantity confirmation and adjustment at receipt

- Purchase Order History fact boxes

Receiving
Freight Tracking

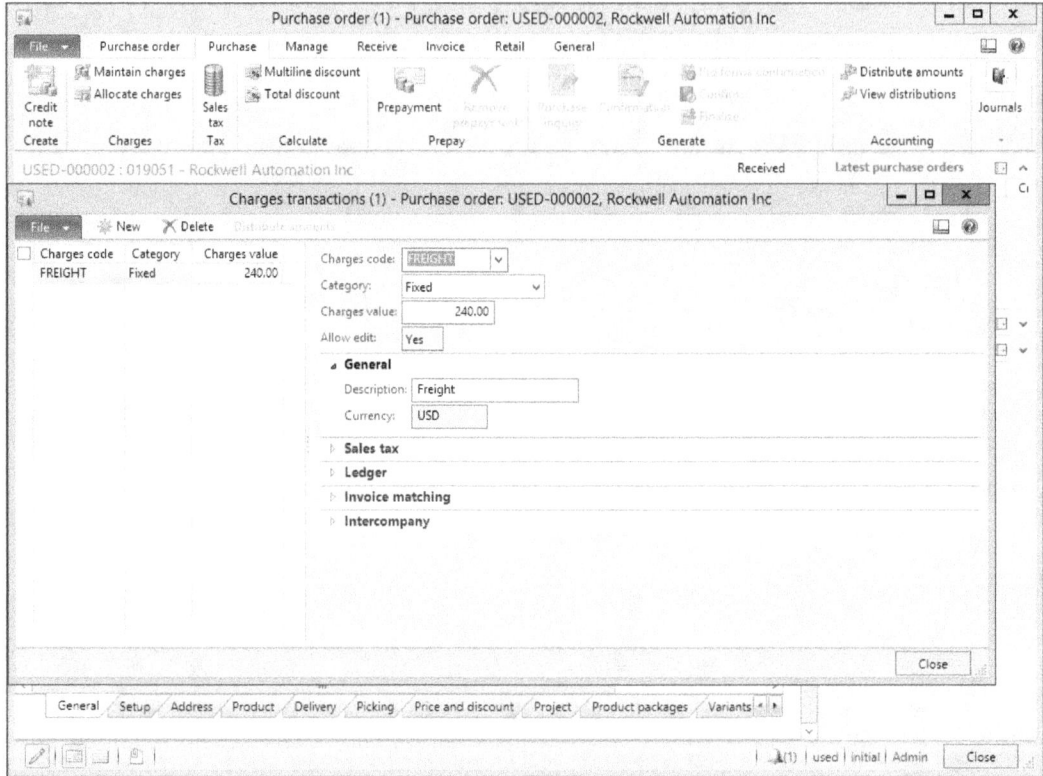

Key Features

- Freight charges tracked against Purchase Orders

Receiving
Cross Docking

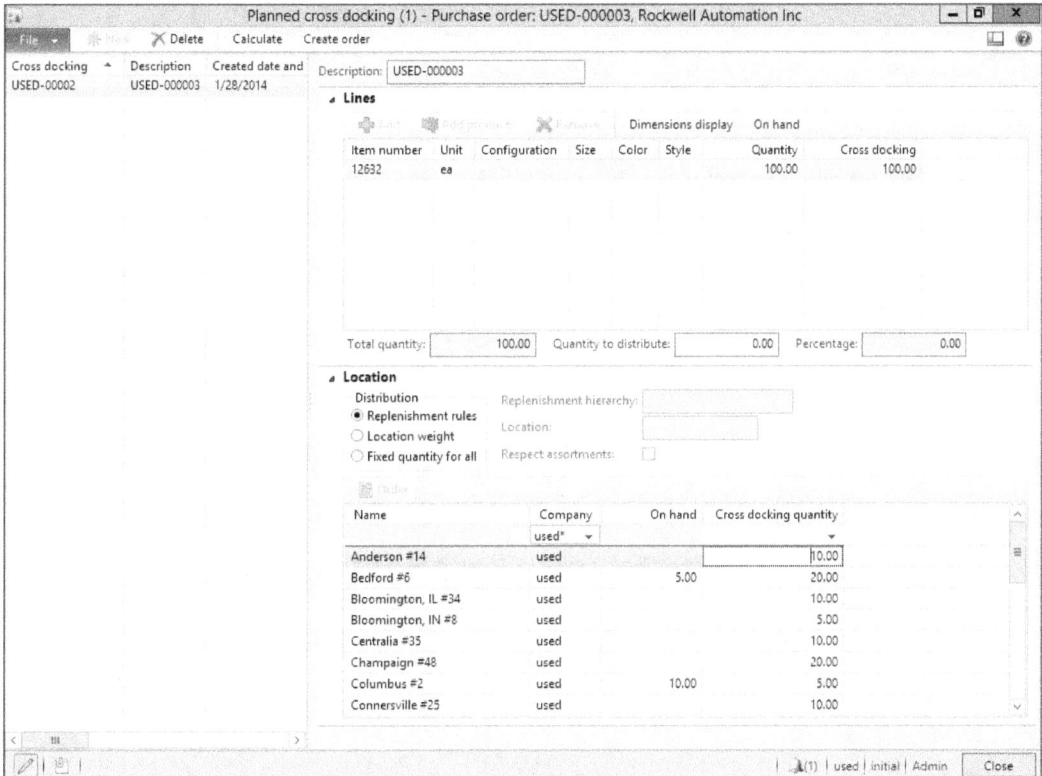

Key Features

* Allocation manually, by weight, or evenly

Payables Management
Invoice Matching

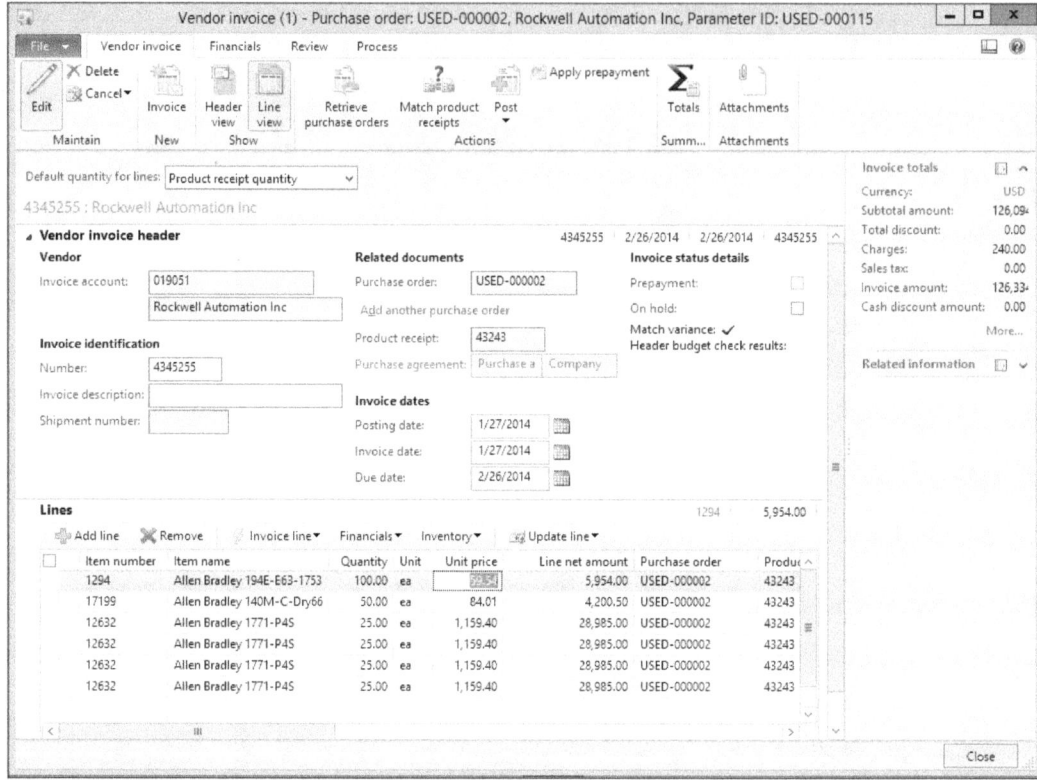

Key Features

- Two & three way matching policies with tolerances

- Invoice lines generated from actual receipt quantities

Payables Management
Invoice Matching Policies

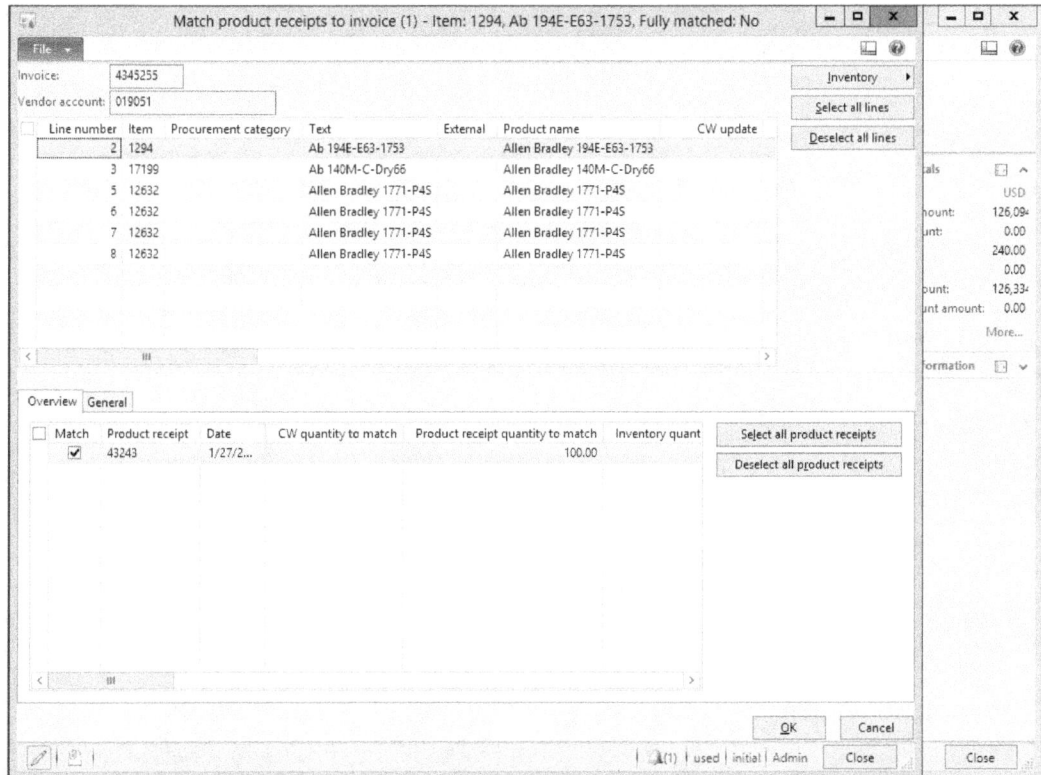

Key Features

- Matching policy violations listed & require approval

Payables Management
Payment Processing

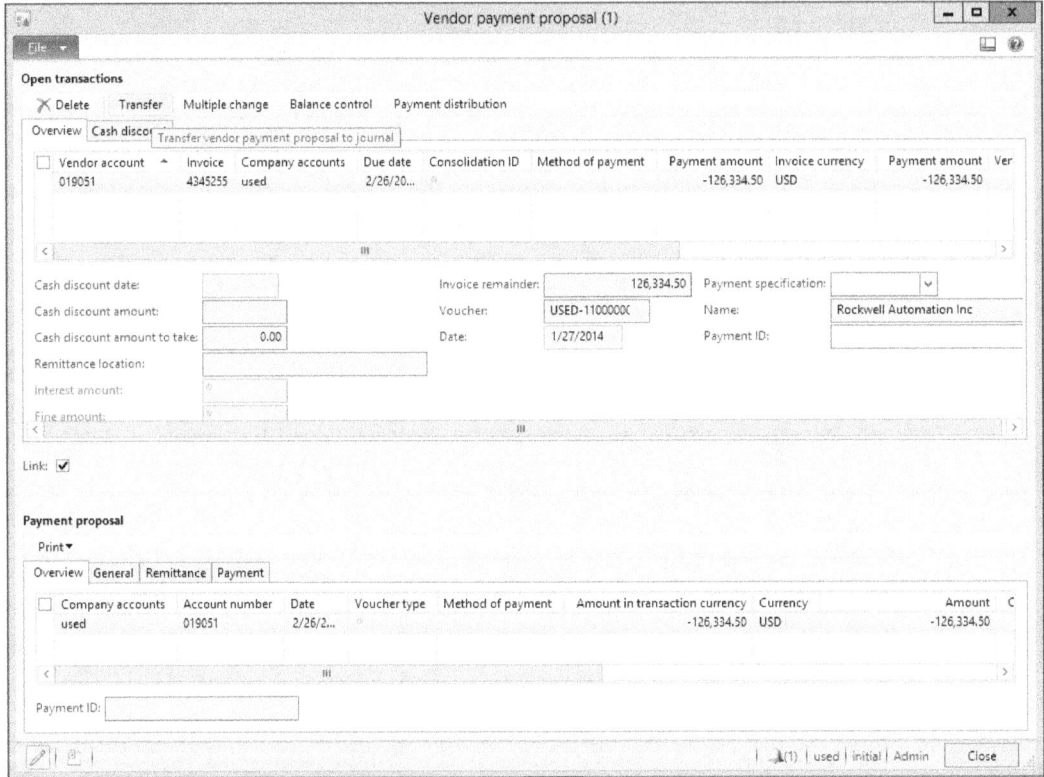

Key Features

- Balance control parameters

- Payment selection based on filter

Payables Management
Check Generation

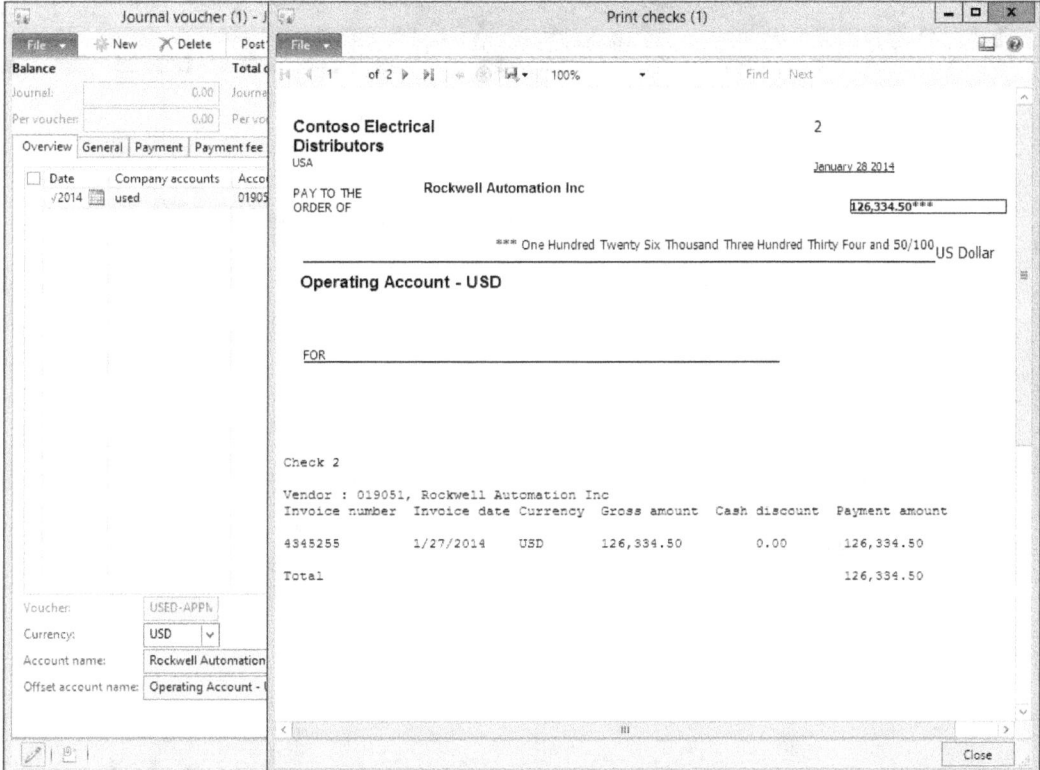

Key Features

- Check formats defined by bank

Portals
Vendor Self Service Portal

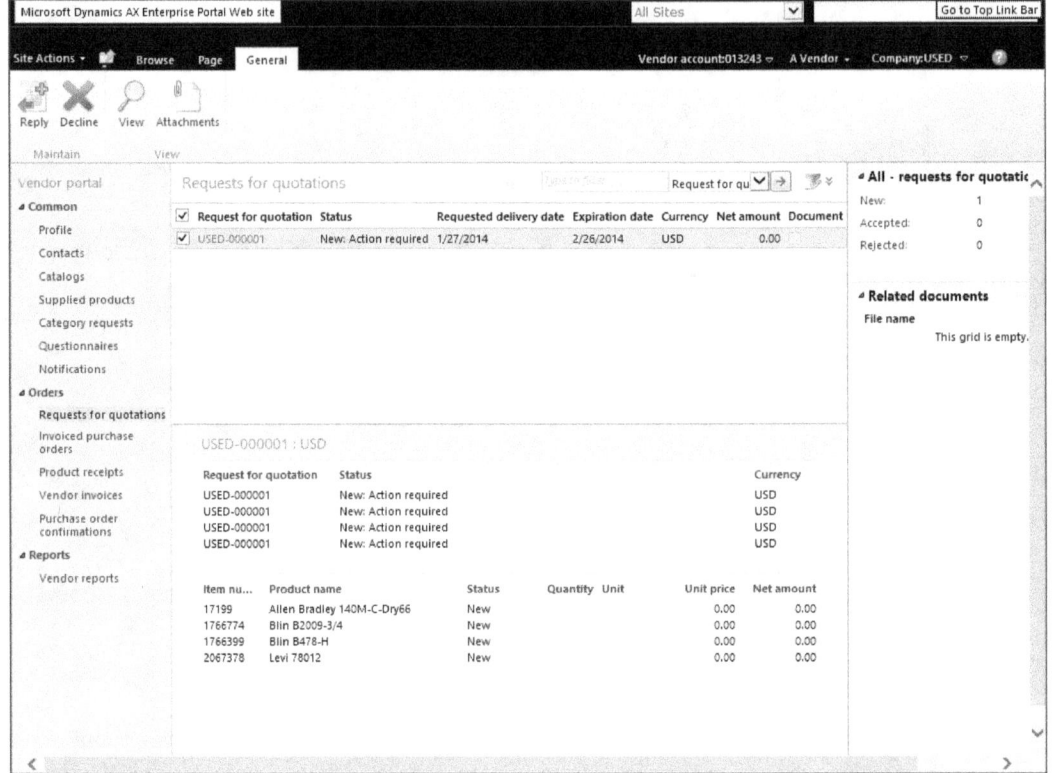

Portals
Procurement Portal

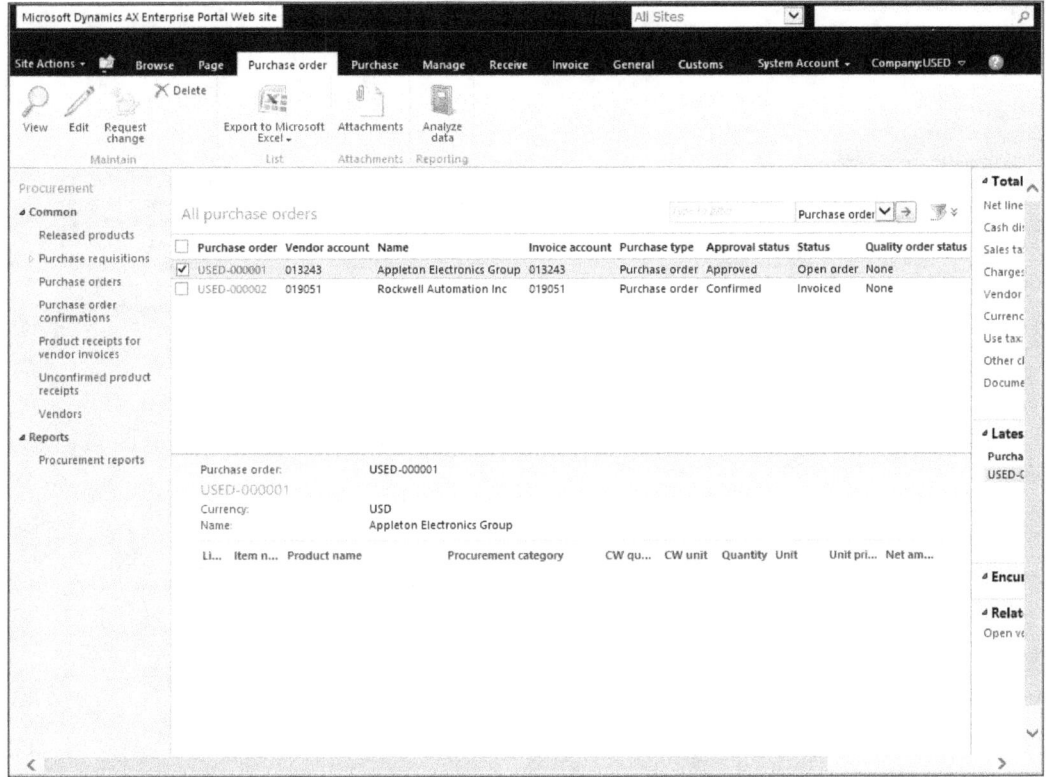

Reporting
Vendor Performance Criteria

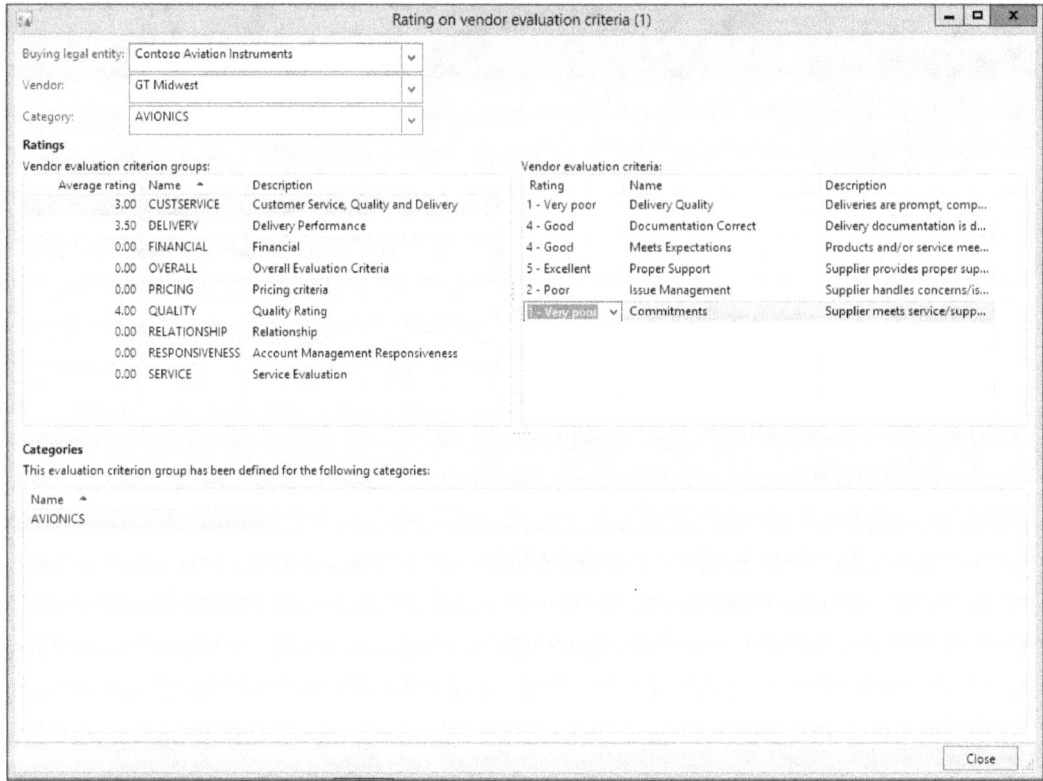

Project Management

Dynamics AX has an integrated Project Management module which is tied directly into the Employee time and expense reporting, and also the payables and receivables, and numerous other areas of the application.

There is also tight integration to Microsoft Project which allows for the maintenance of the projects to be done through a tool that is familiar to all of the project managers out there.

In this section we will show some of the capabilities of the Project Management module that makes it so useful.

Master Data Management
Project Configuration

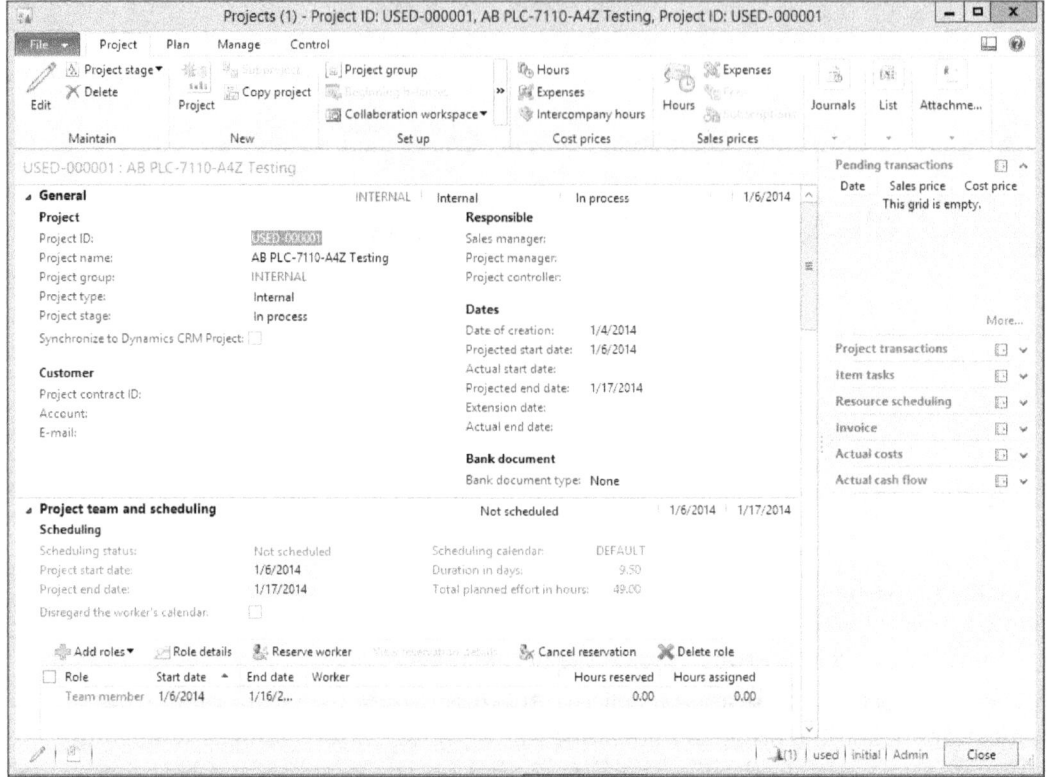

Project Planning
Work Breakdown Structure

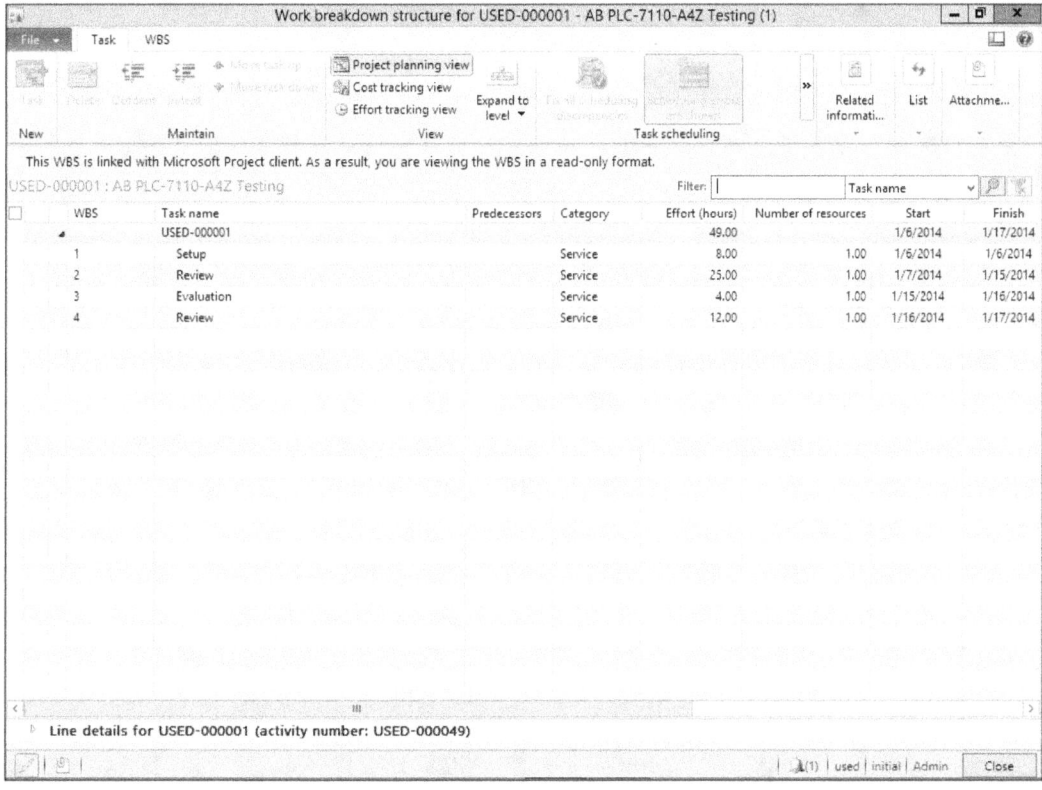

Project Planning
Microsoft Project Integration

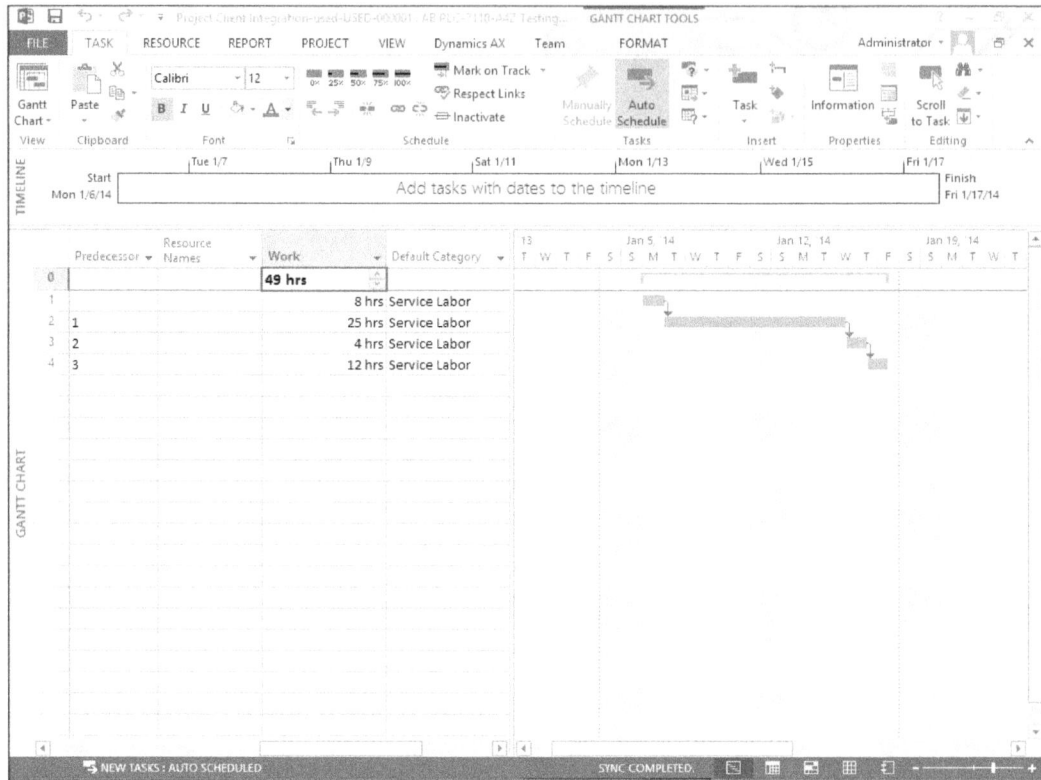

Project Planning
Time & Material Forecasting

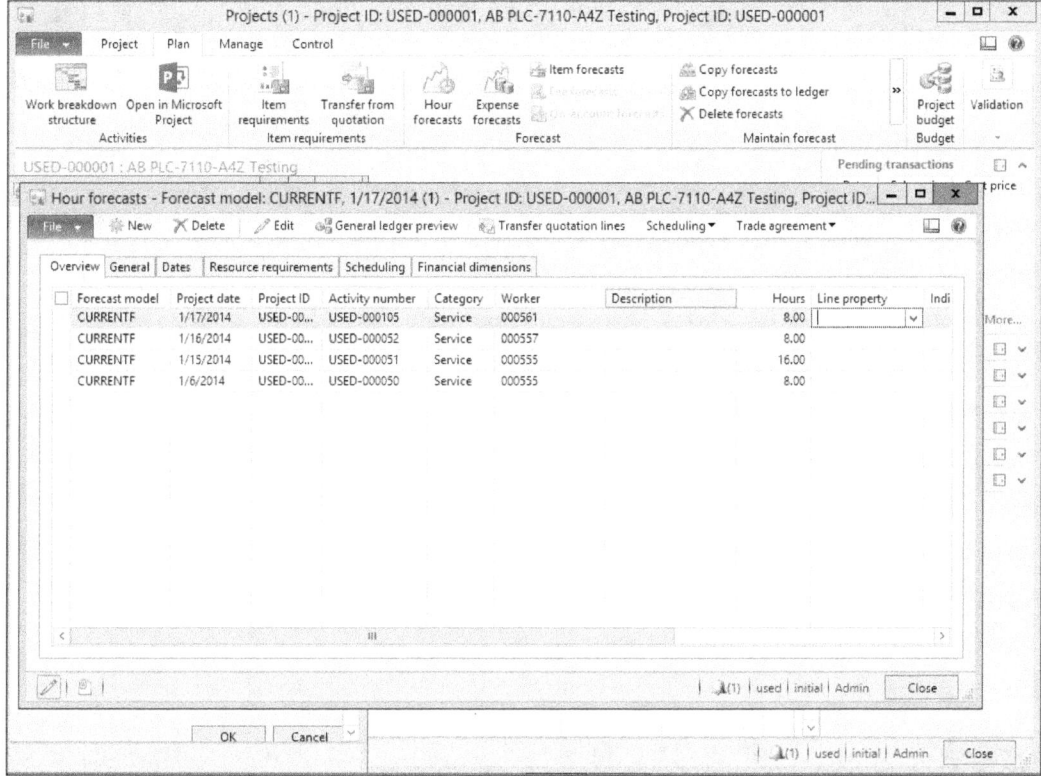

Project Planning
Effort Planning

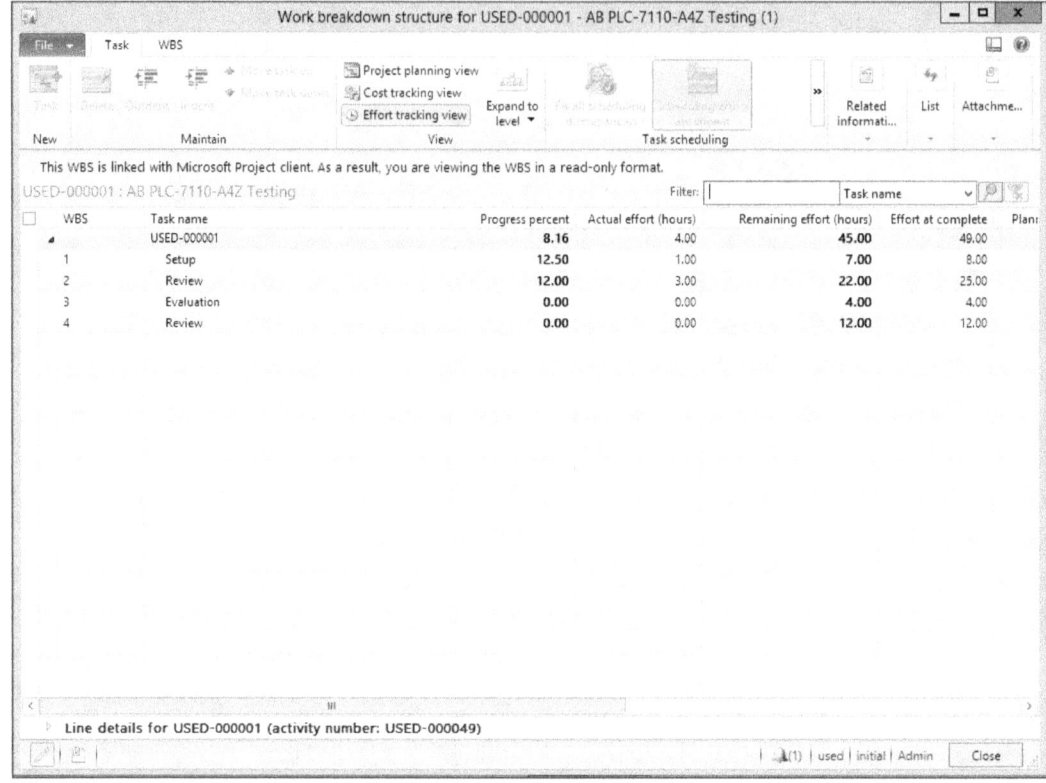

Project Execution
Posting Time Through Portals

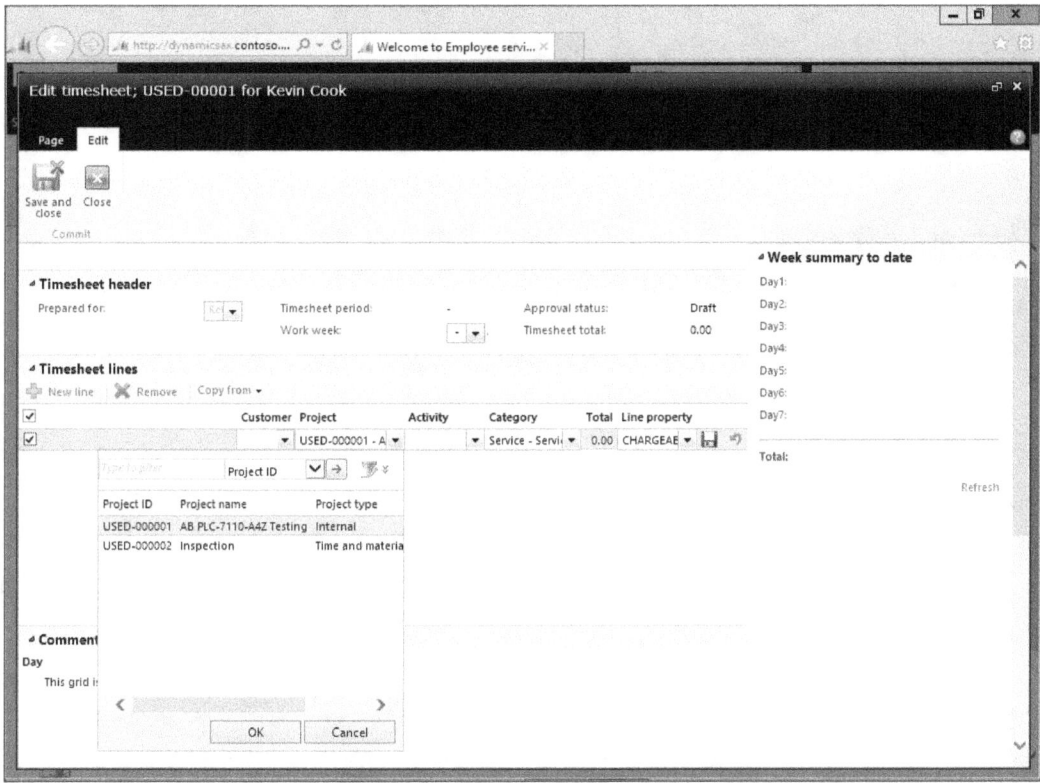

Project Management
Project Statements

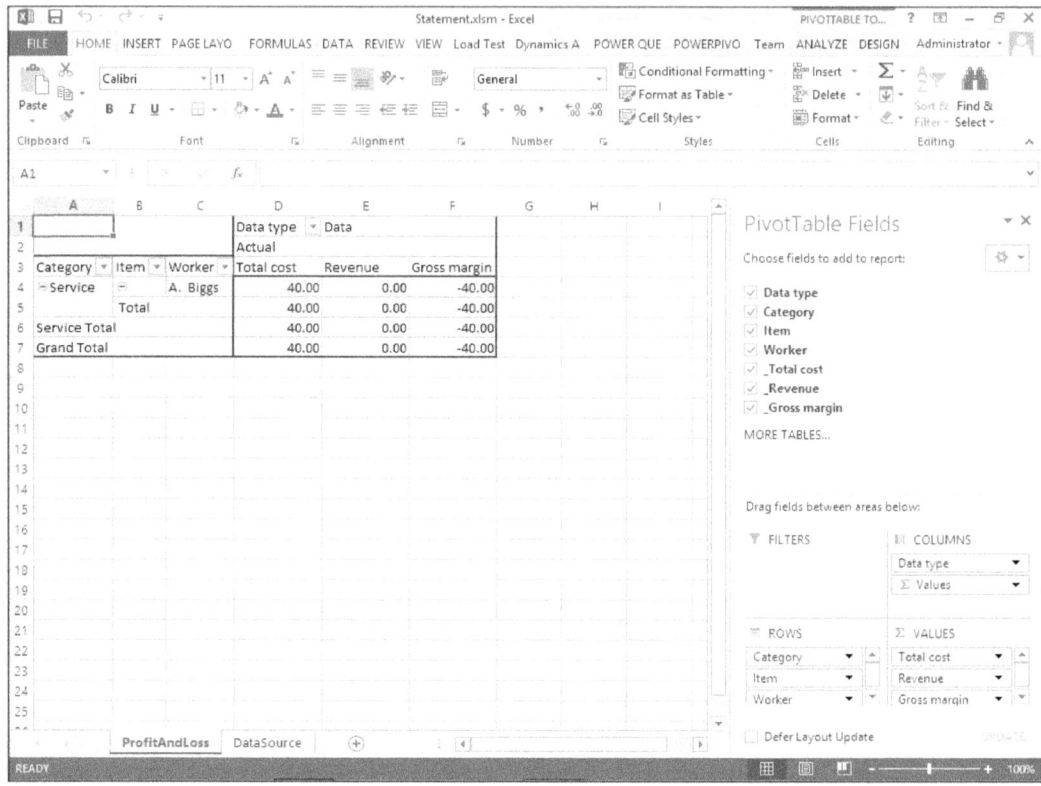

Portals
Collaboration Portals

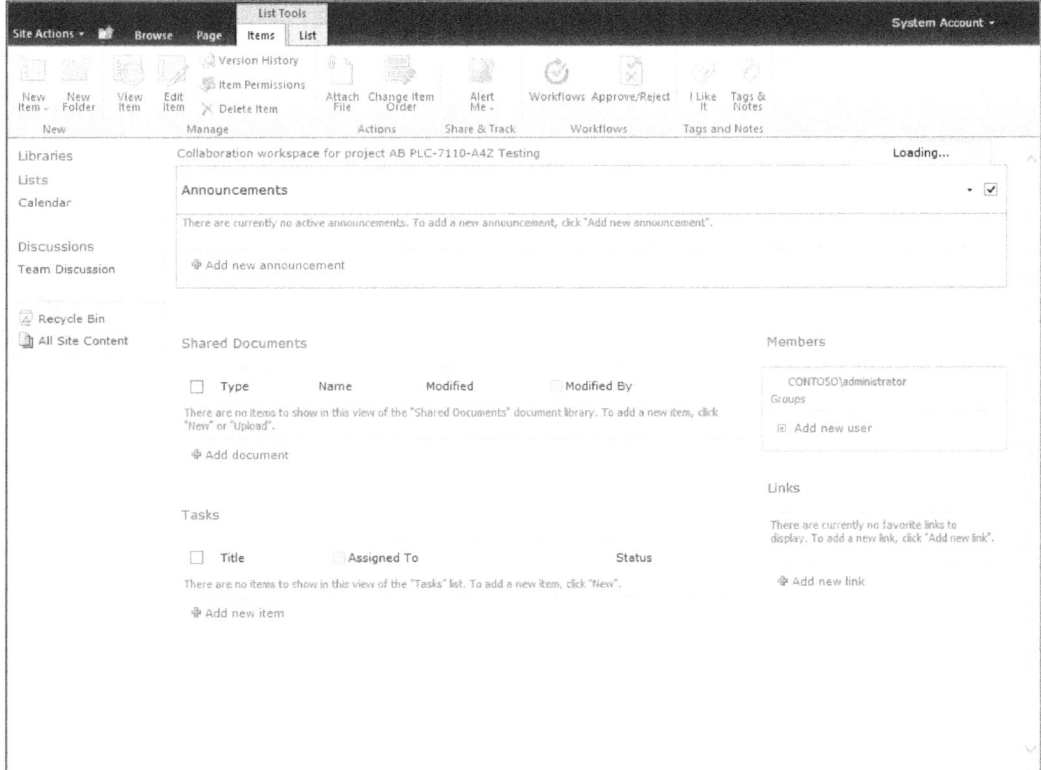

Service Management

The Service Management module within Dynamics AX manages all of the service orders, service agreements, scheduling, and billing requirements that are needed for your field service team.

It is built upon the Project Management module, and leverages a lot of it's capabilities to make the time and billing a seamless feature of the application.

There are other features such as the service object tracking and the repair analysis than can also be used for maintenance tracking within Dynamics AX.

In this section we will show some of the capabilities that are built into the Service Management module.

Master Data Management
Service Agreements

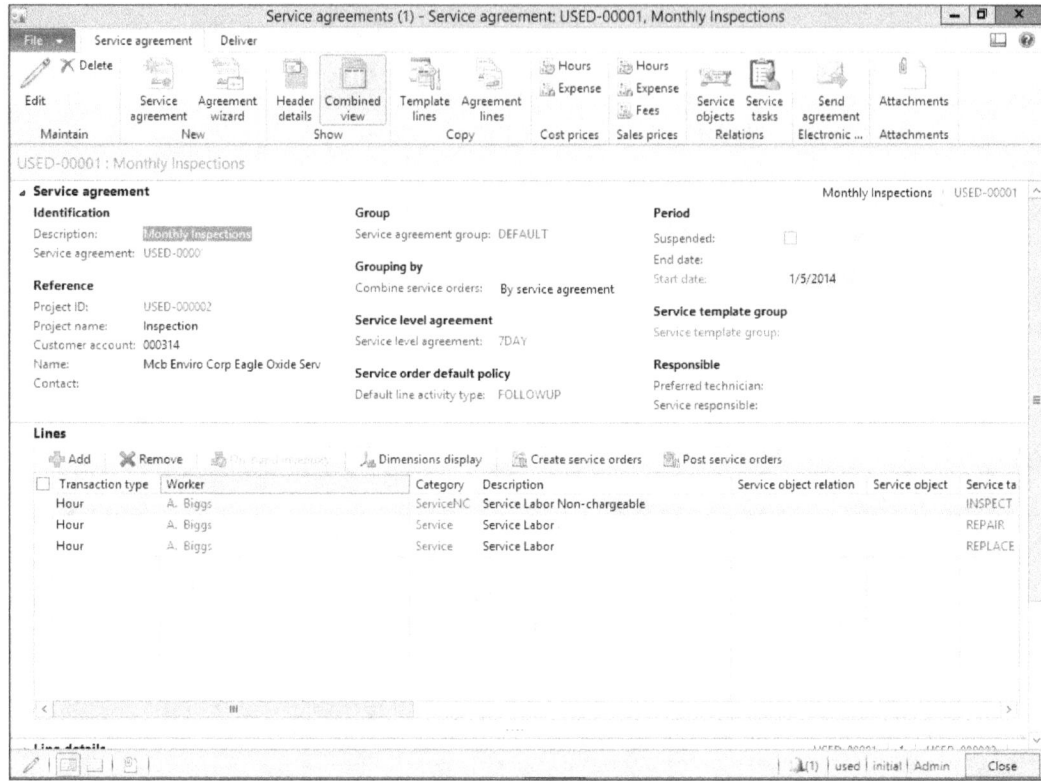

Master Data Management
Service Subscriptions

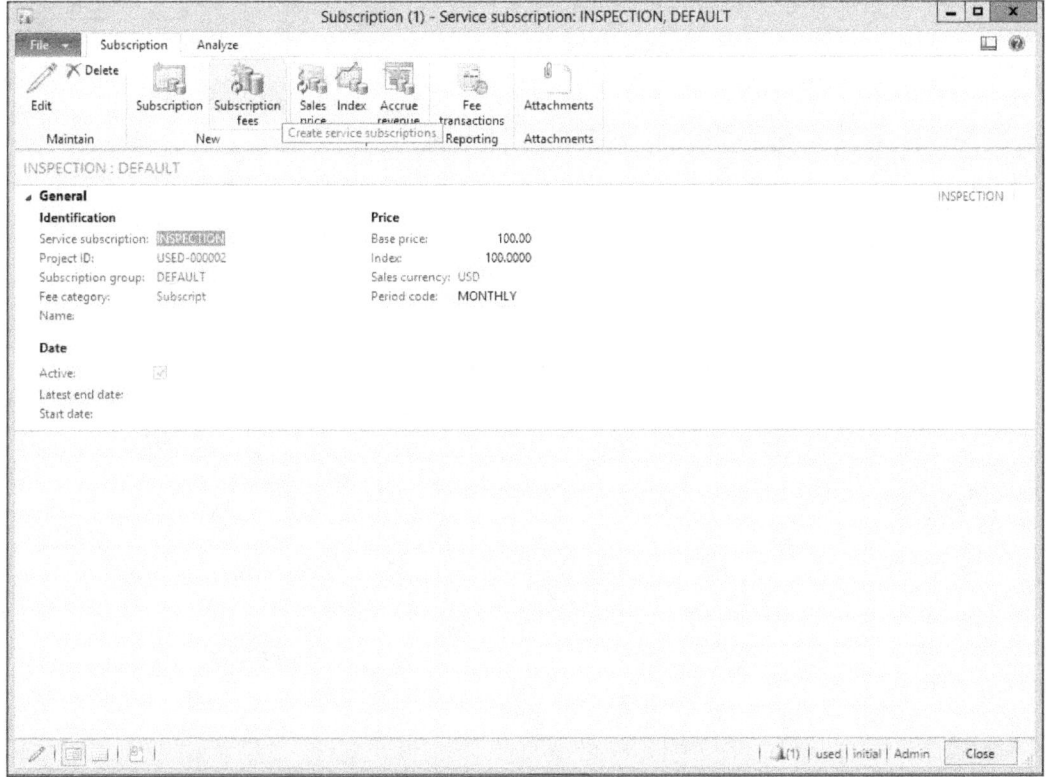

Master Data Management
Service Orders

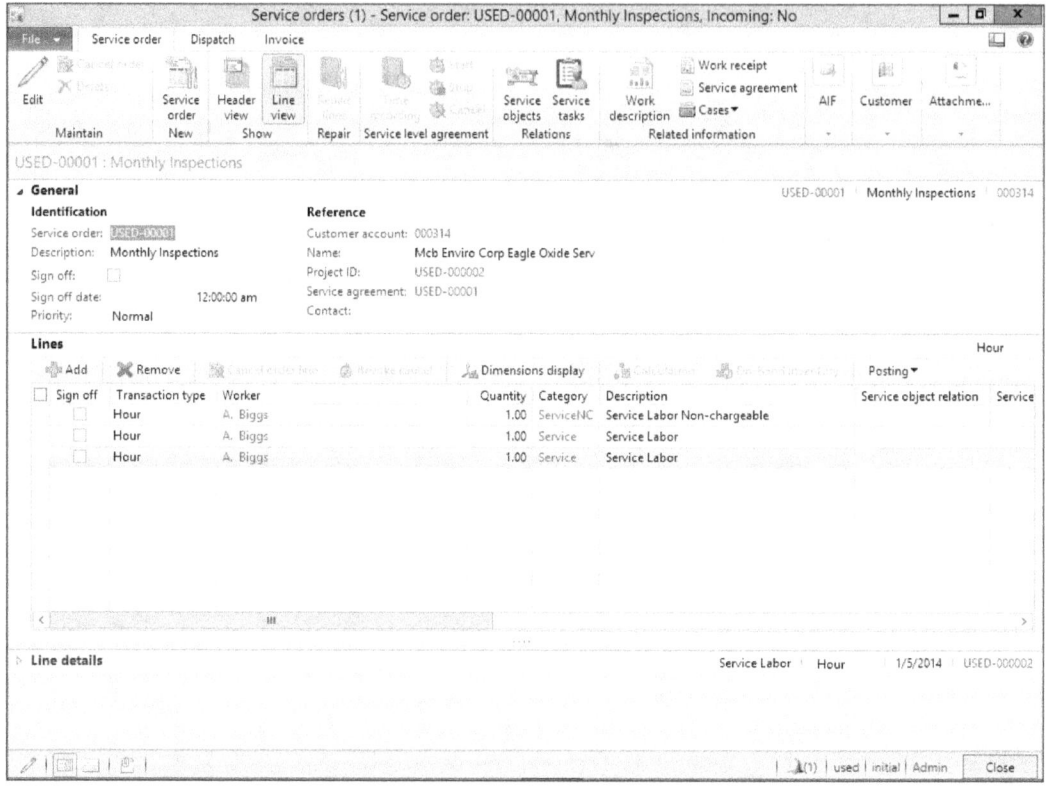

Resource Management
Dispatch Board

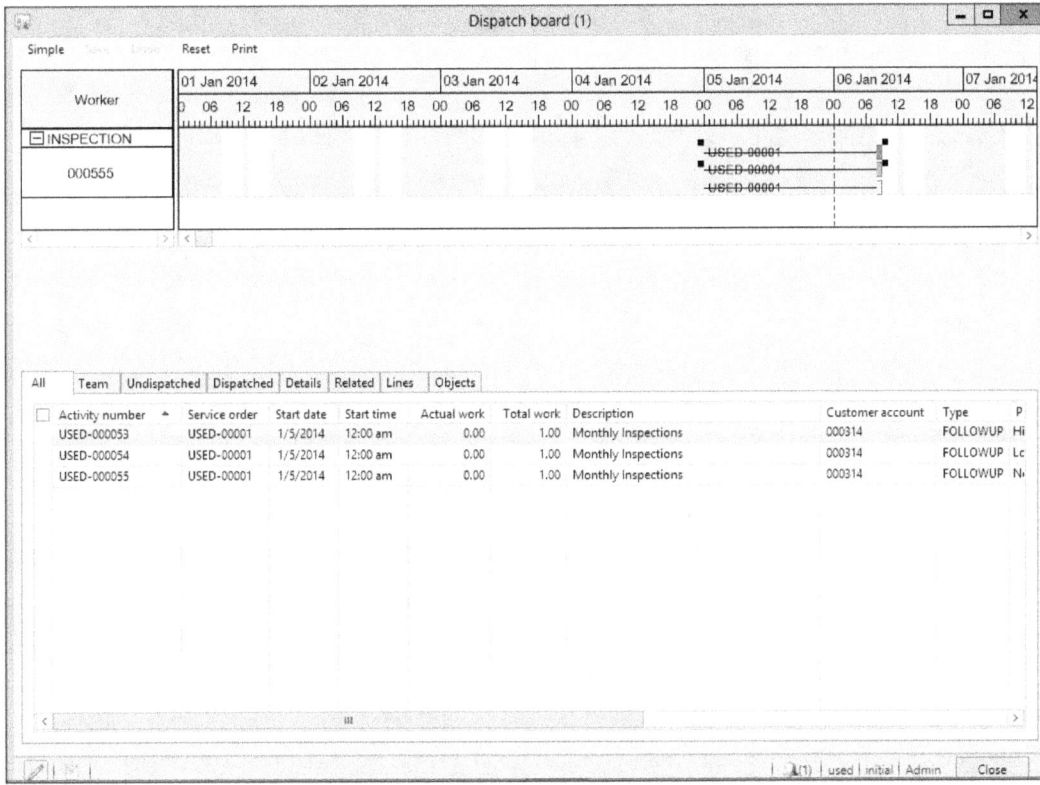

Service Order Management
Time & Material Posting

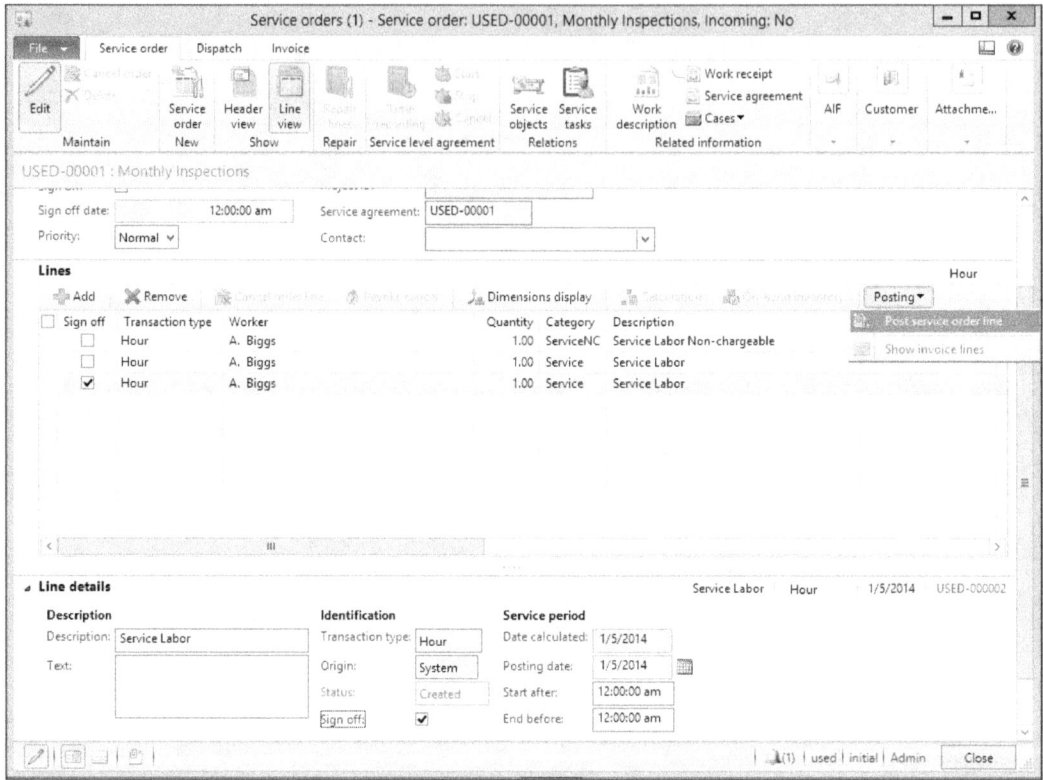

Finance

The Finance area of Dynamics AX includes the General Ledger, Cash & Bank Management and Budgeting modules, and is the backbone of the system. Although you may think that all financial systems are alike, there are a number of features within Dynamics AX that makes if much more flexible than the ones that you may have seen in the past.

In this section we will show some of the more important features of the financial modules within Dynamics AX.

Master Data Management
Ledger Dimensions

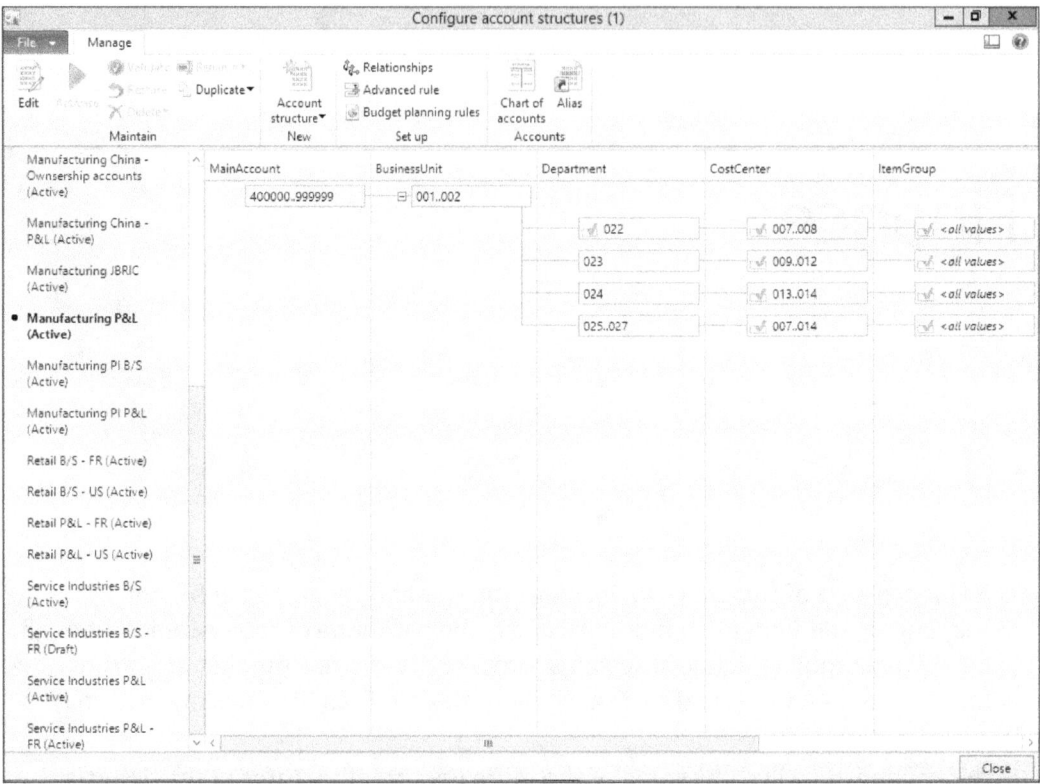

One of the strengths of the General Ledger is the dimensional structure which makes the requirement for a fully qualified account a thing of the past, and also means that you have the flexibility of adding additional ledger reporting elements, without the overhead of having to define all of the values.

Key Features

- Multiple dimensions in GL Account Structure

- Multiple versions of account structures

- Conditional validation rules based on dimensions

- Optional dimensions

Master Data Management
Main Accounts

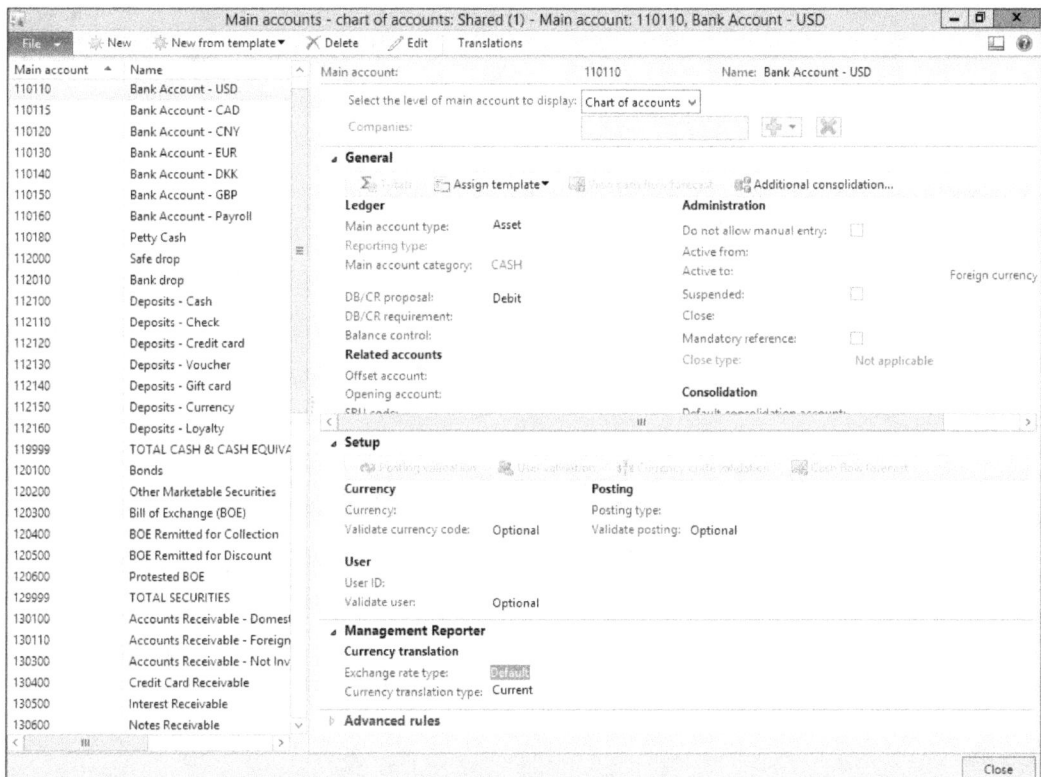

Key Features

- Main accounts definition

- Account management categories

Master Data Management
Calendar & Periods

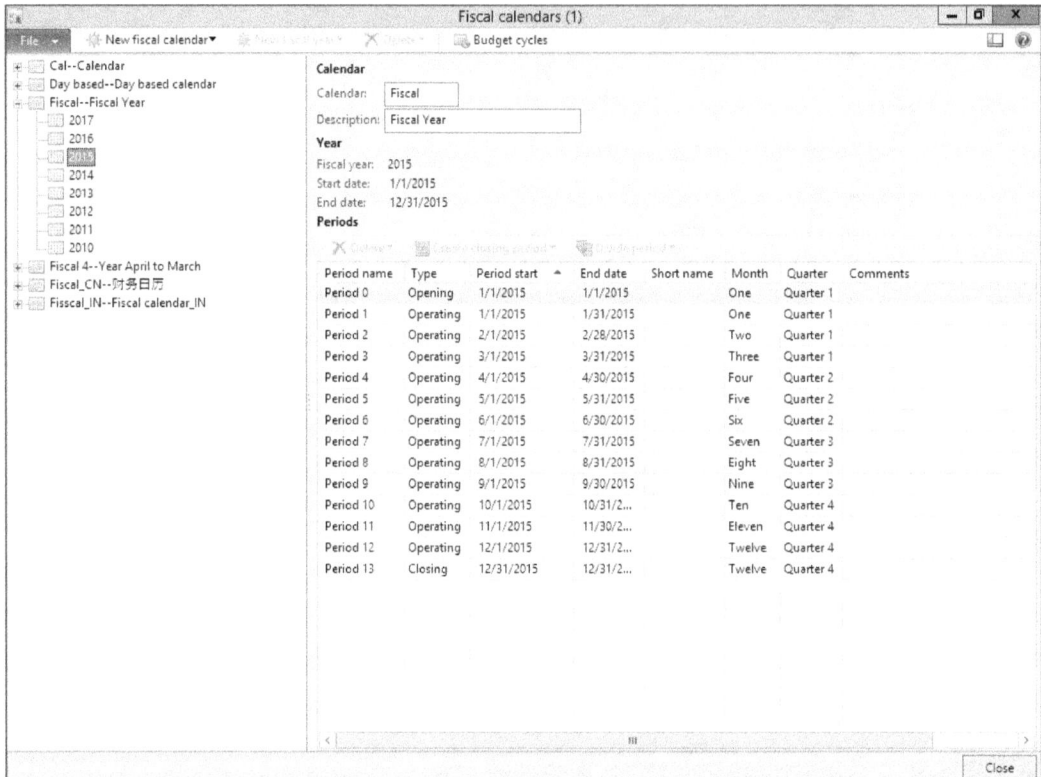

Key Features

- Multiple fiscal calendars

- Flexible period definitions

Organization Management
Organizational Hierarchy

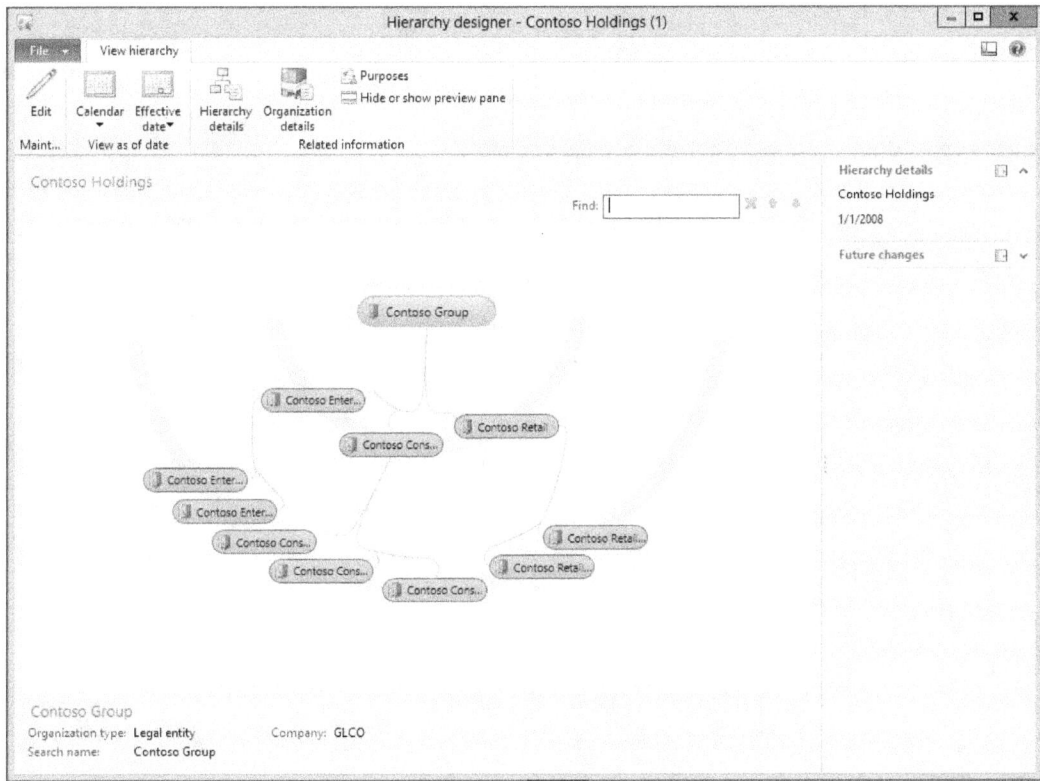

Key Features

- Organizational hierarchy definition used for reporting

- Parent/Child drill through structured

Organization Management
Organizational Hierarchy

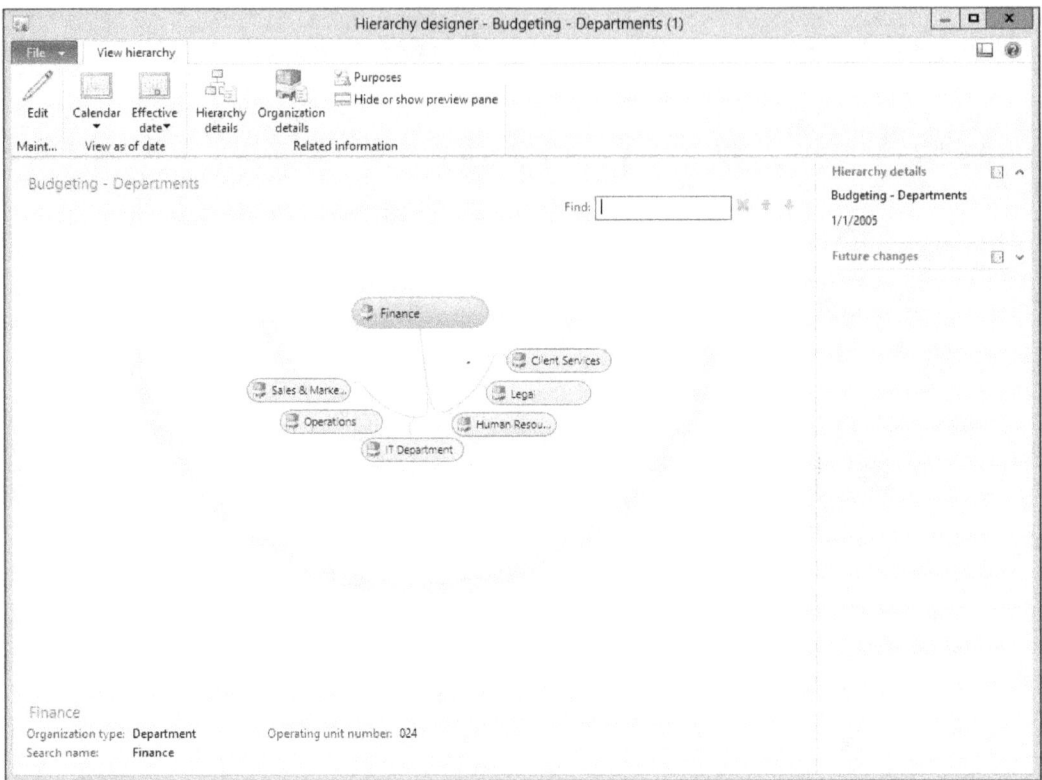

Key Features

- Organizational hierarchies for departments and cost centers

Journal Management
Journal Processing

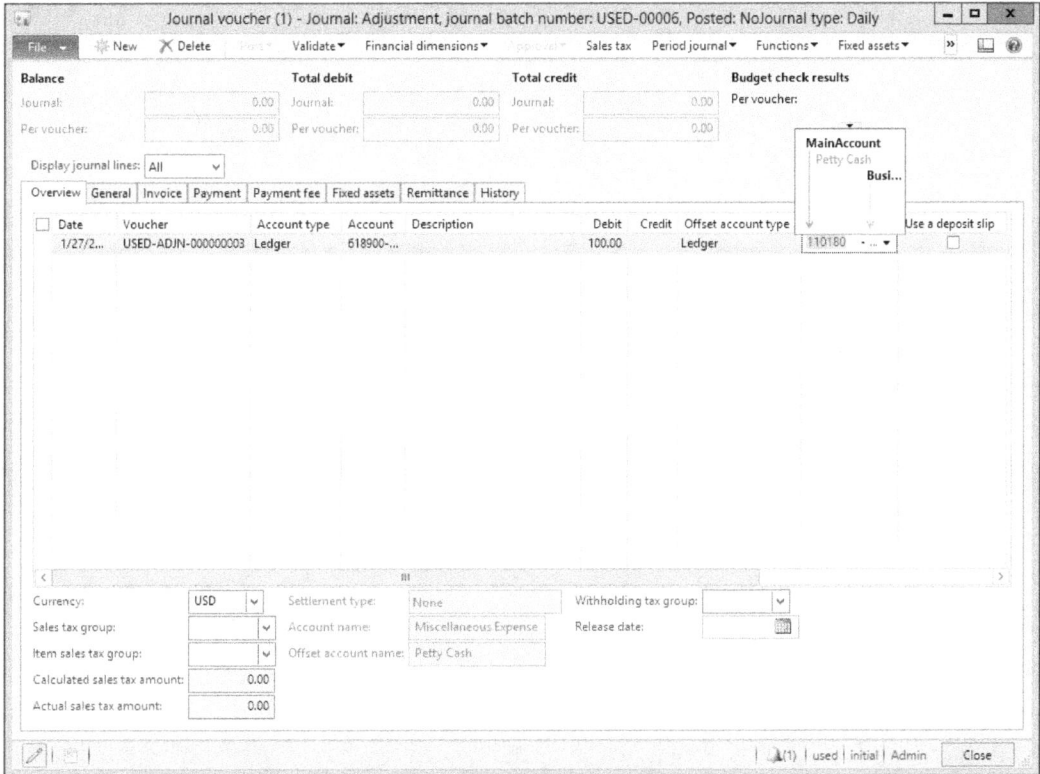

Key Features

- Batch journal posting

- Single line journal postings through offset accounts

- Wildcard search for accounts

Journal Management
Journal Approval Workflows

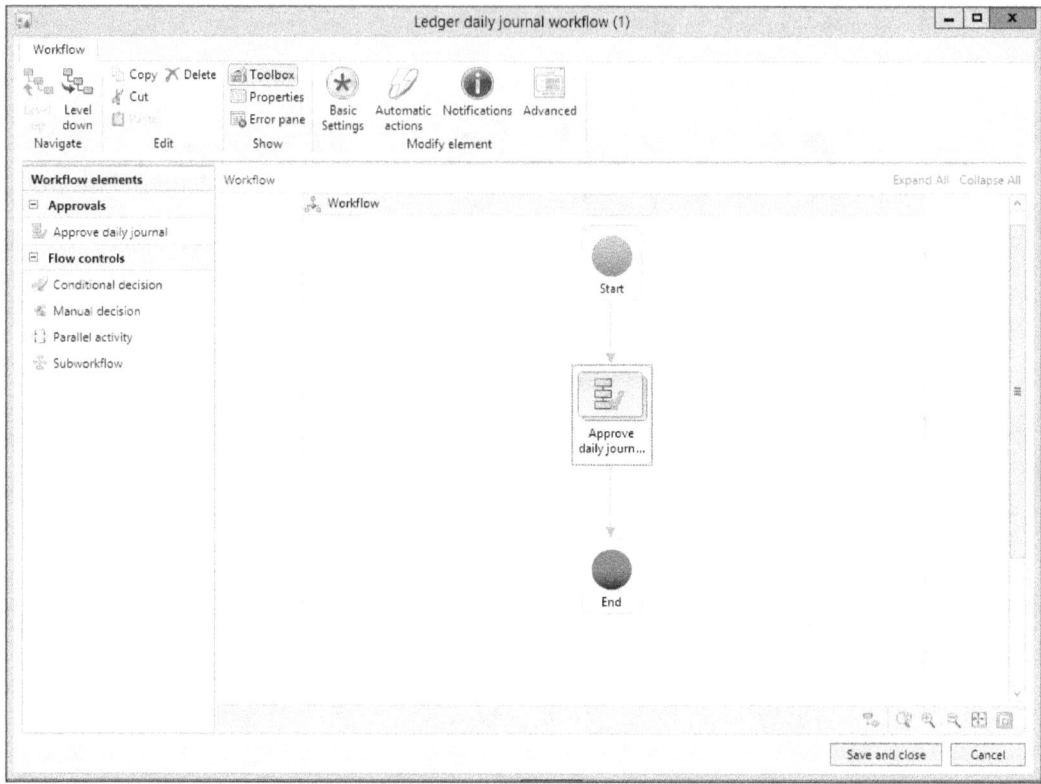

Journal Management
Journal Import Through Excel

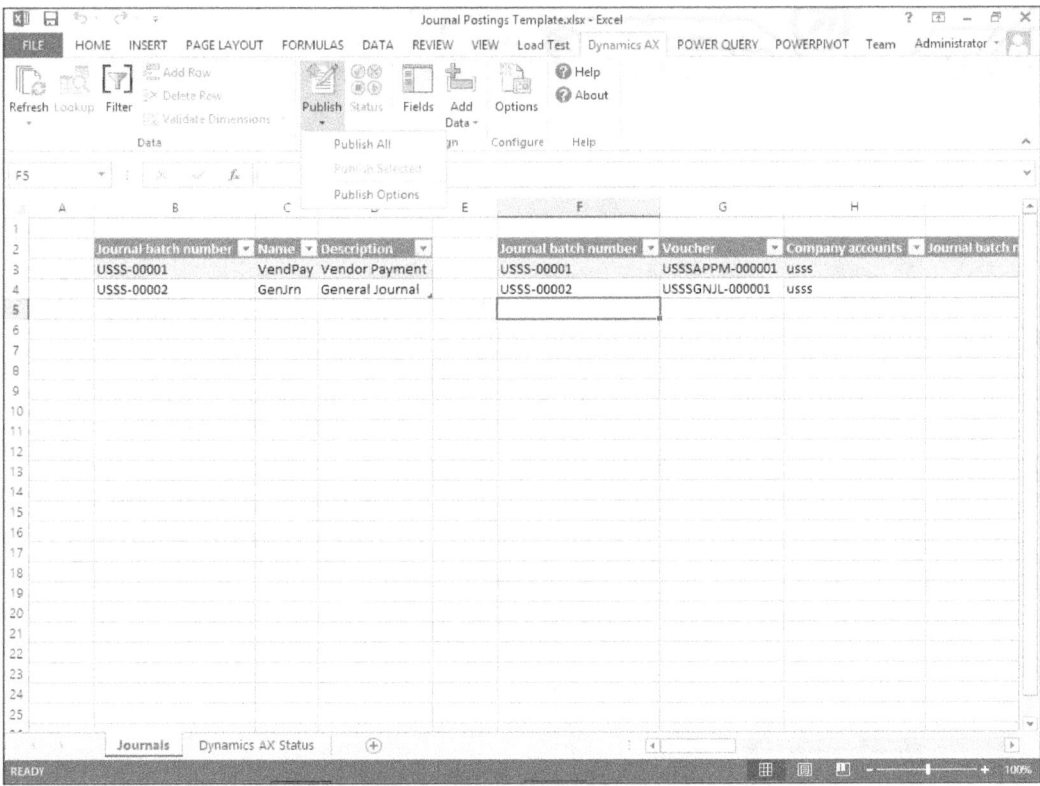

Key Features

- Dynamics Ribbon Bar in Excel

- Postings updated through Excel with validation

Budgeting
Budgeting Portal

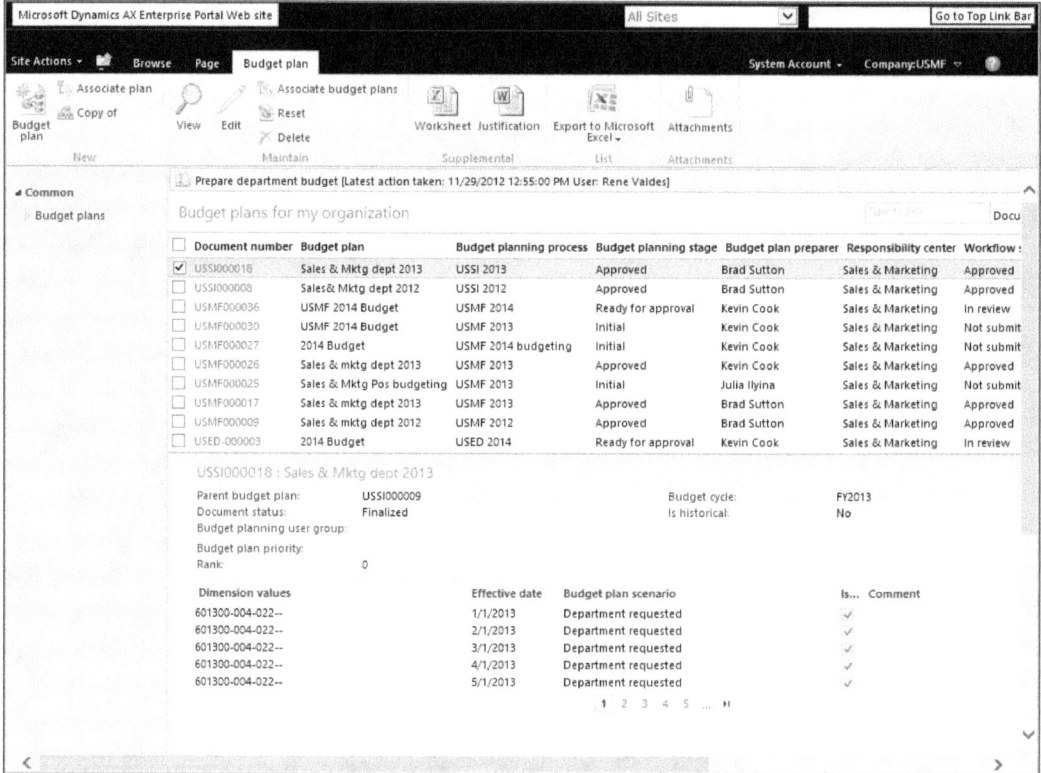

Key Features

- Budgeting Role Centers
- Budgeting analysis reporting

Budgeting
Budget Planning Models

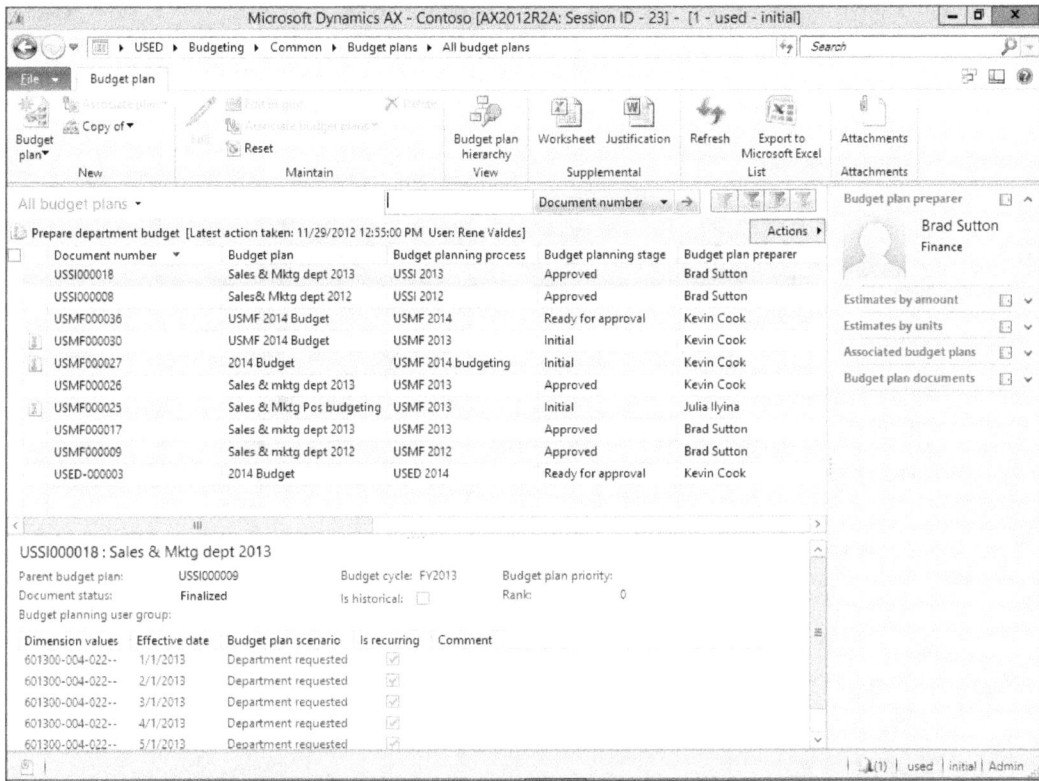

Budgeting
Budget Entry Templates Through Excel

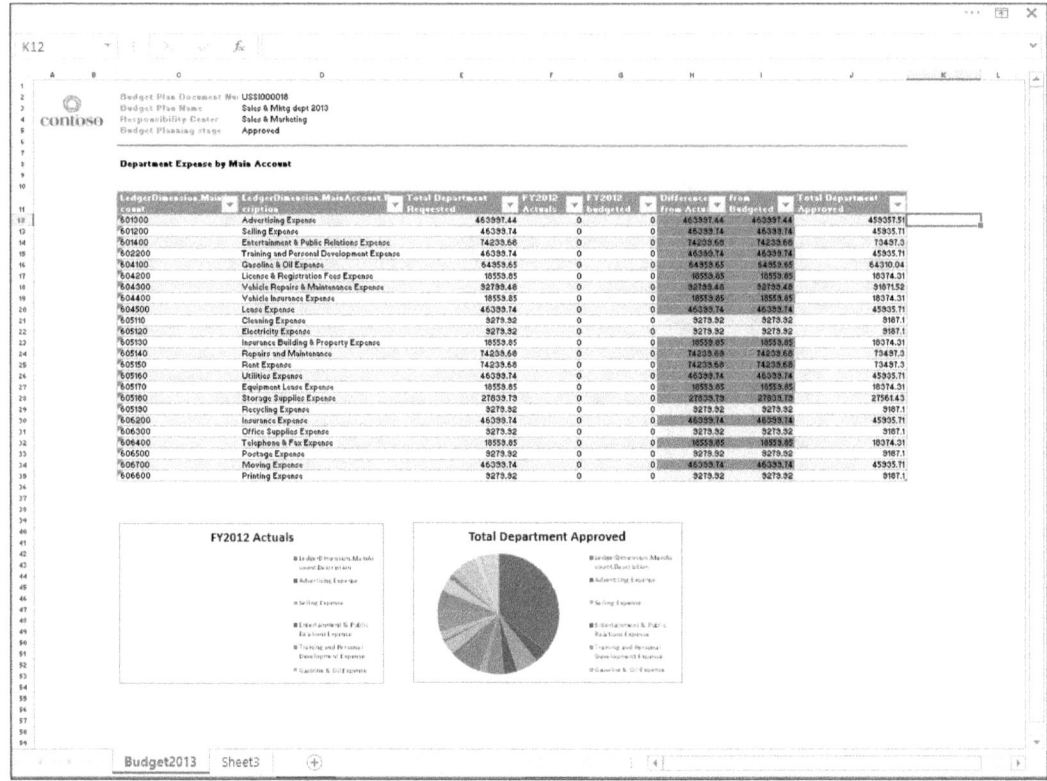

Financial Reporting
Financial Reports Portal

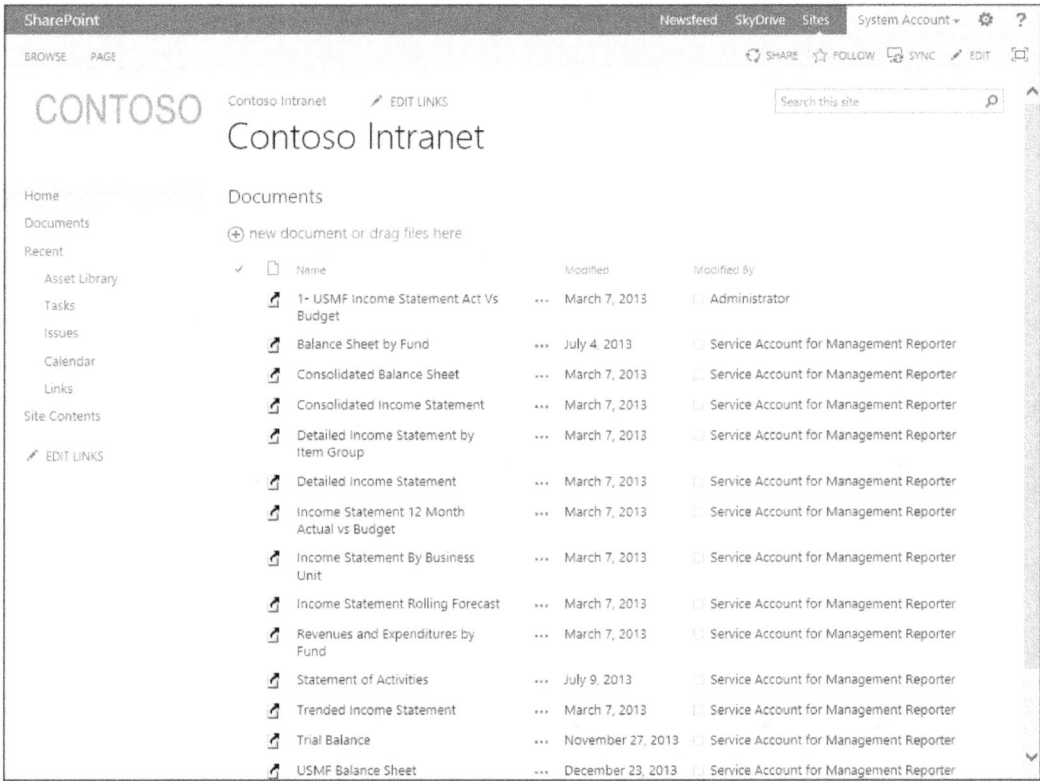

Key Features

- Financial Portal for published financial reports

Financial Reporting Web Interface

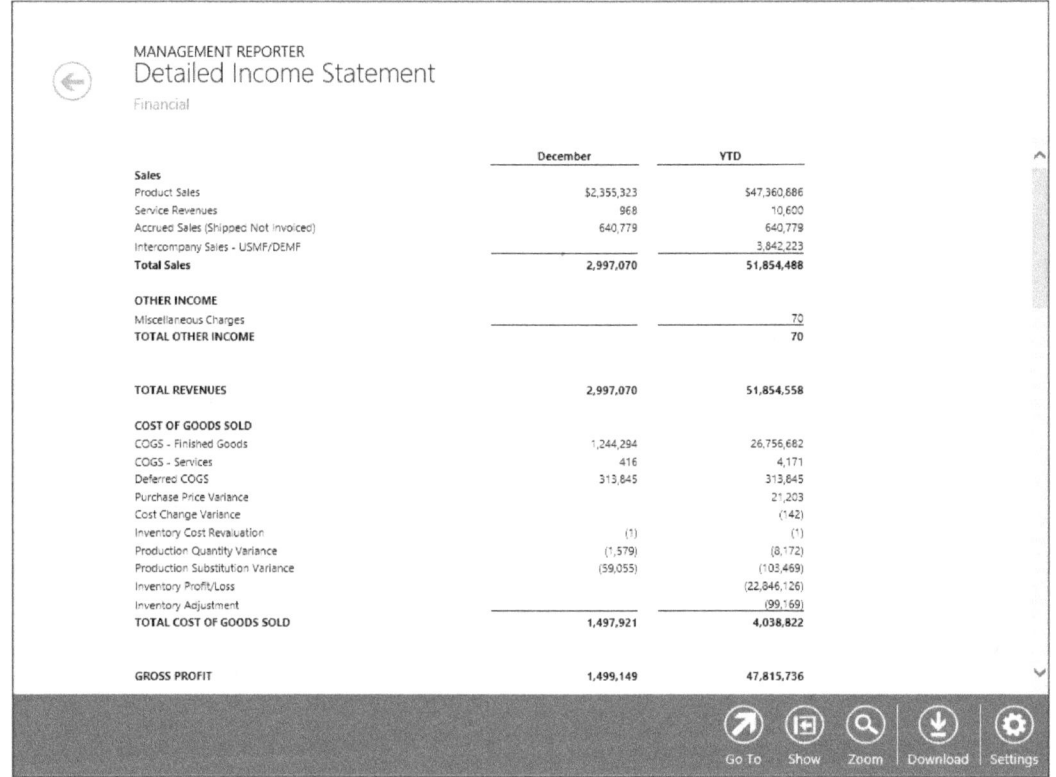

Key Features

- Drill through reporting structure

- Drill from balances to source transactions in Dynamics AX

- Download transactions

Financial Reporting
Drill Down Detail

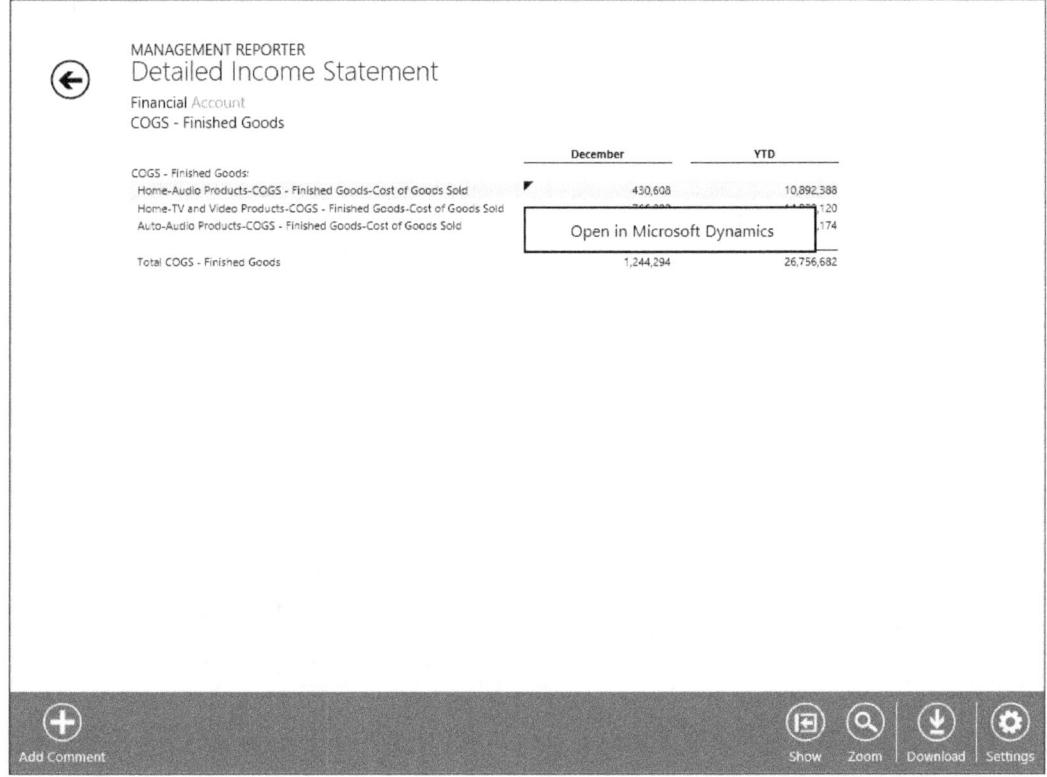

Key Features

- Drill through from journals into journal lines

- Access to original documents

- Access to original transactions from postings

Financial Reporting
As Of Date Reporting

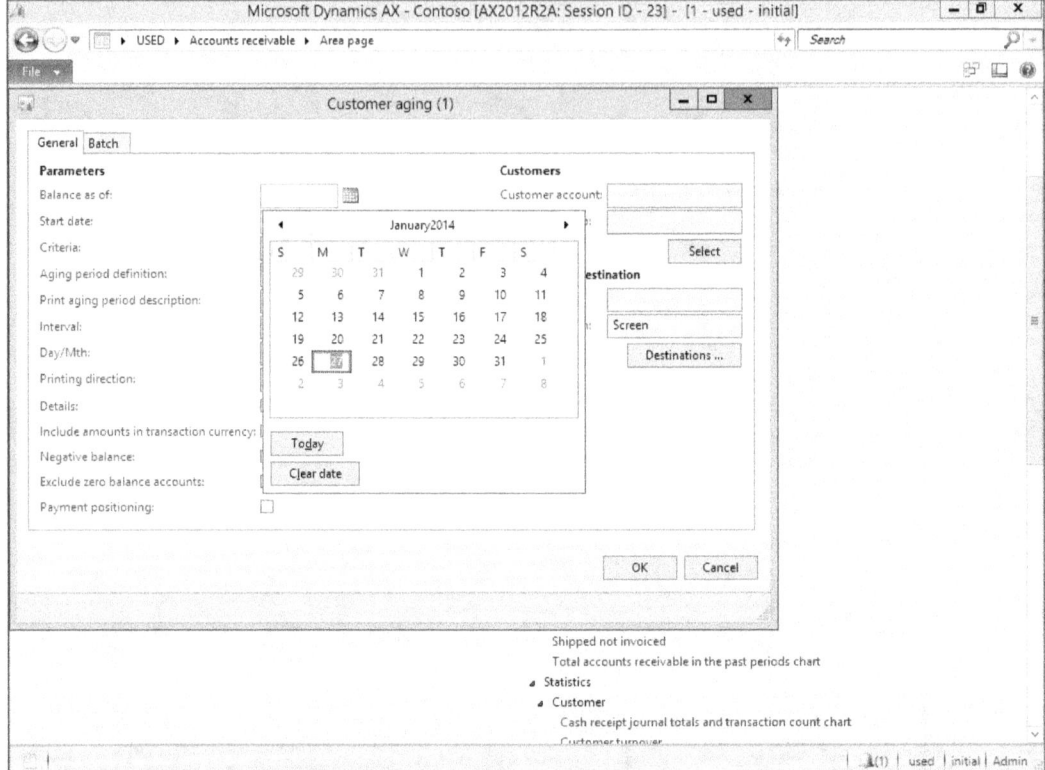

Key Features

- Run reports as of specific dates

Cash Management
Bank Reconciliation

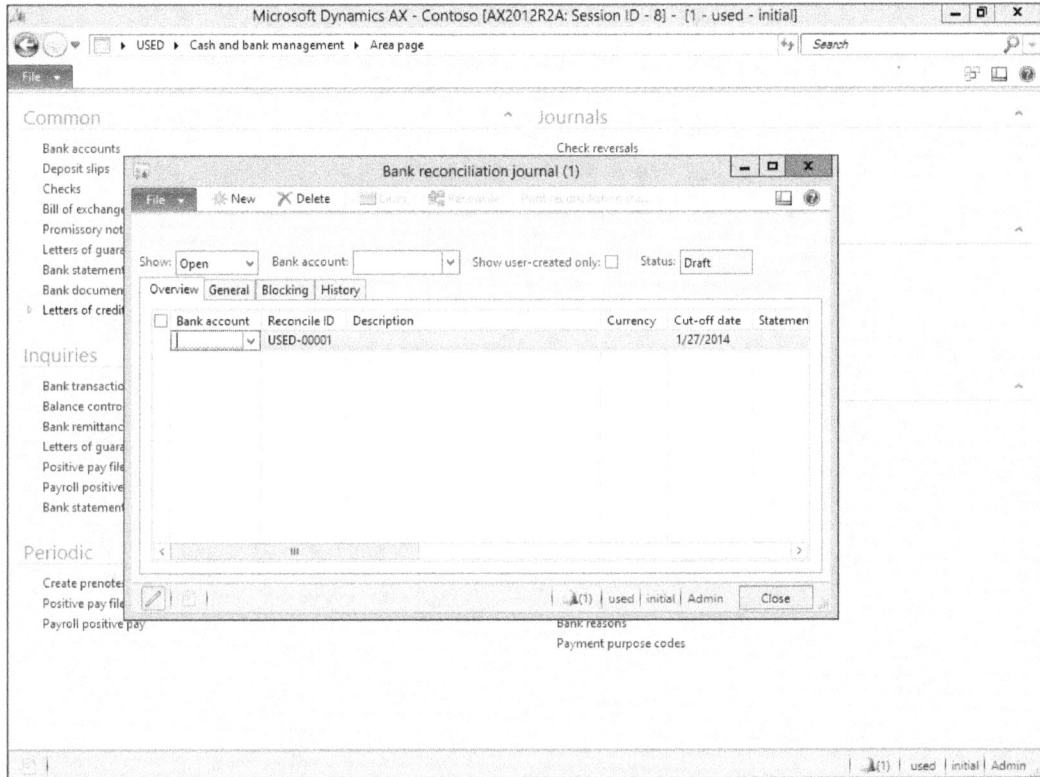

Key Features

- Bank reconciliation capabilities within Cash Management

Human Resources

The Human Resources module within Dynamics AX is fully integrated within the application, and allows you to manage your employees, track training and certifications, allows you to document "discussions" and also provides portals for the employees to access their information on-line.

You may not use all of the Human Resources module right away, but you will use some of it for sure. This is because it is leveraged by all of the other modules within Dynamics AX to manage worker details and also tracks team memberships and also retail privileges.

In this section we will look at some of the features of the Human Resource module and uncover some of the features that make it so useful.

Master Data Management
Organizational Hierarchy

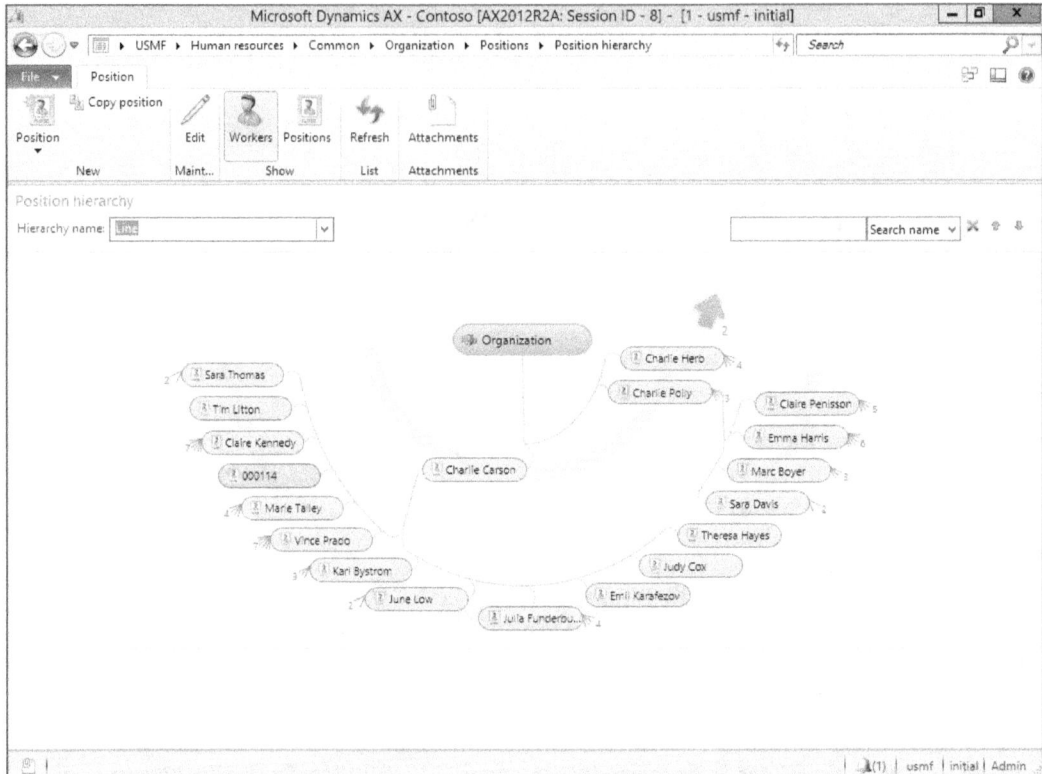

Key Features

- Adapts to your ever changing organization

- Provides a single, unified view

- Delivers timely, accurate information

Master Data Management
Position Management

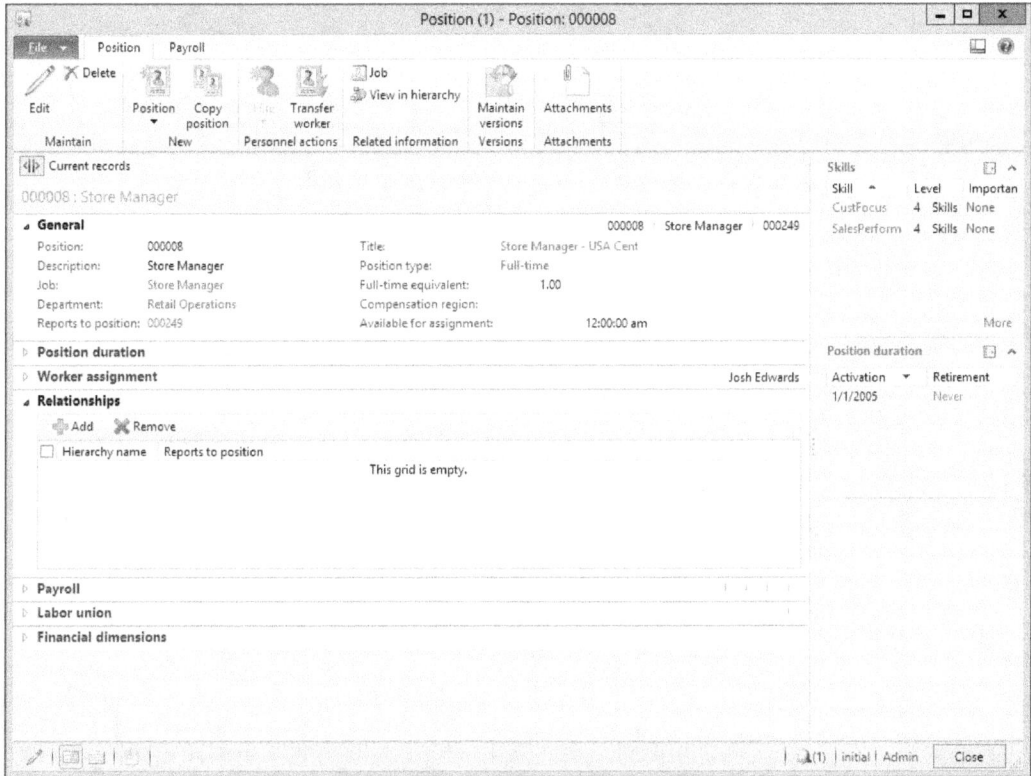

Master Data Management
Employee Management

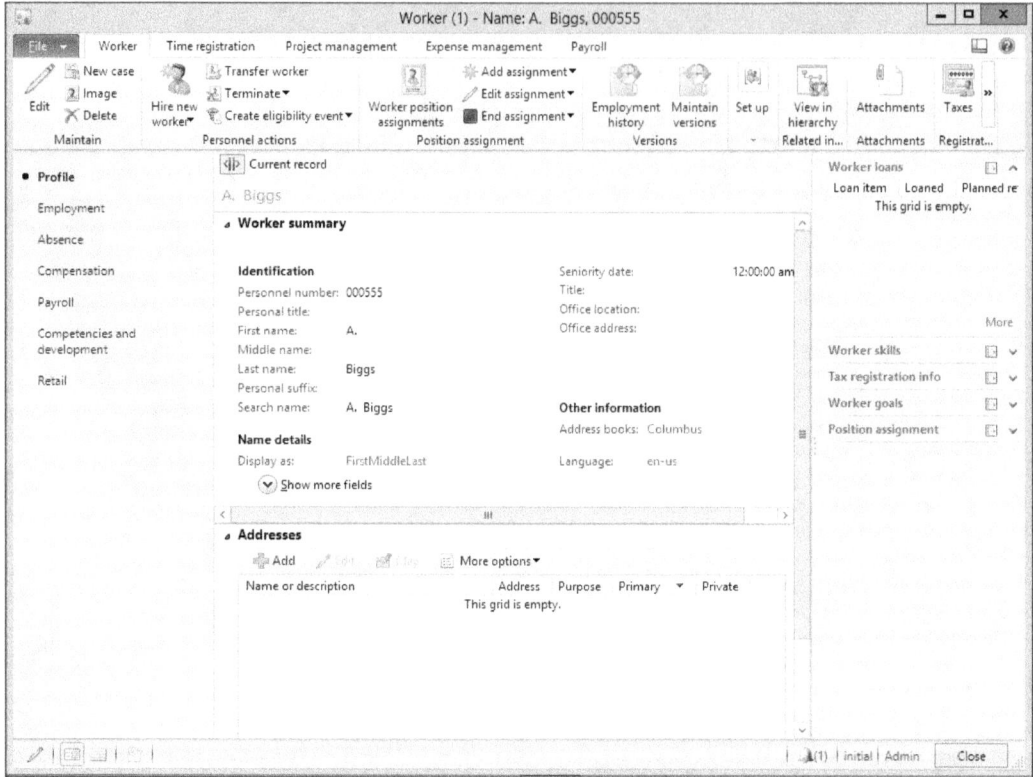

Recruiting Management
Applicant Tracking

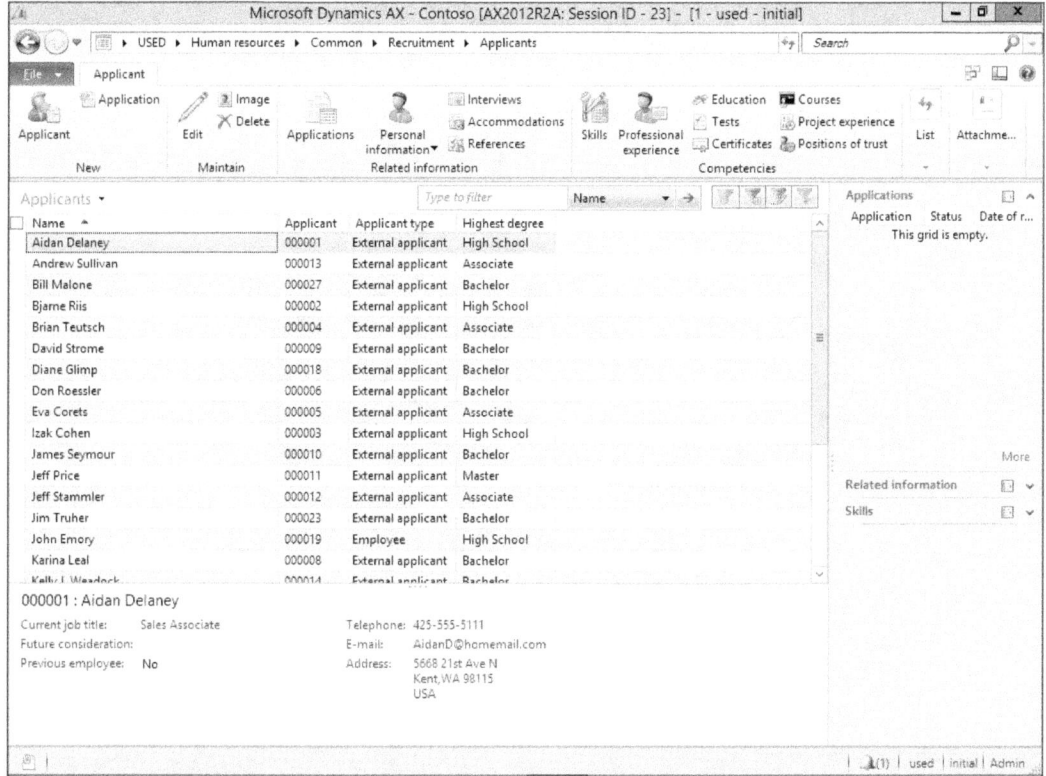

SUMMARY

We have shown quite a lot of Dynamics AX throughout this book, but we have really just scratched the surface. When you dive deeper into the individual areas of the application you will find that there is much more that you can do that we didn't talk about… so that you're not overwhelmed… and so that the book would be a manageable size…

Now that you have a foundation understanding though you can start your journey through Dynamics AX.

Want More Tips & Tricks For Dynamics AX?

The Tips & Tricks series is a compilation of all the cool things that I have found that you can do within Dynamics AX, and are also the basis for my Tips & Tricks presentations that I have been giving for the AXUG, and online. Unfortunately book page size restrictions mean that I can only fit 50 tips & tricks per book, but I will create new volumes every time I reach the 50 Tip mark.

To get all of the details on this series, then here is the link:

http://dynamicsaxcompanions.com/tipsandtricks

Need More Help With Dynamics AX?

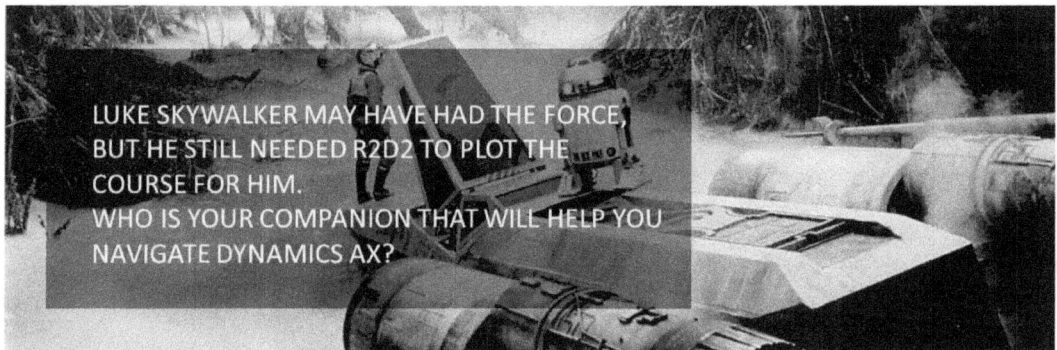

After creating a number of my walkthroughs on SlideShare showing how to configure the different areas within Dynamics AX, I had a lot of requests for the original documents so that people could get a better view of many of the screen shots and also have a easy reference as they worked through the same process within their own systems. To make them easier to access, I am in the process of moving all of the content to the Dynamics AX Companions website to easier access. If you are looking for details on how to configure and use Dynamics AX, then this is a great place for you to start.

Here is the link for the site:

http://dynamicsaxcompanions.com/

About Me

I am an author - I'm no Dan Brown but my books do contain a lot of secret codes and symbols that help guide you through the mysteries of Dynamics AX.

I am a curator - gathering all of the information that I can about Dynamics AX and filing it away within the Dynamics AX Companions archives.

I am a pitchman - I am forever extolling the virtues of Dynamics AX to the unwashed masses convincing them that it is the best ERP system in the world.

I am a Microsoft MVP - this is a big deal, there are less than 10 Dynamics AX MVP's in the US, and less than 30 worldwide.

I am a programmer - I know enough to get around within code, although I leave the hard stuff to the experts so save you all from my uncommented style.

WEB	**www.**murrayfife.me
EMAIL	murray@dynamicsaxcompanions.com
TWITTER	@murrayfife
SKYPE	murrayfife
AMAZON	www.amazon.com/author/murrayfife
WEB	www.dynamicsaxcompanions.com

www.ingramcontent.com/pod-product-compliance
Lightning Source LLC
Chambersburg PA
CBHW080234180526
45167CB00006B/2266